A
GIFT FROM
BEA KAHN-BOYKOFF

Leonard & Shirley Linde

Alvin F. Kahn

9-4-02

Jewish Voices
of the
California Gold Rush

Jewish Voices
of the
California Gold Rush

A Documentary History, 1849–1880

Edited with an Introduction by Ava F. Kahn

Wayne State University Press   Detroit

American Jewish Civilization Series

Editors
Moses Rischin
San Francisco State University

Jonathan D. Sarna
Brandeis University

A complete listing of the books in this series
can be found at the back of this volume.

Library of Congress Cataloging-in Publication Data

Jewish voices of the California gold rush : a documentary history, 1849–1880 /
edited by Ava Kahn.

    p. cm. — (American Jewish civilization series)

    ISBN 0-8143-2859-8 (alk. paper)

    1. Jews—California—San Francisco Bay Area—History—19th century—
Sources.   2. Frontier and pioneer life—California—San Francisco Bay Area—
Sources.   3. San Francisco Bay Area (Calif.) —Ethnic relations.   I. Kahn,
Ava F.   II. Series.

    F869.S39 J55 2002

    979.4'6004924—dc21

00-011104

To Seymour Fromer,
director emeritus of the
Judah L. Magnes Memorial Museum,
whose foresight in collecting
and preserving western Jewish history
made this book possible.

Contents

Part I
Looking West

Part II
San Francisco:
The Instant Pacific Metropolis

Contents

Part III
Personal Struggles

Contents

Part IV
Gold Rush Country

Contents

Part V
Group Relations

Contents

Contents

Contents

Illustrations

Illustrations

Illustrations

Maps

Foreword

THE DOCUMENTARY HISTORY IS A GENRE WITH SPECIAL ATTRIBUTES. Its cardinal virtue lies in its fidelity to presenting a series of original sources arranged in a measured sequence designed to afford maximum justice to its central theme.

Jewish Voices of the California Gold Rush does just that, intimately depicting for the first time the great Jewish migration to the thirty-first state as it was admitted to the Union and at once assumed mythic status. European adventurers, freedom seekers, reconnoiterers, and heralds of extended family chain migrations in the offing—all would be caught up in the fever of the great Atlantic crossing and all would be imbued as well with the epic western spirit and the search for a better life that would carry them, along with a cadre of native-born Jews, to the far reaches of the newest America. There new European immigrants and westward-bound old Americans would meet on common ground. In this wide-ranging volume, Ava Kahn illumines the Jewish, European, American, western, Californian, and world dimensions of this journey by bringing her mastery of the historical record to bear on every aspect of her subject.

Like no other event in our nation's nineteenth-century history, the California Gold Rush galvanized the imagination of the world and incited a worldwide outpouring of treasure seekers bound for the American El Dorado. On the threshold of events that would tear the great American republic apart and even threaten its extinction, the new nation-state of California and the freshly minted potential world metropolis of San Francisco, only a few years earlier an obscure village called Yerba Buena, were simultaneously catapulted into global renown. It was as if California had become a metaphor for a new age of American creation, shoring up the libertarian American image about to be threatened to its core by the bloodiest war in the young nation's history. If the unruly new state was so impossibly remote as to drive lonely young Americans back to their families in the east, this was less true for many Jewish newcomers who had journeyed so much farther. Their new home in California was the only America that most of them knew, and turning back would have been far more difficult and problematical. And many who persevered, buoyed by a sense of ethnic community, were rewarded for their steadfastness. By 1880 San Francisco had become the ninth-ranking city in the country and the Pacific Rim's uncontested metropolitan hub. With 233,000 residents, the great majority of them foreign born or of foreign-language parentage, the city accounted for well over a quarter of the state's population, with 16,000 Jews, who were exceeded in number only by the Jewish inhabitants of New York City.

Foreword

Ironically, Kahn notes, the "new western historians" have been remiss in incorporating the multiethnic Euro-American immigration story, whether urban or rural, into their narratives, prompting Frederick Luebke, a leading western and immigration historian, to lament that "European immigrants are the forgotten people of the American West." The Jewish story, at least, for the crucial third quarter of the nineteenth century in northern California, has found its chronicler in Ava Kahn. Her documentary provides the ideal medium for rendering in their own words the inner lives and richly textured experiences of unknown or barely known witnesses to the past. Almost every page of this volume vibrates with the everyday hopes and fears of flesh-and-blood human beings trying to find their way in a promising but hazardous strange new world. Not only diaries, letters, memoirs, and newspaper reports but also court proceedings, congregational minutes, benevolent society charters, and synagogue constitutions reverberate with their distinctive voices.

Nothing in this volume more poignantly evokes the everyday joys and sorrows of men and women separated by thousands of miles from home and kin than the tales of rites of passage that celebrate the dignity and selfhood of each and every individual whose journey is documented here. The accounts of pregnancies, circumcisions, bar mitzvahs, weddings, and deaths are paramount. The fitful commemoration of the fasts and feasts of the Jewish calendar, honored more often in the breach than in the observance, constitute a quasi-liturgical refrain, registering the ebb and flow of the secularizing and marginalizing pressures on Jewish religious habits and traditions that is rarely portrayed so candidly, directly, and matter-of-factly in works of modern Jewish history. Echoing the griefs of parenthood, especially of motherhood, are the earliest cemetery headstones, their laconic inscriptions memorializing one by one the high incidence of infant and early childhood mortality. At a happier remove, indicative of the welcoming fraternal impulses of the era, was the covenantal rite of circumcision in 1867 San Francisco of Abraham, Isaac, and Jacob Danziger, triplets on whom were respectively bestowed the middle names of Lincoln, Andrew Johnson, and John Conness, the last the U.S. senator from California and a principal in the ceremony. Attended by California's governor-elect, a throng of religious, military, and political notables, and a multitude of other invited guests, this religious rite-cum-civic spectacle seemed to epitomize the age and place.

The story told in this meticulously annotated volume resonates with the experience of firsthand informants. Europe's image of Jewish California—the crossings by land and sea of immense distances, the settlement and building of San Francisco, the Gold Rush mining towns, and the river supply towns—is amply spelled out and illustrated. The founding and functioning of early religious, educational, cultural, and communal institutions, the trials, tribulations, and triumphs of the emergent business and commercial community, and the obligatory round of family engagements and responsibilities are all richly set

22

forth with great insight into the priorities and rudimentary infrastructure of Jewish community institutions. No less faithfully than for San Francisco, if less elaborately, the stories of Sonora and Placerville, Nevada City and Jackson, Sacramento, Stockton, and Marysville are each given their due. The attitudes of Christians to Jews and Judaism in the abstract and the particular are illuminated. The Jewish Sabbath, Sunday Laws, and prayer in the public schools, the role of Freemasonry, the reverence for the martyred Abraham Lincoln, and the Chinese enigma are given careful attention. And religious and cultural obligations to the wider Jewish world—the American Jewish duty to aid the poor Jews of Palestine, the Mortara kidnapping, the plight of the Jews of Romania and Morocco, and the role of the Alliance Israélite Universelle—project a proverbial Jewish concern for beleaguered and less fortunate Jews everywhere denied the benefits of democracy. All shed light on a burgeoning multiethnic and pluralistic new California that a first generation of Jewish newcomers was helping to define for itself and for others.

Jewish Voices of the California Gold Rush is the first full-blown documentary history to profile a multi-voiced American, Jewish, European, and regional culture in its founding years that is attuned to our contemporary sensibilities and grounded in the soundest historical scholarship. At the opening of the third millennium, this volume should help all Americans, most especially Californians of diverse origins and heritage, to better understand their variegated selves and better perceive the connectedness of all our group and individual pasts. Blessedly, the barbaric treatment of the Indians, the cruelties wreaked upon the Chinese, and the rejection of other nonwhites—all parts of the California heritage reaching back to the Gold Rush years—have been repudiated and disowned at every level of American life. Without in any way diminishing the historian's commitment to studying the non-Euro-American dimensions of California and western history, we should be in a position to look more closely and imaginatively at the Euro-America represented in California and western history. Americans all—German, Irish, and Italian, Mormon, Catholic, and Jew—must be envisaged in terms of their full historical complexity in relation to one another, both at odds and in accord with the other, ever in flux, and ever shaped by the contingencies of time and place. *Jewish Voices of the California Gold Rush* should help to expand our capacity to do so.

By the opening of the twenty-first century, over 70 million newcomers, both native-born and immigrant, will have peopled, repeopled, augmented, scouted, and traversed California continually for seven generations. For two-thirds of the nation's history, old Americans and new, sojourners, and tourists have come to California without cease. By far the leading state in the nation, both in its immigrant and its total population, and second to none in its diversity, California, despite the problems and volatility inherent in a state that is sixth among the nations of the world in productivity, continues to be energized by clusters of Americans from all the nation's states and from most of the nations of the world, including a lively Jewish cluster second only to New York in its numbers and vitality.

In our era of unprecedented globalization, high-tech communications, and the prodigious mobility and acute interdependence of peoples and persons, the epic story of Jewish migration and settlement in the tempestuous Gold Rush era, and of the mutual bonds forged among newcomers, has many lessons to teach. *Jewish Voices of the California Gold Rush* makes transparently and vividly evident why they are important lessons.

Moses Rischin

Acknowledgments

THIS BOOK WAS CONCEIVED UNDER THE WATCHFUL EYES OF SEYMOUR Fromer, director emeritus of the Judah L. Magnes Museum, while I was a research associate at the museum's Western Jewish History Center. Seymour's fervent wish was that I write about California Jewish history so that others would become aware of its longevity and importance. This mission was reinforced during a research trip to Boston when Jonathan Sarna, professor of American Jewish History at Brandeis University and an editor of this series, suggested that a documentary history could fill a hole in a neglected area of American Jewish history. I therefore undertook the challenge of bringing the dramatic history of far western Jewry out of the archives and into a more convenient format for use by historians, students, researchers, and all interested in American, Jewish, or community history. For too long, American Jewish history has been centered on the East; this documentary demonstrates the distinctiveness of the West.

In the spirit of a detective, I began searching for the beginnings of California Jewry, assuming I would find few surviving documents. I soon learned that I was mistaken. The collections of the Western Jewish History Center of the Judah L. Magnes Museum, the Bancroft Library of the University of California, and the American Jewish Archives have abundant collections documenting Jewish life during the Gold Rush era. The following is a mere sample of the significant and evocative materials available for the study of California Jewry, for I was forced to exclude many more documents than could possibly be encompassed in one volume.

For help in determining the scope of this book, my gratitude goes to the series editors. Moses Rischin went well beyond the call of duty, suggesting documents, reading numerous drafts of the manuscript and giving his time and expertise to ensure that this work met his high standards. Jonathan Sarna, with his lightning-quick replies to e-mail, was always just one click away with wise advice and constant encouragement. His friendship and encyclopedic knowledge are one of the bonuses of working in American Jewish history.

I am very grateful to the staff of the Western Jewish History Center of the Judah L. Magnes Museum. The center provided me with a home during the early stages of compiling this manuscript, and the staff took an intense interest in my project. Early drafts of this work benefitted immensely from the input of my colleagues at the center. Archivist emerita Ruth Kelson Rafael's love of western Jewish history was reflected in her attention to me and my research. It is due to her care that many of the documents in this collection were preserved in the first place. Laura O'Hara, formerly photo archivist, and Tova Gezit, formerly associate archivist of the center, provided important research assistance. Laura's computer abilities saved me a great deal of time and energy and helped early drafts proceed efficiently. Research assistance and steadfast enthusiasm during the first stages of the project, and continued administrative support in its final stages, were supplied by Susan Smith Morris, now director of the Judah L. Magnes Museum. Her exuberance invigorated this book. The center's volunteers, especially Hank and Mary Hoexter and Ruth Steiner, also aided me by locating materials and translating documents. For their help in finishing the manuscript, I would like to thank the more recent staff of the center, Julia Bazar, Jordi Jones, and head archivist Kim Klausner. Their quick work and attention to detail was very much appreciated. While I was a research associate at the center, my work received the support of the Columbia Foundation, Fleishhacker Foundation, L. J. Skaggs and May C. Skaggs Foundation, and most notably the Koret Foundation. My thanks for their interest in western Jewish history and their appreciation of the time necessary to produce a history of this scope.

Other archives as well preserve the history of the western Jewish community. For their special consideration I would like to thank Susan Goldstein, City Archivist at the San Francisco History Center; Pat Keats of the California Historical Society; Mickey Knapp of the Sacramento County Historical Society; Bernard Rabinstein and Allan D. Satin of Hebrew Union College; the History Room, Yuba County Library; El Dorado County Free Library, Placerville; Kim Walters of the Southwest Museum; Rabbi Yaakov Rosenes, Judaica Archival Project, Jerusalem, and all of the archivists and staff at the Bancroft Library, University of California, especially Bonnie Hardwick and Susan Snyder. A special category needs to be invented for Kevin Proffett, Chief Archivist of the American Jewish Archives, who was always able, with great speed and good cheer, to provide me with what I required. Without the help of archivists and others, often anonymous, this book would never have seen the light of day.

For their help in obtaining illustrations, I thank Marianne Babel and Charles Riggs of Wells Fargo; Kathleen Digiovanni of the Oakland Public Library; Pat Akre of the San Francisco Public Library; Larry Cenotto, Amador County Archives; and for outstanding photographic work, I thank Ben Ailes and David Peterson (who in addition to photographic work supplied enthusiasm and computer services).

Special thanks to the former editors of the *Western States Jewish History*, William M. Kramer and the late Norton B. Stern, for publishing primary documents, some of which are reprinted in this volume. During my undergraduate years, this journal first acquainted me with California Jewish history, and William Kramer always encouraged my interests in the field.

This book would have been a much more difficult project without the annotated bibliographies prepared by Sara G. Cogan; her work made this book possible. Fred Rosenbaum, Glenna Matthews, Barbara Loomis, and students

Acknowledgments

Lynne Young and Joshua Wolfson kindly read drafts of parts or all of the manuscript; their time and consideration is appreciated beyond measure. Among the many people who answered my questions along the way, I want especially to thank Harriet Rochlin, Tony Fells, Judith Edmonson, Mike Richman, Rabbi Stuart Kelman, David Weinberg, and Ida Selavan Schwarcz for their specialized assistance. The Lucius N. Littauer Foundation helped with final book preparation. I am most grateful to the foundation and its program officer, Pamela Ween Brumberg. In addition, I shall always be indebted to Wayne State University Press for its commitment to this book and to Kristin Harpster Lawrence of the press for her attention to detail. Yehudit Goldfarb lovingly prepared the index for this volume. I thank her for her commitment to California Jewry; readers will appreciate her indexing skills for years to come.

Last but in no way least, thanks to close friends who took an interest in this book from the beginning. It is my pleasure to express gratitude to Pam Morgan for her superb technical reading skills. She aptly decoded the handwriting of nineteenth-century authors and evaluated other parts of the manuscript. Ruth Haber not only read the manuscript several times but also shared my enthusiasm for the documents. Ruth was once my teacher; now she is my friend. To all unnamed friends and family, I hope that now I will have time for you again. A very special thank you to my husband, Mitchell A. Richman, who has helped in innumerable ways to bring this book to fruition.

Chronology

This chronology is not a complete listing of all the Jewish organizations of the period; rather, it gives signposts to put Jewish history in context. Bold type indicates important dates for the Jewish community.

1654   **First Jewish settlers arrive in New Amsterdam (New York City)**

1776   Founding of the Mission Dolores and the Presidio of San Francisco

1824   **Reformed Society of Israelites, the first Reform congregation in the United States, organizes in Charleston, South Carolina**

1836   **European Jews begin to migrate to the United States in significant numbers**

1839   John Sutter starts northern California's first inland settlement at the Sacramento and American Rivers

1843   **B'nai B'rith forms in New York City**
        The *Occident and American Jewish Advocate*, first Jewish English-language newspaper, begins publication in Philadelphia

1846   War between the United States and Mexico begins
        Bear Flag Republic is declared in California
        American Flag is raised in Monterey
        Donner Party is trapped in the Sierra Nevada Mountains

1847   San Francisco's first newspaper, The *California Star,* is published
        Yerba Buena is renamed San Francisco
        Plans are made to lay out San Francisco streets at intersecting right angles, American style

1848   Treaty of Guadalupe Hidalgo is signed, ceding California to the United States
        First commercial bank is started in San Francisco
        Gold is discovered in Coloma
        The brig *Eagle* brings the first Chinese to San Francisco
        San Francisco newspaper prints first story of gold strike
        May—Eight hundred men are looking for gold
        June—Approximately two thousand miners are working in the foothills
        Newspapers suspend publication in San Francisco as men head for gold
        July—Four thousand miners established in foothills
        News of gold discovery reaches west coast of North and South America
        October—Eight thousand miners search for gold
        December 5—Gold fever begins; President Polk announces discovery to Congress and gold dust is put on display
        French miners find gold near Mokelumne Hill
        Hangtown (renamed Placerville) is a town of fifty log cabins
        Mexicans from Sonora, Mexico, settle Sonora, California, to mine gold

1849   Regular steamboat service to California begins, bringing first '49ers
First clipper ship arrives in San Francisco
San Francisco burns
Organized wagon trains start out for California from Missouri
Four thousand miners leave Sonora, Mexico, for California
July—Six hundred ships have arrived in San Francisco Bay
October—Europeans arrive by ship
Chinese Camp is settled
First log cabin is built in Nevada City
November—State constitution is ratified though California is not yet a
state
By the end of 1849, approximately forty-two thousand people have
arrived in California by land and thirty-nine thousand by sea
First High Holiday Services are held in San Francisco and Sacramento
The First Hebrew Benevolent Society is formed in San Francisco

1850   First daily newspaper in California, the *Daily Alta California,* begins
publication
National Theater opens in San Francisco
Columbia is established as gold is found
Foreign Miners Tax of twenty dollars a month is legislated
City of San Francisco is incorporated
San Francisco burns
First brick building is built in San Francisco
California is admitted to the Union, thirty-first state
Jenny Lind Theater opens in San Francisco
Fifty-five thousand people arrive overland, thirty-six thousand by sea
Camp town is begun in Grass Valley
Post Office opens in Nevada City
Eureka Benevolent Association is established in San Francisco
Jewish cemetery is dedicated in Sacramento
Congregation Ryhim Ahoovim (later Temple Israel) is organized in
Stockton
Hebrew Benevolent Society is formed in Sacramento
Cholera epidemic; San Francisco Jews unite to provide medical assis-
tance for poor Jews

1851   First orphan asylum founded in San Francisco
Foreign Miners Tax repealed
Fire destroys most of San Francisco
First Committee of Vigilance is established in San Francisco
Congregations Emanu-El and Sherith Israel are formed in San Fran-
cisco; together they purchase land for a cemetery
Sonora community celebrates High Holidays (possibly celebrated in
1850)

Cemetery land is consecrated by the Hebrew Congregation of Sonora

High Holidays are celebrated in Marysville

1852 Three-dollar fee is required of all foreign miners

First High Holidays are celebrated in Placerville

Congregation B'nai Israel of Sacramento buys a building, becoming the first western congregation to own a synagogue building

High Holidays are celebrated in Nevada City

1853 Ladies' Protection and Relief Society is established in San Francisco

Street signs at selected crossings are authorized in San Francisco

The Metropolitan, the first theater to be lit by gas light, opens in San Francisco

San Francisco Verein is organized

First High Holidays are celebrated in Columbia

Marysville establishes a cemetery

Cemetery land is consecrated by the Hebrew Benevolent Society of Sonora

Shaar Hashamayim is established as the first Sephardic synagogue in San Francisco

1854 Alcatraz Lighthouse is built

Rabbi Julius Eckman arrives in San Francisco and helps lay the cornerstones of Emanu-El and Sherith Israel

Sherith Israel moves into its first permanent building on Stockton Street between Washington and Jackson

Congregation Emanu-El moves into its first building on Broadway

Nevada Hebrew Society is established in Nevada City

Placerville Hebrew Benevolent Society is established

1855 Paving of San Francisco streets begins

Ladies' Society of Israelites (Israelitische Frauen Verein) is established in San Francisco to assist Jewish women

Ladies' United Hebrew Benevolent Society is organized in San Francisco to help poor and needy Jewish women

B'nai B'rith Ophir Lodge is chartered in San Francisco, the first lodge on the Pacific coast

Ladies' Hebrew Benevolent Society is organized in Sacramento

Shaar Zedek Hebrew Society is organized in Grass Valley

1856 Second Vigilance Committee is established in San Francisco

James P. Casey and Charles Cora are executed by the Vigilance Committee

Hebrew Observer begins publication in San Francisco

Sonora Hebrew Benevolent Society is organized

First known High Holidays are celebrated in Jackson

Torah of the Nevada City Jewish community is destroyed by fire

Young Men's Hebrew Benevolent Association is started in Sacramento

Grass Valley Jewish community organizes and consecrates a cemetery

1857 Concert Hall opens at the corner of Clay and Sansome in San Francisco

Rabbi Julius Eckman begins publication of the *Weekly Gleaner* in San Francisco

Chebra Bikur Cholim Ukedisha is organized in San Francisco

Synagogue is built in Jackson

1858 Placerville synagogue is consecrated

B'nai B'rith is started in Sacramento

Hebrew Ladies' Society of Sacramento is formed

1859 Sonora and Columbia Hebrew Benevolent Society is organized (previously the Sonora Hebrew Benevolent Society)

Jewish cemetery is established in Mokelumne Hill

Congregation Emanu-El-San Francisco sends $3,700 to the Jewish community of Morocco

1860 Clipper ship arrives from New York in eighty-nine days

First Pony Express rider from Missouri reaches San Francisco

Telegraph line opened between Los Angeles and San Francisco

I. J. Benjamin arrives in California

Chebra B'rith Shalom Society is organized to aid the sick in San Francisco

Congregation Beth Israel is founded in San Francisco

Congregation Shomrai Shaboth exists in San Francisco

Rabbi Elkan Cohn becomes the rabbi of Emanu-El in San Francisco

Hebrew Benevolent Society established in Mokelumne Hill

Sacramento sends relief to the Jewish community of Jerusalem

The Jewish community of San Francisco dedicates a new cemetery near Mission Dolores

1861 Civil War begins

Chebra Benai Yisroel Society is organized in San Francisco

Ladies' Hebrew Benevolent Society is organized in Placerville

Synagogue B'nai Israel is built in Placerville

B'nai Israel of Sacramento celebrates its first confirmation class

Jewish community of Grass Valley purchases land to build a synagogue

Garizim Lodge 43 of the B'nai B'rith is established in Grass Valley

1862 Direct telegraphic communication starts between New York and San Francisco

Chebra Achim Rachomin Association is organized in San Francisco

Ladies' Hebrew Benevolent Society is organized in Mokelumne Hill

Oakland Hebrew Benevolent Society is founded

1863 Ferry and railroad connection between San Francisco and Oakland begins

The Cliff House opens in San Francisco

32

B'nai B'rith Grand Lodge 4 is organized in San Francisco
The *Hebrew* begins publication in San Francisco
High Holidays are celebrated in Oakland by the Hebrew Benevolent Society

1864   Ohabai Zion is established in San Francisco for support of the Jews of Jerusalem
Congregation Ohabai Shalome is founded in San Francisco
First Hebrew Ladies' Mutual Benefit Association is organized in San Francisco
Young Men's Literary Association is founded in Sacramento
Congregations Emanu-El (Sutter Street) and Sherith Israel (Post and Taylor) lay cornerstones for new synagogue buildings
B'nai B'rith lodge founded in Marysville

1865   President Abraham Lincoln assassinated
An earthquake devastates San Francisco
Civil War ends
Placerville Hebrew Benevolent Society becomes affiliated with the national Board of Delegates of American Israelites
Order of Kesher Shel Barzel (Band of Iron) is established in Sacramento

1866   Paid Fire Department in San Francisco is begun
Temple Emanu-El is dedicated on Sutter Street in San Francisco

1867   Mokelumne Hill Hebrew Benevolent Society is reestablished
Bar Mitzvah ceremony is conducted in Placerville during High Holidays

1868   Earthquake strikes San Francisco
First baseball game is played in San Francisco
Eureka Social Club is founded in Nevada City
Rabbi Nathan Notkin of Jerusalem travels through gold counties to seek contributions for the Jews of Jerusalem

1869   Transcontinental railroad is completed
Free Postal Delivery starts in San Francisco
Washington Lodge 56, Order of Kesher Shel Barzel, is founded in San Francisco
Hebrew Ladies' Sewing Circle is organized in San Francisco

1870   Anti-Chinese agitation grows statewide
Golden Gate Park opens
Chevra Kadusha, Free Burial Society, is organized in San Francisco
Jewish Orphan Asylum and Home for Aged Israelites opens in San Francisco
Congregation Sherith Israel dedicates a new synagogue at Post and Taylor in San Francisco

1871   First annual meeting of the California Woman Suffrage Society is held

Pacific Hebrew Orphan Asylum and Home Society is organized in San Francisco

Congregation Shaari Zedeck is organized in San Francisco

1872 Cornerstone is laid for San Francisco City Hall

Bohemian Club is established in San Francisco

1874 **Chebra Ohavai Shalom Society is organized in San Francisco**

1875 **Hebrew Union College is established in Cincinnati**

First Hebrew Congregation, later renamed Temple Sinai, is founded in Oakland

B'nai B'rith is started in Oakland

1876 San Francisco gets its first public electric lights

Los Angeles and San Francisco are united by the Southern Pacific Railroad

Diphtheria epidemic occurs in San Francisco

Jewish Ladies' Relief Society is incorporated in San Francisco

Daughters of Israel Relief Society is founded in Oakland

1877 **Joseph Seligman is refused admission to the Grand Union Hotel in Saratoga, New York, because he is Jewish**

Young Men's Hebrew Association is founded in San Francisco

1878 First San Francisco telephone book is published

B'nai B'rith lays cornerstone on Eddy Street

1879 Chinese Exclusion Act is passed by Congress

Jewish Young Ladies' Leap Year Club of Oakland is established

Young Men's Hebrew Association is founded in Oakland

1880 Public Library opens for book borrowing in San Francisco

Introduction

TO STUDY THE TOTAL EXPERIENCE OF THE JEWS OF THE GOLD RUSH era and beyond in northern California is to share in much of the optimism and excitement of the mid–nineteenth century. It was a time perhaps similar to the launching of the American space program a century later. Just as people in the mid–twentieth century learned that it was possible to travel to the moon, so men and women in the mid-nineteenth century learned that they could break previously proscribed boundaries, communicating instantly by telegraph across immense distances, traveling over vast oceans on steam-powered ships, and even crossing formerly almost impassable continents by rail. This era of innovation was also the era of the first great migration to the United States, and Jews participated significantly. For many of them—dizzied by the lure of the Gold Rush—California would be the ultimate destination.

In 1848, the year of the initial gold strike, California had no more than 100,000 inhabitants, but within four years the population of the eight Gold Rush counties alone had exploded to 123,822 and the state had taken a prominent place on the world stage.[1] Similarly, the number of Jews in the United States—only 50,000 in 1850—multiplied threefold by 1860, thousands emigrating west to the new El Dorado.[2]

Looking at how California's communities sprang up, developed rapidly during the first rush to the goldfields, and then declined as gold fever waned and the economy shifted provides us with an excellent paradigm for studying how pioneer Jewish religious and social institutions took shape. Furthermore, it creates an opportunity for examining how Jews of this time and place became one with American life. It also enhances our perspective on the complex process of migration, immigration, and urbanization during the years that saw the lightning-quick rise of San Francisco.

This documentary history provides students of California and the West with an intimate portrait of Jewish life at a critical period in the history of the state and nation. The documents take the reader from Europe to California's towns, goldfields, and nascent religious communities, and from the founding of the Jewish community to its maturity. Most notably, the documents reveal the instant city of San Francisco, which emerged in little more than a quarter-century as the nation's and the West's incontestable metropolis and most cosmopolitan city.

While it is part of the total American Jewish experience, California Jewry also needs to be seen in its own terms. Just as historians of the West have generally viewed California's Jews as indistinguishable from others of European origin, so until recently historians of American Jewry have scarcely mentioned California in their accounts. Focusing on universal Jewish commonalities throughout the United States, they have given little attention to regional differences. But because of the rapid growth of a multiethnic population in an era of mass immigration, California Jewish history took a new direction. Jewish men and women were less restricted in their pursuits than they had been in Europe or in the eastern United States, and also may have been able to participate more effectively in the development of its Jewish communities. In the East, where they arrived in large numbers in the 1840s, Jews had to accommodate themselves to a preexisting Jewish social and religious structure. In the Pacific West, all was their own creation.[3]

European Jewry

As the first reports of gold set in motion a worldwide frenzy, central Europe was entering the throes of a modernization process that affected all segments of society. Especially unsettled by the changing political economy were young Jewish men and women. Whether craftsmen, tailors, seamstresses, or small merchants, they often found that the new economy had no place for them.[4] Although Enlightenment concepts were beginning to break down anti-Jewish occupational and residential restrictions in some western European countries, Jews were simultaneously losing the security provided by traditional Jewish community structures. The disruptions caused throughout western Europe by the failed revolutions of 1848 sent some Jews fleeing political repression as well as economic discrimination.[5] Others fled to escape military conscription in armies whose governments and military oppressed Jewish recruits.

This repression in much of central Europe included increasingly restrictive laws that made it difficult for a Jew to acquire a residency permit to own a business, marry, and establish a family.[6] In Bavaria from 1813 to 1861, for example, Jews could not move from one town to another without authorization, which virtually stifled their chances for employment. A Jewish marriage was permitted only after one Jewish inhabitant had died and thus made room for another on the prescribed town list of Jewish families. Not surprisingly, many young men and women were eager to seek their spouses as well as their fortunes in the United States.[7] In the 1840s, nearly as many Jewish women as Jewish men left Bavaria's towns for America, with most women traveling to California with their husbands, brothers, friends, or other family members.[8] Of two brothers who left Württemberg's small village of Jebenhausen in 1846, Moses Einstein, a twenty-year-old butcher, became secretary of the Hebrew Benevolent Society in Sacramento and a spokesman for its Jewish community. A study of emigration from this village concludes that more than half of the 207 Jews who came to America from Jebenhausen before 1870 consisted of brother-and-sister family groups.[9]

These young people had been born during extremely difficult times, and repression and turmoil provided a catalyst for many of them to pursue new opportunities in the United States, a country that welcomed Jews as no nation ever had. As faster and safer transportation made travel easier, men and women also left their homes with less fear for their lives and more assurance that communication with their loved ones at home could be maintained.

The Birth of Community

"Among all the areas in the world, California is possibly the one in which the Jews are most widely dispersed. I do not know of one village, one hamlet, one *settlement* of any kind . . . where they have not established themselves," wrote Daniel Levy from the Gold Rush town of Indian Diggings in October 1855.[10] Far from their origins in Europe or the eastern United States, Jews sought kinship and familiar rituals with their coreligionists during this chaotic time. With a sense of urgency, many communities founded societies and Jewish newspapers to disseminate news and give new immigrants a feeling of community. Associations became the primary social agencies and caregivers, as there were few family members, cultural activities, or community structures to offer support, provide companionship, care for the sick, or even bury the dead. In some instances, Jews in California organized burial societies and obtained cemetery land before their non-Jewish neighbors had done so. Women too were an integral part of the history of the West, becoming wives, mothers, teachers, and shop owners. Although we have yet to discover the letters of a Jewish Dame Shirley, the documents of the era vividly describe Jewish women's activities in synagogue life, as volunteers, as choir members, as religious school teachers, and as members of their own benevolent and mutual aid associations. If Alexis de Tocqueville, who noted the spirit of voluntarism in American, had visited California during these years, he would have admired the many voluntary associations founded by Jews from different parts of the world.[11]

On September 22, 1849, the year 5610 of the Jewish calendar, San Francisco's Jews, including one woman, assembled to celebrate their first Jewish High Holiday service in a wood-framed tent-store. Less than two years after failing to unite, San Francisco Jewry formed two congregations, Emanu-El and Sherith Israel, which adhered to different Jewish traditions or *minhagim*—the Ashkenazi, or German, and the *Polen,* or Polish. Conducting services largely in German, Emanu-El's membership included a majority of Bavarian Jews and those who identified with them from other German states, as well as American Sephardim and French Jews. Among the members of this congregation were men who would become the elite of the Jewish community. Sherith Israel, known as the Polish congregation, did not have as distinctive an ethnic identity, most of its members coming primarily from England, Poland, Russia, and the eastern and southern United States.[12] The two pioneer congregations, eager for instant recognition and status, named themselves after the leading German and Sephardic congregations of New York City, replicating the rivalry of these paired religious traditions.

37

These two San Francisco congregations joined sixteen new congregations founded in the United States during the 1850s whose members came from a variety of European backgrounds. Six were Polish while only three were German.[13] While historians have traditionally labeled the European Jewish migration of the mid-nineteenth century the "German wave," more recently scholars have questioned the accuracy of this designation. Immigration officials often recorded a person's nationality as German if the immigrant spoke some German and held documents from a German port, but many of these immigrants were from Prussian Posen, a densely populated Polish Jewish settlement culturally different from Germany.[14] Moreover, because German nationality was considered more prestigious, Jews of Polish origin often chose to identify themselves as German.

It is clear that pioneer California's reputation for religious apathy is unfounded. Yet, as contemporary commentators observed, it was often difficult if not impossible for religious leaders to enforce observance by all Jews. By the 1860s, there were four regularly meeting congregations and several smaller, provisional ones in San Francisco.[15] In Sacramento, Placerville, Sonora, Marysville, Nevada City, Grass Valley, Mokelumne Hill, Stockton, and Jackson, services were well attended at least during the High Holidays and Passover, when Jews from the mining camps and small towns would seek to take part in services that reminded them of the way they were observed in their former homes.[16]

Yet some new Californians were genuinely observant, and their traditionalism is well documented. Their maintenance of Jewish dietary laws, their celebration of Jewish holidays, and their adherence to Jewish rituals, even during long sea voyages, is incontestable. Once in San Francisco, newcomers established kosher butcher shops and boarding houses where Jewish dietary laws were observed. Indeed, the San Francisco congregation split in two after its members failed to agree on a proper *shochet* (ritual butcher). In short, traditional Judaism found its place in the cities and towns of Gold Rush California because some of the pioneers were religiously knowledgeable Jews, able to build a *mikvah*[17] and provide the skills of the *shochet* and the *mohel,* as well as proficient prayer service leaders who were committed to keeping Jewish ritual and worship alive, no matter the obstacles.

Although there was concern for preserving traditional religious practices in California, Judaism was changing. Over the millennia Judaism has always adapted to its host culture.[18] In the United States, this meant a pervasive American Protestantism, with its emphasis on innovation, decorum, a weekly sermon, and women's participation in congregational life. Encouraged by the absence of a well-educated, authoritative rabbinate, Judaism followed suit and became increasingly American. Yet reforms came slowly and were adopted by only a few congregations at first. While these trends influenced newer and older congregations alike throughout the United States, including some in California, it was in the East that change came first. In 1851, when Emanu-El of San

Francisco was founded as an Orthodox congregation, Emanu-El of New York was already beginning to initiate reforms. By the 1860s, however, abridged prayer services and family pews at San Francisco's Emanu-El were becoming accepted practice. More resistant to change, Sherith Israel's congregation waited until 1870, upon moving to a new synagogue building, before eliminating the *mechitsa* (partition) separating men from women. More substantial modifications in traditional religious practices had to wait until the end of the nineteenth century. The same was true of other congregations in the region.[19]

As the community grew and prospered, most notably in San Francisco, so did its need for larger and more fashionable places of worship. San Francisco's two premier congregations first met in rented quarters, then constructed their own modest structures, and by the 1870s both were housed in impressive new synagogue buildings. In the period of avid synagogue and church building that followed the Civil War, San Francisco rivaled New York, Cincinnati, and Philadelphia in erecting impressive, often Moorish-style synagogues.[20] Completed in 1866, a year before its New York namesake, Emanu-El's Sutter Street temple, with its 165-foot-tall twin spires, could be seen for miles by ships sailing into San Francisco Bay, gracing the city skyline and attracting "the eye before all of the Christian churches."[21]

San Francisco became the center of Jewish life, as it did of California life. By the 1870s, a distant, drowsy California outpost had become "the City," a center of Jewish journalism and publication second only to New York City, as well as home to debate and literary societies, clubs, libraries, an orphan home, and a host of fraternal and benevolent organizations.[22] The pride of its inhabitants, both Jewish and gentile, San Francisco became not only the great metropolis of the West but one of the nation's greatest cities. Only one generation after California achieved statehood, its "Jewish population . . . was to stand second to that of New York State, [and] San Francisco's . . . second only to that of New York City."[23]

But San Francisco was not New York, and the distance from Jewish religious authority only exacerbated congregational conflict. In Cincinnati, when a question arose over the certification of a *shochet,* the *shochet* was sent to Baltimore or New York to be examined.[24] This was not an option for Californians, who had to rely on a single rabbi whose impartiality was not always universally trusted. Ultimately, laity had to make decisions on their own. Inevitably, synagogue leaders in California became more independent than their eastern counterparts and had no inhibitions about speaking up or standing out. At times the community was nonconformist in its practices. Such anomalies as the recitation of the Kaddish, or mourner's prayer, in tribute to the memory of an admired non-Jew, reflected an ability to synthesize Jewish traditions with a new, American way of life.

In California as elsewhere, Jews found they could remain Jews while adopting American ways. They joined with coreligionists to form the Concordia and other social clubs, to found literary and debating societies, and to establish B'nai B'rith and Kesher Shel Barzel lodges, among other fraternal organizations. In these associations, small merchants could meet independent of the religious and family constraints of the synagogue.[25] Developing at the same time that the synagogues were becoming more family- and less male-centered, fraternal associations afforded members freedom to gather on their own. In the same way charity balls, with their elaborate dinners and dances, gave men and women a new way to socialize. In adopting this American custom, California Jews also interjected philanthropic elements all their own.[26] In the gold country, where distances curtailed frequent socializing, events like these balls gave men and women from small towns and the surrounding gold camps a welcome chance to meet.

Jews and Gentiles

Although a number of Jews became miners, most newcomers schooled in commerce became shopkeepers, furnishing the mining and supply towns with a wide range of dry goods, clothing, and all manner of services, and brought the amenities of the city to the isolated mountain regions. With miners and merchants converging on California from every corner of the globe, their diverse ethnic identities and cultural values could not but come into play in their social and business relations. Because of the transient population, neighbors were less likely to know one another personally than they were to be aware of an individual's ethnicity. As Matthew Frye Jacobson has noted, "an earlier generation of Americans saw Celtic, Hebrew, Anglo-Saxon or Mediterranean physiognomies where today we see only subtly varying shades of a mostly undifferentiated whiteness."[27] This diverse group of newcomers impeded the enforcement of uniform American values and fostered a more open society in California than elsewhere.[28] Most Jews found acceptance because of the generally acknowledged value of their mercantile skills and their adherence to family and community life.[29] The often haphazard peopling of the mining towns brought the new inhabitants into relations of amiable interdependence, so that Jews could more readily assume middle-class roles than could newcomers in the older eastern cities. Also, eager to embrace their newfound nationality, Jewish immigrants were quick to join with other Americans. The Odd Fellows and the Masons welcomed Jews to their lodges, while gentiles were often invited to Jewish social events. One such ball held in the supply town of Marysville in 1856 attracted seventy couples for a dinner dance benefitting the Hebrew Benevolent Society. By 1880, 812 Jewish men had become naturalized United States citizens in the eight counties of the Mother Lode and the northern mines alone, a pattern that was doubtlessly duplicated many times over in San Francisco.[30]

New ways of socializing in California led to new kinds of business associations as well. In the West as in the East, merchants generally went into partnership with family members or coreligionists. But in the West, Jews entered into business associations with non-Jews, often fellow migrants, with greater frequency. Upon reaching Sacramento in 1849, for example, after crossing the Great Plains together on horseback, Louis Sloss, Dr. Richard Hayes McDonald, and Dr. C. H. (Judge) Swift opened a store together.[31] As the business community developed, Jews entered into partnerships as importers, or in the case of several native-born Americans, as lawyers. Especially prominent in this respect was Solomon Heydenfeldt, a native of Charleston, who not only entered into partnerships with non-Jews but became prominent in public life. Heydenfeldt, an early justice of the California Supreme Court, was only one among a number of able native-born Jews to attain public office immediately upon coming to California. Among those early elected to city and state offices were Jews of Sephardic heritage. Abraham Labatt, a merchant and the first president of Congregation Emanu-El, became an alderman for the new city of San Francisco, and Isaac Cardozo, an uncle of U.S. Supreme Court Justice Benjamin Cardozo, became a state assemblyman.[32] Jews not only entered public life as individuals, they affirmed their identification with their new country as members of Jewish organizations. Upon Abraham Lincoln's assassination in 1865, members of the B'nai B'rith lodges paid tribute to the martyred president by marching shoulder to shoulder with all of San Francisco in a symbolic funeral procession.

After the Civil War, "all who lived in America, alien-born and native-born, were resolved to become one people."[33] This was certainly true of the Jews of northern California, as was dramatically made clear in the unprecedented public circumcision in 1867 of a set of Jewish triplets in San Francisco. Naming their sons Abraham Lincoln Danziger, Jacob John Conness Danziger, and Isaac Andrew Johnson Danziger, the triplets' parents honored their new American and Californian godfathers along with Israel's ancient patriarchs.[34]

A Multiethnic Society

Jews flourished in California and especially in San Francisco because the new pluralistic, heterogeneous society accepted and even celebrated economic and religious freedom. Unlike the eastern United States, with its deep-rooted Protestant hegemony, the West allowed Jews and other European newcomers, notably Irish Catholics, to lay equal claim to acceptance and instant belonging.[35] Although anti-Semitism was not unknown in the West, Jews were readily incorporated into the ranks of the Euro-Americans. As historian Laurie F. Maffly-Kipp has argued, "cultural mobility and exposure to disparate societies are precisely what made frontier California exceptional."[36] The absence of a single dominant culture gave newcomers a sense of great freedom.[37] While many Jews came to California directly from Europe, others were native-born or had lived briefly in the eastern United States. Most Jews were first-generation immigrants and intended to settle permanently in the United States, whether in California or elsewhere, although many would visit Europe to maintain family and business relationships. Few were likely to return to live in an oppressive

Europe. In this respect, they had more in common with American farmers destined for Oregon than with the many single young Americans for whom the Gold Rush was but a passing adventure, after which they returned home to assume their family responsibilities in the East.[38]

Irish immigrants, even more than Jews, found a second home in California from which there was no returning. The most numerous ethnic group in San Francisco, they made Roman Catholicism the largest religious denomination in the state. While the Irish suffered nativist persecution elsewhere in the nation, in San Francisco they, like the Jews, benefitted from the city's ethnic diversity and cosmopolitanism. In a society lacking an established social order, Europeans and Euro-Americans, despite the differences among them, could assert their claims to public place and recognition to an unusual degree, which put the Irish community of San Francisco "a generation ahead of so much of the remainder of the United States."[39]

Far different was the position of non-Europeans, especially Chinese, Hispanics, and blacks. Even worse was the fate of Native Americans, who were forcibly removed from their lands and often hunted down like wild beasts. The most numerous of the non-Europeans, Hispanics and Chinese were victimized especially in the mining camps, where competition for gold exacerbated xenophobic fears that led in 1850 to a state law imposing a foreign miners' license tax designed to make mining an "American only" occupation.[40] Californios and Mexicans who had reached the foothills in the first few months of the Gold Rush were particular targets of violence. Although they had arrived ahead of most Americans, all Spanish-speaking people, including the native Californios, were labeled aliens.[41] Subjected to violence, threatened with lynching, and forcibly removed from their claims, they fled the gold country almost entirely. The Chinese, legislated to the margins of society, remained segregated, while the experience of blacks, of whom there were only five hundred in San Francisco in 1852, "resembled . . . the plight of the Chinese."[42] Until the passage of the Fifteenth Amendment in 1870, the new state legislature prohibited blacks from voting, and San Francisco schools were not integrated until 1875.

The Documents

This documentary presents the stories of the new Californians in all their diversity and complexity. In their letters, diaries, memoirs, in court and news reports, and in photographs, we learn of the public and private moments of their individual lives. In their institutional, synagogue, and organizational records, we learn document by document how they saw themselves and were seen, and how they built their lives and communities.

Part 1, "Looking West," begins with the first descriptions of California Jewish life to reach Europe and concludes with sojourners' and immigrants' accounts of their journeys to the Pacific coast. Chapter 1 introduces California to the Jews of Europe and the eastern states. The five accounts reproduced here, published in Germany, France, England, and the United States, informed readers of Jewish life in California and let prospective immigrants know what they might expect there. These stories reveal both the promises and the perils that California held for newcomers. The authors of the memoirs in chapter 2 were probably influenced by such accounts in their decision to migrate to California. In this chapter, "The Westward Journey," which describes the reasons and motives for emigration to California, Jewish men, women, and one teenager depict their travels in spirited detail, often recounting the strict observance of Jewish religious practices along the way.

Part 2, "San Francisco: The Instant Pacific Metropolis," documents in two chapters the creation of religious and communal institutions in San Francisco. Through an examination of letters and synagogue records, chapter 3 chronicles the difficulties entailed in forming new congregations at a time when American Judaism was in flux, newcomers at loose ends, and California and all of its inhabitants experiencing the boom-and-bust cycles of a turbulent economy. Sermons and lectures show the concern of religious leaders for congregants who were neglecting Judaism for financial gain. Synagogue documents attest that Jews heeded the warnings of their leaders by promptly establishing two Orthodox congregations in San Francisco. But it would be the laity, not the rabbinate, that would determine both the leadership and the membership criteria. In California, the rabbi, or *hazzan,* had to apply for the job, to speak English, to lecture, as did Protestant ministers, and to be a worthy ambassador to the non-Jewish world. In an era when traditionalism was giving way to new religious practices, congregations encouraged American-style prayer services that emphasized decorum and organization. Choirs and organs were introduced, and seating segregated by gender was replaced by family pews; thus were synagogue services brought more closely into line with the American model.

Although Jews usually migrated as individuals, they soon banded together to build Jewish organizations and associations. The first of these, as we see in chapter 4, were initiated primarily by single men living in their tent-stores or boarding houses. As early as 1851, there were two kosher boarding houses in San Francisco where roomers could gather to eat a kosher meal, exchange news about family, friends, and business, play cards, and plan for the future. Like other newcomers who longed for familiar activities in a still lawless and primitive city, they soon found ways to entertain themselves and to care for one another. As the constitutions of the initial societies reveal, they met such immediate critical needs as the nursing of the sick, the burying of the dead, and the care of orphans, widows, and the poor. Newspaper advertisements and community directories highlight the educational aspects of the social clubs, including the scheduling of lectures and debates. These societies, like those formed for religious worship, were often founded by men from the same region of Europe, who assumed the burden of caring for their fellow members' essential needs.

Part 3, "Personal Struggles," records business successes and failures and the everyday and extraordinary moments of family life. Letters, public records, memoirs, and advertisements—the subject of chapter 5—acquaint the reader with the goals, rewards, and hazards faced by Jewish merchants whose small businesses were so vital to the economic health of the cities. Gold Rush California proved especially attractive to immigrants because they brought with them skills that were highly valued in the West. Merchants who could turn to friends and family for financial aid did not have to rely on the powerful credit agency, R. G. Dun and Company, which discriminated against Jews.[43] Similarly, family ties enabled Jewish men and women to import goods from Europe and other parts of the United States. They also were able to change occupations, progressing from peddler to storekeeper or manufacturer more readily than was possible elsewhere.[44] Despite many failures, they were able to improve themselves occupationally and financially to a remarkable degree. Having arrived in California with the right skills at the right time, they settled in communities where a laissez faire climate prevailed, rather than a tyrannical government that set the terms for business. Since Americans of the nineteenth century admired self-made businessmen and valued family and religious life, Jews fit in well to this new world and were usually a welcome part of the mercantile community's leadership.

Chapter 6 portrays family life. While the first Jewish immigrants were almost entirely single men, by 1852 women and children began to immigrate in greater numbers. In the 1850s the minute books of Congregation Sherith Israel recorded many marriages and noted women's contributions to religious life, including the fashioning of decorative ritual objects. The joys of courtship, marriage, childbirth, and family life-cycle rituals became a part of everyday life, as did the tragic frequency of child burials. As the community grew and prospered, family celebrations often became public displays of status and family position. Toward the end of this period, as merchant princes emerged, especially in San Francisco, a new western Jewish society was born in which families competed with each other in hosting the most elegant events.

Part 4, "Gold Rush Country," documents how Jewish life in the mining and supply towns developed differently from life in the city. As chapter 7 demonstrates, for almost three decades the mining towns of northern California, in spite of ups and downs, continued to thrive, and Jewish merchants played a significant part in their growth. Each town was distinctive, as was each town's economy. Some were based entirely on mining, while others were important for farming and trade as well. Each town also had a distinctive ethnic mix. Gold, deposited in uneven quantities, at varying depths, and in different forms throughout the area often required specialized mining techniques. Settlers tended to be drawn to areas where special skills learned in their native countries were in demand. Miners and townspeople usually were identified by ethnic origin. In Grass Valley, the Cornish, who were skilled tunnel miners, set the tone, while in Nevada City the Chinese mined the more accessible placer.[45] Letters and newspaper reports tell of the settlers' struggles, defeats, and triumphs. In a society where gambling, thieving, violence, murder, and vigilantism were prevalent, Jews, here as elsewhere, instituted their time-honored traditions of benevolence, *tzedakah,* and religious observance, debated the need to reform Jewish observance, and fulfilled their obligations to aid coreligionists in parts of the world where Jews were less fortunate.

Although the mining towns had much in common with the supply towns on California's waterways, Jewish life in the boom-and-bust mining towns was always unstable, whereas community life in the supply towns was steadier. Chapter 8 details the history of Sacramento, Stockton, and Marysville, the major conduits between the mining towns and the great port of San Francisco. Here the stores of Jewish merchants provided both everyday necessities and luxury goods imported from the eastern states and Europe that would be sold to miners, farmers, and housewives. Letters, newspaper reports, and advertisements tell of the growth and development of business, and of social and religious life in these small towns. Unlike the inhabitants of the mining towns, Jews in these larger and less chaotic communities generated a substantial, consistent organizational life that included several fraternal associations, such as Kesher Shel Barzel and B'nai B'rith, which sponsored well-attended community events, including Purim celebrations. In addition, these towns were frequently visited by rabbis from San Francisco who traveled up the rivers to lecture, teach, officiate at religious ceremonies, and help to establish congregations. But as river travel declined and railroads gained in importance, the supply towns too lost their primacy and fell into decline.

Part 5, "Group Relations," examines how Jews became part of the diverse new West and how the young Jewish communities sustained ties with Jews elsewhere in the world. In the cosmopolitan atmosphere of these years, Jews were accepted and respected by their neighbors despite persistent Old World stereotypes. Chapter 9, "The 'Mythical Jew' and the 'Jew Next Door,'" demonstrates how Jews as individuals and Jews as a group were often stereotyped.[46] The documents here reflect the ambiguities, contradictions, and inconsistencies in the thinking of many Christians who held a damning Christian image of the Jew that contrasted with the often likable individuals from whom they purchased mining supplies.

Chapter 10, "The Wider Community," illustrates how Jews built legal, political, and personal alliances with gentiles. As court cases and civic activities show, Jews quickly became a visible public presence in California life. At times, events elsewhere also affected the status of Jews in the state. During the Civil War, the patriotism of the Jewish community was called into question, as some of California's Jews were of southern origin and not above suspicion in a profoundly partisan, predominately pro-Union state.

During these formative years, Jewish Californians first established relations with the larger Jewish world, as we see in chapter 11. Northern California communities responded to the plight of less fortunate Jews by collecting funds for Jewish causes and showing a special concern for the impoverished, dependent Jews of Palestine. Newspaper reports and letters, as well as a constant stream of visitors and newcomers from near and far, sustained an abiding concern with the condition of coreligionists abroad.

Part 6, "Looking Backward and Forward," views the Jews in the West through the eyes of two outstanding visiting rabbis, Max Lilienthal and Isaac Mayer Wise. Both American rabbis wanted to tell the world and their fellow Jews what they had observed and to analyze the growth of the singular community that westerners were creating. Written in the mid-1870s, when San Francisco was attaining a new maturity despite problems intensified by depression, their accounts celebrated individual Jewish economic achievement, the Jewish community's high standing in the larger society, and the importance of maintaining Judaism in the face of sporadic religious indifference and ethnic division.

Chosen for their intrinsic interest and for their value in demonstrating the many facets of the emerging Jewish community, most of these documents appear between the covers of a book for the first time. Arranged in chronological order, they differ in length and in format. Dates cited in the document titles are those described by the document, not always the date the document was published. While some selections have been abridged by inserting bracketed ellipses [. . .], all are printed in their original or translated form so as to preserve their flavor and authenticity, except where grievous errors or anomalies in grammar, syntax, or spelling call for editorial emendation or explanation. A [sic] was used only when a spelling or grammatical error could be perceived as a typographical error. Offensive language was not altered. Where a single word or phrase is translated or transliterated, its language of origin is placed in brackets.[47] Names are spelled as they appear in the original language; thus *Eckman* in English becomes *Eckmann* in German publications.

Notes

1. Leonard Pitt, *Decline of the Californios* (Berkeley: University of California Press, 1971), 43; Robert Levinson, *The Jews in the California Gold Rush* (Berkeley: Commission for the Preservation of Pioneer Jewish Cemeteries and Landmarks of the Judah L. Magnes Museum, 1994), 127.

2. These population figures are based on contemporary estimates, which vary considerably. See Jacob Rader Marcus, *To Count a People: American Jewish Population Data, 1585–1984* (Lanham, Md.: University Press of America, 1990), 239.

3. Beginning in the late seventeenth century, Sephardic Jews established congregations on the East Coast. By the 1840s the Sephardim, who faced expulsion when they first arrived in New Amsterdam, were well established in business, social, and religious life. Shearith Israel, North America's first synagogue, was built in New York in 1730; its Sephardic form of worship was ethnically foreign to later Ashkenazi immigrants.

4. Hasia R. Diner, *A Time for Gathering: The Second Migration 1820–1880* (Baltimore: Johns Hopkins University Press, 1992), 47.

5. Bertram Wallace Korn, *Eventful Years and Experiences: Studies in Nineteenth Century American Jewish History* (Cincinnati: American Jewish Archives, 1954), 1.

6. Germany was not united until 1871. The treatment of Jews differed in the various states of Bavaria, Hesse, Baden, Swabia, Posen, and Silesia, as well as in Prussia, where by 1871, 70 percent of the Jews in the "German" territories made their homes.

7. Diner, *A Time for Gathering,* 16.

8. Diner, *A Time for Gathering,* 47.

9. Diner, *A Time for Gathering,* 48; Stefan Rohrbacher, "From Württemberg to America: A Nineteenth-Century German-Jewish Village on Its Way to the New World, *American Jewish Archives* 41:2 (1989): 163. Einstein signed a public letter protesting anti-Semitic comments by California House Speaker William W. Stow.

10. Daniel Levy, "Letters about the Jews of California, 1855–1858," *Western States Jewish Historical Quarterly* 3:2 (1971): 93.

11. Alexis de Tocqueville, *Democracy in America* (1835) (New York: Vantage Books, 1956), vol. 2, 114.

12. For a discussion of the relationship of German and Polish Jews in the United States, see Rudolf Glanz, " 'The Bayer' and the 'Pollack' in America," *Jewish Social Studies* 17 (1955): 27–42.

13. Diner, *A Time for Gathering,* 50. This period also saw the establishment of the first Russian congregations in the United States.

14. See Norton B. Stern and William M. Kramer, "The Major Role of Polish Jews in the Pioneer West," *Western States Jewish Historical Quarterly* 8 (1976): 326–44; Diner, *A Time for Gathering,* 49–56.

15. In the 1850s and 1860s there were several short-lived congregations, including two founded respectively by American Sephardim and Eastern European Orthodox Jews. Beth Israel, founded in 1860, was the most Orthodox of the regularly meeting congregations. Ohabai Shalome was founded in San Francisco in 1864 by former members of Emanu-El.

16. Sacramento, Placerville, Stockton, and Jackson erected synagogue buildings.

17. *Weekly Gleaner* (Apr. 17, 1857, 8) announced that Hebrah Shimra Shabboth had built a *mikvah* in North Beach. This small Orthodox congregation

of Russians and Poles, according to I. J. Benjamin, held services Monday, Thursday, and Saturday in addition to holy days (*Three Years in America, 1859–1862,* trans. Charles Reznikoff [Philadelphia: Jewish Publication Society of America, 1956], vol. 1, 210).

18. See Joseph Blau, *Judaism in America: From Curiosity to Third Faith* (Chicago: University of Chicago Press, 1976).

19. Congregations in the East sometimes moved into church buildings with family pews, which led to the adoption of family seating. In the West, where everything was new, Jews more often built their own synagogues. See Jonathan D. Sarna, "The Debate over Mixed Seating in the American Synagogue," in *The American Synagogue,* ed. Jack Wertheimer (Cambridge: Cambridge University Press, 1987), 363.

20. In 1864 Keneseth Israel of Philadelphia started the Moorish-style synagogue-building trend in the United States, modeling its structure after the Temple in Kassel, Germany (Alan Silverstein, *Alternatives to Assimilation* [Hanover, N.H.: University Press of New England for Brandeis University Press, 1994], 20).

21. Moses Rischin, "The Jewish Experience in America: A View from the West," in *Jews of the American West,* ed. Moses Rischin and John Livingston (Detroit: Wayne State University Press, 1991), 35.

22. Rischin, "The Jewish Experience in America," 34–36.

23. Rischin, "The Jewish Experience in America," 35.

24. Karla Goldman, "In Search of an American Judaism," in *An Inventory of Promises: Essays on American Jewish History: In Honor of Moses Rischin,* ed. Jeffrey S. Gurock and Marc Lee Raphael (Brooklyn: Carlson, 1995), 142.

25. Leon Jick, *The Americanization of the Synagogue, 1820–1870* (Hanover, N.H.: University Press of New England for Brandeis University Press, 1992), 180.

26. Diner, *A Time for Gathering,* 104.

27. Matthew Frye Jacobson, *Whiteness of a Different Color: European Immigrants and the Alchemy of Race* (Cambridge: Harvard University Press, 1998), 10.

28. Laurie F. Maffly-Kipp, *Religion and Society in Frontier California* (New Haven: Yale University Press, 1994), 10.

29. Ralph Mann, *After the Gold Rush: Society in Grass Valley and Nevada City, California 1849–1870* (Stanford: Stanford University Press, 1982), 121.

30. Levinson, *Jews in the California Gold Rush,* 63.

31. For more about Louis Sloss and his journey west, see chapter 2 and Frank V. McDonald, *A Biography of Richard Hayes McDonald* (Cambridge: John Wilson and Son, 1881).

32. Fred Rosenbaum, *Architects of Reform: Congregational and Community Leadership Emanu-El of San Francisco, 1849–1980* (Berkeley: Western Jewish History Center, Judah L. Magnes Memorial Museum, 1980), 5, 16.

33. Marcus Hansen, *The Atlantic Migration, 1607–1860* (Cambridge: Harvard University Press, 1945), 306.

34. The Irish-born John Conness represented California in the U.S. Senate from 1863 to 1869.

35. See Glenna Matthews, "Forging a Cosmopolitan Civic Culture: The Regional Consciousness of San Francisco and Northern California," in *Many Wests: Place, Culture, and Regional Identity,* ed. Michael Steiner and David Wrobel (Lawrence: University Press of Kansas, 1997).

36. Maffly-Kipp, *Religion and Society in Frontier California,* 10.

37. Maffly-Kipp, *Religion and Society in Frontier California,* 117.

38. Maffly-Kipp, *Religion and Society in Frontier California,* 133.

39. R. A. Burchell, *The San Francisco Irish* (Manchester: Manchester University Press, 1979), 3–4, 184.

40. Pitt, *Decline of the Californios,* 57.

41. Pitt, *Decline of the Californios,* 53.

42. Albert S. Broussard, *Black San Francisco: The Struggle for Racial Equality in the West, 1900–1954* (Lawrence: University Press of Kansas, 1993), 15.

43. Peter R. Decker, *Fortunes and Failures: White-Collar Mobility in Nineteenth-Century San Francisco* (Cambridge: Harvard University Press, 1979), 100.

44. For a discussion of capitalist possibilities in California, see Richard A. Walker, "California's Debt to Nature: Natural Resources and the Golden Road to Capitalist Growth, 1848–1940," *Annals of the Association of American Geographers* 91:1 (2001): 167–99.

45. A placer is a deposit of gravel or sand containing gold that can be washed out. See Mann, *After the Gold Rush,* 198.

46. See Jonathan D. Sarna, "The 'Mythical Jew' and the 'Jew Next Door' in Nineteenth-Century America," in *Anti-Semitism in American History,* ed. David A. Gerber (Urbana: University of Illinois Press, 1986).

47. Hebrew words can be transliterated differently, with "b" and "v" interchanged as in "chebra" and "chevra."

Historical Overview: The Rush for Gold

EXCEPT FOR FLEETING VENTURES BY EXPLORERS, CALIFORNIA RE-
mained remote and virtually unknown to the world until the Gold Rush. For
millennia, Native Americans—Coast Miwok, Miwok, and Ohlone—had led lives
untouched by outsiders. Only in 1776 did the Spanish found Mission Dolores
and the Presidio at a site they named Yerba Buena, subsequently renamed
San Francisco, the name given to the bay itself. Spain's control of this distant
outpost remained weak, and throughout the brief period of Mexican rule no
more than seven thousand non-native men, women, and children lived in
California. After the short-lived Mexican war (1846–48), California was ceded
to the United States by the treaty of Guadalupe Hidalgo; it achieved statehood
in 1850 without first becoming a territory.

On May 12, 1848, three months after the treaty had been signed, a merchant,
real estate speculator, publisher, and elder of the Mormon Church set the Gold
Rush in motion. After receiving payment for goods in gold, Samuel Brannan
made his plans. Stocking his store at Sutter's Fort with all the supplies a gold
miner would need, he proceeded to San Francisco, where he announced the
stupendous news. The actual discoverer of California's gold, James Marshall,
a master carpenter, had come upon the nuggets four months earlier while
inspecting construction work on a sawmill on the American River. But Marshall
and the mill's owner, Swiss immigrant John Sutter, had agreed that completing
the sawmill was paramount and that until then the discovery would remain
confidential. With Brannan's announcement, the secret was out. News of the
gold strike spread like a flash fire. Within a few weeks the two San Francisco weeklies, the *Californian* and the *California Star,* closed down, as staff,
subscribers, and advertisers all left for the gold mines. "The whole country,
from San Francisco to Los Angeles, and from the sea shore to the base of the
Sierra Nevadas, resounds with the sordid cry of gold, GOLD, GOLD! while the
field is left half-planted, the house half-built, and everything neglected but
the manufacture of shovels and pickaxes," announced the *Californian* just
before it ceased publication.[1]

As Samuel Brannan had anticipated, the rush for gold created a prodigious
demand for everyday necessities, from eggs at $12 a dozen to shovels priced
at $10 each. Six thousand men, mostly from the western regions of North and
South America, hastened to the Sierra hills during the next twelve months.
The following year many thousands of Americans, Europeans, and Chinese
traveled great distances to reach the golden hills. Immediately upon landing in
San Francisco, captains, crews, and passengers alike abandoned ship, leaving

vessels to rot in the harbor while they "went to see the elephant," California's metaphor for a phenomenon that drove men to risk their lives and livelihoods in the goldfields.

With adventurers from every corner of the world flocking to the hills and down the streams of the new gold country, the *California Christian Advocate* described California's transformation as "the birth of a nation in a day."[2] Upon the lands of the Californios, Miwok, Coast Miwok, and Ohlone descended American Protestants of every sect and men of no religion at all—Germans, French, English, and Italians, Chinese Buddhists, Irish Catholics, Jews of diverse origins, and representatives of all peoples who dreamed of gold, prosperity, and adventure. Would-be miners, merchants, and sundry sojourners made the long trek to the Land of the Gold Mountain, as the Chinese called California. Together, amid turmoil and strife, they inadvertently founded a new cosmopolitan society, establishing overnight the governmental, commercial, and religious foundations that would change California's physical and cultural landscape forever. Soon Spanish, Chinese, French, German, Yiddish, and of course English, spoken in a variety of accents, were heard throughout the gold country, most especially on the crowded, muddy streets of San Francisco.

Once a sleepy little port town, San Francisco was reborn as a city in the blink of an eye. From a mere 850 inhabitants in 1848,[3] the city had become, two years later, "a boiling mass of people of all nations," its population exceeding 20,000.[4] According to the first official state census, that number had grown to 35,000 by 1852. And by 1870, San Francisco had become the tenth largest—and the most diverse—city in the nation, with almost half of its inhabitants foreign born and a high percentage of the rest first- and second- generation Americans.[5] An "instant city," it lacked traditions "and learned to adapt" to the "immediate needs" and customs of its diverse residents.[6] By 1880, this remarkable city and its environs sustained no less than a quarter of a million people.[7]

It was a different story in the mining districts. With the waning of the Gold Rush, many of the inhabitants of the mining towns moved on to more promising places. The fall in population of the eight mining counties, from a high of 123,822 in 1852 to 85,026 in 1880, registered the general decline.[8] As the economy of the region shifted from mining to agriculture and specialized business, the small general merchandise stores that had supplied miners with food, clothing, and other necessities became obsolete.[9]

Significantly, the end of the Gold Rush era did not come simultaneously to all mining camps, and outward migration was a gradual and individual process. Some merchants, seeking new prospects, headed for new mining regions farther north in California, or to Nevada, Colorado, or Canada. Some returned to the East or even to Europe. But the great majority migrated to the growing population centers of California and other western states. Whether they remained merchants, ventured into manufacturing, or invested their capital in other enterprises, most were attracted to the burgeoning metropolis of San Francisco.[10]

With a Jewish population of sixteen thousand in 1880, San Francisco was a magnet for single people and families alike.[11] By then the settled cosmopolitan society boasted an established Jewish elite and an ever growing variety of religious and social organizations. The demographic changes that had taken place there since 1850 were dramatic, whether measured by origin, gender, class, occupation, family structure, or social and economic status. In 1852 four out of ten residents were foreign born; in 1880 only two out of ten fit that description. In 1852 there were 6.5 males for every single female; by 1880 males and females were equal in number. San Francisco had not only become a Jewish family town but in many respects had come to resemble the larger Irish community. However different from each other, both communities found themselves largely in step with what in these years had become the nation's most cosmopolitan city and one that was also imbued with a heightened class consciousness. In 1879 a newly published *Elite Directory* was uniquely divided into a Christian "Calling and Address List" and a "Jewish List," with Jews making up nearly 20 percent of the directory's entries though they constituted only 7 percent of the city's population.[12] On the "Christian List," not the Jewish one, were the names of Levi Strauss and the dry goods importer Abraham Weil. This curious accommodation to social prejudice demonstrated the deference accorded men of wealth who also happened to be leaders of the Jewish community, as well as reflecting prevailing social boundaries. "The remarkable achievement of the San Francisco Jewish community," concluded historian Peter Decker, "was the speed and success with which they organized to protect and insulate themselves from the excess of laissez-faire capitalism" while gaining for themselves "a respect and admiration from virtually all segments of the city population on the strength of their voluntary associations and finally, their achievements in the merchant businesses."[13] Although by the 1880s there had been repeated ups and downs in the new state's economy, San Francisco's Jewish community had weathered the storms and had attained economic and social stability.

Notes

1. Walton Bean and James Rawls, *California: An Interpretive History* (New York: McGraw-Hill, 1988), 85.

2. Maffly-Kipp, *Religion and Society in Frontier California,* 49.

3. Roger W. Lotchin, *San Francisco, 1846–1856: From Hamlet to City* (New York: Oxford University Press, 1974), 8.

4. Alex Friman, "Two Swedes in the California Goldfields: Allvar Kullgren and Carl August Modh, 1850–1856," *Swedish- American Historical Quarterly* 34:2 (1983): 108.

5. R. A. Burchell, *The San Francisco Irish* (Manchester: Manchester University Press, 1979), 3.

6. Gunther Barth, *Instant Cities: Urbanization and the Rise of San Francisco and Denver* (New York: Oxford University Press, 1975), xxii.

7. Burchell, *San Francisco Irish,* 3.

8. Levinson, *Jews in the California Gold Rush,* 127.

9. Levinson, *Jews in the California Gold Rush,* 126.

10. Levinson, *Jews in the California Gold Rush,* 127–30.

11. Jacob Rader Marcus, *To Count a People: American Jewish Population Data, 1585–1984* (Lanham, Md.: University Press of America, 1990), 28.

12. Peter R. Decker, "Jewish Merchants in San Francisco: Social Mobility on the Urban Frontier," in *The Jews of the West: The Metropolitan Years,* ed. Moses Rischin (Berkeley: American Jewish Historical Society, Waltham, Mass., for the Western Jewish History Center of the Judah L. Magnes Memorial Museum, 1979), 22.

13. Decker, *Fortunes and Failures,* 211, 238–39; Decker, "Jewish Merchants in San Francisco," 21–23.

I
Looking West

I
Europe Discovers California

THE UNITED STATES, WITH ITS PROMISE OF ECONOMIC OPPORTUNITY and religious freedom, had been drawing large numbers of Jewish immigrants from Europe for more than a decade before the first gold was discovered in California. Word of the Gold strike only increased the appeal of this new "promised land."

Jewish periodicals in England, France, and Germany carried the news from California, and their reports both catalyzed emigration and provided a picture of how the new American communities were viewed abroad. Jewish immigrants, on arrival in California, sent letters home describing the new land, while others wrote reports for European periodicals. Those at home were hungry to know what California was really like and wondered especially whether Jews could maintain their religious traditions in such an utterly alien environment. One of the most important newspapers, the Leipzig *Allgemeine Zeitung des Judentums* (General Journal of Judaism) regularly carried news of the growth of the California community.

When an early Jewish immigrant, Samuel H. Cohen, sent his sister in London a description of San Francisco life, Jewish interest was so great that the *Jewish Chronicle* of London published his letter in full. Abraham Abrahamsohn's even more expansive account of western life carefully detailed the physical appearance of San Francisco and the mining towns and described his life as a miner and a Jew. So avid was the interest in news from California that Daniel Levy, an active member of the San Francisco Jewish community and a correspondent for *Archives Israélites,* regularly sent descriptive letters to the

Paris publication.[1] A friend of Levy's, I. J. Benjamin, the eyes and ears of the European Jewish community, came to California on a self-appointed mission to report on Jewish and secular life, a visit that culminated in the publication of *Drei Jahre in Amerika* (Three Years in America), which concentrates on the time he spent in California.

While they were addressed to Jews in the three European countries and written in German, English, and French, these reports focus on similar themes. They describe the role of Jews in commerce, demonstrate strong ties to Jewish tradition, and, perhaps especially significant for their readers, show how California Jews were forming congregations and other organizations necessary for Jewish observance. Because they were written by people of different backgrounds, ages, and religious practices, these reports present readers with divergent interpretations of Jewish life.

---

1. *Archives Israélites,* a widely read French Jewish reformist weekly, was first published in Paris in 1840. In 1849, after being refused a teaching position due to Catholic opposition, Isadore Cahen succeeded his father as editor, using the periodical as an outlet for his activist views (Paula E. Hyman, *The Jews of Modern France* [Berkeley: University of California Press, 1998], 64).

1
Views from Germany, *Allgemeine Zeitung des Judentums*, 1850–1856

The following entries informed German-speaking Jews about the growth of the Jewish community in California. Founded in 1837, the *Allgemeine Zeitung des Judentums,* "a non partisan vessel for all Jewish interests," was the first Jewish weekly to focus on contemporary Jewish life. Read throughout the Jewish world, it published news reports from Jewish communities near and far, accounts of cultural events, and items of literary interest. Its diverse articles about California came from a variety of sources, most notably translations of American and French Jewish periodicals and signed and unsigned correspondence from Jewish émigrés. Most were from anonymous correspondents and focused on particular issues or events.

The last article in this chronicle was written by Rabbi Julius Eckman, the first rabbi to lead a congregation in San Francisco. It was the most significant article sent to the *Allgemeine Zeitung des Judentums* from San Francisco during this period. The pious Eckman described the community and all its organizations and stated his specific contributions to West Coast Judaism. Although Eckman regularly sent correspondence to American Jewish newspapers critiquing San Francisco Jewry, this letter, printed in a German Jewish newspaper, not only reported to European Jewry on the condition of the community and the American reality of voluntary adherence to Judaism and community but also showed how news of San Francisco Jewry's internal struggles could be disseminated worldwide.

From these articles the reader learns not only of religious developments but of outside events that affected the Jewish community. Future immigrants and European family members alike learned of the benefits and pitfalls of life in the far West.

March 18, 1850
America

In California, to which many Israelites have emigrated, several congregations have formed.

Source: *Allgemeine Zeitung des Judentums,* Leipzig, 1850–63, trans. Mary A. Akatiff: 14:12 (March 18, 1850), 138; 15:29 (July 14, 1851), 345; 16:34 (August 16, 1852), 402; 18:11 (March 13, 1854), 132; 19:22 (May 28, 1854), 287–88; 20:11 (March 10, 1856), 151–52; Rabbi Julius Eckman, 20:13 (March 24, 1856), 173–76.

July 14, 1851

San Francisco, April 30th. In my earlier letter of March 21st I told you of the movement that is taking place here to build a synagogue; but this object did not preserve the harmony that was desired; national antipathies came between things and thwarted the union that would have done so much good for the Israelites here, whose number is not all that large, and who mostly consist of merchants who have lived in the southern and southwestern states for many years. At the end of many private negotiations and at one stormy public meeting two congregations [Sherith Israel and Emanu-El] were formed, of which one is already incorporated. This situation brought with it another problem. The pious Sir Moses Montefiore sent Mr. Davidson, the agent of the Rothschild estate in California, a valuable Torah, with glorious gold jewelry, as a free gift for the first congregation to be established in San Francisco. Even though there was a congregation for communal prayer [Sherith Israel], it was not incorporated, and thus this newly formed congregation had to give the beautiful Sepher to the German congregation [Emanu-El] which already possesses 5,000 for the building fund. (Asmon.)

August 16, 1852

Jews Leave Havre for San Francisco.

A ship recently left here for California with many Jews as passengers. They had with them a Chasan, a Shochet, Mohel, two Sepherim, all the accouterments of Judaism. (Arch. Isr de Fr.)

March 13, 1854

America

San Francisco. On the 18th of September, the "New Portuguese Congregation" held a meeting at the house of Mr. Jacob Dessau, elected their administrators, and collected an impressive sum for the building of a synagogue.[2] (One sees that with this synagogue old inherited fissures are eternalized [naturally very innocent ones], but the name "Jacob Dessau" shows that they are no longer tied to their heritage.) (Editor) [Isaac Leeser] (Occident)

---

2. The Sephardic congregation of Shaar Hashamayim met for a short time in San Francisco. Some of its members had previously belonged to Congregations Emanu-El and Sherith Israel. Jacob Dessau, formerly of Philadelphia, was married to a Sephardic woman (Norton B. Stern and William M. Kramer, "The Historical Recovery of the Pioneer Sephardic Jews of California," *Western States Jewish Historical Quarterly* 8:1 [1975]: 5).

May 28, 1854

North America

San Francisco (California) in April. (Private communication). Here as well, the persecution-thirsty pietism, under whose larva even more and more envy and begrudging sentiments lie, has attempted to make its voice heard. The question of whether Jews should be forced to celebrate Sunday, that is, to abstain from all work, the congressman Stow of Santa Cruz County said the following in the Assembly session of the State of California:

> I have no sympathy with the Jews, and would, were it in my power, enforce a regulation that would eliminate them from not only our county, but from the entire state. I am for a Jew-tax that is so high, that [Jews] would not be able to operate any more shops. The basis of republican institutions is the Christian Sabbath and the Christian religion. The Jews must join the majority. They are a class of people who come here only to make money, and who leave the country as soon as they have money. They do not invest any money, and they do not erect any of the beautiful houses that decorate our country. They all hope someday to settle in their Jerusalem. The Bible is the basis of our institutions, and the law making process must support its commandments.

General protest rose up against this speech, which was printed in the following article in a California newspaper, and this deserves mention in your paper as well:

> So this is how far we've come, that such things can be said publicly in the halls of our lawmakers: "The Bible is the basis of the constitution in America!" Whoever asked the representative from Santa Cruz County [to speak on] such a thing (in which a few business-men feel themselves to be oppressed through Jewish hard work). He admits himself at the beginning of his speech that it is only the right of the majority that gives the Christians legal priority and not the very basis of the constitution. Therefore, if tomorrow the majority of citizens are Jews, then we will celebrate Saturday and, were there a Turkish majority, then Friday. Finally this party showed its true colors, that is, that they are not concerned with the observation of the Sabbath alone, but that this is about religious persecution. Therefore, a Jew-tax, such as in the dark middle ages, was suggested in the halls of the law-makers in California. A Jewish Quarter will follow, into which, at night, the slaves of the Holy Roman Empire will be locked; the persecution of other Christian sects will follow. California, the youngest state of our republic, had to experience the

61

degradation of seeing such rules defended for the first time in its halls; one saw the phantom rise from the dark grave of the middle ages that has already flooded Europe with blood. [. . .]

A Jewish judge sits in the bench of the Supreme Court, in all branches of administration we meet Jews, their benevolent organizations are better administrated than any others, and the poorest, least educated Jew in the state would easily be a wiseman like Solon[3] compared to the representative from Santa Cruz County. [. . .]

In our cities the Jews build Synagogues of stone, in which no dissident is crushed, in which poisonous religious fanaticism is not promulgated, but rather simple morals taught. Jewry would expel a man such as the Senator of Santa Cruz County, who, in such a way, crushes those who think differently, so branding them with the name of his own religion.[4]

March 10, 1856

America

California (Arch. Isr de Fr.) During a recent crossing of the steam ship, "Uncle Sam" from Saint Jean to San Francisco, cholera broke out on board with great force and in twelve days snatched away one third of the passengers and crew; the survivors themselves had to fear that they all would die, and in this horrible "he who can, save himself" atmosphere, everyone thinks only of his own salvation. The dismay and horror were at their peak; but one of the passengers, the Dr. Israel Moses, stayed awake four days and four nights without rest, barely time to eat, in order to serve the well being of all; a good many people owe their lives to him; however, his comportment was not once the object of praise in all of the California press, and as if the Divine plan wanted to praise so much sacrifice, Mr. Moses was spared from the horrible illness.

March 24, 1856

From California, San Francisco, 5. February

The status of Jewish affairs in California

[by Rabbi Julius Eckman]

---

3. Solon (639–559 BCE) was an Athenian lawgiver and poet who freed those in debt from slavery and reformed the oligarchy, allowing men of all classes to sit in the court and in the assembly.

4. For more on the Sunday Laws and the reaction of the Jewish community see chapter 10.

Rabbi Julius Eckman, Emanu-El, 1854–55. From Jacob Voorsanger, *The Chronicles of Emanu-El* (San Francisco: Emanu-El, 1900). Courtesy of the Western Jewish History Center, Judah L. Magnes Museum.

Already for quite some time I have found myself wanting to take care to communicate to my European comrades in faith a short portrayal of our social and religious affairs; I was, however, up until this point hindered from being able to fulfill this duty. I will now hope that the content of this will be not without practical uses for some readers; some of the data could be of use to historians as well.

Should the following truthful and unexaggerated portrayal not meet expectations, the reader so inclined should consider that we have settled here only in the past few years; and that institutions cannot be brought into existence within a single day nor can they be brought to completion.[5]

And, therefore, I will continue with the comment, that the lure of gold, which brought people from all lands in 1849, also brought with it a number of Abraham's progeny, who have in the meantime expanded their population to such an extent that there is no town in California where not a few of our

---

5. For more about Rabbi Julius Eckman and religious life in San Francisco see chapter 3.

brothers are settled, and who are dedicated to the most various occupations. Especially high in numbers are the populations of Stockton, Sacramento and San Francisco. In the latter city there is perhaps not a single street that cannot claim one or many Jewish inhabitants. Their numbers in the state, or even in the cities, cannot be supplied any more exactly, because the census does not take into consideration denominational differences under the population, and the lack of our religious organization also prevents us from learning of a more precise number. Nevertheless, the number of them in San Francisco alone is probably around seven thousand individuals.[6]

Their social status does not form any especially remarkable characteristics. We have a Jewish judge in the Supreme Court, Judge Heidenfeld [Heydenfeldt],[7] whose understanding for law and justice has found general recognition; beyond that we had a Jewish County Treasurer in 1853 and in 1852 a City Councilman.[8] At the present time we number two or three civil servants in the Custom House. Other than these individuals there are many doctors and lawyers of our faith.

In commercial respects, they exercise an important influence here. A few branches of trade are almost exclusively in their hands. However, following from various crises and the constant fluctuation of all conditions here, our position is less than brilliant, and there is much worry here, and even poverty. Especially in the past eighteen months or so, a poorer class of people settled here, who have difficulty supporting themselves. Nevertheless, the employed and useful immigrants will probably have an easier time getting ahead here than in other countries.

However, it is painful to comment that the progress of religion has not held pace with that of other concerns. A massive indifference rules almost everywhere here. Usually, the first step toward the religious life begins with death. In places where a considerable number of Israelites live, the start up of a Jewish cemetery is the beginning of a future congregation; then follows the union for benevolence; after which there begins, or there is loaned the sepher, in order to make Minyan on Rosh Hashana and Yom Kippur—then a synagogue is built—and this external materialistic building is the highest point that we have reached thus far. There is not yet a trace of inner spiritual stirring.

---

6. It is difficult to know the exact Jewish population for these years as there was much coming and going within California and in the region as a whole.

7. Solomon Heydenfeldt was a member of the California Supreme Court from January 1851 to January 1857, when he resigned. In 1858 he successfully defended Mr. Newman, a Sacramento merchant who was convicted by a lower court of selling merchandise on Sunday in defiance of the Sunday Law. Heydenfeldt was also the presiding officer at the 1859 Music Hall meeting protesting the Mortara abduction. See chapter 10.

8. Two Sephardic Jews, Abraham Labatt and Joseph Shannon, both served as presidents of Congregation Emanu-El. In 1851 Labatt was elected one of eight San Francisco aldermen and Shannon was elected county treasurer.

Thus we have, outside of our societies in Los Angeles, Sonora and elsewhere, a wooden synagogue in Stockton, and a second one in Sacramento, and two of stucco in San Francisco. [. . .]

It is often to be regretted that this people, who already have to fight against prejudices in this country coming from the outside, also has to have its strength split by small internal national prejudices. In the entire area of the United States, the Bavarian and Alsatian immigrants are in conflict with those from Poland to such a degree that even marriages between them are formed very seldom.

This antipathy became visible from the earliest times up until the present to such a degree that, of the few creations that we have brought to pass, all are duplicated each time—two synagogues, two support unions for men, and likewise, two for women. Each one is apparently a repetition, a complete duplicate, both serve the same purpose, the only difference being that one is for Germans and the others for Poles (including Russians, Prussians, Bohemians, etc).

We want to describe this more closely now.

1. The Polish synagogue, Schaarith Israel [Sherith Israel], has around seventy contributors, of whom each individual one pays a sum of two Talers.[9] This income is increased through the renting of seats, each of which brings in about 5 to 15 dollars per year (seats in churches bring in about 100 to 200 dollars per year). This income is enough to pay the monthly interest on a mortgage, and to pay yearly about 1000 dollars into the same, so that after about 4 or 5 years the debt is paid off. Until then the synagogue does not keep a Rabbi, Preacher, Teacher (for the children) nor a Chasan; no, not even a Schamasch [shammash]. The whole undertaking of this synagogue (which names itself a congregation) is limited to gathering a Minyan on the Sabbath and holidays. The Minhag and other duties of the same are in every way Polish Minhag.

2. The German Synagogue, Emmanuel, now has around 120 contributors, each of whom pays two dollars per month, and the other income of the same equals around 1500 dollars per year. This synagogue was built about a year and a half ago on stocks so that it is in debt about 20,000 dollars, that is to be paid off in ten years. [. . .]

It was decided for such a building to acquire a preacher, and so one was engaged for three years with a yearly salary of 3500 dollars. On the recommendation a Dr. Steinberg from Munster was chosen. At the same time, one sent a circular out to the Occident without noting

---

9. The *taler* was a German currency between the fifteenth and nineteenth centuries.

that one had already found the object of the choice and that only in the case that the Dr. [Steinberg] should not accept the position would there be a vacancy. Dr. Julius Eckmann,[10] previously a preacher in Charleston, later a Rabbi in Mobile, was moved to introduce himself personally, rather than to write, and undertook the trip, being not a little surprised on his arrival in San Francisco to hear that the choice had already been made, almost simultaneous with the time of the publication of the circular. Dr. Steinberg did not accept the position. Eckmann had come to San Francisco on his own accord and served the congregation for a year. However, the congregation did not renew Rabbi Eckmann's contract and they decided to engage a [different] preacher, and to announce such a position in Germany right away.[11] [. . .] This is the current condition of the Synagogue Emmanuel. Now we will come to the New Congregation.

3. Organized about three months ago, with a small number of members, and only the small contribution of two dollars monthly, it suffers a lack of everything. We have here neither pious men who could bring up sacrifices for the religion, nor do we have an understanding of community or sense of refinement that distinguishes the Israelite congregations in the older countries. Here it might be commented upon that the ritual of this congregation, with a few changes, is Portuguese.

4. Religious School. Right at his arrival, Dr. Eckmann endowed a school for all Jewish children which is enjoying only after eighteen months a thriving condition. Until now the lessons were free of charge, but now because the new congregation is not strong enough to pay a spiritual leader, and that school is generally effective, there is to be established a fund for the school, to which general contributions can accumulate. The children are taught four times weekly the following subjects: 1) biblical history, 2) biblical archaeology, 3) Catechism, 4) Ethics, 5) Hebrew. The presentation is made in the English language.[12]

---

10. In German publications Eckman is usually spelled *Eckmann*.

11. The congregation was divided as to whether or not to renew Eckman's contract. The contingent led by the Bavarians and Alsatians prevailed over the American-led faction. It was then decided that while they waited for a rabbi who would be more suited to the congregation (a German with prestige who would introduce reforms), they would hire a *hazzan* to lead the congregation. They first hired Herman Bien as "lecturer and teacher"; when he did not meet their needs, they hired Daniel Levy, an Alsatian, as *hazzan* (see document 4). (Fred Rosenbaum, *Visions of Reform: Congregation Emanu-El and the Jews of San Francisco, 1849–1999* [Berkeley: Judah L. Magnes Museum, 2000], 27–28.)

12. See chapter 4.

5. and 6. The First Hebrew Benevolent Society, and the Eureka Society, both to support those needy and sick; to the former belong all those who are not German, and its effectiveness reaches everyone who bids help, without consideration of nationality. On the other hand, the Eureka Society is exclusive; it supports only Germans.

7. and 8. The Ladies Hebrew Benevolent Society and the German Women's Union. About six months ago there was a plea to women to gather in the form of a society. The first of the aforementioned society formed then. But there, too, entered the spirit of conflict. The Alsatian and the Bavarian womenfolk excluded themselves at this meeting from the English, the Polish and the others, and formed shortly thereafter the German Women's Society.

9. The Young Men's Mutual Assistance Society. This organization has as its duty to create mutual support for its members, mostly very young people. In addition, it also has a social tendency: in its rooms they keep newspapers and they have otherwise appointed the rooms such that evenings can be pleasantly spent there. This union has the unusual feature that the young people are left to their own devices. The have turned to neither experienced nor learned men for matters of advice, instruction, entertainment or teaching.

Finally, I must comment in general, that there is yet much to be desired. We have here neither Orthodoxy nor Reform. The formal aspects of our religion are generally neglected. The Sabbath is generally not observed. In my considerable knowledge of the local area I know only two merchants who close their shops on the Sabbath. The laws of eating are also not observed. Only exceptionally, at weddings (and then only by Beriths) are kosher dishes brought to the table. Even at the occasion of the dedication of the synagogues the dishes at the ball were delivered by Christian restaurateurs. That the often held balls of the benevolent societies are also catered in this way it is probably not necessary to mention. The synagogues are only opened on the Sabbath, holidays and fast days, as is the general custom in the United States. Moreover it is only on Rosh Hashanah and Yom Kippur that they are visited, on normal Sabbath days the synagogues are little visited.

It is also to be mentioned that the synagogues have not yet realized the importance of accepting the appropriate synagogue authority. The whole undertaking of the self-named congregations attempts nothing more than to read prayers and to gather a Minyan. The care of the old men is not the business of the congregation; neither is the undertaking of the dead; the education of the youth has been up until now also not an affair of the congregation. Couples have been married by unauthorized individuals. Until last year there were no divorces. Since then, Dr. Eckmann has granted three widows. He denied a fourth

בשר

☞ The MEAT properly killed and Inspected is
to be had only at the following places—

LEVI & WOLFE,
Y. ABRAHAMS,
M. BECK,
M.HAYMAN,
I. GOLDSMITH.

je19

The *Shochet* debate was fought on the pages of the *Weekly Gleaner*, Oct. 30,
1857. Advertisements were placed by different factions of the community;
each believed that only their selected *shochet* could provide truly kosher meat.

case because the woman was insane, and the husband wanted to push her away
heartlessly [. . .]

The Schechitah [koshering of meat] here is also not under the domain of
the congregations. Up until 15 months ago the Schochat of each synagogue
received 12.5 dollars per month. However, because he was not a German, the
German synagogue (Emmanuel) looked for a German to engage. They turned
to Dr. Eckmann for Rabbalah for a young man who wanted to function as the
congregation Schochat for no pay. The former did not at first want to let himself
be misused in that way, because it was known to him that the young man had
taken [unkosher] meals daily on the steamship during his trip, and that on
his arrival here he had similarly lived in a treppha boarding house, and then
had a fight on the Sabbath, and also later, on the same day, just like on all
others had his shop open and worked. [. . .] Dr. Eckmann, on the request of
the Parnass of the Polish synagogue, explained in the newspaper (so as not to be
too personal) that only Mr. G. [Isaac Goldsmith][13] was the dependable Schochat,
the synagogue Emmanuel was so upset about it, that they immediately called a
congregation meeting, where Dr. Eckmann was taken from his office. Because
this was impossible to do, they gave the Rabbi a vote of censure.

To finally come to the end, it must be commented upon that time itself must
bring all things to fruition, and that, in consideration of the fact that seven

---

13. The Polish-born Goldsmith arrived with his family in 1852. See chapter 3.

years ago there was not even a trace [of] any institution, they will, God willing, conduct themselves much differently in a few years, and on the whole we have little to complain about. And if God should grant us his blessings, so we may raise ourselves with eagles' wings and follow our brothers in the east in all things good, Golden, and holy.

    J. E. [Rabbi Julius Eckman]

2

"We Have Kosher Meat,
a Burial Ground, and a Synagogue"

Samuel H. Cohen, *Jewish Chronicle,* London, 1851

In this letter to his sister, Samuel H. Cohen, a young English immigrant and the first secretary of congregation Sherith Israel, describes his religious observance. The four men mentioned in the letter were involved in preliminary meetings held to establish a single congregation for the community. Cohen, with Mark Isaacs, was appointed to find a place of worship for the 1851 observance of Passover. However, before Passover they broke into two congregations, and Cohen's hostility to the members of Emanu-El probably was due to that split.

San Francisco.—As every matter relating to this part of the world is of interest, we give an extract of a letter from Mr. S. H. Cohen to his sister, under date of 8th May, 1851:—"We have Kosher meat,[14] a burial-ground, and a synagogue [Sherith Israel] which was formed, three days before Passover, by twelve single young men and one married man. We have now forty-two members, principally English, and we have some old married men to lead us the correct way. Our form of prayers is that of the Great Synagogue [of London]. We voted in our officers, who are all married men except two. I was elected honorary secretary, and had thirty-eight out of forty-two votes. There was a congregation formed last year but they could not agree; they have, however, again formed themselves into a congregation [Emanu-El], and number sixty members, Germans, Portuguese and Americans, but it is not supposed it will last long. Ours is considered the correct congregation, as we have a Shochet [written in Hebrew], but for which office they have no competent person. Our president is Mr. Joseph, an American; our treasurer, Mr. Hart, a Pole.[15] Mr. Isaacs, of Brown's Lane, baked the matzos for Passover, with whom twelve of

---

Source: Samuel H. Cohen, *Jewish Chronicle* (London), July 18, 1851, 327.

14. Cohen is probably referring to the meat supplied by B. Adler (see illustration from Alexander Iser, *The California Hebrew and English Almanac for the Year 5612 [1851–52]* [San Francisco: Albion Job, 1851].)

15. Henry Hart, who would become the vice president and treasurer of Sherith Israel for two years, was appointed to the 1851 committee to arrange for the baking of matzoth. Hart was also the founding treasurer of the First Hebrew Benevolent Society of San Francisco and head of the committee that raised $4,000 for the first Jewish cemetery there.

כשר

BOARDING HOUSE,

By E. Alexander, Battery street, near Washington street, at Mr. Prag's building.

כשר

BOARDING HOUSE,

By Rubenstein, Montgomery street, between Pine and Bush streets. Meals at all hours, and at moderate charges.

כשר

BEEF, VEAL, AND MUTTON,

Of the best quality, killed by a competent and qualified שוחט, always obtainable, at the corner of Sacramento and Dupont streets, by B. Adler.

מצות

Cakes for next פסח will be baked by Mark Isaacs, Bartol street, Broadway. A competent משגיח will be in attendance. Board over פסח at moderate charges.

Advertisements from the *California Hebrew and English Almanac for the Year 5612* (San Francisco: Albion Press, 1851). Compiled by Alexander Iser. Courtesy of the American Jewish Historical Society.

us youngsters passed the festival. I do not think that the Jews in any part of the world could have kept the Passover more strictly than we did, and I am happy to say he intends to keep a Kosher house all the year round, so that we shall be enabled to eat lawful meats."[16]

16. Like Cohen, Mark Isaacs was probably from London. There must have been a large demand for kosher-for-Passover foods, for Isaacs hired an assistant, Abraham Abrahamson (see illustration from Iser's *Almanac*). Also in 1851, Philip Mann's Hebrew Boarding House hosted Jewish activities (*Western States Jewish Historical Quarterly* 7:1 [1974]: 7).

3

"America . . .
Where No Kind of Work Is Ever Shameful"

Abraham Abrahamsohn, 1856

Abraham Abrahamsohn, a wanderer and adventurer, dictated this account
to Friedrich Mihm in 1856, three years after returning to Germany from his
extensive travels. In 1849, upon leaving his wife and children in West Prussia,
Abrahamsohn set off for America. After spending a year and a half in the
eastern United States, he sailed for California, arriving in the spring of 1851;
he stayed for a little over a year. A jack of all trades, he became a miner, a
merchant, a tailor, a baker of matzoth, and a *mohel*. An avid gambler, he left
California in 1852 to try his luck in Australia, returning to Germany a year
later.[17]

As told to Friedrich Mihm.

Foreword

The traveller, now a resident of Erfurt, was lying comfortably on the couch
in his robe, aromatic cigar smoke drifting from his bearded lips, with a crystal
pitcher of Coburg beer in front of him. He told of his travels and his life
in foreign countries, and I, sitting across from him, made notes of the most
interesting parts.

The sketches related to me are true, completely true. Whether or not I have
been able to depict them well and interestingly is to be decided by indulgent
experts; I am only certain of the diligence and honest care I applied.

The traveller did not keep a diary. During his long and distant trips he
did not have the least intention of making observations for a literary work,
but purely and solely set out to earn a fortune. Thus, many things will have
been observed and interpreted lightly and fleetingly. Despite this, the work is
not lacking in individual sincerity. The proper names are given as they were
pronounced to me.

SOURCE: Abraham Abrahamsohn, *An Interesting Account of the Travels of Abraham
Abrahamsohn to America, Especially to the Goldmines of California and Australia*
(Ilmenau, Germany: Carl Friedrich Trommsdorff, 1856), translator unknown. Western
Jewish History Center of the Judah L. Magnes Museum, Berkeley, California.

17. The foreword, translated by Marlene P. Toeppen, was printed in the *Western States
Jewish Historical Quarterly.* The translator of the main body of the book is unknown.
A typescript of the volume is held by the Western Jewish History Center of the Judah L.
Magnes Museum in Berkeley (hereafter the Western Jewish History Center).

The traveller does not intend to move in high-flown tirades and phrases, loaded with a geographical mess stolen from other books, but means to present to the eye of the reader, briefly and vividly, all that he saw, heard and did.
Friedrich Mihm
Coburg, 1856

* * *

With a golden hope in my breast I came to the country and the city [San Francisco] and took lodgings in a guesthouse on the dock, a big wooden stall, until I should have the opportunity to find a store to rent. So I had time to look around the city. There was no trace of houses such as we see in Europe except for a few stone public buildings. Frames of narrow boards and lath, covered with many-colored thin cotton cloth on the sides and over the top, generally a mounteback firm with giant letters over the entrance make up the dwellings of the people; the unpaved streets must be bottomless when it rains; mostly the shacks had steps like ladders made out of old barrel staves, and the floors likewise. On the floors lay, even at night, great heaps of goods of all kinds, and it was said that robbery was uncommon since punishment for stealing was the gallows and for even petty theft there were lashings and ears cut off. Such severity was necessary with the enormous hordes of rabble, and up in the gold region lynch law provided quick justice as we shall see later. The shacks were expensive to build because of the high price of wood brought from afar by ships.

On all the faces of the people I met, and as well from their bearing and their business, one distinctly saw the desire to get rich in this Eldorado as soon as possible and to leave still sooner. Many people went about the streets, carrying great goldpieces, which looked like gilded iron dross, or with bags of grains of gold and strutting about. They had come from the mines in order to lose in one night in the gambling hells, what they had gained either with ease, or great labor, and to enjoy themselves, then to go back to the mountains to burrow for more gold.

But the town was also crowded with gambling houses from which came noisy music. For drums, trumpets, violins, flutes and guitars endeavored to make passersby curious and to entice those who came in with heaps of silver and dubloons. If the instruments made a deafening noise the people were happy. Many of my countrymen appeared in such places as musicians, especially with flute and guitar. Beautiful girls, mostly French, and brown black-eyed Mexicans with fragrant flowers in their hands and at their bosoms, coquetting with word, smile and glance, offered to all who came in Ale, porter, different wines, punch and grog, white bread, butter, cheese and indeed—free. Here they played Faro, 21, blind-hooky, dice, roulet and Monte, a Mexican game like *Landsknecht.*

The gaming houses like the restaurants, fancy-goods stores, cafés and fine bakeries, were mostly run by the French; the many Germans had the better sales places; the Jews usually handled clothing, and the Chinese, many of whom lived here, had eating houses, which because of their respectability and

74

cheapness were very well patronized. The population of the city, chiefly from the United States, is difficult to estimate because of the coming and going; but it must be at least 30,000.

Labor was enormously high, also rent and food. A day laborer received 6 dollars a day, a craftsman 10 to 18 and a billiardmarker [scorekeeper] made more than $100 a month. A stall, called a room, cost 20 to 30 dollars a month; place for a trunk cost 1 to 2 dollars, and people were happy to be under a roof—of sail cloth that is! The price of goods and food was sometimes more, sometimes less, according to the traffic but always expensive and this can be seen from the fact that I had to pay $1 for an egg.

My goods finally arrived the 15th of April on the ship *Schallhorn* and now I rented a place for $30 a month. It consisted of 4 bare wooden walls, covered inside with colored paper, the wooden floor had cracks as wide as your finger, the roof of canvas protected against the sun and insufficiently against rain. It stood on the dock which extended a halfmile over the sea and at high tide, the salt water came into my house. In short order I unpacked my boxes, and decorated the store with clothing, and on the first day I took in $86 with a fair profit. As my business was good, I soon found I had to replenish my wares every evening. In short I was in a position to send to my wife $100 through Davidson,[18] the agent here from Rothschilds in London, and to send her the thrilling news that I was in California. I had not done this before, so that she would not worry. Now I had a well-stocked store.

However, my luck didn't last long. On the first of May, a date often fateful in my life, at 2 o'clock in the morning a fire broke out at my neighbor's and this spread lightning fast through the wooden houses so when the cry of terror woke me from soft sleep there was nothing to do but jump out of the window of my blazing hut in my under clothes.[19] In spite of the most earnest pleas of the householders, a whole row of houses was torn down to halt the raging flames— even the planks in the street turned to glowing coals. All of S F except 10 to 12 houses burnt to the ground in a few hours. The night before I had spent all my money for new goods and was now burned out and a beggar. Thus I stood, full of anxiety in this foreign city, the dwelling place of avarice, the gold fever, the most unfeeling self-interest. About me were ashes, and waste and poverty. Then a good friend came to me in my need: Saul, from Markolni in Posen. He offered me the needful clothes, hose, boots, a blue woolen shirt, a wool cover, a cap, a leather belt, and a pick, shovel, a pan, a strong knife and said: "Abrahamsohn, There is nothing for you to do, but to go to the mines and try your luck. Here is $10 travel money and best wishes for a happy return."

18. Benjamin Davidson had been in San Francisco since 1849.
19. The correct date for this fire is May 4.

I knew well that gold digging was not such an easy thing, and I must now do what the quarrymen do in Germany with the sweat of their brow. But necessity forced me to bite into this sour apple, so I found 9 companions and traveled with them to the wonderful shimmering blue mountains to the gold mines. Wherever the eye fell, there were gorgeous flowers, which cannot be imagined. At night the heavens were our roof, the wool cover our bed.

On the second day we spent the night under a mighty hollow oak, with thick foliage. Soon we had a fine fire for preparing the commonly used coffee and the welcome evening meal in iron pots. I went to the brook for water. Then there was a sudden cry of fright from my companions. I looked around and saw a grizzly bear running around and then away. Our fright was great, for this animal is considered the most savage in the country. From reliable sources I heard that this grizzly bear, as it is called, is stronger and more savage than the black bear; may be 9 feet tall, weigh 12 to 14 hundred pounds, has huge paws with sharp claws, a long-haired dark brown fur with pale ends, and lives on animals and if those are lacking on berries and roots. The Indians and also the settlers fear it as the smartest and most dangerous robber, which attacks buffaloes with its jaws. If he is excited, he attacks the hunter, and it takes strength and cleverness to overcome him with a hunting knife. The Redskins wear his claws around their necks as a sign of valor and make their children fear him. Our sleeping neighbor had been in the hollow tree and frightened by the noises and the fire had crept out and fallen suddenly among my comrades. To all appearances he was a young one. During the night we were disturbed by the howling of the coyote, a kind of jackal which lives in the ground. They are little bigger than our fox.

On the third day we came to the mountains and reached Beavertown, a place made up of straggling tents of miners and gold diggers where the red white and blue flag of the American Union waved over many stores or shops. The curse of San Francisco, gambling dens, was here, too, and since coins were seldom seen gold nuggets were used. In a circle of one mile (English mile) 1000 men worked. Here I bought a hatchet and heavy canvas for my tent, took leave of my companions, to be on my own, and went to the upper part of the ravine— the lower part was already torn up with a hundred men working busily. My first work was to set up my dwelling. My hatchet got me 3 stakes, over which I spread the canvas, made a bed of leaves covered with my woolen cover. The workers themselves made a rule that each person had the unquestioned right to a place 16 ft. long, 8 ft. wide and 3 ft. to throw the earth, to dig as deep as he wants, and then to find another place. Usually they dug 16 to 28 ft. down where in white or blue loam soil the most gold is found, but it also occurs in the upper layers of sand. Some dig as deep as 40–100 ft. After I had broken the upper layer with the pick, and thrown the earth out with my shovel, I took a sack of that clay earth to a brook a half mile away, put it in the flat iron vessel (washpan), set it in the water and mixed the earth with my hands. This made the water run away and the heavy gold remained behind. It was in little pieces, grains and nuggets. On the average, the highest daily take is one ounce or 16 dollars, the lowest $3. Many find nothing. On the 1st day I made enough so that I went to the store, where besides food and drink, you can buy clothing and all kinds of tools, for an enormous price, and bought myself 1 lb. salt, 1 lb. sugar, 1/2 lb tea for $1, 4 lb. potatoes, 2 lbs. beef, and 8 lbs flour. Naturally the price depends on the greater or less demand, and the number of miners. On how high it is may be seen from the fact that a pound of wheat flour (there is no other kind here) costs 3/4 to $1, 1 lb salt $1, a lb of beef $2, a little glass of whisky in a liquor store 45 cents, later 25 cents or 35 Kreuzer. With that purchase I had enough for a week. I mixed the flour with water and made a sour dough in flat round cakes and baked them in the hot ashes.

My surroundings were magnificent. The vegetation of the fragrant mountain had all kinds of pine trees, alder and hazelbushes, and were at the top were gorgeous cedars and redwood trees and oaks where spotted wildcats and panthers prey on the deer and rabbits. Bushy partridges went clucking through the thickets and larks soared into the lovely blue heavens and awoke me to my difficult task. [. . .]

After eight days I was heartily sick of the work so I went into partnership with a cartwright from Schwabia and with a wheelbarrow in the burning sunshine we carried the dirt from the mountain down to the brook. From the extraordinary exertion, my eyes were bloodshot and my hands so sore that every night I had to soak them in water, to cool them a little and alleviate the pain. Oh, how I remembered my confectionery store in Germany. I worked thus for 3 months and my share came to $40. [. . .]

One day I had a message from a tailor, a companion from Posen, by the name of Harris, who lived in Sacramento City and to whom I had lent $20 in New York for the trip to California. He had learned that I was in the mines, and invited me to come to him as he was doing well.

As I was already long-since fed-up with the hard work, bringing in only a paltry return, I decided to answer the call from my friend. So I sold my gear, bought provisions, and after a hearty farewell from my comrades started off. On the way I saw my first California Indians. They were copper-brown, short and strongly built, some naked and some with a blanket, others with shirts, pants, vests and caps, a red scarf flung around the waist. The gayer the colors, the better they liked them. They had black eyes, chin tattooed with blue, a proud nose and their long black hair was ornamented with pins, feathers and glass beads. Their appearance in general is good-humored and trustworthy. Weapons: Very cleverly worked bows and arrows, and also flints. Their women, Squaws, sometimes with beautiful figures and pretty faces, wear only a little apron, some have many-colored mantillas. They gather the food and prepare it. In love and loyalty they are very indulgent and the men flare up dangerously with jealousy. Fish, game and acorns made into mush, nuts, wild cherries in bunches, gooseberries, redwood berries, strawberries, and raspberries as well as wild grapes are used for food. Where they can, the redskins beg for wheat and food and similar presents. Pointed-looking black and white dogs are their constant companions and are very good at hunting. The Redmen, unfortunately love their poison, brandy. It weakens their virility and the day is not far off when the last Indian will follow to the grave those already there.

Sacramento City lies north of SF on the not unimportant, widely-traveled Sacramento River from which it is separated by a thicket of tall trees, and like every other city, consists of tents and wooden shacks, which are lost under those trees. I soon found the tailor in a room 10 ft square sitting on a crude table and busily plying his needle. As lively as a goat he jumped up and hugged me, crying "Abrahamsohn, are you finally here?"

"As you see, soul and body," I replied, and further said "What kind of a profitable business are you doing here?"

"Well, I sew old clothes, pants and jackets and shirts of all the nations on earth," and he regarded me with an animated look.

"And what shall I do here, as I do not understand how to sew on a button?" I asked softly, for my heart had sunk to my boots.

"Oh, a lot, my dear friend! You shall go from house to house and ask if clothes should be repaired or altered. You recommend me as one of the best artists in this line; you bring the clothes and then deliver them to the customers."

"But, my God," I cried, "here I left my homeland more than two years ago, I am in America—in California, full of gold, and I should do something like this?"

"What did you do in the mines? Nothing, and besides you had sunburn, and privation and toil. And who knows you here? Moreover, are you not in America, where no kind of work is ever shameful? Abrahamsohn, Abrahamsohn, really I thought you were smarter."

So I made my decision, procured some courage in a liquor store and went to find customers. Since I found many, within 3 weeks I had earned $92 and really very easily. I went about and recommended, and the tailor sewed at home. But our mutual success did not last long. The man with the shears and the needle began to find fault with me in every way; first, I had quoted too low a price and he thought I was getting a cut; or the price was too high and then the clients did not patronize us and the silk-thread tailor's reputation would be lost. Finally I couldn't do anything right for him, gave him half of my savings—I had the money on deposit—and asked for the return of the $20 New York loan. He retorted that I had earned $92 only because of him and he would not give me a cent more, and the long-legged spider threw me out.

I knew that I had worked for him honorably as an honorable man and had not taken a penny from him. So I thought of revenge. Across the street there was a place to rent and I rented it and put up a huge sign over the door "Decart" or, "Tailor and Mender" The next day I had customers, the old ones knew me already. At night I cleaned and mended, for I had learned much of the trade from the ill-tempered tailor, and in six weeks I had made $300. My neighbor across the way, however, who almost burst with rage, had almost no customers, began to drink and gamble and was a lost man. Soon I had all the trade.

Once I got into trouble because of my vaunted skill, but my audacity helped me out. A rich merchant had come to me to have a coat lined with silk. I tried very hard but the stitches were a yard long, as I did not know how to sew a fine seam. When the gentleman looked at the coat, he shook his head, and said: "My grandmother could have done it like this."

But I answered him saucily: "I'm not here to sew, but to make money." He looked at me for a moment, then slapped me on the shoulder and said "You're a clever fellow and you'll get ahead here." [. . .]

In Germany, I had practiced circumcision on Jewish boys, an honorable, holy profession, which is never paid for there. A Jew from Regensburg who lived in San Francisco, and had seen my certificate asked me to come to San Francisco for the circumcision of his son. I received $60 for this and $10 for travel expense. After I came back to Sacramento City, I bought all that I would need and set myself up in business in San Francisco as a circumcizer, charging $50 for each child. Through this religious profession I had access to the richest and most prominent families. Since the Jews in this city were competing with their elders in Egyptian lands in the matter of offspring, I had much to do and in about half a year had laid by a profit of 800 Dollars.[20]

My assets were now $1200 and I prepared to reap a rich harvest. Within 24 hours I built a wooden stall in the California manner on the dock, furnished it with chairs, tables, mirrors, shining tablecloths, plates, glasses, bottles etc. and the restaurant was ready. I had a French cook, three waitresses and a dishwasher, and this was a fine restaurant. In Germany, however, no respectable man would have entered it. With many customers, and my circumcision busi-ness, I would do very well, though I had to pay high wages. [. . .]

A foolish man trusts his hardwon capital to the stormy sea, the boat sinks and he stands on the shore wringing his hands. I put all I possessed into the restaurant and on April 1, 1851, in the morning there was a cry of "Fire" in the city and in half an hour my possessions had been burnt down and ruined and I had nothing but my clothes and $150. It burned up a good part of the city; but in 8 days there was nothing to see of the destruction. Everywhere new and better dwelling had been built and out of the gambling houses came the sounds of violins and guitars the cold even-toned cry of won or lost.

I went to a German missionary who had given up his calling and sought fortune in the mines. I went to him in my doubt, a passion that was wholly foreign to me. To force Fortune, I began to gamble and lost all my money in

---

20. Abrahamsohn is referring to the biblical period when Jews lived in Egypt.

one night. The next day I had a circumcision and the money disappeared that night at the green table. So I lived through Hell, unhappy with my better self, and though I had the best intentions during the day, in the evening witchcraft drew me to those accursed houses if I had any money. I look back on that time with horror. [. . .]

It was almost time for Jewish Easter [Passover], and the newspapers carried an ad for a man who could bake Easter cakes and *Mazzen* [*matzoth*]. I went to the Jewish baker Eisacks [Isaacs]²¹ who wanted help and for a daily wage of $8 and living expenses—I still lived with my missionary—from six o'clock in the morning to 6 at night, I shoved Mazzen in the oven to bake. The last day before Easter I got $5 for a half-day's work and saved this. The rest of my wages had already disappeared over the green table. [. . .]

The thought that in California my luck was not blooming, that I would do better to leave and go to Australia came to a head. The newspapers which sang the praise of the Australian goldmines, my missionary talking interminably, my gaming vice which threatened not to leave me here—were important reasons. I paid my passage on an English sailboat to Sydney on the coast of New South Wales in Australia, or as it is commonly called in Germany, New Holland, for $70 and in May left San Francisco Bay with about 200 passengers—mostly unlucky Californians, men who had searched in vain for luck.

I have given a true account of the life, customs and inhabitants of Upper California, as well as of my activities I can confidently advise anyone who has a sound, stalwart body, knows how to endure trouble and privation and does not fear the hardest work, to come to California. But he who thinks roasted doves fly about here with golden wings asking to be plucked and eaten, should stay at home. I saw not a few such persons. [. . .]

California will be truly a blessed land, if the thirst for gold is stilled, and together with agriculture, the flowering of social life, manufacturing, trade, science, and art come to pass.

---

21. This was clearly Mark Isaacs, who advertised matzoth and board over Passover in the 1851 Iser *Almanac*.

4
"Rapid and Glorious Results"
Daniel Levy, *Archives Israélites,* Paris, 1855–1858

Daniel Levy's career and education set him apart from the many Jewish merchants who settled in San Francisco. Born in Luxheim in Lorraine in 1826, he studied at the University of Paris and became a teacher of languages. Sent by the French government, he served as the principal of a public school for Jewish boys in Oran, Algeria.[22] There he was jailed briefly for printing a cartoon satirizing Louis Napoleon in *La Lune,* which he edited.[23]

In 1855 Levy joined his brothers in San Francisco, where he became the reader at Congregation Emanu-El (1857–64). In addition, he taught languages at San Francisco's Boys' High School and later at the academy headed by Rabbi Elkan Cohn. Active in many French organizations, including the French Hospital, the French library, the Alliance Française, the Ligue Nationale, and the Cercle Français, Levy also was the author of *L'Autriche-Hongrie ses Institutions Et ses Nationalites (1871),* and *Les Français En Californie* (1884). He received the Cross of the Legion of Honor for his service to the French government in 1909 and died in San Francisco the following year.

The following letters were written to the editor of the *Archives Israélites* in Paris by one of California's most cosmopolitan chroniclers.[24]

1

Indian Diggings, California, Oct. 30, 1855.
To the Editor of the *Archives Israélites.* Sir,
Among all the areas in the world, California is possibly the one in which the Jews are most widely dispersed. I do not know of one village, one hamlet, one *settlement* of any kind, either in the North, the mining area, or the South, the region of ranchos, where they have not established themselves. Germany

---

Source: Daniel Levy, *Archives Israélites* (Paris), 1855–58. "Letters about the Jews of California: 1855–1858," *Western States Jewish Historical Quarterly* 3:2 (1971): 86–112. Copies of the letters in the original French are held by the Western Jewish History Center of the Judah L. Magnes Museum, Berkeley, California.

22. For more about Daniel Levy, see *Western States Jewish Historical Quarterly* 3:2 (1971): 86.

23. Martin Meyer, *Western Jewry: An Account of the Achievements of the Jews and Judaism in California* (San Francisco: Temple Emanu-El, 1916), 119.

24. The letters were translated by Marlene Rainman for the *Western States Jewish Historical Quarterly.*

Daniel Levy, journalist, teacher, and reader for Congregation Emanu-El. From Martin Meyer, *Western Jewry* (San Francisco: Emanu-El). Courtesy of the Western Jewish History Center, Judah L. Magnes Museum.

and Poland furnish the largest contingents, and this is understandable. In no other area of Europe is the legal and extra-legal oppression weighing on our coreligionists, so strongly and painfully felt. Thus, they only wait for a favorable occasion and the means needed, to leave the countries that treat them so infamously, in order to go to America where they find freedom, equality, and the rest. Having arrived here, our coreligionists, no longer paralyzed by any obstacles, can fearlessly give in to the fervor of their spirit of enterprise and give flight to all the moral and industrious energy, that is the endowment of their race. Well-being frequently and opulence occasionally, crown their efforts, without public opinion making it a crime as in other places.

In California, and especially in San Francisco, the German and Polish Jews form two distinct communities, each with its own temple and distinctive regulations. The French, for the most part from Alsace or Lorraine, do not actually form a real group and are integrated into the mass of their nearest European neighbors.

I am unable to give even an approximate figure for the number of Jews in California. Those of San Francisco are estimated at more than three thousand. There may be as many as that scattered about in the interior. But whatever the number, it seems to me of greater interest to follow the various phases of their religious organization, and to sketch in quick lines the strange and picturesque lives of those who have fixed their choice not on the mines, but the miners.

As soon as the first mad excitement of the gold fever had passed, the Jews of San Francisco bethought themselves of the duties that their religious origins imposed on them and as a result, they opened places of prayer to observe their religion. But their spirit of brotherhood showed itself first by the establishment, as early as December, 1849, of the First Hebrew Benevolent Society, the earliest of all the welfare organizations which abound on these newly discovered shores. Another one, called the Eureka Benevolent Society, followed in short order. In time, as the number of families increased, the ladies joined together and founded a society to help the poor and the sick. Finally, just recently, the young people organized a literary and mutual aid society, which is destined to have a great development and success which is highly desirable, since it is a case of welfare and intellectual and moral culture at the same time.

As you can see, dear sir, we have here rapid and glorious results, and a number of creations which would do honor to the oldest and most important communities of Europe. Let us add that two beautiful temples, one for the Germans [Emanu-El], the other for the Poles [Sherith Israel], were built two years ago and are already too small to hold the influx of the faithful on High Holy Days. We will also say that a functionary, serving in the three capacities of rabbi, teacher and hazan, has been practicing for a year, that kosher meat is available, and that, in other words, all the facilities are here for those who wish to lead a perfectly Orthodox life.

Now a few words about the synagogues. The German one, built of brick and located on Broadway (not as grandiose as the famous street of that name in New York), is spacious and elegant. The exterior style is so-called Gothic, as are all the buildings of this type in the United States. Two wide and high flights of steps lead to the vestibule in front of the hall. This, very simply decorated, has as its only remarkable feature a beautiful Brussels carpet covering the entire floor and a magnificent chandelier which, if I remember correctly, cost $400.00. The platform for the officiating minister occupies the center of the hall and around it, there is an attractive gallery for the ladies. There are no innovations

Emanu-El (1854–63) on Broadway in San Francisco. Courtesy of the Western Jewish History Center, Judah L. Magnes Museum, Emanu-El Collection.

in the synagogue services. They are more or less as are still found in our more humble villages. As to the officiating minister, he carries out his various duties as best he can. I am told that before his nomination he was a peaceful farmer in one of the Southern States of the Union.[25] The history of those famous Roman generals who were taken from the plow and put at the head of armies, is thus not so extraordinary. As a rabbi, the aforesaid dignitary preaches three or four times a year, in German or English. As a teacher, he teaches Hebrew reading, the rudiments of religion and Jewish history, for a few hours a week. Finally, as a hazan, he officiates on Friday evenings, Saturday mornings, and on Holy Days. The rest of the year the synagogue remains closed.

My first visit to the temple was on a Friday night. The benches were almost entirely empty. However, little by little they were filled, and finally I counted about thirty individuals present, although there is room for four hundred people. Unfortunately, the officiating minister is lacking all the good qualities of

---

25. The minister referred to here is Rabbi Julius Eckman. He was not a farmer.

his position. All he has is a dignified bearing and that is not enough to attract the crowds. As I said, the ceremonies are not special in any way, except for the recitation of the *Yigdal,* which the hazan and the congregation chant alternatively verse by verse, and also the suppression of the *Bema [Bammeh] Madlikin.*

The Saturday morning service does not have anything worth mentioning either. The honors of the Pentateuch, instead of being sold at auction, belong to all the members present.

The expenses of the congregation are covered by a monthly assessment with the uniform figure set at four dollars. Thus, as you can see, there is still much

In 1854 Rabbi Julius Eckman of Emanu-El dedicated this first permanent building of Congregation Sherith Israel (1854–70) on Stockton Street in San Francisco. Courtesy of the Western Jewish History Center, Judah L. Magnes Museum, Sherith Israel Collection.

that needs to be done. But one must remember that the community is still in its formative period. I do not doubt that many improvements will be introduced into the general organization of the group, as soon as the weight of the heavy debt incurred by the building of the temple and the purchase of a cemetery is lifted.

The synagogue of the Poles, located on Stockton Street, has an exterior architecture similar to that of the Germans. However, instead of having its bright-red and picturesque bricks exposed as the latter has, it is covered by a grayish cement facing, much in use in the United States. It also is smaller and less elegant inside. On the other hand, its members are more assiduous, without having a titular cantor. But they do the unforgivable wrong of making their fervor too loudly vocal. You are familiar with the classical and venerable uproar in the synagogue in the good old days of the faith. The Poles have not fallen away.

As to the ladies in general, American customs do not permit them to mingle publicly in business affairs, but nothing can keep them from visiting the temple and in fact they are seen there in quite large numbers. More pomp and solemnity during the ceremonies of the faith would attract them in even greater numbers. [. . .]

Please accept, my dear editor, the assurances of my sincere affection.
Daniel Levy.

2

San Francisco, December 20, 1856.
Dear Mr. Editor,

The Jews of California do not offer the scholar, the historian or the tourist, the same degree of interest as do our Algerian coreligionists who, with their original costumes, their Hebrew-Arabic traditions, their tormented past, and above all their customs in the home, show such a different physiognomy, such a marked contrast. Thus your readers must not expect to find in these letters anything but the simple details of the public worship and the social position of our brothers in California.

Public worship (see my first letter) is still in the process of being organized, and it will only arrive at the more or less perfect condition reached by some communities in Europe, when there is a rabbi deserving of the name and capable of carrying out the complicated functions which are his. I say complicated, because he will not only have to preach, but also to establish on a solid basis the religious fabric, which is still only in the building stage.

The rabbi will not find here the inert resistance, more powerful than the most active opposition, known as religious indifference. No. America, if not bigoted, is at least very conscious of externals, and it is known that our coreligionists, no matter where they may be living, are always subject to the prevailing ideas. Thus, I am convinced that were it not for financial interests, the Sabbath services would always bring a large number of worshipers. But the store prevails over the temple, even among those who, through piety, abstain from eating *trafe,* and who close on Saturday. If one is an American, as well as a religious man, one is more the former as a practical man and one holds very strongly with the Yankee maxim: Time is Money (time is golden) and, going even farther than that, with the older classic saying of our neighbors across the Rhine: *Morgenstunde Tragt Gold im Muncle.*

There lies the problem. The golden calf has its home built right across from the home of Jehovah. It is up to the future rabbi, as was done long ago by the prophet Elijah, to bring back the strays and draw them to his side.

These thoughts naturally bring me to the social situation, which is the other side of the coin that I had undertaken to describe. In San Francisco, if one goes through the quarter specially set aside for wholesale commerce, where vast quantities of merchandise imported from the principal manufacturing centers of the world are stored in immense warehouses, one can see on both sides of the streets, especially on Sacramento Street, an endless series of signs, for the most part displaying in shiny gold letters Jewish names, almost all of them deriving from Jewish families of Europe. Naturally, the German names predominate, some retaining their German spelling, others Anglicized. There are only three companies belonging to French Jews. They are those of the brothers Lazard, Charles Schmitt, and the brothers Godchaux. It is true that this number is proportional to this group in the population.

A few years ago, only a spark was needed to destroy in one hour all the riches accumulated in this district and to spread ruin, but not despair, where life and human activity reigned. Fire was so frequent and always so terrible in its ravages that it ended by being accepted as a sort of enemy to be vanquished by means of perseverance and stubbornness, or as a kind of business contingency which, like profits and losses, had its place in the account books.[26] The fight was long, fierce and implacable, but man won out; he bested the element. Instead of the old wooden barracks built in great haste, which the California Minotaur swallowed in a mouthful, there are now strong buildings constructed like forts, out of brick and iron, defying both fire and thieves.

There is one branch of business for which Jews seem to have been given the password. They have cornered it, made a specialty and almost a monopoly of it, and they exploit it at every level, wholesale, retail, commission and peddling. It is the business of textiles and ready-made clothes. This preference for dealing in soft goods has reached the point where, in some mining areas, where there are convenient terms for everything, these types of stores have ended up by

---

26. In San Francisco, Sacramento, and all of the mining towns, the threat of fire was constant, and being burned out and starting over was part of every businessman's experience.

being called *Jewshops,* even when run by Christians. After this favorite line come cigars and tobacco, foods, groceries, liquor, etc. Then come the manual occupations: tailors, shoemakers, butchers, jewelers, etc. The tailors are almost always Polish, and I will add with no less truth that all the Poles are or were tailors, at least when they are not or were not shoemakers. They are truly wonderful men, knowing a little about everything and embarrassed by nothing.

The Jews do not refuse the roughest work in order to make a living or to amass dollars. They gladly become stevedores, porters, water-carriers, etc., convinced that there is no demeaning job, especially in California where, with luck, all roads can lead to fortune.

The Jew as a citizen is distinguished by a rare quality for which one should be grateful, even if it is only negative. He is not, like too many Americans, a politician by profession, continually lying in wait for the big chance, intriguing, corrupting and corrupted, ready to do anything to court public favor and to have his share of the rich spoils of the public monies. He minds his own business, according to the hallowed expression. That is, he takes care of his own affairs, although he may be the first to pay with his coin or his person, when his civic duty demands it. The last popular movement, famous under the name of the Vigilance Committee [1856], has shown it clearly. The Jew is a little like the ant: active, organized, foresighted, thrifty. His goal is to become rich, and he reaches it by patience and effort more rapidly than the tortoise of the fable, but not as fast as the hare, the speculator and the gambler who expect to reach there in one leap.

Nevertheless, in the last elections, two Jews were nominated: one, Mr. Miro, German by birth, to the legislature; the other, whose name escapes me, to the office of clerk of the Superior Court. A third coreligionist, Mr. [Solomon] Heydenfeldt, has for several years occupied the high post of Judge of the Supreme Court, and both as a man and as a magistrate, he enjoys the highest and most deserved reputation.

Two lawyers, Messrs. Labatt, father and son, hold an honorable position among their many colleagues.[27] I say many, because in California the law, like medicine, is a career that is not only liberal, but free, open to anyone, so that these gentlemen multiply in a distressing fashion and become a real social plague. You already know that the younger Mr. Labatt, together with Rabbi Bien, publishes a newspaper, *The Voice of Israel,* which appears every Friday, and of which you must have received the first copy.

This publication appears to be born viable. Since until now it is the only one of its kind, it should be quite successful. As far as the press is concerned, this

---

27. Abraham and Henry Labatt were originally from Charleston, South Carolina. They both served as officers of Congregation Emanu-El.

observation must be made: in France, and in Europe generally, a newspaper only lives by its literary merit and the popularity of the opinions it espouses, whereas here, it lives by its advertisements. Thus you see three-fourths of the columns filled, crowded, overloaded with advertisements, some of which surpass in conceit, absurdity and charlatanism, anything of this kind that could appear in your moderate European publications. [. . .]

Now, before closing, let me add a few words about two Jewish societies, which appear characteristically American. The first one is secret, organized along the lines of Freemasonry, and it has its ceremonies, initiation tests, passwords and recognition signs. It is the B'nai B'rith society.[28] Its main lodge is in New York. The second, which you already know by name, is the Hebrew Young Men's Literary Association. The purpose of this organization is not so much welfare, as instruction, or, to make myself clearer, the perfecting of the members in the difficult art of public speaking. In this country of unlimited liberty and of self-government, everyone is more or less connected with publicity and occasionally with oratory. Therefore, our young people meet every other week and hold debates on a prearranged subject. These are always questions of history, politics, social economics or religion, or else of practical philosophy, and they are posed in such a way as to invite two answers, one affirmative and the other negative.

The last issue to be considered was whether "Wealth Makes A Man Happier." Three members took the affirmative side and three the negative. A jury was selected to decide which side's arguments carried more weight. The discussion lasted about three hours, and the battle, vigorously carried on between the two sides, interested me very much, as I had the honor of sitting as one of the judges. Well, can you guess what was the unanimous decision of the jury and the general opinion of the audience? It was that wealth does not make a man happier, and this verdict was rendered in California, by young people who came here to get rich and therefore be happy in the quickest way. People might say: what bitter disillusionment, or else, what open contradiction between opinion and behavior. My goodness, no! It is just that the negative side found better grounds of attack and defense than the affirmative, as well as that at times, it is difficult to disprove the evidence. The association already owns a fairly large and well-chosen library, housed in a large and comfortably furnished hall where the meetings are held, and which may be visited at any time of the day or evening, to read the periodicals or the books. [. . .]

Goodbye, dear sir. I crave your forbearance and remembrance.

Daniel Levy.

---

28. The B'nai B'rith was founded in New York in 1843. The first San Francisco lodge, Ophir, was chartered in 1855.

3

San Francisco, June 5, 1857.
Here I am too far removed from the central observation point to study the nature and public spirit of the American Jews, in order to make comparisons between them and our compatriots. The first striking thing [. . .] is the difference in the administrative organization of religion. Whereas in France, all the synagogues accept a single superior authority, in America, where centralization is against the principle of the Constitution, they are all independent of each other, and are only answerable to their collective memberships.

This independence of the congregations, permits the religious spirit to soar and convictions to be translated into actions. As in any city, a certain number of Jews find that they have the same principles and views on religion and worship, and behold, they promptly hold a meeting, adopt resolutions, form a congregation, assess themselves to build a new temple, name a committee qualified to revise the ritual and remodel the religious ceremonies, another committee to hire the salaried officials, such as the teacher, of ficiating clergyman, and others. All this is done without the government having anything to do with it,

Rabbi Henry A. Henry, 1857–69, Sherith Israel (painting). Courtesy of the Western Jewish History Center, Judah L. Magnes Museum.

with complete independence of action and spirit and without any concern for murmurs, the disapproval of the ignorant masses, or for the bitter criticism and the cries of anathema of the Orthodox fanatics. Doubtless it is regrettable that this freedom of initiative and isolated action, outside of any concerted movement, breaks up the unity or rather the uniformity of worship in the synagogue. But if one bears in mind that the future belongs to Reform, and that changes made or to be made are the result of recognizing a few basic principles, then one can easily see that today's broken uniformity will end up by being reestablished as the Reform movement spreads. The minority will become the majority and one day will be universal. This is according to the inexorable law of progress. [. . .]

At the present time a choir is being organized [at Emanu-El], to consist of members of both sexes and to be accompanied by an organ. One had already been formed for the High Holy Days of last fall, but now there is the desire to form a permanent organization.

The Polish congregation [Sherith Israel] now has Mr. [Henry A.] Henry as rabbi, who, as teacher and officiating minister, seems to suit his congregation perfectly.[29] He is strictly orthodox.

I shall here end my letter. I am aware that it is much too long for its content. But as always, I know you will be indulgent and treat this communication with your customary hospitality.

Daniel Levy.

4

San Francisco, June 20, 1858.

Anyone leaving California in those days [early 1850s], not so long ago in time, but far removed by events, and returning today, would certainly not recognize it. Instead of the social chaos he had left, he would be pleased and delighted to find about a thousand Jewish families with pure morals and with homes that contained all the conditions necessary for comfort and even luxury. In place of the old and miserable hovels, ravaged by vermin and constantly exposed to total destruction by fire, he would see elegant brick homes or

---

29. Rabbi Henry A. Henry was hired by Sherith Israel in 1857. Born in London in 1806, Henry attended the Jews' Free School, where he later served as headmaster. In 1842 he became a rabbi at the Western Synagogue in London but left that position in 1849 to come to the United States. From 1849 to 1857, Henry served successively as rabbi for the B'nei Yeshurun congregation in Cincinnati, the Synagogue Concord in Syracuse, and the Sharay Zedek Congregation and Rodef Sholem in New York. He was the rabbi of Congregation Sherith Israel of San Francisco until 1869. An author and compiler of books on Jewish practice and prayer, Henry was a frequent contributor to journals and newspapers.

Dinkelspiel daughters at the piano, 1872. Painting by a young Toby Rosenthal. Courtesy of the Judah L. Magnes Museum, painting collection.

dainty and graceful cottages, hidden among trees and flowers; charming nests for people, where Americans have learned so well to shelter their domestic bliss.

These families are linked by bonds of neighborliness and friendship. The ladies, almost all of them young, well brought up, more or less musical (there is a piano in every parlor), get together either for Saturday or Sunday visits, at the Temple, at dances or at the theater, or for their charitable meetings. All this creates a charming and serene social life. I do not think that many European communities can boast of as large a number of young and happy households living in affluence. The influence of family feeling has restrained the former passionate fervor and led men back to the true path in which human society should move.

In an earlier letter I spoke of the various welfare and other societies that were formed almost by magic. I shall only mention that marriages have become very frequent, and this is explained by the great number of young people who, realizing the impossibility of returning home quickly with a readymade fortune, prefer to settle down here and enjoy family life. Another more remarkable and less easily explained fact is the enormous imbalance between the boys and girls that are born. In the eight months that he has been in office, the president of Congregation Emanu-El has registered twenty-seven children, twenty-four of whom were boys. [. . .]

Daniel Levy.

5
Wanderings in the Mining Districts
Israel Joseph Benjamin, *Three Years in America*, 1862

Israel Joseph Benjamin was born in 1818 in the Turkish province of Moldavia. After receiving a traditional Jewish education, he became a lumber dealer, but when his business folded he chose a life of travel.[30] Emulating Benjamin of Tudela, who had written about Jewish life during the twelfth century, he called himself Benjamin II and proceeded to Vienna, where he raised funds for his trip to Egypt, Syria, Babylon, India, and Afghanistan. After his return, he set off again, this time for Italy, Morocco, and Algeria. There Benjamin met Daniel Levy, whom he would meet again in San Francisco. In 1859, after raising funds and gaining sponsors for his next project in Germany, Benjamin left for the United States. He spent a year in the east, then set out for California by sea, traveling by way of Panama. Over the following months, he traveled widely, ever the participant observer. Arriving after a decade of California's growth, Benjamin was able to capture the whole settlement experience. The following account further documents the settlement of families with children in the mining towns as well as the beliefs of some Jews that they would leave these towns as soon as the mining ended. The contemporary records generally corroborate Benjamin's observations. Soon after his return to Germany, Germans were able to read about faraway California. Again, Benjamin set out to see and document world Jewry, but he died in London in 1864 just as he was about to begin.

On the twenty-fourth, at about eight o'clock in the morning, we sailed through the Golden Gate and an hour later landed at the great capital of the West—San Francisco.

After I had worked my way successfully through a mob of drivers of carriages for hire, agents for hotels, and others who crowded about us, I made my way to the New York Hotel on Battery Street. That very morning I visited Dr. Julius Eckmann [Eckman], publisher of the *Gleaner,* as well as Mr. Daniel Levy, a native Frenchman, who, in Algiers in 1854, translated my first travel-book into French. The joy of Mr. Levy and myself was great as we met again after our

SOURCE: I. J. Benjamin, *Three Years in America, 1859–1862,* trans. Charles Reznikoff (Philadelphia: Jewish Publication Society of America, 1956), vol. 1, 115, vol. 2, 3–10, 26–28, 94–96.

30. For more information on the life of Israel Joseph Benjamin, see Oscar Handlin's introduction to *Three Years in America,* by I. J. Benjamin and trans. Charles Reznikoff (Philadelphia: Jewish Publication Society of America, 1956), vol. 1, 1–36.

Israel Joseph Benjamin, author of *Drei Jahre in Amerika, 1859–1862*. This photograph was taken in New York during his visit to the United States.

long separation, twelve thousand miles from the place where the brief time we spent together had securely tied the bonds of our friendship. There is really something wonderful in a friendship formed in a foreign land, then broken off for a time through circumstances, and renewed again in another foreign land; it becomes warmer than ever. We sat and gossiped; we had so much to tell each other we did not notice how soon the day passed; but we did not stop talking, as though we feared to be parted for ever and that if every minute were not utilized it would be lost eternally. My stay in California, however, was fortunately prolonged beyond my expectations so that not a few evenings were devoted by Mr. Levy and myself to the memories of the past. [. . .]

NOVEMBER 6, 1860, will be recorded as a most noteworthy day in the history of the United States. It was on that day, namely, that the election of Abraham Lincoln to the presidency of the United States decided the fate of the country. Men were well aware of the significance of the day, and the seriousness of it dominated every one. The places of business were closed, work was suspended, the ceaseless bustle took a holiday, and the only rivalry was in working for the election of the man considered most suitable to take the wheel in that stormy time.

It was indeed a day that I will long remember, for I had never seen an election and all its attendant circumstances: its excitements and its tricks and crookedness. Fully impressed by this singular spectacle, I went on board the splendid

steamer *Chrysopolis*. The Rev. H. A. Henry, preacher of Congregation Sherith Israel, went along with me to Sacramento, in accordance with a resolution of his congregation, to introduce me to the Israelites of that city. About two hours after we left the bay, we reached Benicia at six o'clock in the afternoon. [. . .] From Benicia we continued up the Sacramento River and, after about three hours, reached the little town of Rio Vista. Here, to our great fright, the ship ran aground on a sand-bank. The water of the river was very low and it took the crew almost an hour before they could get the ship afloat again. At about three in the morning we reached Sacramento, "the city of the plains," a name it received because it is on a level expanse of ground.
[. . .]

Sacramento has about five hundred Jewish residents. They formed a single congregation at first. Later, there was dissension among them and a number formed a separate congregation. This happens quite often in America.

Congregation B'nai Israel was organized in 1859 and soon built a synagogue with the same name. The German and Polish Jews were at first united but separated because of the *Hazzan* (cantor) whom the Germans did not like. They left the synagogue to their Polish brethren and formed a new congregation called B'nai Hashalom. By this time it has three thousand dollars in its treasury and will soon build a synagogue. In this brief time of its existence, the B'nai Israel congregation has had no less than four preachers. I could not find out who was to blame for this frequent change.

The B'nai Hashalom congregation celebrates New Year's and the Day of Atonement in a rented house; and this is almost all it does by way of religious services.

The Hebrew Benevolent Society was organized in 1850 and has, at present eighty members. They have three thousand dollars in their treasury.

A social club of young Jews was organized in July 1855. It has forty members. They meet monthly for social entertainment and the exchange of ideas. The club is highly thought of for its benevolence.

I. O. Bnai Brith

was founded on the first of January, 1859, and has forty-five members. [. . .] I saw as little of religious life of the Jews of Sacramento as I heard of their charity. [. . .]

I left Sacramento [. . .] and went by railway to Folsom—a distance of twenty-two miles. This was my last stop before Placerville to which the road ran through a hilly and mountainous district. On this trip I passed through Mud Springs. This place owes its name to the mud through which a man must actually wade in the rainy season. It has 700 inhabitants, mostly Chinese and a few Irish families.

Two miles farther is Diamond Springs, a flourishing little town of 400 inhabitants. The town has its name from a clear well, eighteen feet deep, which provides the inhabitants and the gold-miners with fresh and pure water. Diamond

Springs has six Jewish families consisting of thirty-two Jews. My old friend, Daniel Levy, who is now a *hazzan* in San Francisco has brothers and sisters here. I let myself be persuaded to spend a day with them. The place is proud of its profitable gold-mines and the land about it is very suitable for cultivation.

In the evening I came to Placerville, one of the oldest towns in the hills and, because of its location, one of the most important, Placerville is the capital of flourishing Eldorado County. It lies on Weber Creek, a branch of the southern fork of the American River, and is divided into two parts—Upper and Lower Placerville. The place was first built in 1849 and became important at once because it was the point to which immigrants first pushed on when they came to this land. For a long time it was known by the pleasant-sounding name of Hangtown, a name it received because of the many hangings that took place there under the laws as laid down by "Judge Lynch." In 1850 it was given its present name and, ever since it received a respectable name, it rejoices in a respectable standing.

Since Placerville is on the route between California and Utah, it has become a kind of center for the trade of Carson Valley and a depot for the silver ore of Washoe, as well as for the necessities of the people in the mountains there. Placerville, like all other towns, has had to suffer disasters by flood and fire. The last severe trial of this sort took place in July 1856, when almost the whole town was changed into a heap of ashes. Since then it has been rebuilt, for the most part with fire-proof buildings. It has almost four thousand inhabitants, two newspapers published twice a week, as well as several schools and four churches. There are good places in its neighborhood, as well as rich and extensive mines. The ore of these provides much work for several mills of the town.

It is due to its location that Placerville became so quickly a town of great importance. Its prosperity does not depend wholly on the mines of the neighborhood, and it would suffer no damage in case these were to become exhausted. The suburbs have beautiful gardens and orchards. These provide the residents of the city with fruit and repay with great profit the labor expended on them.

Placerville has only a few public institutions. It has a hospital, two public schools and three private ones: that is all this wealthy town has to show. But there are other institutions to be found, public enough not to be lacking in influence upon the ways of the place, and these are—the gambling houses! Some of them are open day and night, as used to be the case in the good old days of '49 and '50. Here the most expensive games of chance are played and many a miner goes in a rich man and comes out a beggar. It is true that gambling is permitted throughout the State but in many places it is conducted more privately; here all the laws of morality are openly scorned. The cards, however, are treated with as much favor as if the dealer were put there by the State to cheat poor simpletons and squeeze them dry of their hard-earned earnings.

Five companies of militia, four belonging to the town, should likewise be included under the heading of "institutions," since they were organized for the general good.

The Masons and Oddfellows are well represented. They have their lodges and gather substantial funds in their treasuries. A new society, called "Druids," was recently organized. They received their "privileges" from St. Louis. Since they keep their affairs secret, I know nothing of their purpose and heard only that all their members are Germans and that they trace the origin of their organization back a thousand years to the time when the druids were exterminated in England. [. . .]

Placerville has seventy Jews. They are almost all members of a charitable organization that they organized. The president is Mr. Cohn.[31] Otherwise, little is known of them and a cemetery is practically all that discloses the presence of Jews. Public services are held on New Year's and on the Day of Atonement; during the rest of the year no one thinks about performing Jewish ceremonies. However, they are planning to build a synagogue very soon: its success as a unifying center is to be most ardently desired. If there is a house of prayer, there must also be a teacher; and the Jewish children of the town will at least have some idea, if only a weak one, of what Jewish character should be and of Jewish religious services, almost completely neglected by their fathers.

The Israelites here are well off. They do a great and good business and several have interests in the neighboring gold and silver mines from which they receive handsome dividends. [. . .]

I reached Mokelumne Hill around half-past three in the afternoon. This town lies on a hill, four miles south of the Mokelumne River, in the center of a rich mining-district. A single mine-claim in that neighborhood, in the spring of 1850, brought in the vast sum of $78,000. Mexicans and natives of Chile began to build the place in 1851 and, in the early days, very unpleasant disagreements arose with Americans and French about the right to claims. Both sides took to arms. The disputes, however, were soon settled without an outbreak of fighting and the contestants concluded a peace. The population of the town is about a thousand. It is the county-seat of Calaveras County.

In 1854, the town was so badly damaged by fire that only fifteen houses remained standing. But it was rebuilt later and the little town has a pleasant appearance.

The thirty Jews of Mokelumne Hill are almost all in good circumstances. At my request they met in Odd-Fellows' Hall. In a speech I urged upon them the necessity of establishing a charitable society and I found, thank God, no ear deaf to my plea. This society was really established and, because there were no

---

31. Most probably Louis Cohn or Jacob Kohn; see chapter 7.

poor among them, its funds grew to such an extent that in the course of time they could build a synagogue from the dues that accumulated gradually. When the society was organized, I was elected an honorary member.

In most places in California, if any Israelites live there at all, their first care is to provide themselves with a cemetery. No matter how indifferent and cold in many places our fellow Jews are towards their religion, nevertheless they are never so completely estranged from all religious feeling that it is a matter of total indifference to them where they bury their dead. And so in this town, too, the Jews have a place provided with an enclosure and set aside as a place of eternal rest.

An event, in itself of no importance, is closely connected with the purchase of this cemetery and may therefore be mentioned here. When two brothers, the richest Jews in town, were approached to contribute their mite for the purchase of the cemetery, they, to everybody's astonishment, flatly refused. The reason they gave was that they considered it quite unnecessary to do anything for the matter for they had no intention whatever of remaining in Mokelumne much longer. Soon afterwards, a child of one of the two died. His fellow Jews refused to let the body be buried in their cemetery, and he showed himself callous enough to have the body buried elsewhere. This is the way a rich Jewish father in California acted and even found satisfaction in doing so. But this was not all. Soon afterwards his only remaining child, a child of ten, became sick and died. This aroused the indifferent father and he pleaded with his fellow Jews to allow his dear child to be buried in the Jewish cemetery and at the same time offered a sizable sum for the privilege. At almost the same time, his brother also lost his only child.

Although these brothers were subjected to severe trials, they became neither more humane because of them nor of gentler disposition. The people of this land are entirely too much interested in gold—although I must add to the credit of some that this is not true of all. Unfortunately, it is true of the majority.

2
The Westward Journey

FOR JEWS LURED BY THE CALIFORNIA GOLD RUSH, THEIR FIRST PROB-
lem was how to get there. Travelers from the eastern seaboard in the 1850s
could choose between land or sea routes. To go overland, one could join either
an emigrant caravan or travel with a small group on horseback. European Jews
who made their way to California were familiar with sea travel, for they had
already crossed the Atlantic. The sea route also presented different options.
Jews departing from the eastern U.S. coast could sail around Cape Horn of
South America, which took over four months, or to the east coast of Central
America, either to the Isthmus of Panama or to Nicaragua. There they would
cross overland by mule or on foot and then resume their journey by steamship.
The Isthmus routes took from five to eight weeks, depending on the availability
of ships at the western terminus.

Sometimes travelers were forced to camp out for weeks waiting for their
ships, which were often delayed or damaged at sea. During the long waits,
Jewish passengers frequently sought each other out to share kosher food,
celebrate Jewish holidays, and establish friendships. In 1855 the opening of
the Panama Railroad made the crossing easier and shortened the trip by a
week. Although the passage around the Horn took longer, the Isthmus crossing
was more hazardous, as travelers were susceptible to the many diseases of the
region. Whatever the route taken, the trip was long, hard, and often hot, and
death was a frequent companion. According to an 1852 survey, one out of ten
passengers who booked passage to San Francisco by ship died before setting
foot on California soil.[1] Abraham Abrahamsohn remembered that during his

---

1. Louis J. Rasmussen, *San Francisco Ship Passengers List,* vol. 4 (Colma, Calif.:
San Francisco Historical Records, 1970), vi.

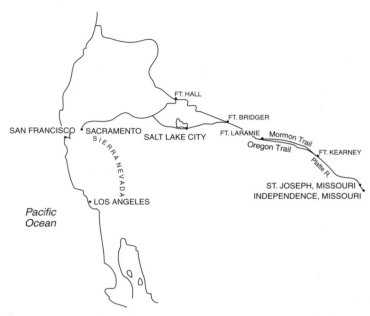

Overland trails to California from the eastern United States

"storm-free trip an old Jew died and was buried at sea according to Jewish religious customs."[2]

Written by Jewish men and women who came from a variety of backgrounds and who left Europe at different times, the following selections portray common experiences. Young people left to seek adventure and economic improvement. Their odysseys are documented in their diaries, letters, and memoirs. Louis Sloss set out for California by wagon train in 1849, but after much hardship he left the train with two companions and continued to Sacramento on horseback. Fanny Brooks and her husband headed for California in 1854, also by wagon train. Educated and adventurous, Mr. Brooks joined the Gold Rush for the same reasons many men did: who wanted to sit at home when an exciting new life beckoned? Fourteen-year-old Myer Newmark kept a diary of his 1853 journey around the Horn in which he described Sabbath study and the teaching of

---

2. "Interesting Accounts of the Travels of Abraham Abrahamsohn," prepared from the oral account by Friedrich Mihm, translated from the German by Marlene P. Toeppen and edited by Norton B. Stern, *Western States Jewish Historical Quarterly* 1:3 (1969): 139.

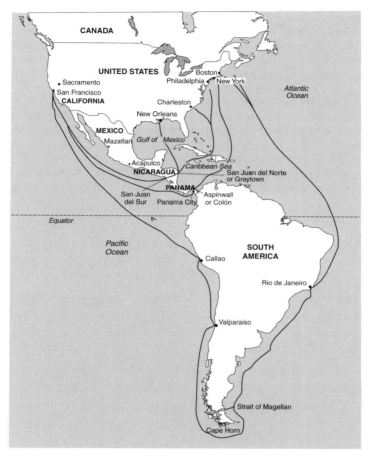

Sea routes to California from the eastern United States

Hebrew, along with the more monotonous aspects of the trip. The possibility of a freer life motivated Henry Cohn, who left Germany to avoid induction into an army that offered Jews few prospects. After spending a few years in the eastern United States, Cohn traveled to San Francisco in 1855 by way of the Isthmus of Panama. Upon returning to live in Germany, Cohn set down his memoirs for family and friends.

Hanchen Meyer Hirschfelder was able to shorten the journey by traveling on steamships and the new Panama Railroad in 1856. She wrote of her Yom

Kippur experiences aboard ship and described the many ports she visited on the journey. Eugene Meyer also crossed the ocean to get to California, not to pan gold but to start a new life as a merchant. He left France in 1859 with an introduction to a prominent West Coast business family and, once arrived, quickly became part of the French Jewish merchant community in San Francisco.

In 1876 Rabbi Max Lilienthal left Ohio for California by a different means of transportation, thanks to the completion of the first transcontinental railroad in 1869. In order to perform the wedding of his nephew in San Francisco, he traveled by train from Cincinnati to Utah on the Union Pacific and then on the Central Pacific to Oakland, where he boarded a ferry for San Francisco. By 1869, just twenty years after the beginning of the Gold Rush, the railroad made a short visit to California practical.

6
West by Horseback
Louis Sloss, 1849

Counted among the '49ers, Louis Sloss (1823–1902) was born in Bavaria; he emigrated to the United States in 1845 and settled in Kentucky. When he learned of the discovery of gold in California, he made his way to St. Louis and, for a fare of $200, joined the Turner and Allen Pioneer Train.[3] There he met Dr. Richard Hayes McDonald and Dr. C. H. Swift (also referred to as Judge Swift), who would become his traveling companions.[4] Once in Sacramento, Sloss first went into business with McDonald and Swift, then established a store with Simon Greenwald. Lewis Gerstle joined the firm in 1851, and in 1860 they moved to San Francisco. The Alaska Commercial Company was formed in 1868, and Sloss became a successful businessman, selling fish and furs from Alaskan waters.

In 1855 Sloss married Sarah Greenebaum, a Jewish woman from Philadelphia; together they had six children. Among a variety of religious, charitable, and social organizations, Sloss was a member of Congregation Emanu-El and a contributor to Jewish organizations.

The following selection was edited by Richard Hayes McDonald's eldest child, Frank V. McDonald, one of Louis Sloss's traveling companions. His trip was marked by many of the hardships commonly described in overland travel diaries and reminiscences: overloaded wagons, sickness, especially cholera, and a generally uncomfortable trip.

Of the party [in the Turner and Allen Pioneer Train] was Mr. Louis Sloss, who had moved to Mackville, Ky., not far from the McDonald homestead, after Dr. McDonald had left there, and had become well acquainted with all his family. He introduced himself to Dr. McDonald, who was delighted with this chance meeting with one from the home he had not seen for five years.

In due time the procession started on the long and hazardous trip; but before travelling twenty days, it became evident that the wagons were overloaded and the preparations inadequate to perform the stipulated trip. Dr. McDonald,

---

SOURCE: Frank V. McDonald, *A Biography of Richard Hayes McDonald* (Cambridge: John Wilson and Son, 1881), 60–75.

3. It is estimated that thirty thousand people came west overland in 1849, but only four thousand had made the journey in 1848 (Lillian Schlissel, *Women's Diaries of the Westward Journey* [New York: Schocken Books, 1992], 24).
4. Swift became mayor of Sacramento, an office he held for eight years.

fearing some failure in the programme, had taken his horse, having him cared for in the extra stock, and thus he could ride horseback or in the vehicle at will.

The cholera prevailed all along the emigration line, and of the number in this train, passengers and teamsters, about one hundred and sixty-five in all, forty-two died before reaching California, nearly all of cholera.[5] [. . .]

Seeing the confusion that was daily increasing in the train, and realizing that their chances for reaching California by that route were small, the two friends, with Mr. Sloss, determined to give up their seats as soon as their [medical] services could be spared. At Fort Laramie, [. . .] [t]he soldiers not only protected the emigrants from the Indians, but supplied them with food, shelter, and kindly care, that gave them a new lease of life for the long and exhausting trip before them.[6]

By this time the train began to pass the vanguard of the emigrant parties, for its lighter conveyances moved much faster than the heavier horse and ox teams. As they approached the foot-hills of the Rocky Mountains, called the Black Hills, which they had long been making every effort to reach, the cholera gradually disappeared. This decided change for the better had been anticipated by Drs. Swift and McDonald, and had induced them to remain longer with the train than they otherwise would have done; when about two hundred and fifty miles from Omaha the improvement was noticeable, and, feeling that their services could soon be dispensed with, they, with their companion, Mr. Sloss, determined to purchase extra stock from emigrants on the road, and "pack" across to California. [. . .]

They rode up and down among the different emigrant trains until they had obtained the stock they desired. They found one party of two with only two horses, all packed, who were trying to reach California by alternately riding and leading their animals; they had experienced great hardships journeying in this way, and were glad to exchange their animals and equipments for two of the seats in the train, giving in addition a double-barrelled gun with one shot and one rifle bore. Our party had now three horses, and an opportunity soon offered to increase the number to six,—three for riding and three for packs; they had only two pack-saddles, but for the third they built a very good substitute of sticks; their supplies they bought from the overloaded teams. Thus equipped they left the Turner and Allen Pioneer Train, and rapidly passed ahead of all team emigration, for it was much easier for packhorses to climb the steep grades and travel over the rugged ways than for any loaded vehicle on wheels.

---

5. In 1849 there was a cholera epidemic along the trail. For further information, see Charles Rosenberg, *The Cholera Years: The United States in 1832, 1849 and 1866* (Chicago: University of Chicago Press, 1962).

6. At Fort Laramie, the travelers were about 635 miles from their starting points along the Missouri.

Traveling companions R. H. McDonald, Louis Sloss, and C. H. Swift. From Frank V. McDonald, *A Biography of Richard Hayes McDonald* (Cambridge: John Wilson and Son, 1881). Courtesy of the Western Jewish History Center, Judah L. Magnes Museum.

They started together, and kept together through all the sufferings and perils of the long journey; together they entered Sacramento, together commenced business, and were in partnership for a year; and, unbroken and unaltered, their friendship has continued from that time till now.

At their start the little band of three agreed that all disputed cases should be settled by the two-thirds rule. About the time and place of starting, resting, and other matters, they, like all travellers, would frequently differ, and would, perhaps, argue the point fiercely; but the question was invariably settled by applying the two-thirds rule, and, whether satisfactory or not, the resulting decision was always accepted. In fact, most of their differences, as well those occurring in general conversation as those bearing directly on methods of travel, were finally settled by the application of this rule. [. . .]

When they reached the North Platte they found the waters had been swollen unusually high by the fast-melting snows and the recent warm rains. The ford was in a narrow, deep, and turbulent part of the stream, which had not even subsided from the effect of the spring freshets. It was useless to attempt their customary mode of passing, and they had almost decided to go higher up the river in search of a more favorable place, when Dr. Swift, an excellent swimmer, determined to try and take the animals and packs across by swimming and guiding them. With considerable difficulty, Mr. Sloss and Dr. McDonald drove the horses in,—for neither of the two could swim,—and Dr. Swift, seizing the tail of the first horse, led the way. The current, however, in the middle proved too rapid, and resisted all efforts to cross. The horses were carried back to the same bank from which they had started; Dr. Swift lost his hold, was caught in the rushing eddy, and so whirled about that he was unable to swim, but fortunately drifted on some rocks in the river, where he rested, regained his strength, and avoiding the current made his way back to the shore. Realizing the impossibility of crossing at this point, they started up the river in search of another ford. Higher up they found a temporary bridge across a very narrow part of the river which a party crossing had built for their own convenience and had then converted into a toll-bridge. Our party thankfully paid the reasonable charge, and, with much less peace of mind concerning their future, continued their journey, turning their faces from the fertile valley of the Platte to the lofty passes of the Rocky Mountains.

Their route thus far had been principally on the table-land or continuous plateau through which the Platte winds its way; they had been always in sight of the waters, and oftentimes on the banks of the river. The valley proper of the river is extensive, and forms a pleasant panorama from its upland borders, its rich, fertile soil, covered with its sweet prairie grasses, affording abundant food for the stock. At short intervals, herds of buffaloes, thousands and thousands in number, reaching at times as far as the eye could see, hardly looked up at the travellers' approach; they had not yet been molested, and were as unsuspicious and almost as peaceful as domestic cattle. They fed and moved always in one direction, and gave little heed to the advancing van of the emigration. [. . .] The sight of these buffaloes grazing in such immense herds, from fifty to one hundred thousand at times together, was to our travellers most wonderful. [. . .]

One of the many mistakes of the thousands who left their Eastern homes for California, the first year, was the universal overloading of teams. While on the level plains, the burden did not press so heavily; the roads were fair, the grass good and abundant, and water within easy reach, so that their stock could stand it; but on reaching the mountains, where the road was steep and rugged, water and forage scarce, and long marches necessary, they found it impossible for their overloaded teams to proceed, and were obliged to lighten them. First they dispensed with all luxuries, then they remembered that "half a loaf is better than none," and often were forced to the final conclusion that they would do well to get through with their lives.

The goods thus discarded by the emigrants strewed the way for hundreds of miles, and every variety of article was to be found among them: in one place, furniture and household ornaments; in another a barrel of flour; in another canned meats and bacon; here, a fine selection of books; there, cooking utensils and stoves. In nearly every case they were neatly arranged by the roadside, and were often labelled,—"Overloaded and compelled to throw away," "Take all you can carry," "Help yourself to what you want and leave the rest for others"; or, perhaps, more briefly, "Could not carry, help yourself," or simply "Help yourself." Here and there among them were humorous lines, and occasionally on some ludicrous object might be seen a classical salutation, such as "Have valeque" (Hail and farewell), the first word, "Have," evidently bearing the meaning its English form suggested as well as its Latin signification. The passers-by made judicious exchanges or additions to their loads from these abandoned goods thus pressed on their attention, often only to leave them in their turn on the dreary Humboldt Plains, or even before they reached that distant place. [. . .]

On reaching the picturesque Donner Lake they turned aside from the regular trail into the grove at some little distance to examine the place where the Donner family had suffered that awful winter, and where all but one of those who stayed behind had perished. The bones of the unfortunates lay bleaching around the cabin, the skeletons yet continuous in their parts. The bones of the animals were also all perfect. They were perhaps the first visitors to the place that year, and no one had disturbed in any way the landmarks of the catastrophe: the trees were yet barked and showed the height of the snow, and the stumps above which the trees had been felled spoke more plainly of the depths to which it fell over the captives. [. . .]

From here they entered California, and kept on their way to Sacramento. They left the summits of the mountains and came down into "Steep Hollow," near Nevada City, California. [. . .] Their journey from here was through a series of mining camps until they reached the flats of the American River in the vicinity of Sacramento. At their long journey's end, they stopped at Norris's Ranch, on the other side of the American River, where they made their camp-fires, picketted their stock in good grass, and waited a few days before moving into Sacramento.

They hired a little one-horse wagon to take them and their effects into the city. It was, of course, necessary to ford the American River, and provision had been made for this; but they had forgotten to calculate for the rise of water, due to the influence of pressure from the tide-water at San Francisco Bay, which, at that time, made a difference of from one to two feet. As it happened, they crossed at high tide. All their personal effects were carefully placed on the bottom of the wagon, among them a half-dozen new and elegantly finished shirts, which Dr. McDonald had brought to wear in California; these shirts were damaged by the water. This was looked on with merriment by his fellow travelers, as now he would have to wear the same type of flannel shirt as everyone else! [. . .]

On arriving in Sacramento, they stopped at the corner of 6th and I Streets, built their camp-fires, and entered into an agreement to transact in partnership whatever business they should decide upon as the most advantageous. [. . .]

With a capital of about $2,500 in which each was to share equally, they sought an opening for their energies.

Sacramento, which was on General Sutter's claim, was laid out in blocks and lots, but contained only one wooden building, which was about half finished; all other dwelling-places were in tents. There were from fifteen to twenty thousand people already there, and the number was fast increasing, as this was the nearest starting-point for the mines.

The furnishing of miners' outfits seeming to our party to offer the best business-opening, they prepared for that. They rented a seven-foot space between two tents, [. . .] The labor was equally divided among the partners, each assuming the duties which by taste or training he was best fitted to perform. Mr. Sloss was auctioneer, Dr. McDonald was buyer, and Dr. Swift was business manager,—taking charge of the store, looking after details, keeping the accounts, and generally overseeing and directing.

The partnership was, as may be supposed, a most harmonious one, and the business, thus conducted, proved very remunerative, enabling them to divide the large amount of $17,000 profits in seven weeks. [. . .]

Sacramento City was then on a bluff, and the river flowed far below, in no respect a source of danger, even when at its highest. The mountains, however, which the miners soon washed into the rivers, filled up the channels, changed the course of the water, and brought upon the city the calamities which deprived it of its first rank, and drove its business men and capitalists one by one to San Francisco.

To the three friends this winter's flood brought surprise and disaster; it swept away their stock, and destroyed all their earnings, leaving them worse off financially than when they arrived in California.

They knew that another year would materially decrease the profits to be realized from the business, as too many were entering into it; and their stock having been destroyed, their preparations for a second year of partnership were useless: so the partnership was dissolved by mutual consent, with the friendliest of feeling, with the pleasantest memories of their long and intimate companionship, each thereafter to follow the dictates of his own judgment, and occupy his time as inclination should direct or opportunity offer.

7

A Woman's Wagon Train Adventure

Eveline Brooks Auerbach, ca. 1853

Like many Jewish immigrants, Julius Gerson Brooks (changed from Bruck) returned home to find a bride, in this case his sixteen-year-old niece, Fanny, in Breslau. Fanny (Bruck) Brooks told her daughter Eveline the exciting story of the ocean voyage and the 1854 wagon train trip across the Great Plains from Nebraska to California. After living briefly in Marysville, Timbuctoo (where Eveline was born), San Francisco, and Portland, the Brooks family settled in Salt Lake City, where Julius Brooks became a successful merchant. In their later years, Fanny and Julius vacationed in Europe. Julius died in San Remo, Italy, in 1892 and Fanny in Wiesbaden in 1901; both were buried in Salt Lake City. In 1879 Eveline Brooks, their daughter, married Samuel Auerbach, another Prussian immigrant whose family also lived in California before settling in Utah.[7]

Writing in her sixties, Eveline Brooks Auerbach recorded her mother's account for future generations. The account is of special interest because it is one of the few we have of a Jewish woman venturing west by wagon train.

My father Julius Gerson Brooks was born in the year 1825, at Frankenstein, a small village near Breslau. [. . .] Father never was a great student and at an early age was apprenticed to a trade, as a weaver of cloth. He received no money but had to pay a few guldens (a gulden being equivalent to forty cents American money). He said the hours were long and tedious and his food poor; many times he went to bed hungry. When his two years were up he quit and went to work for a tanner. He met there a peddler who told him what fun it was to travel and the many beautiful places to be seen, also what a lot of money he made. Father

SOURCE: *Frontier Reminiscences of Eveline Brooks Auerbach,* ed. Annegret S. Ogden (Berkeley: Friends of the Bancroft Library, University of California, Berkeley, 1994), 19–39.

7. Samuel Auerbach, with his brothers Fred and Theodore, operated stores in mining towns before settling in Salt Lake City, where the brothers became merchants and founders of a department store chain that bore their name. Active in the Jewish community, Samuel Auerbach was a founding member and served as the 1884 president of B'nai Israel Congregation. For more about the Auerbach family, see *Frontier Reminiscences of Eveline Brooks Auerbach,* ed. Annegret S. Ogden (Berkeley: Friends of the Bancroft Library, University of California, Berkeley, 1994) and *Utah Pioneer Merchant: The Memoirs of Samuel H. Auerbach* (1847–1910), ed. and intro. Judith Robinson (Berkeley: Bancroft Library, University of California, Berkeley, 1998).

was now getting a few gulden in addition to his board, which was good, but the work was hard, so he decided to run away. He did not write his mother, for he knew that if he did, she would make him go back to work. So he took his few belongings, tied them up in a square green cloth with a stick through it, put it over his back, and he was off. He went straight to Breslau, bought such notions as pins, hairpins, threads, needles, shoelaces, pearl buttons, etc., and started out. [. . .] He soon had more orders than he could fill. After nine months he decided to visit his mother who was delighted to see him. [. . .]

In 1847 Father [. . .] decided that he would go to the New World, and with the little money he had saved up bought his ticket on a sailing vessel. He paid about $35.00. His mother was very set against his going, but having his ticket, there was nothing to do but consent. Father took the few clothes he had, put them in a carpet bag, as in those days there were no trunks. Being very religious, he took some crackers, sausage, cheese, and black bread in a box, as he had heard that mostly bacon and ham were served on the boat, but he said there were plenty of things on the boat that he could eat. Part of his food got moldy, and he threw it into the sea. He took his straw bed and blankets with him. This on landing was thrown overboard. The little vessel was old and rocked from side to side; Father being more in his berth than on deck. He was five weeks on the water. He surely was happy to see the beautiful harbor of New York, Castle Garden, and said like Robinson Crusoe: "I'll go to sea no more." [. . .] He bought merchandise and went to the New England states to open a little shop, as they were the most populated. [. . .]

[In 1848] was the first gold excitement. All the papers were filled with thrilling tales of the wonderful country. [. . .] Father wanted to go to California, too, but had not enough money; besides, he was getting homesick and was saving money to go back home. Father stayed here five years and returned home. Everyone from near and far came to visit his mother and hear about the wonderful New World. Father was a wonderful exaggerator and told how money was found in the streets; Indians on the war path, fighting on the streets, carrying their bows and arrows on their backs, pistols around their waist, also the scalps of white men. Everyone believed him, and each and every one was willing to sell their all and go back with him. In 1853 while Father was home there was again great excitement. The papers were full of wonderful discoveries, so that the people believed everything Father said. Among the listeners was a young girl, Fanny Brooks (my mother), who was just out of college.[8] She said to him: "Julius, do take me with you to America." "Well," said Father, "the only

---

8. This was probably a form of post-elementary education. An early draft of the memoir read: "The children had been given a good education, something unusual for Jews even in those days as only few Jews were allowed in schools" (Ogden, ed., *Frontier Reminiscences,* 112).

way you can come is to marry me." "Well, if my parents do not object, I will." It was customary in those days to give a dowry, and as Father did not ask for one they gladly consented. [. . .]

Mother had just graduated with high honors. She spoke a beautiful German and French and had some knowledge of English. She played the piano and guitar and sang very beautifully. Mother said Father was a fine looking man and that any of the girls would gladly have taken him. Besides all her accomplishments, Mother was tall, dark haired, with dark eyes, and very fine looking. They were married August 18, 1853 and sailed at once from Hamburg. The whole town came down to the train to see them off for Hamburg, bringing rice, flowers, old shoes, this being the custom, and calling after them "Good Luck," "God-Speed," "Safe Voyage," and "Early Return."

They took quite a large boat for those days, but Mother said it rolled like a drunken sailor and most people were dreadfully sick. She was not sick a moment but helped entertain the crowd in the evening with her German and French folk songs, and jokes. Father was a good talker but a dreadful sailor, and most of the time found him in his berth. It took them three weeks to cross. [. . .] My parents stayed in New York about five months.

In the spring of 1854 they left New York for Galena, Illinois, where they heard that a company was leaving the following June for California. In order to reach Galena they had to go by boat. Galena was then an important commercial center, and large supplies for the west-bound emigrant trains were obtained there. In those days a number of large sized steam-boats operated between Galena and St. Louis, also between St. Louis, St. Joseph, and Fort Leavenworth. They had to remain in Galena until the following June. [. . .]

In June 1854 they heard of a train leaving Florence, Nebraska which they were permitted to join. They had to go by boat from Galena to Florence, where they purchased a covered wagon and two little mules, in order to be comfortable; otherwise they would have been compelled to walk.

Ten individuals were the number allotted to a wagon and one tent. One hundred pounds of luggage, including beds and clothing for all persons over eight years of age; fifty pounds to those between eight years and four years; all under four years of age had no luggage privileges. The wagons were ordered in Cincinnati and St. Louis and were brought by steamer to the camping ground. The wagon bed was 12 feet long, 3 feet 4 inches wide, and 18 inches deep. Boxes were made to fit inside the wagons to put utensils and clothing in. Cattle was purchased from cattle dealers in Western settlements and driven to the camping grounds. Tents were made of very superior twill cotton brought from England. For the emigration of 1854, it was supplied before their departure, and they made the tents and covers on the voyage; and thus saved expense. A common field tent was used. The material was 27 inches wide, and 44 yards were used for a tent, 26 yards for the wagon cover. The cost for the tent and the wagon cover was $40.00. The pole and cord were purchased by agents in the U.S. Each wagon this year cost $65.00. They were supplied with 1000 lbs. of flour, 50 lbs. of sugar, 50 lbs. of bacon, 50 lbs. of rice, 30 lbs. of beans, 20 lbs. of dried apples, 20 lbs. of dried peaches, 5 lbs. of tea, 1 gallon of vinegar, 10 bars of soap, 25 lbs. of salt. These articles and the milk from their cows, the game caught on the plains, and the fresh water streams furnished them better food and more of it than the emigrants had had in their native land.

As soon as a sufficient number of wagons could be gotten together, that is a hundred or more, they moved off under their respective captain. [. . .] In those days women could use fire-arms as well as men; in fact, it was required of them. The men carried a belt of cartridges around their waists, powder-horns, a bow-knife and a large pocket-knife, a whiskey flask, and a quid of tobacco. They wore heavy leather boots, corduroy pants tucked into their boots, denim shirts, slouch hats, and heavy overcoats of cow-hide or buffalo hide. The women were plainly dressed, with tight fitting waists, long tight sleeves, full skirts of calico or delain with a deep hem, and a small shawl, which they made themselves, about their shoulders. Some wore a calico or gingham sunbonnet, some a large flat Milan straw hat, heavy cow-hide shoes, and all wool underwear. Several pairs of shoes were taken along. The roads were so dusty, full of stones and brush that their shoes were worn out very quickly.

Mother tells that after crossing deep streams they had to take off their clothing and put on a calico wrapper, hang their clothes on lines strung from the wheel of one wagon to the wheel of another wagon, and hang their shoes on the sagebrush to dry. When they came to a small creek they would wade in it to relieve their feet of the soreness. The dust was terrific in the hot summer and after a rain or thunderstorm the roads were impassable, and the poor animals could barely pull their load. They were forced to remain over a couple of days to rest. After a storm everything was drenched, sagebrush, bunchgrass, and bush. It was almost impossible to make a fire, the smoke would stifle them. They then had to eat bread, raw bacon, and tea. The utensils for cooking were a large iron pot for boiling meat, etc., an iron frying pan, a skillet for baking bread (a skillet resembles a deep frying pan with a lid on it). The dough was put in it, placed on the fire, and the lid put on, and on that lid hot ashes were placed and left on and replenished until the bread was baked. It took about an hour for the bread to be baked. Most of the dishes were of tin, such as tin cups, dishpans used for washing dishes and mixing bread, a wash-basin, a grid-iron or flapjack pan. Flapjacks are griddle cakes made with flour and water, baking-powder, and a little salt. A tea and coffee pot, a wash tub and wash board, knives, forks, and spoons of the cheapest grade. A couple of wooden three-legged stools and a rocking chair the only luxury. Every wagon had a rocking chair. Their bedding was wrapped in black oilcloth during the day to keep it free from dust and water. The men were required to walk, but most of the time the women also walked unless they were sick or invalids. The entire cost to cross the plains per person was about $65.00. To each emigrant as he traveled his wagon served as a bedroom, parlor, kitchen, some times as a boat. The average day's journey did not exceed thirteen miles, though the trains were in motion from sunrise to sunset, stopping for their midday meal in order to give the animals time to graze. Some caravans consisted of several hundred wagons. Some wagons were drawn by six or eight oxen or horses. It was a grand sight to see this vast train with hundreds of men, women, children, and cattle and wagons going across the desert like a lot of ants. At times the heat during the day was terrific and the blow flies annoyed the cows and horses to death. The teamster had a stick with four leather straps nailed on with which he drove the flies off. At times blackbirds would sit on the cattle's backs and eat the flies. [. . .]

By the second of September they were in Laramie. From there they went to Independence Rock and then to Sweet Water. It was gradually getting colder; their bedding and clothing were insufficient to keep them warm. Cold weather, scarcity of food, and fatigue soon produced their bad results. Many were taken ill, and several died; amongst those who died was my mother's first baby. Along the route were many graves of former emigrants. Thousands of skeletons of animals lay bleaching in the sun. [. . .]

The overland route to California followed the old Oregon Trail from St. Joseph or Independence along the Platte River to Fort Laramie, then on to a point about one hundred miles from Fort Hall, then to the head waters of the Humboldt River; landed on the north side of the mouth of the Platte, followed the stream to the fork 400 miles. In this distance there is only one stream where a raft would be needed and that near the Missouri; all the rest are fordable. At the forks take the north side. It took fourteen days travel to the Black Hills, leaving the river bank going northwest to the Sweet Water Trail. [. . .]

Mother said they did not suffer as many hardships as the previous trains had suffered as they were better provisioned and had less illness and were not molested by the Indians. They had a few dreadful thunderstorms which ruined their food and clothing. Mother's first hardship was the lack of bread. After she ran out of hard tack, an army bread, she found herself without any bread. As she had never baked bread before and was too bashful to ask any of the other women, she decided to try her luck. She put the flour and water in a pan, added some salt, and started to knead it as she had seen the other women do. She worked it an hour until she was tired, covered it over as she had seen the other women do, left it to stand overnight to raise. Next morning, bright and early she was up, put the dough in the skillet, and started her fire. She piled sagebrush, broomgrass, and buffalo chips below and above and watched it patiently for an hour. All at once she smelled something burning and found it was her bread. It was solid as a rock and black as coal. She was so tired and disheartened she sat down and cried. Her neighbor saw her and asked her what the trouble was. Mother told her. Her neighbor said: "Never mind, I have some nice biscuits and will give you enough for your breakfast, and tonight I will show you how to mix bread. No doubt you forgot the yeast." Mother had no idea that yeast was needed. That evening she was shown how to bake bread, she soon had as nice a bread as any of the women and taught the other women how to make German coffee cake, which she had eaten but never before baked.

Mother said they were all just like one big family, dividing their joys and sorrows together. The evenings were spent in singing and dancing and playing different instruments, the jewsharp, the accordion, the bugle, the cornet, the fiddle, the banjo, and guitar. If anyone were taken sick, sage tea was resorted to and had wonderful results. Mother said her little team was the envy of the camp. The little mules were never tired and trotted along at a good pace, while often the horses balked and refused to move. The government at that time had station houses every ten miles on the road. The station house was a frame building. There were two men in charge of it. Its only furniture were a stove and two long benches. Whenever they came to a station the men would come out and offer to unharness the mules. Mother told them that she did not think that they could do it. They said: "You come inside and rest, and we will attend to them." Mother had barely turned her back when Father called: "Fanny, Fanny, come here"; she turned around and both would-be gallants were on the other side of the fence, where the mules had gently placed them. Mother said they were gentle as lambs when she was near, but Father dared not go near them, and they refused to start when he took the lines.

Fording the rivers at times was very difficult. Some rivers were very deep and swift, and often driver and horses were washed down the stream for over a mile. The company then had to wait for them. Mother said that often the bottoms of the wagons were filled with water, and clothes and provisions would get wet. They would have to take out everything and dry it. Mother said they had a few Indian scares, but they turned out to be peaceful Indians who were hungry and left after they had been well fed. One day they suddenly saw a big black cloud which frightened all very much, as they feared it was a band of Indians, but it turned out to be a herd of buffaloes. Their fear was not without foundation, for the previous train had been set upon by the Indians, and the whole train had been practically wiped out. Women and children went to sleep at nights while the men kept watch with loaded rifles, as they neared the Indian country, ready to shoot Indians or wild beasts. The men slept during the day, while the women drove the teams. Hyenas would come in packs, sometimes a mountain lion, deer, eagle, or hawk. Everyone was dusty and dirty, half starved when they arrived at Laramie. There was no wood or sagebrush. Children gathered buffalo chips so that the fires could be started and the cooking of the food begin. [. . .]

In Salt Lake City they arrived at the Haymarket Square, which occupied a square block on West Temple and First South. It was used by emigrants for camping purposes. It was also a general market place; here hay was sold, animals bought and exchanged, vegetables and fruits exchanged with the emigrants going West, who gave clothing, sugar, tea, and coffee in exchange.

They had just finished feeding their horses and built their camp fires to make supper, when a curious crowd of Mormons, who were the only inhabitants of Salt Lake at that time, among them a small thin man measuring five feet, with a round ruddy face, sharp eyes, and a briar pipe in his mouth, who came up to Father and said to him in German: "Who are you? From where do you come?" Father answered: "My name is Brooks. I came from Breslau with my bride, and we are making a wedding trip through to California." Niebaur said: "I, too, come from Breslau. Your aunt married an uncle of mine."[9] He knew quite a few of my parents' people. As he was a Jew, Mother and Father were surprised to hear that he had joined the Mormon Church. He said he had studied to be a rabbi. He was well versed in the Talmud but was a dentist by profession. His roving disposition caused him to leave Germany and wander to England, where he met his present wife. He said the missionaries told him of the wonderful climatic conditions and that milk and honey flowed through the streets. As to gold, it was so plentiful that you could pick it up in the street. No one needed money as ground cost nothing. One could have a home for very little, raise all your own vegetables, fruit, and cattle. "We (Niebaur) were poor, had nothing to lose but everything to gain, and we found conditions better than we had expected. We have a nice adobe house of twelve rooms and keep boarders. Would not you and your wife like to board with us over the winter?" Father said: "No, we are going through to California." "You can't do it," said Niebaur. "It is late in October, and already the snow has fallen in the Sierra Nevada." (Sierra Nevada means Mountains of Snow.) "The drifts are already forty to fifty feet deep. Your whole company will have to stay in Salt Lake over the winter until next spring." Father said: "If that is the case, come on over, and I will introduce you to my wife." Mother was very happy to meet someone who could talk German and who knew her folks in Breslau. Niebaur said that Mother was the first Jewish woman to cross the plains. It had taken them nearly four months to cross the plains. Mother said that Mrs. Niebaur was a nice, trim-looking English (Christian) woman. She kept a few boarders; she was only a fair cook. But she gave mother some very good advice. Mother was then only seventeen years old and badly in need of advice. Later Mother and Father discovered that Niebaur was a close friend of Brigham Young. As Niebaur was well versed in the Old Testament, Brigham Young had him translate some parts of the Old Testament into the Book of Mormon. Besides, he was interpreter to the emigrants. He met every train. He spoke German and French, Hebrew and a splendid English. He also started the first match factory in Utah and was by profession a surgeon and dentist.

---

9. Alexander Niebaur was born in Ehrebreitstein in 1808, received a Jewish education, and was fluent in several languages. He married an Englishwoman and they immigrated to Salt Lake City (Ogden, ed., *Frontier Reminiscences*, 113).

The winter had been very severe, but they were very comfortable and did not mind the fact they were housed up most of the time: they enjoyed sitting at the log fire and listening to Mr. Niebaur's stories of his boyhood days. When the spring came they hated to leave Salt Lake. The cost of living there was nominal. They left in May with a heavy heart but promised to return someday, little dreaming they would return so soon.

They started for California with most of the train that had crossed the plains with them, but a few remained behind. They encountered very bad roads; the snow was still quite deep in the mountains and the drifts at times impassable, which necessitated many detours. It was uphill all the way to Truckee but an easy trip from there on, as the beautiful scenery, the wonderful pine and oak, fir and maple made the trip seem much shorter.

When they reached the Sacramento River, the heat was unbearable. If the distance had not been so great, they would have returned to Salt Lake. They stopped at Marysville, a town on the Feather River, which was then, and now, a great grain and fruit country. The climate was mild, but there was a great deal of rain. Father opened a general merchandise store, but the town was small, and it was not a good business center, as most people went to San Francisco for their goods. My little sister Amelia, one and one-half years old, died there; my sister Cecilia and brother George were born there.

8

A Boy's Trip around the Horn

Myer Newmark, 1853

From December 1852 until April 1853, fourteen-year-old Myer Newmark kept a diary of his trip from New York to California with his mother, younger brother, and sisters to join his father in California.[10] Born in New York in 1838 to Joseph and Rosa (Levy) Newmark, Myer was the second of six children.[11] His father, an observant Jew, came from a long line of rabbis in Poland and Germany. Myer was educated in New York and England, where he lived with his maternal grandparents, attending grammar school and later New York's Columbia College for a short time. He celebrated his bar mitzvah a year before making the voyage to California.

In California, Myer Newmark lived in both San Francisco and Los Angeles. In 1859 he became a practicing lawyer in Los Angeles at the age of twenty-one, returning in 1863 to San Francisco, where he entered a law partnership with Henry J. Labatt and Robert T. Payne. Moving back to Los Angeles in 1871, he went into business with Harris Newmark. In June of 1874, Myer Newmark married Sophie Cahen, a recent French emigrant. Together they had three children. Newmark died in 1911 in San Francisco, the city to which he had retired four years earlier.

The following excerpts are taken from Myer Newmark's travel diary, in which he wrote almost daily while sailing on a clipper ship from New York to San Francisco. It was not uncommon for children and adults to keep diaries of their trips as a record for their families. As Newmark was born and raised in New York, his perspective as a native-born American and as a teenager makes this account unusual. Newmark's poor spelling and grammar may reflect his age and lack of education. It is especially interesting to note the development of the children during the voyage, the observance of the Sabbath, and the teaching of Hebrew.

---

10. It was common for a husband to establish himself in the West before sending for his family. An edited version of the diary was printed in 1954 by Donald Price Germain in memory of his grandmother, Emily Germain, daughter of Matilda Newmark, sister of Myer Newmark, for use by his high school students and relatives. This version was later republished in the *Western States Jewish Historical Quarterly* 2:4 (1970): 227–45.

11. See *Western States Jewish Historical Quarterly* 2:3 (1970): 136; Leo Newmark, *California Family: An Intimate History* (Santa Monica: Norton B. Stern, 1970); Harris Newmark, *Sixty Years in Southern California, 1853–1913* (Boston: Houghton Mifflin, 1930).

California-bound immigrants on a clipper ship rounding Cape Horn of South America. L. A. Fleming, *California, Its Past History, Its Future Prospects* (London: self-published, 1850). Courtesy of the Bancroft Library (F865.C17), University of California, Berkeley.

Ship's Log around the Horn
Kept By
Myer Newmark

Incidents of a voyage from New York to San Francisco around Cape Horn in the good ship "Carrington," F. B. French Commander, commenced December 15th, 1852, ended April 20th, 1853.[12]

Wednesday December 15th, 1852

We went on board with expectations of leaving, but in consequence of the absence of the steward and cook we were detained until the following day. We all remained on board the ship, cleared into the East River.

SOURCE: Myer Newmark, Ship's Log around the Horn, 1852–53. Myer Newmark diary, MS 725. Courtesy of the Southwest Museum, Los Angeles, California.

12. Although the Newmark family left in the winter, it was summer in the southern hemisphere, where they would have spent much of the trip.

Thursday, December 16th

We sailed at 8 o'clock A.M., Uncle John escorted us as far as the tow boat went, past the Highlands of Neversin and then we were left to our reflections to travel for sixteen thousand miles. In the afternoon, taking benefit of the leisure time laid before us, our whole party set to and cast up our accounts. Caroline[13] commenced, and I was the worst of the lot; however, we continued to sail brightly along.

Friday, December 17th

A great storm arose against us about the middle of the day, and we covered the blankets over us glad to get into our births. In the night our steward unfortunately fell down and almost broke his leg. The sea was mountains high, and the two life-boats was carried off, together with a large portion of the fresh stores and, worst of all, our Christmas turkey. The sea came in our cabin and relieved us of our stove-pipe. In attempting to save one of the boats, the capitain almost fell overboard. [. . .]

Thursday, December 23rd

As for winds and weather it is just the same as yesterday. Meats, bread, pies, puddings, apples, figs, go from our eyes to our mouths like chaff before the wind and we all feel very happy and comfortable.

Friday, December 24th

The wind shifted around, but it is still in our favor and in this short space of time we have run 1800 miles from New York. The weather is delightful and the beautiful moonlight nights we spend on deck are really sublime. We are all in fine spirits and pass our time very happily. We continue to run at a great rate, the only thing we miss is the milk. Have nothing particular to write.

Saturday, December 25th, Christmas Day

It is a beautiful day and are going very fast. The sea and sky are a most beautiful blue, and everything looks happy, merry and cheerful. We all did justice to the dainty dinner set before us, which consisted of roast and boiled fowl, vegetables, plum pudding and applesauce, fruits and cider, and altogether spend a very pleasant day.

Sunday, December 26th

We can not wish for better winds and weather, everything is very quiet while all hands are reading. We are in the trade winds and our course liest south by south-east.

---

13. Myer's siblings were Matilda, born in 1837; Sarah, born in 1841; Caroline, born in 1845; Edward, born in 1851; and Harriet, born in 1852.

Monday, December 27th

Fine weather still enlivens our spirits. The wind is high and are going at a great rate. This morning we had a good ducking on deck from a spray which covered us. The children are very cross, particularly Edward; so much so that we threatened to put him in the hole. We are at the moment enjoying the merry tones of the Piano Forte, played by the captains daughter, Miss French. [. . .]

Saturday, January 1st, 1853

We had a codfish dinner, consisting of boiled cod-fish with butter, fish balls, boiled onions and patatoes, pickles, pancakes and fruit at 11 o'clock P.M. Dear Mamma cut up our New Year's cake! and gave all hands on board a piece with a glass of Port wine. The weather is the same as yesterday though the wind is fair and we are going fast. We are now 4000 miles from New York. [. . .]

Friday, January 7th

There is no alteration in the wind or weather and if it continues so till tomorrow evening, we may be on the line [the equator]. The Captain says it is one of the quickest runs he ever made, five thousand miles in twenty-three days; it is near one third of our journey. We live first rate, this morning we had buckwheat cakes for breakfast and pea soup and fowl for dinner; in the morning after breakfast the children are dressed and go on deck. Mamma and Matilda sew till it is time for dinner, previous to which we put the two young ones to bed, who as you may suppose, are the whole time squalling. Harriet must have very strong lungs to remain well with the noise she is all the time making, and if it was not for those two we would spend a very plesant time. [. . .]

Monday, January 10th

The weather is very fine and we have a good steady breeze going from five to six knots an hour. We lost three chickens overboard, they got loose from the coop. [. . .]

Wednesday, January 12th

A good steady breeze still continues to carry us toward Cape Horn. The ship that I mentioned yesterday to have been ahead of us we came up to at 12 oclock today. She was a Scotch Bark from St. Andrews bound for the Sandwich Islands. Before seeing her closely, we knew her to be English, as she hoisted her flag, while with delight we unfurled the pride of the world—the Stars and Stripes. However, we left her in the shade and at 4 oclock in the afternoon we were 6 miles ahead of her; across the line, a good steady breeze all well, plenty to eat and beat a Johnny Bull [British ship] does first rate and we are all very well satisfied.

Thursday, January 13th and Friday, January 14th

The same steady breeze still continues and the weather is beautiful. Dear Mamma has been very industrious and made the children two dresses, one for Sarah and the other for Caroline. [. . .]

Tuesday, January 18th

We are not going as fast as yesterday still the weather is quite as fine as previous. In the morning we passed an English ship, she was to windward of us and could have easily spoken, but like all Englishmen, he was obstinate. She was [a] very pretty ship, not quite as large as ours. About five in the afternoon (we have daylight till seven) we came near to a whaler; we hoisted colours. She was an American. They immediately lowered a boat and sent us six men and the mate. Her name was the Garland, Captain Hoye (?) of New Bedford, she had been out twenty-one months. We gave them a lot of tobacco and a sack of potatoes and onions, late papers, and a letter directed to dear Grandma, which they promised to forward if they spoke to any ships homeward bound or went to any port. They said they had been very unfortunate this year in whaling. They gave two whales teeth, one to Matilda, the other to Miss French. [. . .]

Thursday, January 20th

No change has taken place either in the weather or the wind. We are now abreast of Rio Janeiro About dusk this evening we saw an English bark a short way from us; she was homeward bound. I pass my time reading and talking and taking care of Edward. I have been reading Percival Keene, David Copperfield by Dickens. I am trying to teach Caroline reading and writing and Sarah Hebrew. [. . .]

Saturday, February 5th

Last night about 11 oclock the wind changed quite fair. We had a breeze going from eleven to twelve knots an hour till about twelve o'clock to-day when it changed ahead and has remained so all day. We past the day [as] usual, praying,[14] reading etc. We had a first rate dinner, consisting of fish balls, boiled codfish with eggs and butter, potatoes, onions, salad and apple fritter. We live very well indeed. [. . .]

Friday, February 11th

We will have a fair wind but it is so light it is almost a calm. The weather is beautiful this morning. At about 11 o'clock we saw a penguin; they are only seen in the vicinity of Cape Horn. We cannot be a great way from it. We have been 56 days out and will soon pass the Horn. [. . .]

Monday, February 14th

Wind still fair and we are going at the rate of nine knots an hour. The weather is beautiful and we are no more than two hundred miles from Cape Horn. All on board that have been around say they never experienced such beautiful weather as we have. This morning we came across the American bark "Douglass" from

---

14. It is Saturday, the Jewish Sabbath.

Boston, bound for San Francisco. The means by which we knew her name and particulars are that Mr. Ellery, our mate, has travelled on her. Dear Mama is not at all well to-day and intends taking three antibillious pills. This evening all the rest of us are thank God well. [. . .]

Friday, February 18th

A light but fair wind took us along slowly this morning, but it changed this afternoon to a strong head wind. We sighted two islands called the Diego Ramesis to the eastward and Cape Horn to the westward. After writing yesterday, we saw the Hermit Islands on our weather bow. We are now at the extreme point of Cape Horn and the weather is cold, stormy and disagreeable and we all wish ourselves in San Francisco, California. [. . .]

Saturday, March 5th

The weather remained the same as yesterday till 12 oclock noon, since which time there has been but very little wind and that is ahead. Our course is N. W. by N. It is a beautiful day and we are all on deck. I should have very well liked being in New York yesterday as it was the inauguration of OUR DEMOCRATIC PRESIDENT.

FRANKLIN PIERCE

and Vice President, William R. King for the ensuing term of four years. [. . .]

Thursday, March 24th

It is useless to criticise any longer on the winds and weather, for we are in the trade winds and they are always the same. Today we are setting up the main or middle rigging. Yesterday the Capitain presented dear Mamma a drawing of the "Carrington" in full sail, beautifully executed by himself. We are now about five degrees from the line. I trust that this day three weeks hence, we shall be with dear Father. [. . .]

Thursday, March 31st

The Capitain says we have now caught the trades, we are all the time going 8 and 9 knots an hour. Today I have commenced "Crichton," by W. Harrison Ainsworth and have just finished the "Vale of Ceders [Cedars]," by Grace Aguilar,[15] our Jewish authoress. If this should continue for twelve days we shall be in San Francisco, please God.

Friday, April 1st

Today being all fools day we kept it up. Mr. Ellery, our Mate, made a hollow tube in immitation of a flute and told me to blow it in Miss Palmer's ears as hard as I could. I done it thinking it was to make a fool of Miss Palmer, instead

---

15. Grace Aguilar (1816–47), a Sephardic English author, wrote many novels with Jewish themes.

of which I got my face filled with powder and looked like a white nigger. We are going very fast indeed and it is a beautiful day. Blessed Harriet has cut two eye teeth so easily that dear mother did not know anything about it till they were through. [. . .]

Monday, April 18th
All sign of the gale has vanished and we have a fine steady breeze going from 6 to 7 knots an hour. Towards evening we were in sight of a Fierre Lone [Farallon] Islands. Trust tomorrow we shall be very near San Francisco, being near the land. The Captain abacked the main yard and lay to all night for fear of running ashore.

Tuesday, April 19th
This morning the whole of the mainland is clearly seen together with Point Ray [Reyes], which is exactly 37 miles from the town of San Francisco, but there is no wind and we are not likely to get in today. In the afternoon about 3 oclock a fair but light breeze sprung up, but the tide being so strong against us we are not going very fast. At five o'clock we hoisted our Union Jack and soon got a pilot from the Fierre Leone [Farallon] Islands. He said there had been no fires in San Francisco and nothing particular occurred.

San Francisco, 1851. Courtesy of the Bancroft Library (1963.2.127-A), University of California, Berkeley.

Wednesday, April 20th, 1853

At 2 o'clock this morning while we were yet asleep, dear Mama heard the pilot call "Port." Of course, she was up in a minute and called us. We dressed ourselves and waited till morning, when at ten o'clock dear father, Mason, Uncle Sylvester, Lewis Isaccs and Mr. Brush came out in a boat. Then you can easily imagine our feeling. We then went in a little boat ashore; once more on land my task is done. Trusting you will excuse all imperfections, allow me to subscribe myself.

Yours truly,

Myer J. Newmark.

N.B. My dear relatives: You will please exscuse the dreadful scrawl and numerous other faults which are to be found in these pages, as I was so much hurried I could not well avoid it; you must therefore take the will for the deed, and for the same reason, I am prohibited from corresponding to any of you.

Myer J. Newmark

9

"I Had the Intention to Emigrate"

Henry Cohn, ca. 1855

Henry (Heiman) Cohn, born on April 14, 1831, in Dobrzyn, a small town on the Polish-Prussian border, made two trips to the West Coast. After spending three years in New York, he made the first trip west in 1852, becoming a citizen of the United States in Downieville, Sierra County, California.[16] But Cohn was ambivalent about settling permanently in California and in 1862 he returned to Europe to visit friends and family. After a brief second trip to California, in 1864 Cohn returned for good to Germany, where he married and entered the wholesale wine business in Stettin.

In this account, Cohn describes his early life and Jewish education in Dobrzyn, his apprenticeship, his travels in the company of other Jews to the United States, his life in the East, and his first trip across the Isthmus to California. As a peddler in the eastern United States, Cohn became acclimated to American business practices before opening a store in California. He wrote this account in 1914, on his fiftieth wedding anniversary, for members of his family.

[. . .] My parents lived in those days very much in the same general fashion as everybody else in Dobrzyn. They and their eight beautiful and well-behaved children lived in a dwelling, which had a living room, salon, bedroom, kitchen, pantry, etc. this also contained the shop, all this in a space of maybe four meters by four meters. In the middle of which yet a great bed with a canopy and solid roof, which also served as counter to show the leather skins. Next to this universal room was another large space which served as stockroom for the leather and to lodge eventual guests which happened frequently. [. . .]

Friday was always the best business day for my father, because this was the day of the weekly market. Saturday the shoemakers could not do business and they also observed Sunday.

SOURCE: Henry Cohn, "Memories from Yesteryear on the Occasion of My Golden Anniversary Dedicated to My Descendants." Stettin, Germany (May 24, 1914), trans. from the German "Jugenderinnerungen" by Lisette Georges, daughter of Erwin Blumenfeld, whose mother Emma was Henry Cohn's daughter. Western Jewish History Center of the Judah L. Magnes Museum, Berkeley, California.

16. Arnold H. Zweig supplied additional information about his great-grandfather, Henry Cohn. He has completed a translation of the *Jugenderinnerungen* and collected the personal documents of Cohn. For Henry Cohn's life as a merchant in a mining town, see chapter 7.

My father often literally had to throw his clients out, Friday afternoon, when the Sabbath obliged him to go to Schule.

My mother in spite of all this business was able to prepare the usual Sabbath dishes in the corner of their dwelling, usually consisting of, Fish, meatbroth and vegetables (tsimmes). A beautiful bread (challah) of course was always served.

"Schabbes" was really a blessing and the only rest we had during the whole week, while traditional and festive and also most enjoyable. At the beginning of the Sabbath all our worries were forgotten. Upon our return from "Schule" the room was clean and tidied and clean sand on the floor. The traditional Sabbath lights competing with the sparkling dishes and white table and bed cloths. These and the afore mentioned delicacies and often beer or Meth, made this into a real festivity. When the first and joyous Hebrew prayers started all present fell in and soon everybody was happy and cheerful.

I do not have a happy memory of my Schule or Cheder years. When I was only four years old, I and all the other boys my age had to get up in the early morning when it was still dark to go "Cheder."

We of course all brought our own lights [candles]. We were taught to read and pray in Hebrew. The teacher usually a down and out Chassid without any knowledge but Hebrew, was after the small and big boys from early morning to late in the evening. [. . .]

I absolutely did not want to study the Talmud and informed my father when I was fourteen that I would much rather learn a trade or handicraft, than to continue to visit Cheder.

After a few weeks my mother took me to Rypin to my brother-in-law, Feibusch Wilk, who was a furrier. I was to be an apprentice and live with my sister Henne, a pretty and nice woman, and I was not unhappy. My brother-in-law Feibusch although a good, adept and hard worker who knew his trade, was very young and inexperienced and naive which gave me the feeling that my sister and he were not matched too well. He worked very hard in the summer to prepare the skins which he then worked into furcoats and hats during the fall. Aside from that he also made different kinds of hats for the yearly markets. [. . .]

In Poland, in those days there was no regular conscription, but young men of military age, would be pointed out by the local mayors and burgomasters. And one night all over Poland, these youth would be gotten out of bed by the police and gendarmes, sometimes even chained and handcuffed and would be delivered to military centers as recruits. My elder brother Chaskel, who was then of military age, was already safely on the other side of the frontier in Prussia, I have to add to this that until then all young Jews from Dobrzyn had managed to escape and that not one had served as a soldier. In the year 1847 the levy took place during Springtime. The mayor of Dobrzyn, Moczikowski and his secretary Teitscher, with whom my father was on very friendly terms, gave my father a discrete wink, on what night the raid would take place. Although

I was not yet to be picked up, I was living since my illness with my brother Itsche, whose home was close to the Drewenz [River]. The next morning we heard who among the youths they had been looking for, and it turned out, that at my parents place they were not after my brother Chaskel, but after me. This meant that I had to get across the border as quickly as possible. Brother Itsche, a very big and strong man, took me on his back and brought me wading and swimming across the Drewenz. So now I was safely in Gollub, a little Prussian border town. During the next fourteen years I did not set foot in Dobrzyn.

This was the beginning of a new serious part of my life. I would like to say that from now on I did not think too much but acted instinctively. I waited for several months in Gollub to see what would happen to brother Chaskel and myself. Had I given myself up, I probably could have given my liberty in favor of brother Chaskel, but I decided not to try; at which brother Chaskel returned to Dobrzyn totally unmolested, and where after a few months he became engaged to the daughter of one of the foremost citizens of Dobrzyn, counselor and burger, Michael Roina. [. . .]

In the fall of 1848 I went to Strasburg in Western Prussia to become apprentice to a furrier Hirsch Joseph. I liked Strasburg, it was a quiet, clean and pleasant little city. I lodged, actually mostly slept at night over with my uncle Marcus Joseph, brother of Hirsch's and lived next door. Marcus was an honorable and respectable man, who left the upkeep of his household entirely to his wife Rebecca, my father's sister. This very good and energetic lady had a well going business selling household goods, she kept house, went to buy food at the market as well, which earned her respect from the entire family. [. . .]

On the 18th of April 1852, I passed the examination of furrier's journeyman, received my certificate and walked as was the journeymen's custom to Gollub with half a dozen friends and companions, they went as far as Ostrowit, which was about half way to Gollub. I had the intention to emigrate to America. My parents were very much against this idea. My mother cried bitterly and begged me to change my mind. I stood firm, and explained to her and to my father, who did not even come across the Drewenz to Gollub, that I had decided to emigrate and that if he would not give me the money for my trip, I would myself earn enough for a passport and fare to get to England, where I would make enough to work my way over to America. But in that case he would never hear from me again. My strong convictions convinced them, with the result that I received the next day sixty Taler from my father, and three from my brother Chaskel. My mother took care of the linen [clothes] for my trip, and after a moving farewell party from my relatives, I took off for Hamburg at the end of April. I only bade my father farewell from across the river Drewenz.

As my money was not sufficient for a steamship crossing to New York, I was forced to take a sailing ship. And so on May 5, 1852 we sailed, on the Two-masted "Lewizow Lelkendorf" whose captain, Günther, was a good natured and gentle soul, for New York.

The passengers, of whom there were about two hundred in all, stayed in a large space.

Aside from the Germans, many with their wives and children, there were twenty Jews. There was only this one room. The beds consisted of large open bunks, built two or three on top of one another. Each bunk was furnished with two to four mattresses. The passengers had to bring their own pillows and blankets. These beds were not assigned but each person arranged things for themselves as well as possible, [including] husbands and wives. The Jews of course kept to themselves and paid little attention to the others. We had to rise early in the morning and everybody had to go up on deck, weather permitting. Even the seasick or the slightly ill had to get out, or they would be smoked out with cayenne pepper.

Food was eaten on deck. I cannot actually remember much about the food. It was not very good, particularly since I only ate kosher. I do remember that we Jews were given special permission to cook a dinner prepared with plums and meatballs in the honor of "Shauvot."

The weather was good in general. No bad storms, but the wind was mostly against us, so to make any progress at all we had to tack. The passengers got along well, and time was shortened by several interesting natural occurrences, jokes and fun, and so after sixty four days, on July 8, we finally arrived in the harbor of New York.

In New York, I stayed with a family from Dobrzyn, who lived there already for many years. [. . .] After eight days of rest, I found a job with a furrier who I knew from Strasburg. But I soon found, that my friend was taking advantage of me. And so I looked around for another occupation, when, quite by chance I met a young man by the name of Flatow, who also came from Strasburg, who made his living as a peddler in the surrounding country[side]. Flatow suggested I do the same, and even most generously offered to take me along and show me the way.

With the money I had brought, 10 shilling which were $2 1/2 and the salary for the four weeks of work at the furrier's, I now had a capital of $9–, besides which a young man I knew from Dobrzyn, who had been in New York for six years lent me another $6–. With this I bought a basket and cover, needed for the merchandise and also at Ullmann at Bowery street about $12– worth of wares, consisting of hardware, notions and haberdashery. Early Monday, Flatow and I took a boat across the river Hudson to Newark in N.J. and from there by railroad about two stops inland. Flatow by the way was a very good looking and imposing man of about twenty two, who had been living for several years in America.

When we got off the train, I believe the place was called Dover, Flatow said to me: "Here is a map for this week, [. . .] I noted where you should spend every night, and on Sunday in a week I will rejoin you." At this we started off down the road and went on for another two hours, until the road split. Then he said, after he wished me good luck: "You take this road, and I [will] take that one. On Sunday we shall meet again. Goodbye." I shall never forget how I felt. As long as I could see Flatow, I kept going. But as soon as I lost sight of him, I sat down on the first stone in sight and wept bitterly.

When finally I had no more tears left, I took courage and continued walking, but never offered my wares to anyone that day.

I spent the night with a friendly farmer, and the next morning after breakfast when I got ready to pay, the farmer's wife told me, with words and sign language, that she would not accept money, but that she would like to see my wares. Whereupon she picked several items and paid me for them. Moreover she picked a few more small things, like needles and thread etc in payment for my overnight lodging. So these few "cents" were my first business transactions. Many farmers in those days gave overnight lodgings to peddlers, and under those circumstances one was always well taken care of. [. . .]

During the Jewish holidays I stayed in New York and tried my luck in between by selling here and in Long Island some writing material, but without any success. Being a "Greenhorn" I was not up to the smart townfolk's tricks and especially not up to those of the Jews. I bought goods and necessities for the next trip, but this time instead of the basket, I now got a pack and straps, and at Ullmann's I bought somewhat better quality merchandise on credit, which they offered and I gratefully took advantage of it. [. . .]

David Wollenberg [a *cheder* companion from Dobrzyn] wrote from California, that all went well in California, and that he already had entered into a business in Folsom, Sacramento County.

In the spring around the month of April, I got prepared for the voyage, a decent looking Jewish man paid me a visit and told me that he heard I was leaving for California. He himself had intended to go and had bought a ticket for passage on May 5th, but his mother had written him from Berlin unexpectedly that urgent family matters made it necessary for him to return to Berlin. So he could let me have his ticket for a very low price. At first I told him off very positively, but the man came back and made me such a good proposal that I finally agreed that I would buy the ticket from him, if the ticket would be put in my name. We then both went to the ticket office of the shipping company, but the gentleman did not go into the office with me but waited outside. When I showed the ticket to the collector, he asked me where I had obtained it, and when I explained the provenance, he told me I was very lucky to have shown him the ticket first, because I would surely have been put off the ship, because this was a stolen ticket. I told the official that the man who sold me the ticket was sitting outside waiting for me, and he was taken away. I never found out what happened after that.

The Pacific Railroad was not yet in existence in those days, and steamboats to California left only every two weeks. So I bought a steamboat ticket for San Francisco over the Panama Isthmus and left New York on May 5th on a beautiful day. The boat trip to Aspinwall called Colon today took about eight days and it was an excellent and most interesting trip. All berths on the boat were taken and the passengers were, thanks to the good weather, in a good mood and very good-natured. Aspinwall was a very lively town because of the many immigrants, and also on account of the Isthmus R.R., was being built, which at this time was almost half finished. Right upon our arrival we were put on the train and expedited to the terminal station [end of the line]. Some of the passengers got on donkeys' I and the others walked a stretch until evening. We spent the night together in the open and we posted watch against any possible attackers, because in those days the road across the Isthmus, about 47 English miles in length was supposed to be very dangerous, although less so for those arriving than for those returning from California. The night however went by without incident.

We started the next morning very early, so that we arrived very tired at about four in the afternoon in Panama. My luggage which I and some friends had entrusted to an almost naked Mexican kid with a donkey was found again in Panama. To our great disappointment we learned that the Steamer "Golden Gate" which was supposed to have picked us up, had been pirated. Consequently we were forced to spend fourteen days in this very unhealthy and uncomfortable Panama City, while we waited for the next steamer to pick us up. I did not see much of interest, apart from a great many worthwhile large Catholic churches, very dirty streets, and beggars in rags.

I used this time, to sell as much of the wares I had brought along. With this I was so successful that I practically paid my expenses for the trip in this manner. We were finally rescued at the expected time by the arrival of the beautiful steamer "Sacramento." This trip on the Pacific Ocean, with the exception of the stretch of the Gulf of California, mostly on the coast of the southern states, was exceptionally hot but glorious. The time passed quickly and agreeably, and so we arrived in about twelve days, around the 10th of June in San Francisco, where I right away met several relatives and quickly got used to life there.

These were bad days in California, and especially in San Francisco. Moral conditions especially in the better circles had deteriorated badly. Theft, murder and corruption were everyday happening and the criminals went mostly free, because the judges were all corrupt. Because of these conditions, an opposition party, created a vigilante committee, which exercised rigid lynching justice. Many of the accused were arrested, among them even a judge, and after a short trial, three of them were hanged in broad daylight on the railing [of the balconies] of Montgomery Street, the main thoroughfare.

This incident caused great unrest and excitement. Soon however people became reassured, when the committee of the vigilantes asserted itself and put in different judges. And so the situation soon improved again.

San Francisco situated in the hills was even then a really beautiful city. It had lots of beautiful stores and lots of traffic. The climate with summer and winter almost equally mild is glorious. Never once did I experience rain in California from April till September. Like in the East, I started immediately to peddle my goods, especially in the surrounding country.

Starting out from Sacramento, I soon found my friend David Wollenberg, who lived in Folsom, Sacramento County, and who had together with a fellow Dobrzyner a very good business. I myself set up shop there and went out into the surrounding countryside where the farmers and gold diggers lived, with much success selling my goods.

10

Accompanying Her Husband to Gold Country

Hanchen Meyer Hirschfelder, 1856

Born in Karlsruhe, Germany, in 1837, Hanchen (Johanna) Meyer married Emanuel H. Hirschfelder before migrating to California, where they had three children. Emanuel's shop in Downieville sold "All Kinds of Ladies' and Gentlemen's wear, from bonnets to gaiters, and from hats to boots."[17] In the following letter, Hirschfelder describes to her family in Europe the trip with her husband by ship and by the Panama Railroad to California. The Hirschfelders' voyage was unusual in its luxury. Hanchen Hirschfelder died in 1869 at age thirty-two and is buried in the Jewish cemetery in Marysville.[18]

Dear Mother and brothers and sisters-in-law,

In accordance with my promise and your wishes I am sending you the notes I took during our trip from New York to here. Our trip was, with God's help, one of the best and most beautiful that has been made in a long time. On Sept. 20th at two in the afternoon we left New York on the *George Law*, a big steamer, while a great crowd waved goodbye to us, [. . .] and while the cannons fired off a shot which announced the mail boat. The exit from the harbor was as lovely as the entrance which I recently described to you in detail. We had 700 passengers on board, several of whom my husband introduced to me immediately as friends from San Francisco. They were very friendly and even offered me an armchair, sour pickles, apples etc. [during] the first few days when I was somewhat seasick. The gentlemen had made the trip several times and knew what was prudent to take as precautions. The first few days passed fairly quietly, just ocean. Sometimes we saw sailing boats or fishing boats come relatively close, which we enjoyed. After 4 or 5 days it got so warm in the cabins that many people preferred to spend the nights up on deck, which we also tried. We traveled first class and the price in the upper saloon was $270.

SOURCE: Hanchen Meyer Hirschfelder to her family, 1856, trans. Ruth Eis and Ruth Steiner. Hirschfelder Collection, oversized. Western Jewish History Center of the Judah L. Magnes Museum, Berkeley, California. Reprinted by permission.

17. *Sierra Citizen*, Mar. 11, 1864, 4.

18. For further information, see Levinson, *Jews in the California Gold Rush*. Karlsruhe, formerly the capital of Baden, had a Jewish population of 1,080 in 1862. Anti-Jewish demonstrations there in 1843 and 1848 may have led to Emanuel Hirshfelder's migration to California. Fanny, their first child, made the high school honor roll in Downieville (northeast of Marysville) in 1868. For a photograph of Hanchen Meyer Hirschfelder's Marysville gravestone, see chapter 8.

per person—in the lower saloon $200.—we had to take the latter because first class was already filled. Very few Germans liked the American food, and it takes a long time until one gets used to it. All the waiters and servants were Negroes and sometimes, despite my seasickness, I had to laugh . . . As you know, I don't speak English, but managed to get everything anyway. For example I got ice water ("Eiswasser") and other things very readily from the Negroes. . . . [It was] said to me one day that the Negroes must consider me to be one of them since they were always so friendly to me, and I am really glad, dear sister-in-law, that I don't speak English. [. . .]

On the 24th we saw a lovely rainbow and on the 25th many birds which means that land is near. Toward noon we saw islands which I thought to be Cuba, but when I looked at the map I saw that they were the West Indies, that is a part of them. In the afternoon I saw land on the other side, Haita [Haiti]. The weather was very humid but toward evening it got nicer. The passengers are full of gaiety. Many groups sing, play guitar, and so on. On the 26th we passed Cuba and it is a very large island. Every day we cover about 206 miles; one must calculate 3 1/2 miles per hour. I believe we also passed Havana and in the evening we saw the island of San Domingo at sunset. Very picturesque. On the 27th, beautiful blue sea, reflection of the sky, many islands in sight. About 10 A.M. a Negro ship's pilot came on board and we had a lovely view of Jamaica. At 11 we saw the capital, Kingsdon [Kingston] the fort jutting out into the sea. One cannot see much more beautiful sights than that. The fort in the ocean, the ship near the shore, pastel colored small houses smiling at you, and between and around them palm and coconut trees. One should look at paintings and pictures of this area to see how beautiful it is. Many people on the shore, mostly Negroes. Our ship fired its cannon, and immediately there appeared a French doctor, several English and American officers who are stationed here on two warships, and who came to us in little skiffs. A ladder was let down from the ship and the gentlemen climbed up; however, finding everything in order, soon left. In order to get into port we had to pass the whole town and so we anchored only at 12 o'clock. About 10 Negro boys came swimming to the boat. The passengers threw small silver coin bags to them and they dove for them [. . .] and brought them back up, showed them quickly, put them in their mouths, and the game started all over again. To a lover of beautiful scenery today would be worth the trip. Around 12 o'clock we stopped and took on water and coal. Many Negro women came, in the most outrageous outfits and with vessels on their heads, dancing and singing, to do this job, since the men are too lazy to do this kind of work. After 3 o'clock we and many other passengers went on ashore to spend at least some time in the land where the pepper grows. [. . .] Here it is very hot and the fruits that grow here wild are very tempting—but one must beware of eating them. Maybe the oranges are ok. But pineapple, for a few cents, are not good for your health. Kingston is an old town. The women come to market on mules, laden with fruit, like wild ones,

135

similar to gypsys . . . pipe or cigar in mouth, often wearing ball gowns, checked scarves on their heads, and usually without shoes. [. . .] But you also meet English and German business people. Many "Israelites" live here. A Negro Jew showed us the very beautiful synagogue. We returned early to our ship where I received from a gentleman a pretty shell basket. At 10 o'clock in the evening we left. I forgot: there were many policemen in the street, black men with shiny white trousers and jackets, cloth caps with a big P in the middle. We left at 10 o'clock. The moon made the sea shine like so many lights.

[. . .] Several of the passengers were late and now have leisure to explore the interior of the pepperland, where there are forests of cactus and tropical fruit.

Today [September 29] confusion aboard the ship with weighing of luggage.

This morning [September 30] we see land and immediately thereafter came fog and rain which indicates that we are near the Isthmus. We passed several small islands and land finally, about 3 P.M. in Aspinwall. A wide street, bordered on one side by houses, on the other by railroad cars—in the middle tracks on which all day long the locomotive runs back and forth with a big bell which sounds constantly, so that men as well as animals should make way. We quickly secured overnight beds in Howard House which cost $8.00 per person. . . . October 2—In the morning at 9 o'clock we left on the Panama Railroad via the Isthmus from the Gulf of Darien where it was awfully hot and my arm with which I held the umbrella got blisters. Then we traveled through rain forests, past swamps and the straw huts of the natives, who sat on the floor, practically naked. To the right and left . . . areas with straw huts inhabited by families, and it appeared at times like chaos.

We saw immense trees, palm trees etc., but I did not see monkeys or the like. The train often crosses canyons that make you shudder. A few narrow oaken planks serve as bridge. But inside the car we had wine and other drinks to pass the time, and good company made us forget the scary sights. But this is "gold" compared to earlier days when you had to make the crossing by mule. Many natives, are busy with construction work, whites do not tolerate the climate; 2000 workers died on this undertaking.

About 3 P.M. we arrived in Panama, a Spanish fortress, or rather ruin. Here it is quite nice and we saw Spanish troops exercise. Meat is being sold in strips, about 2 fingerwide bands, and sold by length. We stayed here about 11 1/2 hours and then were taken by small steamboats 2 miles out to the *Golden Age,* a big beautiful steamer that was lying between two mountains. It is nice on this ship and we got one of the best rooms, next to the captain's quarters. Although we were now on the Pacific, several passengers got seasick. The first few days passed uneventfully. Passengers are not allowed to talk with the officers, that is the crew of the ship. Nonetheless, we had many conversations with the doctor and the purser, who talked to us. At night, the men make music on the accordion, and so I had to, despite my protestations, dance a polka with the purser on the foredeck. My husband wanted to take along a young Negro from Panama as a servant. I however did not want to take on a burden to make it easier on myself, and so another man took him along for the price of the passage. On the ship we cover 280 miles per day, and we have very good travel companions. Also several Jewish families. I am very popular on board, so are my husband and Emma.

7th October. This morning huge rocks and islands. We are approaching the American fortress Acapulco. Here, it is very hot and one has to watch out for sunstroke. A lot of small boats arrive, partly to take passengers to land, since the ship stays at sea because of the low tide, partly to sell fruit and shells. I prefer to stay on board. The scenery is very romantic, so that I imagine I am seeing the gulf of Venice . . .

Here again we take on water and coal; however, here the work is done by men. The Mexican men are good looking and muscular with co-colored appearance. The waves are gently caressing the rocks, and after a few hours we left. Water has to be freshened up with ice, which costs 25 cents per portion. The following days we saw islands every day. I got so used to travel by sea, since the pleasant company made the time pass quickly, that it all seemed like a beautiful dream.

Our "Day of Atonement" (Yom Kippur) which was on the 9th, we spent very well. However, the next day I felt somewhat weak. 11th Oct. From Acapulco, we went north, and during the night it was rather cold. We saw land again . . . lower California. We also met a steamer coming from California.

The closer we came to the coast, the colder and foggier the weather. . . . Oct. 14 the ship swayed a lot, a sign of approaching land. [. . .] We came between two high mountains to the Golden Gate, and then we saw from a distance San Francisco which offered a beautiful sight. This, after NY, is the most beautiful approach in the world. The city lay on the mountain like in a sea of fog. About 8 o'clock we arrived in San Francisco where we were met by a cousin Hirschfelder [. . .] however, because of lack of low tide [we could] not land before 10 o'clock. We were so glad to be patient with God's help. In SF, where we stayed for 10 days, I liked it very much and I will, dear mother, describe in detail the interior of Calif, with its gold mines at the next opportunity. For the time it should be enough for you, for my arm is really very tired from writing. With cordial greetings to you and the whole family I remain your loving

Hanchen Hirschfelder[19]

---

19. There is a notation dated November 30 stating that the letter did not make the boat, was returned to them, and was sent out with the next mail. A partial translation of a note by Emanuel Hirschfelder reads: "Our business opened a week ago and is doing well. Emma learns well, is getting tall and pretty. I am expecting mail from you, as well as from Buffalo and N.Y. I talked to Mr. Willstadter who is not inclined to have his family come here, however, if they insist, we will help them. Hanchen is doing well and California agrees with her." Emanuel Hirschfelder Collection, Western Jewish History Center.

11
"I Want to Go to America"
Eugene Meyer, 1859

Eugene Meyer was born in Strasbourg, France, in 1842 to a family with an illustrious Jewish history. His grandfather, Jacob Meyer, had been a rabbi and member of the Sanhedrin called by Napoleon,[20] while his father was the Secretary of the Jewish Consistory of Bas-Rhin and of the Commission of the Jewish Community of Strasbourg. After receiving a religious and secular elementary education, Eugene had to cut his education short when his father died and he was forced to go to work to supplement the family's income. Briefly employed as a clerk in the "fancy goods" business, Meyer was captivated by talk of California and in 1859, at the age of seventeen, he boarded a westbound steamer.

After arriving in San Francisco, Meyer moved to Los Angeles, where he worked as a clerk in the dry goods store of Solomon Lazard, another French Jew, and in 1867 he married Harriet Newmark, Myer Newmark's sister. Before returning to San Francisco in 1883, he served as French Consul in southern California and was a founder of the Los Angeles branch of the Alliance Israélite Universelle. His son, Eugene Meyer, Jr., was to become publisher of the *Washington Post*.

[W]hen my boss Nathan Blum announced that he was going to Donaldsonville [Louisiana], I decided that I wanted to go with him to America and so informed my mother. To this she gave her consent, at the same time obtaining a promise from me, however, that I would not go to the South, or to the region in which yellow fever epidemics occurred.

The newspapers of France of those days (1859) were full of tales of California, which at that time was still a land of romance. There was a lottery in France of which the prizes were transportation to California. There were quite a number of Frenchmen in California, the winners of these prizes, who were known as "lingoes" or "lottery men."

As I was thus prevented by my promise to my mother from going to Donaldsonville or New Orleans, I decided to go to California. The necessary formalities

SOURCE: Eugene Meyer, unpublished reminiscence, 1859. Typescript, Rosalie Meyer Stern Collection, Western Jewish History Center of the Judah L. Magnes Museum, Berkeley, California. Reprinted by permission.

20. The "Great Sanhedrin," which included members of France's rabbinic and Jewish lay community, was convened in 1807 to represent the Jews of France.

and preparation for my journey were soon attended to. I accompanied my employer, Nathan Blum, to Paris and there was introduced by him to Alexander Lazard, of the firm of Lazard Freres who gave me a letter of introduction to Alexander Weill who was with Lazard Freres in San Francisco.

During the month of September I sailed from Havre on the steamship "VANDERBILT," a side-wheeler, but known as a crack boat, in fact the fastest boat of her day. All that I could afford was third class which on the steamer was one hundred and ten dollars. At Havre I had bought a mattress and of course I had blankets with me. To reach my sleeping quarters on the boat I had to go down two flights of stairs. There was little or no ventilation and the surroundings were very dirty. Among my traveling companions were boxes of goods consigned to Lazard Freres and marked "L.F." which I recognized later in the store of Lazard Freres in San Francisco. Although my boss offered to lend me the money to travel second-class, I said I would stick it out as I preferred not to go into debt.

My mother had given me a box of lunch containing, amongst other things, oil, vinegar, and sausage. I met another Jewish boy on the boat and we arranged to have our meals together. We went for our portions and then would make potato salad and add from our boxes some more palatable food.

The steamer arrived in New York in October, 1859, where I remained for a period of about two weeks waiting for a steamer to the Isthmus. Mr. Blum took me to his boarding house in Warren Street. It was a very good place, but I could not afford the price. I stayed there only a short while, until I was called for by an uncle of my brother-in-law, Jacob Loewe, who asked me to stop with him at his house. I was also invited by a nephew of my uncle, Baruch Meyer, to his house. He lived at the time in Fourteenth Street, then considered one of the best residential districts in New York.

There was a steamship rate war at the time between lines from New York to California and prices were so low that I felt warranted in taking second-class passage from New York on the Steamship "AERIAL" to Colon. I crossed the Isthmus on the narrow gauge railroad to Aspinwall.[21] The trip took four hours. The Isthmus at that time was a very unhealthy place. I took the steamship "ORIZABA" from Aspinwall to San Francisco. I had bought a good deal of tropical fruit which I was careful not to eat until the boat was two days out and well beyond the yellow fever zone. The ship stopped at Acapulco and other ports where we took on coal and fresh provisions. In all it took me twenty-four days from New York to San Francisco.

I landed in San Francisco one morning the latter part of November practically a total stranger. I had made no acquaintances among the passengers. The

---

21. Meyer is mistaken; Aspinwall was an earlier name of Colon and is on the Atlantic side of the Isthmus.

boat docked at a short wharf. San Francisco at this time was a comparatively new town with a population of over fifty or sixty thousand inhabitants. Except near the water front, a large part of the city was sand hills. Most of the population lived in the district between the water front and Fifth Street. The What Cheer House was the leading hotel. There was one gambling house after the other where miners with gold-dust used to go to gamble.

I called upon Mr. Alexander Weill who was with Lazard Freres. Their place of business at that time was 48 Sacramento Street, between Sansome Street and Battery Street. The partners of the firm of Lazard Freres, who at that time lived in San Francisco, were: Simon Lazard, Eli Lazard, Sylvain Kahn, a half-brother of the Lazards, and Alexander Weill. The firm imported goods from France, Germany and Switzerland. I may say that I already knew Mr. Weill slightly, having met him in France. He placed me in a clean and comfortable boarding house.

Here I first met Simon Lazard, one of the finest men I ever knew, who acted as a father to all the younger men. He said to me: "Eugene, I do not want you to run around the streets. You are going to work here until I find something for you." Auction houses filled an important role in California in those days. Mr. Simon Lazard used his influence to place me with a large auction house just organized, by the name of Smiley, Yerkes & Voizin. Mr. George W. Smiley was a prominent figure in San Francisco at that time and was Vice-President of the Vigilance Committee.

Mr. Simon Lazard had in the meantime secured for me a place in the home of a very nice family by the name of Barnard. [. . .] The Barnard family lived in American style. On Sunday we had roast beef, on Monday cold roast beef, and on Tuesday roast beef hash. I paid for my board and lodging forty dollars a month. Occasionally I would be invited to dinner by my employer, Mr. Voizin. When I left in the evening Mr. Voizin would ask me if I had anything with me, and if I was unarmed he gave me a knife or a cane to carry, as the streets were not entirely safe. [. . .]

I continued to receive many kindnesses from Mr. Simon Lazard and from Alexander Weill. Whenever they gave a dinner I was sure to be an invited guest.

The firm of Smiley, Yerkes and Voizin were most active and I liked the business. Besides the three members of the firm there were ten clerks, of which I was the youngest. In addition, there were two darkies who acted as porters. The work at the auction house was of an arduous nature as the clerks were often called upon to act as porters and to move the goods from the counter to the shelves. There were three months in the year in which people were exceedingly busy and a period when they were comparatively idle.

The first six months I received a salary of fifty dollars a month, after which I was raised to seventy-five dollars.

12

By Union and Central Pacific to Perform a Wedding

Rabbi Max Lilienthal, 1876

Born in Munich, Bavaria, in 1815, Max Lilienthal, after working unsuccessfully with the Tsarist government to modernize traditional Jewish education in Russia, emigrated to New York in 1845. An ordained rabbi with a German Ph.D., he became a schoolmaster and a congregational rabbi. In 1855 he settled permanently in Cincinnati, where he served the Reform congregation of Bene Israel until his death. Involved in civic activities, a member of the Cincinnati Board of Education, and a trustee of the University of Cincinnati, Lilienthal had a close friendship with Rabbi Isaac Mayer Wise and taught at Wise's Hebrew Union College. In 1876 he traveled west to officiate at the marriage of his nephew, Ernest Lilienthal, to Bella Sloss, the daughter of Louis and Sarah [Greenebaum] Sloss.[22]

OUR BRETHREN IN THE WEST AND SAN FRANCISCO

BY DR. LILIENTHAL.

Home again from California! and I consider it my pleasant duty to send the following report of my trip to the numerous readers of the AMERICAN ISRAELITE.

We live in an age of progress. Though Ecclesiastes says, "There is nothing new under the sun." Did you ever hear that a minister traveled three thousand miles to perform a marriage ceremony? Did you ever hear that the same minister accompanied the young, happy couple three thousand miles on their wedding tour? I am sure it has never happened before; but it has happened now—as I went from Cincinnati to San Francisco to perform the holy ceremony at the wedding of my nephew, Mr. Ernest Lilienthal, with Bella, the daughter of Louis and Sarah Sloss, a prominent member of the Alaska Fur Company.

The journey is a long, and in the warm summer months, probably a tedious one. But we made it in April and May, the fine and cool months of Spring; and I not only do not regret having made it, but rejoice at it, and shall ever cherish the reminiscences of this pleasant, almost wonderful trip. [. . .]

With sleeping berths, meals, trinkets to porters, and other incidentals, the trip to San Francisco on the express train costs nearly $200.

SOURCE: Rabbi Max Lilienthal, "Our Brethren in the West and San Francisco," *American Israelite*, June 2, 1876; June 9, 1876.

22. Bella was the oldest of Sloss's five children. Ernest Lilienthal became head of Crown Distilleries.

We passed through Illinois and Iowa, through towns, cities and numerous villages. But the season was yet backward; hundreds of acres had not yet been plowed, it looked yet barren, though here and there Spring showed it had arrived in good earnest. [. . .]

How I delighted in this sight! God bless our free schools, with their unsectarian character. They have no warmer, more devoted friends than we Jews, and that all over the country. As long as they will flourish, and be not interfered with, either by the Roman Catholic priesthood, or by the men of "God in the Constitution," the liberties of our country will be secured, and our youth will grow up in the strong sentiment of the common American brotherhood.

Another sight that always pleases me when traveling through the country, are the plain, unostentatious churches, without any sectarian sign, either on the steeple or the building. This is genuine American. Only in the last twenty-five years has this sign of religious liberty been encroached upon, and the American heart beats rather uneasily under this display of sectarian division. Well, vigilance in the price of liberty.

For two long days we steamed through Nebraska, Wyoming and Utah, till we reached Ogden, the terminus of the Union Pacific Railroad. In all the little places wherever we stopped we found our Jewish brethren. Wherever there is a row of those wooden country stores, we read on the signs the names of our co-religionists. They cannot be mistaken—Cohn, Levy and a lot of names for the "Israel" are displayed everywhere. Counting from this fact, we may fairly set down the number of Israelites in the United States as at least a quarter of a million, if not more. And I felt sincerely elated that wherever you meet them, they cling proudly to the faith of their fathers. Though secluded in the desert, far away from every Jewish religious institution, they still try to observe as much of Sabbath and holidays as they possibly can. [. . .]

On Thursday afternoon, at three o'clock, we arrived at Ogden, in Utah, at the terminus of the Union Pacific Railroad. Oh! we were highly pleased when we arrived in the land of the Mormons, the land in which we Jews were at once turned into Gentiles! [. . .]

I do not wish to dilate on the granite palisades, through which we passed before reaching Utah. The pioneers have given these wild and weird structures of nature the queerest names—the Devil's Slide, the Devil's Gate, and so on. Endowed with a little poetical imagination one can discern the ruins of temples, fortresses, castles, pulpits and what not, and they reach on some points near two thousand feet above the train, which thunders away between them. But all this monotony passes away as if by a magic wand as soon as you enter Utah. The *Mormons, guided by Brigham Young,* have changed this wilderness into a Paradise.

We had made up our mind to go to Salt Lake City instead of continuing our journey on the Central Pacific Railroad to San Francisco. And we shall never regret this trip. How beautiful is the Salt Lake! how splendidly cultivated the land all along the road! One seems to be in Belgium, where neat, clean houses greet you from all sides, where the husbandman works on his fine fields, where orchards and blooming gardens adorn the neighborhood of farmer's houses.

I will not dilate on all we have seen in the country and the city. I will only mention that we visited Brigham Young, the Tabernacle, that mighty and splendid building, in which 15,000 people can congregate, the Zion's Co-operative Institute, the Mormon's store, larger than any in the West and the Pacific Coast, the theater, the baths, the museum and so on. Think what you may of Brigham Young and his queer doctrines of polygamy, he is a mighty organizer, and one of the remarkable men of the age.

But what we wish to mention and are pleased to mention, is the fact that we found forty Jewish families settled in Salt Lake City, and all of them in good circumstances. We made the personal acquaintance of many of them, and found them ready to organize a congregation, providing they can get a qualified minister. They had, as Mr. Waller [Watters] and others told me, a great many applicants who lectured there on trial. But they were of the usual third-rate, self-styled, white-craveted reverends, and did not suit them.

Brigham Young has cheerfully donated them a piece of ground for a Jewish cemetery. The Mormons wonder what kind of religion our brethren have, as on Sabbath they attend to their business, and on Sundays they hold no religious service. My informants told me that both the Mormons and Gentiles would certainly assist them in the most tangible way, if they were once going to organize a congregation. At present they hold their services in a private room, only on Rosh-Hashonah and Yom Kippur. "The right man in the right place" could easily succeed in organizing a congregation. [. . .]

The trip back to Ogden—the terminus of the Union Pacific Railroad—was a treat in itself, and was hugely enjoyed by all the passengers. We arrived just in time to buy our sleeping-berths on the Central Pacific Railroad, and to arrange our hand-baggage. The porters, after being promised a trinket, such as the Californians pay, are attention itself, and with commendable punctuality attend to all the wants of the "promising and paying" passengers.

The train leaves at 4 P.M., and we had to prepare ourselves for another ride of forty-eight hours, before we could reach San Francisco. [. . .]

Our road on the Central Pacific line now ran continually upward in the heart of the Sierra Nevadas. Two and three engines led the van of the train till we reached near Truckee, the summit of the Sierras. The country begins to change; the sagebrush and alkali fields disappear, mountain ranges begin to surround us, adorned with woods and forests; we are nearer to the promised land of California. [. . .]

It was one in the afternoon when we reached Sacramento City, the capital of California. From the dome of the majestic capitol floated the star-spangled banner; all was life and enjoyment; no traces of a Puritan-Sunday; people and land are cosmopolitan in the Far West! [. . .]

In Sacramento City we were welcomed by our sons, Philip and Leo, and O God, what a hearty welcome it was! My son Philip, the cashier of the Anglo-California Bank, led me around in the splendid depot, where respite of twenty-five minutes was granted to the passengers. He there pointed out to me some of the living wonders of California, the millionaires, both Jews and Gentiles, of the golden coast. They had come down from their mines and banks to spend the Sunday. [. . .]

But there was not much time left for either consideration or admiration; the conductor's cry, "All aboard!" hurried us back into our cars. We passed through Sacramento City and Stockton, where many of our co-religionists are living, and met at St Laura the groom and the bride; her father, Louis Sloss, Esq., one of the principal leaders of Alaska Fur Company, and some of his relatives, the Greenbaums [Greenebaums], the cousins of our old and Rev. friend, Dr. Greenbaum, Rabbi of London. Another hearty welcome, and onward we started to Oakland, the terminus of the Central Pacific Railroad.

Here we took the splendid ferry-boat, which crosses the magnificent bay and brings the passengers over to San Francisco. My Lord, what a sight! There lay the bay, almost an ocean itself, and on its bosom rest a cluster of large green islands, as the Goat Island, or the Yerba Puena [Buena], Fort Alcatraz and others, and to our right, looking over the broad expanse of water, the mountains of Marion [Marin] County loom up in the distance.

The boat drew nearer and nearer to the city, the first building which enlists our attention is the Temple Emanu-el, with its two splendid towers and ten commandments hewn out of stone between them. I greeted it with all my heart, and joyfully and thankfully exclaimed: "How goodly are thy tents of Jacob, thy dwelling, O Israel!" It stands high upon Luther [Sutter] Street and commands a magnificent view.

After seven long days we landed at last, and trod once more on terra firma. Our sons and nephews had engaged rooms for us in the Palace Hotel, the largest and finest in the world—the Grand Hotel of Paris not excepted. It occupies an entire block of ground, 344 by 265 feet, and is seven stories high. The entrance and the court are of surpassing grandeur and beauty; it is another wonder of California!

II
San Francisco:
The Instant Pacific Metropolis

3
Judaism Takes Root

IN SEPTEMBER OF 1849, IN RESPONSE TO A NEWSPAPER NOTICE, THIRTY newcomers gathered in a framed tent on Jackson Street and held the first Rosh Hashanah service in San Francisco.[1] By Yom Kippur, a week later, there were twenty more participants for the Kol Nidre service.[2] Although the gathering included only one woman, three (Mrs. Berg, Mrs. Keesing, and Mrs. Simon) would attend the following year's Rosh Hashanah service at the Masonic Hall on Kearny Street, where participants formed a short-lived, provisional congregation.

The following documents portray the beginnings of religious life in the city. In the first known sermon to be given in San Francisco, Louis Franklin urged those present to build a synagogue and to create a strong Jewish community.[3] Following his advice but unable to agree on worship practices, San Francisco's Jews were to organize two separate congregations in 1851, Emanu-El and Sherith Israel. Three years later, when the city's first rabbi, Julius Eckman, arrived, both congregations were building their first synagogues. Eckman's first duty was to officiate at impressive ceremonies marking the laying of the cornerstones for both congregations.

The members of Sherith Israel chronicled the laying of the cornerstone for the "new schule on Stockton street" in their minute books, which illuminate the

---

1. Rosenbaum, *Architects of Reform,* 3.
2. The High Holidays may also have been celebrated in Sacramento.
3. In 1851, three hundred circulars were printed by the committee to solicit funds for the new congregation (William M. Kramer and Norton B. Stern, "A Search for the First Synagogue in the Golden West," *Western States Jewish Historical Quarterly* 7:1 [1974]: 9).

traditional values of the congregation and reveal the desire to cooperate with Emanu-El in obtaining Passover matzoth and hiring a *shochet*. Its members were probably not as observant as some of its leaders desired, as shown by the severe fines imposed on those who chose not to obey the congregational by-laws. The many written requests found in the minutes from members seeking permission to marry demonstrate the social controls the congregation placed on itself. These entries point to the availability of Jewish women, as well as to the role of the congregation in preventing intermarriage.

From the women's galleries of Sherith Israel and Emanu-El, Mary Goldsmith Prag was an eyewitness to the young Jewish community. Prag's memoir makes it possible to view the congregation as it lived and functioned more than 150 years ago.

A more critical account of the development of Jewish religious practice in San Francisco was provided by Cauffman H. Meyer, a bookkeeper and sales agent for Isaac Leeser's *Occident and American Jewish Advocate* (1843–69).[4] In letters written from 1852 to 1854, Meyer describes to Leeser synagogue attendance, holiday observances, social functions, and the founding of women's associations, as well as business and personal relationships.

Henry Labatt, who also maintained a correspondence with Leeser, made it clear that at Emanu-El, as in other American congregations, the lay member-ship, not the rabbi, made decisions and determined policy. This Rabbi Julius Eckman learned when he was dismissed by Emanu-El, whose members were unhappy with his failure to follow the will of the congregation. Emanu-El needed a different type of rabbi. In a letter asking Isaac Mayer Wise to help them find a new rabbi, the officers of the congregation requested a man who would support reforms.

When they found such a man, the president of the congregation, Henry Seligman, wrote a report to the board welcoming the new rabbi and emphasizing both the reforms he expected and the expansion of the congregation and its new activities. However, some of Emanu-El's members soon opposed these reforms, and in 1864 they founded congregation Ohabai Shalome and reinstated some of Emanu-El's traditional practices, along with its 1856 constitution, minus a women's gallery.

The members of Ohabai Shalome were not alone in rejecting the reforms at Emanu-El, as is evident in the letter of Rabbi Aron Messing of Sherith Israel.

---

4. The *Occident and American Jewish Advocate* was the first American Jewish monthly with a national and international readership. Isaac Leeser, its editor, was also the founding corresponding secretary of the Jewish Publication Society. See Lance Sussman, *Isaac Leeser and the Making of American Judaism* (Detroit: Wayne State University Press, 1995), and Jonathan D. Sarna, *JPS: The Americanization of Jewish Culture, 1888–1988* (Philadelphia: Jewish Publication Society of America, 1989).

A notable change in congregational practice took place in 1870 when Sherith Israel, like Emanu-El, voted to allow families to sit together in its new building instead of requiring women to sit in the gallery.

A fourth congregation, Beth Israel, retained traditional services and customs while instituting strict rules of decorum. By 1880, San Francisco had four synagogues, in addition to a number of seasonal congregations, which between them could please all tastes. This variety of practice was often noted by the satirist Isidor Choynski, a correspondent for the *American Israelite* of Cincinnati. In his regular columns he both chronicled the development of the community and chastised it for its delinquencies. The documents in this chapter contain an unusual number of misspellings and other errors.

13

A Yom Kippur Jeremiad

Lewis A. Franklin, 1850

Born in Liverpool, England, of Polish origin, Lewis A. Franklin (1820–79) arrived in San Francisco in 1849 and opened a tent store on Jackson Street, which may well have been the site of the first High Holiday observances in San Francisco. The following year, at age twenty-nine, Franklin, a highly literate community leader, addressed the short-lived Kearny Street Congregation on Yom Kippur, stressing the opportunity and freedom for Jews in California, the need to build a synagogue, and the congregation's obligation to obey Jewish law.[5] Reprinted in the *Asmonean,* the following letter and sermon demonstrate his devotion to his new Jewish community and at the same time give a sense of the difficulties involved in establishing oneself simultaneously in the religious and the mercantile communities. In this sermon, his first such endeavor, Franklin delivered an admonition against greed to rival any preached in California's Gold Rush–era churches. In 1851 he left San Francisco for San Diego, returning in 1860 to England, where he died in 1879.[6]

San Francisco, Upper California

Sept. 27th, 1850, 5611

To the President and Trustees of the Kearney [Kearny] Street Hebrew Congregation.

—GENTLEMEN—In reply to your esteemed favor of 23rd inst, I can only regret, not having better deserved the flattering encomiums you have been pleased to pass on my humble effort, for the advancement of our Holy Religion, which your own devotion and untiring zeal afforded me the opportunity of exerting.

I feel great timidity in handing you the enclosed copy of my address delivered on the day of Atonement, in compliance with your request, as I find you purpose its publication, for I do not presume to be insensible, that the untutored style, and tone of sentiment, of this, my first attempt at Theological composition, (or even of public delivery) must be subject to innumerable imperfections.

I, therefore, throw myself upon the generous criticism of such as may peruse the effusion of one who enters not the area of public life to break a lance with

---

SOURCE: Lewis A. Franklin, letter and sermon, 1850. *Asmonean,* Nov. 15, 1850, 30–31.

5. For an analysis of this sermon, see Samson H. Levey, "The First Jewish Sermon in the West: Yom Kippur, 1850, San Francisco," *Western States Jewish Historical Quarterly* 10:1 (1977): 3. Franklin's great-grandfather had been the rabbi of Wroclaw (Breslau), Poland.

6. Levey, "The First Jewish Sermon in the West," 3.

more valiant knights; but as one who claims to be a son in Israel, ever-ready to stand forth in the defense of his co-religionists against any foe, whether it be the clamorous tongue of deluded fanatics, or the more insidious machinations of the ruler of England my only ambition is to aid the Jew to remove the odium which his own inertness has cast upon him.

I will only add in extenuation for any error which may be discovered in my language, or the inapplicability of my quotations, that during the few days which I have had to prepare for this occasion I had also to study so as to officiate in the solemn services of the eve of the day of Atonement which you in your wisdom honored me with the request to do (alike for the first time,) and all this, when my mind was somewhat pre-occupied in the contemplation and conduct of my mundane affairs.

In conclusion, I offer you the assurance that I shall date these events as a new era in my existence, the remembrance of which shall be cherished with gratitude to gentlemen for your kind good wishes and shall ever pray "that the God of Israel may inspire us with love and confidence toward His will, as well as to each other, that in our day Israel may dwell securely and the Redeemer come in to Zion." And with best wishes for the realization of your fondest hopes.

I subscribe myself,
Your very faithful Friend and obedient servant,

LEWIS ABM FRANKLIN

A DISCOURSE
delivered in the Temporary Synagogue, San Francisco, California
on the day of Atonement, September 5611–1850
BY LEWIS A FRANKLIN
and published by request of the congregation.

Brethren. I feel myself impelled to ask your indulgence, if in the course of my present appeal, I shall be found rude of speech; for I am unused to the task which my zeal in the cause of our revered Faith has emboldened me to essay. To you all my brethren, I say, look not upon the presumptuous individual who now stands before you with too severe a scrutiny. For he is not unblemished, but an erring and sinful mortal, who like yourselves, is here, this day to offer up a sacrifice for that favor from on high; which shall enable him to blot out his manifold transgressions. Bear with me then, while I strive to awaken within you that repentance, which this day we make a public manifestation of.

I ask you, wherefore are ye assembled? Are ye come cheerful and glad, to make an offering of a contrite heart? Have you well reviewed the past, and resolutely determined upon amendment in the future? Are ye honest and sincere, when ye ask the Supreme King of Kings "This day incline to our supplications, and view our repentance?" Dare ye ask God, "Oh, remember unto us the covenant with our fathers," "happy the man who doth not forget thee, and the son of man who steadfastly believed in thee." To him shall it be said

"Blessed shalt thou be at thy entrance, Blessed shalt thou be at thy departure," but wo! wo! to them who think their task is done, their duty performed when they present themselves at the House of God, once in each year, and then mingle their voices in the shout of praise to the Great Eternal's throne, while they abstain from the ordinary sustenance of their everyday life. Of such I ask if their consciences do not smite them when they so oft repeat the prayers? Are they at all sensible that they stand in the presence of Him who rules their destinies? And who with unerring hand takes note of these things?—From whom naught is hidden—yea! Even to the inmost recesses of man's heart, does He penetrate; and the judgement, which through His infinite mercy He withholds from day to day. He will yet visit upon their heads. That they shall know and fear Him. "For the Lord, He is God."

I shall not detain you my brethren, to dwell on the various ordinances of this solemn festival, this Sabbath of Sabbaths, for I find myself surrounded by those, whose early education has been such, as to satisfy the most skeptical in their fastidious ideas. That your fathers have not been unmindful of their duty, but have instructed you in the paths of righteousness, your gathering here affords abundant evidence. Upon your own shoulders then, will the burthen of sin fall. [. . .]

The plea of ignorance cannot be yours. "Behold the guardian of Israel neither sleepeth nor slumbereth." "The day of retribution will assuredly be to you as a pall, to shroud you in sore affliction, and your awakening shall cause dread and fear, and trembling, that ye be abashed and ashamed one before the other." Too frequently do we meet the response "I am a good Jew in my heart, but I have my living to make, my family to support, the present is my harvest, and I must gather in ere the storm and tempests of life overtake me. I owe it as a duty to myself to secure an independence, so as to be above the frowns of the world. I cannot therefore, now observe the Mosaic Code, but so soon as I have accomplished my present pursuit, then will I be ready to serve my God, with all my heart, and with all my soul." These are but everyday excuses, for constant abrogation of the most sacred duties, and those Divine attributes, which are to every Israelite, a covenant.

How clearly apparent is it that Interest, Wealth, Gold, are the stumbling blocks to the tranquility of the mind, and the rejoicing of the soul. How fleeting and deceptive are the blessings which attend this acquisition of gold. The mind is even harassed by the dangers of speculation, the fury of devouring elements, and the risks of designing men. No day of rest knows the follower of this shadow; continual fever consumes his life, his blood now boiling and coursing through his veins like molten lead in the furnace, speedily cools again, and congeals and hardens into one solid mass, the muscles contract and he stiffens into death. [. . .]

Brethren you cannot be insensible to the benefits you enjoy, in this blessed land of religious freedom. The Jew is as unfettered in this Republican country as though he were again in possession of the Land of Promise. No restraint is he under, neither in the precept, or practice of the religion of his fathers, rather does America invite Israel to become a people in her midst. California, in her infant state asks, your aid to build her cities, and will you not erect such edifices, as your children, and your children's children, from generation to generation shall delight in! And I ask you, shall there be no temple built to Israel's God? Shall there be no watchtower to guide the traveler in his journeying through the thorny paths of life, and direct him in whice [which] he should go? Will you not provide for the wants of hungering thousands, who will crave for the food of religion? Shall their lips be parched and utterance denied them when the heart is bursting with gratitude to all-bountiful Providence? You, yourselves, have reaped an harvest, forget not a tithe for the gleaners—give them food from the dainties of the Law, and drink from the fountains of Divine Inspiration. You yourselves, be their example, and teach them how to live. Yes, bid the mason hew the stone, and the artisan cast the molding, and raise a new house, worthy the crafty work of God's chosen people.

In this far west, as in the east, yea "from the commencement of the rising of the sun, til the going down thereof, let the name of the Lord be praised." Let it not be said that we are excluded from the highest privilege of sinful men, "communion with his Maker." But rather bear evidence, that in this new country, ere civilization with its rapid strides has taken foothold, the Jews, persecuted, though they be in despotic Europe, will never desert the banner of their creed, but fearlessly unfold it before all eyes, that its peaceful, fraternal, and benign influence shall win it adoration. Yes, the prattling babe shall lisp its joy, the youth, be clamorous of its beauty. The virgin shall sing its praise, and the men of years shall delight in its ways, for they are ways of pleasantness. Ere such a blissful state of things can exist, look well into your own hearts, and say if the time be ripe. It is not enough that ye be willing. [. . .]

Now! This present day is the fitting moment to purify yourselves. While here assembled to crave remission of your sins. Your souls affected by fast. Your heart opened by prayer. Your proud spirits humbled to the dust, as with bended knee, ye prostrate yourselves before Almighty God, utter your vows to forsake your iniquitous ways, and pursue righteousness, that they may be registered in the archives of heaven, for here naught is expunged, then—go forth, and with cleansed hands, commence your good work of architecture. Erect each pillar as a monument to Him who has been your Guardian, through the perils of the sea, and the pestilence and dangers of the land—that most trusty Pilot, who has steered you in safety to the haven of your desires on this transitory earth, and who will hereafter conduct you in safety, to that region of bliss, where ministering angels shall attend you to life everlasting.

Make fidelity the keystone of your arches, and brotherly love the cement to bind them. This latter cardinal virtue, belongs to the duties of this sacred-day. If there be any amongst you, who have offended, ask forgiveness, that ye may be forgiven. Let there be no strife between you. He is a veritable coward, who would shrink from an avowal of his offense, if he have acted unjustly towards his fellow man and know it. Brave is he, who blushing for his errors, asks for peace. If any I have offended, I stand before you my brethren full of contrition and crave your pardon.

There is another indispensable requisite, to the due performance of this day's ceremonies which must not be forgotten. It is Charity, a virtue so comprehensive, that I must only point out its leading characters. First then, is a generous impulse, like unto the twinkling star in the firmament which lends its light to other orbs that shine, Second is Benevolence, like unto the north star, which is ever in its appointed place as a faithful guide. Third is Liberality, like unto the moon, which as freely gives of her public strength, as has been bestowed upon her. Fourth is love, like unto the sun, whose resplendent light fills the universe and is but a shadow of God's own repulgent [refulgent] glory.

Man formed in the image of his Maker, has given unto him a portion of this virtue, the practice whereof is entirely within his own control; no teaching can influence him. We can only appeal to him to arouse his latent energies and all will be accomplished. Assign to this sublime moral influence a becoming place in your new synagogue. Inscribe it on your foundation, and seal it in your roof. Adorn your walls with the purity of your motives. Build your cushioned seats with words of humiliation. Dovetail your floors with concord and harmony, that ye may stand firm, and steadfast, before God, and upright before man, and ye will not build in vain. Acceptable shall be your house, for ye will have remembered this day to keep it holy, and ye may repose in the assurance, "Israel shall be saved in the Lord, with everlasting salvation."

14
Matzoth, Marriage, and Reforms
Minutes, Congregation Sherith Israel, 1851–1854, 1870

The Polish, English, and American founders of Congregation Sherith Israel recorded the birth and the development of their congregation in large, heavy minute books. The following selections from the minute books include the Preamble and Article XIV of the 1851 constitution; selected minutes of early meetings; a request from Congregation Emanu-El to jointly hire a baker for the "Passover bread;" minutes of November 24, 1853, which discuss the building of a *schule* and the continuing problem of finding a *shochet*, a request for permission to marry from the secretary of the congregation; a report of the laying of the cornerstone for their first synagogue; and the April 24, 1870, vote establishing mixed seating. All signify the congregants' devotion to Judaism and reflect the changing attitudes of the times in which they lived.[7] A brief analysis of Sherith Israel's preamble reveals that the congregation saw itself as being in partnership with God (spelled with a small "g"), and believed in voluntary membership—unlike the European *kehillah*, which was an all-inclusive hierarchical community. The preamble was based on the principle of toleration and written in the constitutional language of the United States. Through their organization and terminology, the members of Sherith Israel sought to link themselves with other congregations in the United States and England.[8]

1

Constitution

Whereas it has pleased the god of our foreFathers to gather some of his dispersed people in the City of San Francisco, who are taught and used to apply to him for his merciful bounty and his holy name and

Whereas the wise and Republican Laws of this Country are based upon universal toleration given to Every Citizen and Sojourner the right to worship according to the dictates of his Conscience,

---

SOURCE: (1–7) Minutes, Congregation Sherith Israel, minute books, 1851–54, 1870. Western Jewish History Center of the Judah L. Magnes Museum, Berkeley, California.

7. There are many spelling errors throughout this section, as well as many variants of Sherith Israel.

8. For an excellent discussion of synagogue constitutions, see Daniel J. Elazar, Jonathan D. Sarna, and Rela G. Monson, eds. *A Double Bond: The Constitutional Documents of American Jewry* (Lanham, Md.: University Press of America, 1992), 35.

Therefore, We the Undersigned bind ourselves under the name of the Congregation Sheareth Isreal [written in Hebrew and English] to use our best exertions to Support the Synagogue and to worship therin according to the Customs and usages of *Minhag Polin* [written in Hebrew] to be the same as far as practicable and without departing from the form and Custom, now in use in the principle Congregations of the United States and England. [. . .]

Article 14th

The Board of Trustees, or the President of the Congregation as the case may be, shall and is hereby empowered to inflict and levy the following fines, and all such fines other fines as are before recited in these Bye Laws shall become due and payable immediately after the decisions inflicting the same subjecting the persons so fined to all the penalties and disabilities for non-payment, as accrue on the neglect of liquidating all other arrears due and owing to this Congregation.

	$ ¢
For refusing the office of Trustee	10.00
For refusing to serve either the office of Hasan Torah [written in Hebrew] or Hasan Bereshit [written in Hebrew] upon the first ballot	10.00
For refusing either of the said [*Mitzvot,* written in Hebrew] upon the second ballot	10.00
For refusing either of the said offices upon the third ballot	10.00
The [Hasan Torah, written in Hebrew] or [Hasan Bereshit, written in Hebrew] neglecting to attend divine services on [Simchat Torah, written in Hebrew] for each neglect	10.00
For refusing the office of Auditor or Inspector of an Election	5.00
Auditors neglecting or refuseing to make a report each	5.00
Members refuseing or neglecting to appear before the Board of Trustees, when specially summoned	16.00
For the non-attendance of a Trustee after receiving a summons to attend a meeting of the Board of Trustees he shall be fined	3.00
And for leaving the Meeting without permission before adjourned he shall be fined	2. 00
For refuseing or neglecting to serve on a committee	5.00
For non-attendance at a Special meeting after signing a requisition to Convene the Congregation	16. 00
For refuseing to come to order at a Congregational Meeting when requested by the Chairman	1.00
For disturbing divine worship	50.00

For non attendance summonses to be called to the Torah [written
in Hebrew]   3.00
For refuseing to accept a Mitzvah [written in Hebrew]   1.00

2

At a meeting held on Sunday the 26th Dec 1852 [. . .] Wanted by the
Congregation Shereth Israel a compitent person to undertake the office of
Reader and Schamis and Schochet, Aplications for the above received until
the first day of January 1853 by I. Solomon Tr.

No 197 Pacific st.

Resolved that a general meeting be called on Sunday evening next the second
January 1853 at half past 2 Oclock P.M.

S. Hoffman

Sec. Protem

3

San Francisco Novbr 24 /53.

At a special general meeting of the Congregation of Sherith Israel held this
day at our Synagogue It was proposed by Mr Lewis & seconded by Mr. Neuman
that a Committee of 4 be selected to confer with the Committees of the other
Congregations,[9] as to an appointment of a Competent Shochet, & to report their
views at the next general meeting Passed unaninomously. J Myers. [?] L. Levy,
Lesynsky Mr Hochstein & Mr. Lachman were appointed for that purpose.

Proposed by Mr Josephi & seconded by Lachman that we build a shule, & to
raise the Funds shares are to be made at $50. Each, Members Strangers are to
be at liberty, to take as many as they please to be paid in 1/4 instalements Which
is to be repaid to them by Ballot hereafter as funds accrue. The remainder of
Capital required to be raised by public subscription & that a commitee of 10 be
appointed to carry out the above resolution upon which Massrs R Josephi, HM
Lewis, Keesing, Friedlander Joseph Rich, A Marks, Jacob Meyer Blumenthal
Pander, J Lachman were selected. The above was unanimous by paper. Their
being no further Business the meeting adjourned.

Henry Julian

Secty.

---

9. The other congregations were probably Emanu-El, Shaar Hashamayim (a short-
lived Sephardic congregation), and a precursor to Shomrai Shaboth, a small, observant
Eastern European congregation.

מצות
MATZOTH.

PASSOVER BREAD.

T HE undersigned, having received the contract for Baking the Passover Bread for
the congregation Sherith Israel, for the ensuing holidays, is ready to receive orders for the
same.

The community may depend upon their being of superior quality, as he had the baking of
them last year for the congregation Emanu-el,
which gave entire satisfaction.

Orders left at   P. WOOLF'S,
Corner Sutter and Dupont Streets,
And at   MR. ASHIM'S,
Corner Commerical and Leidendorff.

In 1857 Congregation Sherith Israel contracted with these bakeries for their
Passover matzoth. *Weekly Gleaner,* March 19, 1858.

4

At a meeting of the Board of Trusties at the Synagogue Chambers held this
12th day of February [1854], A letter was received from the Congregation
Emanu El this being as to appoint a Committee to act with them jointly on
regulating & providing the Israelites generally with passover Bread Messrs A
Weiss B Keesing & H Julian are duly appointed with power to act jointly with
the Committee of the other Congregation & a letter to that Effect be sent to the
Trusties of the Congregation Emanuel

H Julian Secty

5

At a meeting of this Board of Trusties held this Fourth day April 1854, An
application was received from Henry Julian a member of this Congregation

The favor of your Company
is respectfully solicited to attend
the

Nuptial Ceremony

OF

Miss LOUISA PLATSHEK,

AND

WOLF KALISHER,

On Sunday, October 14, 1860, at
the Stockton Street Synagogue.

Ceremony at 3½ o'clock, P. M.

Invitation to a wedding at Sherith Israel, 1860. Courtesy of the Western Jewish History Center, Judah L. Magnes Museum, Sherith Israel Collection.

for marriage to Miss Rebecca Cardoza which was granted on payment of the usual fee.[10]

H. Julian
Secty

6

Congregation Sherith Israel
Sunday 6th day of Aug 1854

According to previous Arrangements, the corner stone of the new schule on Stockton st, was this day laid The trusties of the Building Committee met the officers of the Congregation Emanuel at our Synagogue, on Kearny St, & at 1 o clock precisily escorted Dr Eckman, to the new Building—where a large Concourse of Ladies & Gentlemen were waiting to see the Ceremony—Dr Eckman first offered a prayer & then made some appropriate remarks suitable for the occasion he then read an account of the formation & progress of the synagogue prepared for the occasion which was the first document placed in the stone then followed the Constitution & By Laws, List of Officers, & Members & list of Donors. The daily papers, the occident & Asmonian of the latest dates, a Jewish Almanack printed in 1851 in San Francisco California & lastly a Box Containing several Coins—Mr Israel Solomon President then closed the stone with a marble slab on which was inscribed the name of the Congregation & date, he then presented to Mr Butler the Architect, with the silver Trowel just used— The Rev Dr Eckman Closed the Ceremony by making some further select & appropriate remarks———

Henry Julian
Secty

7

Congregation Sherith Israel
Semi-Annual Meeting
San Francisco April 24, 5630
1870

The Semi-Annual Meeting of the Congregation was held on the day above stated at the Stockton Street Synagogue & largely attended.

Mr. C. Meyer President in the Chair.

---

10. There were many such requests recorded in the 1853–54 minutes. The laws of the congregation required that members apply to the congregation for permission to marry. The usual fee was $20.

The minutes of the last Annual Meeting, and all the Special Meetings following were read and on motion approved.

The Proceedings of the Meetings held by the Board of Trustees since their Organization till this day were read.

On motion the Resolution introduced at the last Annual Meeting held October 3, 1869 was taken up for action.

The Resolution reads as follows:

Resolved, that compulsary separation of the Sexes during Divine Services in our Synagogue is hereby, abolished.[11]

A motion was made by A. L. Badt seconded by M. Davidson and many others to pass said Resolution, and after the question being first stated by the Chair, it was debated upon by the members at great length pro and contra by the President.

After being agreed upon that it shall be voted on the question by separate votes, the Secretary called the roll of members and each member when his name was called voted.

The Result was as follows:

> whole number of votes cast *105.*
> of which there were   84. ayes
> &   *21. nayes.*

Total as above 105. votes
[followed by a list of those who voted for and against]

---

11. Separation of the sexes at religious services was discussed as far back as 1864, when Rabbi Eckman wrote in the *Gleaner,* "Sherith Israel—This congregation contemplate following the example of the Emanual Congregation, and seat men and women worshippers promiscuously, instead of, as formerly, keeping the female looking down upon the men from the gallery" (Oct. 21, 1864).

15

"The House Was Crowded the Gallery Solely with Women"

Mary Goldsmith Prag, 1850s

Born in Poland, Mary Goldsmith Prag (1846–1935) was six years old when she came to San Francisco with her parents, Isaac and Sarah Goldsmith, and a brother and sister in 1852. Her father, Isaac Goldsmith, was a *shochet*.[12] After graduating from Girls' High School and the State Normal School, Goldsmith married Conrad Prag in a ceremony performed by Rabbi Julius Eckman. She became a teacher at South Cosmopolitan Grammar School, the head of the department of history in the Girls' High School and the school's vice principal, a teacher at the religious schools of Sherith Israel and Congregation Emanu-El (for twenty-eight years), and a member of the San Francisco Board of Education, where she served until her death at the age of eighty-nine. Known as the "Mother of the Pension Movement in California," she fought for a teachers' pension bill, vacation pay and tenure for teachers, and the permanent recording of teachers' certificates. She also worked for the enforcement of a law that mandated equal pay for male and female teachers and headed a group of teachers who defeated a proposal by the Board of Education that would have excluded married women from teaching.[13] Her daughter, Florence Prag Kahn, became the first Jewish U.S. congresswoman.[14] Prag attended her first Rosh Hashanah service at Sherith Israel in 1852. The following account describes this service and another held two years later at Temple Emanu-El.

The first Rosh Hashonah after our arrival, Mother not being able to go, Father took sister and me with him to the evening service at Sherith Israel. The men occupied the main floor, while the women were seated in the gallery. All synagogues at that time had a similar arrangement. [. . .] There were a number of men present at the service this Rosh Hashanah evening in 1852, away from home and friends, they clung more closely together and were more

---

Source: Mary Goldsmith Prag, Early Days. Typescript, Florence Prag Kahn Collection, Western Jewish History Center of the Judah L. Magnes Museum, Berkeley, California.

12. In 1857 Isaac Goldsmith was listed as the *shochet* at B. Adler's San Francisco butcher shop on the corner of Sacramento and Dupont. *Weekly Gleaner,* May 22, 1857.
13. *San Francisco Examiner,* ca. January 1920. Scrapbook, Florence Prag Kahn Collection, Western Jewish History Center.
14. Florence Prag Kahn represented the Fourth Congressional District of California in Congress from 1925 to 1937, succeeding her husband, the late Congressman Julius Kahn.

Isaac Goldsmith, a *shochet* who arrived in San Francisco with his family in 1852. Courtesy of the Judah L. Magnes Museum Painting Collection.

Sarah Goldsmith, Isaac Goldsmith's wife. Courtesy of the Western Jewish History Center, Judah L. Magnes Museum, Kahn Collection.

Mary Goldsmith Prag, who arrived with her parents, brother, and sister at the Montgomery Street Pier in 1852. Courtesy of the Western Jewish History Center, Judah L. Magnes Museum, Kahn Collection.

Notice published for Yom Kippur. Of special interest are the introduction of a choir and the use of English and German. Rabbi Eckman led the services even though he no longer served the congregation on a permanent basis (*Weekly Gleaner,* October 7, 1859).

devoted to the faith of their fathers. There were only two other occupants of the gallery besides ourselves, another big sister and her little sister.[15] We soon became acquainted and a friendship was established which has lasted through more than four generations. [. . .]

Speaking of the Synagogue reminds me of my first evening visit to the Temple Emanuel then just completed [1854] on Broadway above Powell. I was a regular member of the Sabbath School and had attended the Sabbath services, but had never been there of an evening. It was the eve of Yom Kippur, one of our neighbor's children was suddenly taken ill and it was decided to send for the mother who had gone to Schule. Seizing the opportunity I tagged along. It was a warm evening in October, we went upstairs to the gallery to find the mother. The place appealed to us most brilliantly illuminated. (No doubt with candles). The house was crowded, floor and galleries, the latter solely with women. Never shall I forget the impression made upon me as I gazed upon those lovely women garbed, most of them in white or light dainty lawns, white crapte shawls draping many many a form. Light bonnets gorgeous with flowers and feathers decking their heads. They were all young then—there were the two beautiful sister-in-law, Mrs. Isidore and Mrs Simon Wormser, later they moved to New York. There were the two Castle Sister[s], the English brides. There were the Seligmans, the Baums, the Labatts, beautiful Mrs. Henry Cohn, mother of Mrs. Sig. Greenebaum, Mrs. Louis Cohn, and her sister, Mrs. Lewis. The Bergs, the Tandlers, the Jacobys, all in the beauty of their youth. [. . .] I was simply enchanted and when I reached home said "O, Mother, it was just like heaven." Later on as I grew to girlhood, I became a more regular attendant on holidays, but I fear I was more outside in the lobby than inside listening to the service.

It was the custom on Yom Kippur for all the young people to come to the Temple [Emanu-El], and no doubt the other synagogues also in the afternoon to inquire as to how their parents were fasting, and it thus became a popular meeting place.

---

15. The two sisters were the daughters of Israel Solomon, the president of the congregation.

16
"We Have Smart and Leading Men Here"
Cauffman H. Meyer, 1852–1854

A San Francisco bookkeeper, Cauffman H. Meyer also served as a book and newspaper agent for Isaac Leeser (1806–68), editor of the *Occident and American Jewish Advocate*. In addition to collecting payments for Leeser and selling his books, Meyer sent him reports from 1852 to 1856 on the development of the Jewish community in San Francisco and the smaller cities in the region, keeping Leeser, and through him others on the East Coast, informed about the burgeoning West.[16]

1

San Francisco Feb. 15. 1852

Revd Mr. Issac Leeser
Dear friend
I send you enclosed Draft on Mess. M. Cauffman & Co., Phils, Drawn by Roggenburger & Co for $24.00, which I have collected for the Occident, as per enclosed Statement; and enclose you now also a fresh subscription for the O. [*Occident and American Jewish Advocate*]; had I more Time to spare and our Californians would devote more time to reading your intellectual work, I could, no Doubt have sent you a larger list of Subscription.

I have read your letter, and am sorry that I cannot comply with your wishes for informing you how Jewish affairs progress; however that much I can tell you, that Jewish Families are getting quite Numerous in San Francisco, and of late we had also several marriages taking place. The Jewish Population all over California is very numerous, but our Religion is not by any means kept up in generality, as it should be. We have two Synagogues here, one Polish and one German, which are open every [Sabbath, written in Hebrew]; but are not very well attended & it is only on [holidays, written in Hebrew] that you have the opportunity of witnessing the Synagogues crowded, when there is generally not room enough to seat 1/2.

Source: (1–3) Cauffman H. Meyer to Isaac Leeser, 1852–54. Isaac Leeser Collection, Center for Judaic Studies Library, University of Pennsylvania. Microfilm courtesy of Hebrew Union College.

16. See William M. Kramer and Norton B. Stern, "Letters of 1852 to 1864 Sent to Rabbi Isaac Leeser," *Western States Jewish Historical Quarterly* 20:1 (1987): 43–59.

It saves me some trouble if I collect the Subscription immediately, and you will notice several on my ac. who have paid in advance. You will also be kind enough to send me the acs. what Roggenburger & Co. in California owes you.

It was told me by several whose subscription to the O. I have sent the last time, that they have not read the O. You will please therefore, to be exact in making a plain direction; as our Post Office arrangement is none of the best.

Business in general has been very good with us for the last 10 or 12 mos. And in goods almost all Branches have paid well to import; some articles always pay very well in California; as for instance Flour is worth from $40 to $45 per barrel, which cost at home no more than $4.50 per barrel. I could give you more information about business, but I am aware it is of no interest to you. As you are no doubt aware, money making and speculating is all the go—and one's attention is almost entirely directed to that.

Mr. and Mrs. Roggenburger desire their kind regards to you; they have arrived safe; and live very handsomely and very convenient, and enjoy themselves; they live [unclear] and I am boarding with them, which gives me the opportunity of reminding myself that I am a "Jew"—.

Hoping you will soon write to me a large letter As, and this may find you in good health

I remain your true friend
Cauffman H. Meyer

2

San Francisco April 29, 1853

Mr. Isaac Leeser
Dear Friend

I have read Your Letter and also that Book treating upon the Sabbath question, for which I return you my thanks.

I have had no time yet to collect that money nor attending to any of your other affairs. I have been of late so very busy in receiving goods & c.. I wish to tell you about the [Passover, written in Hebrew] which has been kept in a very credible manner in general; the Synagogues have been extremely well attended, and everything carried on in an orderly and fine manner. We have at least now about 50 Jewish families, and there are but very few exceptions which did not have "Mazos." As much as I can learn, even those which don't live [Kosher, written in Hebrew] in general have however had "Mazos." You may well judge that Mazos have been in Demand, from the Fact that they have been sold from 40 to 50 ct. per pound; when the baking at first had been commensed they were sold at 40 ct., and shortly after that they were raised to 45 ct. and 50 ct. per pound. You may perhaps attribute these high Rates to the exorbitant prices of flour, Each which is not the case; the Flour sells from $10 to $12.50.

Our Jewish population is increasing wonderfully; it is to be regretted that we have not a better Synagogue, when the very large numbers of Jews is taken into consideration and we have smart and leading men here, but all seem not to desire to take up such matter, nor to take any other part attending to advance our Position. However, I believe in a short time many Improvements of this kind will take place, the more Families will come here, the more everything will be more regulated; even now you can live here as well [Kosher, written in Hebrew] as in Phila.

Many complain yet that they do not receive the Occident.

The next time I will write you a larger letter.

Mr. Roggenburger and family wish kindly to be remembered to you. In the meantime I remain

Yours Truly

C. H. Meyer.

3

San Francisco March 15, 1854

Rvd. I. Leeser

Dear Friend—

I am in receipt of your letter of the 3d ultc. and also of the books, which were all in good order. Owing to the accident to the Steamer Georgia, which connected[17] with the Steamer Columbia on the side by which I received the books, and the unusual long passage of the Columbia, I did not receive the books till a few days ago; and therefore I could not as yet distribute the books which have been ordered; but after this Mail Steamer is gone I shall attend to. I have sold several D. letters and I have no doubt with three books which are not ordered I can meet with a ready sale, as the books are all got up in a neat and handsome manner. The "Hebrew Benevolent Ball" of which I made mention in my previous letter, has come off night before last; a very large assemblage was present; and the profit at present estimated will be about $1500; really the Ball was an honor to the Jews here and creditable to the Managers; everything passed off to the satisfaction of all present; one unusual feature of the Ball was the large number of ladies, which numbered to about 200. It is due to our Jewish population to say that a great number of our persuasion are very much respected as first-class and prominent citizens.

Mr. Cohen has been to see me and told me a great deal of the China Jews, but as he has given you already much information in that respect, and has told me he would write to you again by next mail, it would be for me unnecessary

---

17. The ships collided.

to say anything upon that subject. I think you would have done wise if you would have advertised in your Occident, that your books could be had by me. I am well acquainted with Mr. Chas. Emmanuel, and he requests me to give his regards to you. Mr. and Mrs. Roggenburger wish kindly to be remembered to you. With my best wishes for your good health and prosperity, I remain yours Truly

Cauffman H. Meyer

17

The Congregation vs. the Rabbi

Henry J. Labatt, 1854

Born in Louisiana, Henry J. Labatt was the son of Congregation Emanu-El's first president, Abraham Labatt, and became Emanu-El's second secretary (1854–60).[18] In addition to practicing law, Labatt became co-editor with Herman Bien of the short-lived *Voice of Israel* in 1856. Active in many Jewish organizations and a Mason, Labatt was an officer of the First Hebrew Benevolent Society and a frequent participant in the activities of the Hebrew Young Men's Literary Association.

An educated American Jew of Sephardic origin, Labatt was an eloquent spokesman for the Jewish community.[19] Like Cauffman H. Meyer, he corresponded with Isaac Leeser, the editor of the *Occident and American Jewish Advocate,* to familiarize him with the condition of San Francisco Jewry, especially of the fate of Rabbi Julius Eckman, the first rabbi to be hired by a San Francisco congregation.

San Francisco, Dec. 19. 1854

Rev. Isaac Leeser
Dear Sir:

I received yours of late date by last steamer and conveyed the various respects to your friends as desired. Mr. Mason's Estate I regret to inform you will not pay even borrowed money & therefore you can scarcely expect pay. However I will do my utmost.

Relative to your letter about ministers let me explain. Dr. Eckman came out here on his own hook & unexpectedly. When he married me in N.O. [New Orleans] I gave him no encouragement for I knew he would not suit our people. I then heard from Mr. Gutheim that a friend of his would probably be taken up. Dr. E. Knew this but took the chances. He was not elected here until we heard Dr. Steinberg could or would not come, for what reasons we are childishly ignorant. Dr. E. only received 26 votes, the 7 others blank. The salary of $3500

SOURCE: Henry J. Labatt to Isaac Leeser, 1854. Isaac Leeser Collection, Center for Judaic Studies Library, University of Pennsylvania. Microfilm courtesy of Hebrew Union College.

18. For more information, see Rosenbaum, *Visions of Reform,* and Stern and Kramer, "The Historical Recovery of the Pioneer Sephardic Jews." For a time in the mid-1860s, Henry Labatt shared a law practice with Myer J. Newmark; see chapter 2.

19. Henry Labatt's article describing the early Jewish commercial community is included in chapter 5.

was reduced to $2000 & the term of 3 years was reduced to *one*. Even at these sacrifices the few who upheld him found it difficult to elect him & we had to debate & debate until eleven o'clock at night & by skill and ingenuity crowd down the opposition. The sequel will prove how worthy he has repaid them their labor. I was, when I saw no other minister on hand, eager to take up the Doctor in order that as a synagogue we might have a head & a respectable one. My father [Abraham Labatt] Louis, Cohn, Sam. Marx & others will attest how earnestly we labored together & fought the Doctor through.

Previous to the building of the Synagogues which exist at present we had one Shochet & each congregation paid $12.50 per month & the butchers so much per head making it sufficient to support a man, but lately the increase in the butcher business has been so great that our congregation determined to suspend the payment of $12.50 & of licensing two Shochtim, as the revenue proved to be by examining the butchers themselves, over two hundred and fifty dollars per month, and in case of *sickness* one could resume the other's position. We gave no preferences, no recommendations. We appointed Mr. Messenger & Mr. [Isaac] Goldsmith[20] and allowed butchers to select their own Shochet, of the two, Mr. M. however belonging to our Synagogue and Mr. G. to the Polish [Sherith Israel]. Mr. M. came to us with three *Robolahs* from Europe and superior recommendations. I myself would not vote for both until I carefully examined & found the business would support two. When we sent to Dr. Eckman to examine those men he refused to examine Mr. Messinger & sent us a long article about the necessary requisitions for Shochet, failing, however, to tell us that Mr. M. had not proved competent. We replied (Dr. Eckman was then & is now boarding at Mr. Goldsmith) that as Dr. E. wishes such a standard for Shochtim & we the trustees believed no man in California was competent to stand the test & we must have a Shochet rather than none, such as we have always had, we appointed three of our congregation to examine the candidates, men who always examined them, previous to the arrival of Dr. Eckman in California. These men examined Mr. Messinger and pronounced him skillful & highly competent. Mr. Goldsmith sent us a communication which evidently was dictated by the Doctor, saying in short that he would not be examined by those men. Wherefore the Trustees rescinded his appointment. What was our astonishment to find Dr. E. publish a card in the morning papers nullifying the act of the Trustees, who created him, and pronouncing against us & in favor of a foreign congregation without our knowledge & consent & virtually injuring *a man* whom *he* did not *deign* to question. Dr. E. said he did not keep his Sabbath previous to election, whereas we know it was utterly out of his power to do so as his bread depended on it. Dr. E. has been coalesced with Shochet Goldsmith

---

20. Isaac Goldsmith was the father of Mary Goldsmith Prag. See document 15.

& has violently opposed his own congregation. A Trustee meeting is to be held & they are the Doctors warmest supporters. I learn they intend to request the Doctor to resign. He who was so unpopular & was elected by such a struggle & such sacrifices has in 6 short weeks make himself outrageously inimical to the whole congregation. I hear but two opinions, one asking him to resign, the other dismissing him from his post.

In a new country it was in the Doctor's province to endear himself to a warm & ardent congregation, but he has chosen the opposite. Yesterday in conversation the Doctor was advised by my father and myself to be careful of his actions that the congregation were very uneasy about the Shochet matter & his position & *might* censure him. He said on that subject he courted their censure & forthwith proclaimed to the world through the papers that we were all fools & knew not what we did that our Shochet was no Shochet & his Shechitah to be Terephah. [. . . publications were enclosed]

I regret to add Dr.'s statement is false in many respects, as probably his information was derived from Mr. Goldsmith.

In the first place the Doctor is not legally our Rabbi, he never was so elected.

In the second, Dr. E. never questioned Messinger, but merely listened to calumny.[21]

In the third, he had no recourse to any expedient. The Trustees did so authorize him to appear before the three members without Mr. Messinger being aware of their action.

In the fourth, the Congregation have adopted to eat meat of no other Shochet than Messinger & we boast as religious men as any in the world, perhaps not more so.

There will be a sequel to this of which I shall keep you advised.

Upon these remarks you may be certain Dr. E. cannot be reelected at the end of the year & if you know of any competent minister who of their own accord or at your suggestion will visit San Francisco & when here will act prudently they would do well to come out.

Yrs truly

H. I. Labatt

---

21. Eckman stated that he had seen Mr. Messinger eat non-Kosher meat.

18
"No Ear for Lectures"
Rabbi Julius Eckman, 1855

Born in 1805 in Rawicz, Poland, Julius Eckman was educated by local rabbis and tutors in Jewish and secular studies. After a short stay in London, he studied in Germany, receiving rabbinic ordination from the rabbis of Berlin and Prenzlau and a Doctorate in Philosophy from the Royal Frederick Wilhelm College in Berlin. In 1849 Eckman emigrated to the United States. First settling in Richmond, Virginia, Eckman subsequently held rabbinic positions in Charleston, South Carolina, Augusta, Georgia, and Mobile, Alabama. In 1854 he came to San Francisco, where he became the first rabbi of Congregation Emanu-El.

After being let go the following year, the rabbi remained in San Francisco, where he founded the Hepzibah and Harmonia Schools and the Hepzibah Synagogue and edited the *Weekly Gleaner,* one of the first Jewish newspapers in California. Although Eckman did not have a regular pulpit, he was at times the only ordained rabbi in San Francisco. In that capacity he was frequently called upon to officiate at weddings, funerals, public meetings, and dedications. During his many years in San Francisco, Eckman was much respected by the city's Christian clergy, with whom he worked closely.[22]

Solomon Nunes Carvalho, a daguerreotypist and artist for Col. John Charles Frémont and a freelance journalist, was a member of a respected Sephardic family. In 1853 he became the first official photographer on the staff of a western exploration mission. When Eckman needed a sympathetic hearing he turned to his friend Carvalho, a proponent of traditional Judaism.

San Francisco March 15, 1855
S. N. Carvalho
My dear Sir!
By this you will have resumed some post to carry on the warfare that this life imposes upon the children of man. The struggle is real and continual; the distant trophies held up by the arm of hope in the skies, vanish in the clouds, and leave disappointment behind them. Happy the man who, for the bare means of life, fully confides in the bounty of the Dispenser of life—his bread shall be given him, and water shall not fail.

SOURCE: Rabbi Julius Eckman to Solomon N. Carvalho, 1855. Western Jewish History Center of the Judah L. Magnes Museum, Berkeley, California.

22. See the comments of O. P. Fitzgerald, a Methodist minister, in chapter 9.

I expect, please god, to receive soon a few lines stating your safe arrival home, and the health of yourself and family.

Here we have had excited times, bancrupies [bankruptcies], reverses; we do not know who is involved, and how matters will end—the return of protested drafts will open a scene to which the failure of bankers was but the prelude. Many sufferers are obliged to keep their accounts covered carefully—The very picture of life. Labor, speculations accumulations, botheration, we at last imagine our deposit safe, ourselves rich the last failure—awakens us from our madness in raving after riches, which, when acquired, we did not know, where we deposit them and how to apply them for *our* use. [. . .]

The late excitement has put all religious affairs into the shade; all is dormant. We can get no ear for lectures, and no persons for attendance: a few stereotype Edition appear every Saturday. Since four weeks there was not even a disposition shown to hear a lecture: the last time such was shown, the Parnas invited the people to stay and the ladies to come down.[23] But on his going to the vestibule to invite them into the interior, he learned that the Steamer had come in,[24] and so he came up to me and apologised "for himself and the house" [the phrase is repeated in Hebrew] like the priest of old [in the] Holy of holies.

There is a strange mode gaining countenance here of celebrating wedding banquets—the feast takes place in some public locality—of course *trafa* [written in Hebrew] as the soirees, and even the Ball on the dedication of the Synag to which they invited Dr. Wise (this was in a Christian establishment). After the last *chuppa*, [written in Hebrew] in the Synag, the parnas invited "the Ladies and gentleman to the "Shepherds" (Mentioning even the name) You perhaps know the German Beer house on corner of Stockton at Jackson. The house has several inscriptions whereby you may have noticed it as Shepherds Brewery, Saloon; Yeast sold here etc. The invitation was called out in the Syn : the room was crowded people got in spirit four Ladies fell headlong to the ground in the room. In charity I will not ascribe it to the mismanagement of the Parnas of the Syn who was the manager of the affair. Jewish weddings-feast in Beer houses? without grace, without a blessing: how beautif are the passages Exod 18: 9–12:/ Sam 9: 12–13.

As for the insertion in the Occid, after mature consideration, I think it better declined for the present. I do not think it will influence them any towards improvement. The only object that I could gain would be, that it would be known why at the expiration of my term I shall have to return to the states. Well, perhaps a few lines hinting at affairs here would be sufficient, and the best would be to give briefly something like the following lines

---

23. In 1855 Emanu-El still had a women's gallery.
24. That is, the arrival of the Pacific Mail Steamer with mail and goods from the East.

San Francisco. We are sorry to hear that both Synag: of that city labor under pecuniary difficulties. The revenue of the Polish Syn [Sherith Israel]: is just sufficient to cover the interest which they have to pay on a mortgage, so they will not be able to engage either Hazan Lecturer or even Teacher for their youth for some years to come. Nor are the finances of the Syn: Emanuel in a better state: a heavy debt on the building of about 18,000 on scrips at 6% per annum; besides about 1500 an year interest on mortgages absorb nearly the whole revenue accruing from the monthly contribution of ["110 to 130" is crossed out] two dollars from about l20 members. However, we are happy to learn that laudable efforts are making to remedy the evil by raising the contributions from two to four dollars monthly till the expiration of the term of Dr Eckman's engagement, which will close ["in the fall" is crossed out] next automn. We are also glad to hear that the children of the School for rel [religious] instruction under the direction of Dr Eckman are improving considerably, and that the children attend regularly.

The Portuguese Syn:[25] at San Francisco has enjoyed only an ephemeral existence: it continued ["only" crossed out] for about one or two months So has the debating Society ceased to exist about nine months ago.

"Laudable efforts" is said above in irony: The object is about 14 dollars a member. They had one plenary meeting at which about 50 ayes: and six nos. But when it came to pay they retracted so they had another meeting last sunday a fortnight and not coming to a conclusion, the meeting was continued last Sunday a week when it was at last adopted, by the majority. Upon which 16 sent in their resignation; so that shamash [written in Hebrew] ordered to take 4 dollars when he can get it; if not to be satisfied with two, and not accept resignation. The above content in the Occid would help me out. I will pay for it. And it is quite enough for present. It admits of curtailment or alteration of perhaps some remarks etc. The last Crisis has given the last blow. Let me soon hear

Yours respectful,

Julius Eckman

Do most Kindly remember me to Mrs Carvalho to the children, to Mr [Isaac] Leeser. David must be a little man by this.[26]

---

25. The short-lived Shaar Hashamyim, or Gates of Heaven, was founded in 1853 by Sephardic members of Sherith Israel and Emanu-El.

26. Carvalho's eldest son, David, was six years old.

19
"A Man . . . of the New School"
L. Tichner, 1857

After the conclusion of Rabbi Eckman's one-year term in 1855, Congregation Emanu-El remained without a permanent rabbi until 1860, when the congregation elected Elkan Cohn to its pulpit. In the quest for a suitable rabbi, the search committee, appointed in 1857, wrote for advice to Rabbi Isaac Mayer Wise (1819–1900), the author of *Minhag America* and editor of the widely circulated *American Israelite* who was fast becoming the leading exponent of Reform Judaism.

The Congregation Emanu-El, San Francisco.

The places of Minister, Preacher, Reader and Hebrew Teacher in this congregation having become vacant, the society herewith solicits gentlemen, desirous to fill these vacancies, to send their applications, accompanied by undoubted and duly certified testimonials of their competency and good moral character to the undersigned as soon as practicable.

None need apply, but those capable to perform all the four above named functions.

The salary at present is not to exceed the sum of Doll. 3000 per annum.

For further particulars apply to the Rev. I. LEESER of Philadelphia, Pa.

San Francisco, Cal, January 1st 1856.

J. BLOOMINGDALE, Pres. C. E. E.

Emanu-El advertised in the United States and Europe for a rabbi. This notice in English appeared in the German newspaper *Allgemeine Zeitung des Judentums* 20:14 (1856): 194.

San Francisco, April 18, 1857.

Rev. Dr. I. M. Wise, Cincinnati, Ohio.

Rev. Sir: We have been appointed a committee on behalf of Congregation Emanu-El, of this city, to correspond with the Atlantic side, on the subject of "Minister," a matter which has occupied our attention for the last two years, and we are sorry to say without accomplishing the much desired result. 'Tis true, we have had gentlemen officiating here, but owing to certain deficiencies in their peculiar capacity, their stay with us has been but limited; but still the congregation highly esteem them as men of learning and moral abilities.[27] Our congregation being composed of men of every age and country, their opinion and feelings as to *Minhags*, appears naturally divided, but 'tis evident from the spirit already manifested, that they are much inclined towards the reform style of service. Orthodoxy seems to have but little sway among us, and, consequently, we have no hesitation in saying that a man to lead our flock should be of the New School; and a man of good talent and moral standing will find but little trouble in gathering a congregation together here that would be a pride to our people, and he would indeed find a home among us.

We have taken the liberty of addressing you on the subject, not doubting that you will give your valuable assistance to relieve us of this present difficulty, and at the same time assuring you, that any recommendation you make, shall certainly take precedent; and Sir, without troubling you with a long letter, knowing that your time is otherwise employed, we will at once come to the point. 1. Qualifications of a Minister. To lecture in the English and German languages, and to superintend a Hebrew School. 2. Term of Office. Two years, to take effect from time of arrival here. 3. Salary. Three thousand dollars per annum, together with perquisites attending the office. 4. Travelling expenses, paid to this place. The applicant must furnish congregation, accompanying their letters all vouchers and credentials as to their capacities of a Rabbi or Minister, and also satisfactory recommendations from the place where they last officiated.

You will perceive that we wish to avoid a lengthy communication, but have been as brief as possible. The material points are all expressed. As to the climate and society of this place, 'tis already known throughout the world. In the event of an election we will inform the gentleman in time, when to draw for his

---

Source: L. Tichner to Isaac Mayer Wise, 1857. *American Israelite*, May 22, 1857, 366.

27. Julius Eckman was the congregation's first rabbi. Twenty-five-year-old Herman Bien was a journalist, playwright, musician, and radical reformer who served the congregation from 1856–57. Bien was not an ordained rabbi, and with his lack of a proper education he did not please the congregation for long. See Rosenbaum, *Visions of Reform*, 27. Daniel Levy also served the congregation as Reader. See chapter 1.

travelling expenses, and would strictly desire *that all applications be made to you.* You to act with us. Of course, all applicants are subject to our choice and election.

We would desire to place an advertisement in your paper relative to the matter in question, say for four months, and also send proof of it to *Occident, Asmonean* and *Sinai*. We leave the composition of advertisement to you and please have all bills sent to your office.

The election will take place as soon as the congregation will have heard from you.

We enclose you a copy of our Constitution and By Laws, hoping that we may have an opportunity of serving you. We subscribe ourselves

L. Tichner, *President.*

Louis Cohn, *Secretary.*

A. Tandler.

Committee.

20
Progress and Reform: President's Report
Heinrich Seligman, 1860

As recorded by I. J. Benjamin, Heinrich Seligman, the president of Emanu-El, delivered the following public report proclaiming the healthy condition of the congregation.[28] Seligman, born in Bavaria, arrived in the United States in the late 1840s, where he joined his brothers in the dry goods business, coming to San Francisco in the early 1850s. He served as president of Emanu-El from 1853–55 and from 1857–62 and played a pivotal role in the construction of its first two synagogue buildings and in the hiring of the congregation's first two rabbis. Much had changed in the first ten years of congregational life at Emanu-El. San Francisco was no longer a primarily male society. Families had become an important part of worship, and reforms were being initiated in the synagogue service. The previous summer, the congregation had named Elkan Cohn as their new rabbi, a position he would hold for three decades.[29]

San Francisco, October 7, 1860

To the Officers and Members of Congregation Emanul-El

In accordance with tradition and in harmony with the principles of our constitution, I beg leave to present herewith my annual report and at the same time offer a brief review of the condition of our organization. I shall try to bring before you a true and impartial description of all that has happened and been transacted since the last annual meeting.

First, and above all, it should be said that we have good cause to congratulate ourselves and to lift up our thanks to the Lord of all creation that He has preserved the lives of all our members during the past year, so that, with the exception of the death of the wife of one of our most respected members, we have, fortunately, no deceased to mention among us. May this continue to be the case and may we continue to be blessed with health and prosperity. However, kind Providence prepared a sad blow for us among the children of the members of our congregation, and many have to mourn the untimely loss of innocent beings who have been called to a better world. According to the report of the

SOURCE: Heinrich Seligman, Congregation Emanu-El, 1860. From I. J. Benjamin, *Three Years in America*, 1859–1862, trans. Charles Reznikoff (Philadelphia: Jewish Publication Society of America, 1956), vol. 1, 205–9. Reprinted by permission.

28. For more about Benjamin, see chapter 1.
29. For more information on Seligman, Cohn, and the history of Emanu-El, see Rosenbaum, *Visions of Reform.*

Henry Seligman, president of Emanu-El from 1853 to 1855 and from 1857 to 1862. From Martin Meyer, *Western Jewry*. Courtesy of the Western Jewish History Center, Judah L. Magnes Museum.

vice-president, eighteen children of the members of our congregation have been buried. As we extend our heartfelt sympathy to those parents whose children have been unexpectedly snatched away, we pray from the bottom of our hearts that Providence will spare us in the future from similar misfortune, so that our young ones will grow up to be the pride of parents and society.[30]

It gives me great pleasure to be able to inform you of the rapid increase of our membership. According to the lists and records, fifty-three new members were admitted; of this number, only two withdrew. There were two resignations, and four names were stricken from the list of members. Thus we have gained forty-nine good members. Our membership is now 227 and, if our number continues to increase as it has in the last twelve months, Emanu-El will soon be the largest congregation in the United States.

I am also glad to be able to make a satisfactory report of our finances. At present our expenses are very great—ever since we had the good fortune to

---

30. The child mortality rate was very high.

acquire our eloquent and learned preacher and leader [Rabbi Elkan Cohn]. Disbursements for the choir have also increased as well as other expenses for the needs of so large a congregation. The board has tried to be as economical as possible but, nevertheless, the regular expenses come to $750 a month and will probably amount to $800 after the establishment of the new school. The sale of seats this year was very welcome in order to cover this great sum and, as you can see from the report of the Seat Committee, $5008 was collected and $60 is still outstanding. This is an increase of almost $2000 above last year. This is more than necessary to meet the additional regular expenses. Many of our members are in favor of dispensing with the *Gaben*,[31] but to bring this about another way must be found to enable us to cover our heavy disbursements. If we figure the monthly contributions of 110 members at $200 every month and consider that our interim loan-certificates are soon due, we cannot easily do without the $2500 or $3000 which the receipt of the *Gaben* amounts to on the average, without increasing the monthly dues; and I do not consider this advisable or just. We have many good and useful members who would regard such an increase as too heavy a tax and—if I may be permitted to express my own opinion—they would be quite right. Therefore, I consider it best to make no change in this respect and let things remain as they are.

Our loan-certificates have, fortunately, been reduced to $5919, including interest—a good sign of the liberality of our members, who have reduced a debt of $35,000 for our building, to so insignificant a sum. You will see, from the report of the financial secretary and treasurer, that there is a sum of $5737 in the treasury, plus the dues for the current month and the offerings during the holidays. And if you add the bills due us and, on the other hand, the bills that have as yet not been presented to the board for payment, the sums will balance exactly, and we remain free of debt. If in addition we consider that since our last annual meeting we have taken out of the congregation's funds approximately five thousand dollars for the cemetery, we may be proud of the satisfactory state of our finances and look forward to excellent prospects for the future.

Furthermore, we cannot overestimate our good fortune in having acquired as our preacher a noble, learned and eloquent man like the Rev. Dr. Elkan Cohn, who now lives among us and with us. I believe I express the conviction of almost all when I say we could have made no better or wiser choice. He is a faithful teacher who shows us and instructs us in the true faith that was given to our forefathers. It is therefore our duty to assist him in his difficult office

---

31. Benjamin inserted the following in his recording of the report: "Upon being called up to the reading of the Torah, offerings are made in many places. In many congregations these amount to a considerable sum" (Benjamin, *Three Years in America*, vol. 1, 206).

Rabbi Elkan Cohn, Emanu-El, 1860–89. From Jacob Voorsanger, *The Chronicles of Emanu-El* (San Francisco: Emanu-El, 1900). Courtesy of the Western Jewish History Center, Judah L. Magnes Museum.

and to offer our aid that we may encourage him in his sacred task, so that this new field—for which he left the place where he was settled, happy, beloved and respected—may prove satisfactory to him, and prove blessed and instructive to us and our children.

The most important task that remains to claim our attention is that of the erection of a school for our children, and it is the wish of our preacher that quick measures may be taken to carry out this most essential objective. At the last quarterly meeting this matter was put before the board for a final decision, but since it was not in its power to appoint teachers and to expend money for salaries, it could not carry out the project. I trust that you will now take all the necessary steps to carry out this praiseworthy work, so that the children will soon derive benefit from the favorable opportunities that will then be offered, and will be able to receive all the instruction necessary to their becoming some day good and useful members of our congregation.

Furthermore, the great growth of our congregation points to the necessity of providing a house of worship adequate for all. It is clear that in a short time our synagogue will not be large enough for our needs, and I take the liberty of urging you to select soon a suitable plot of ground in the center of the city that a new house of worship, enough to meet our needs, may be erected. Then the attempt might be made, if possible, to employ our present house of worship for some other, though similar, purpose. I take the additional liberty of proposing that a fixed sum be set aside from the rental of seats in our present synagogue for the specific purpose of buying a plot so that later, and as soon as possible, the needs of the congregation may be satisfied. [. . .]

I might further suggest that a certain amount be given the Jewish traveler, I. J. Benjamin.[32] I believe that we would be performing a righteous act for our cause here and for the benefit of all the earth if we extend a helping hand to this estimable representative of our cause. San Francisco has rightly erected a glorious memorial for itself by the generous way in which it came to the help of its poor brothers in Morocco[33] and will also, I hope, show its beneficence in this case and not hold back. I will bring this matter up again for your approval.

I take the liberty of calling your attention to another fact. Before we were informed whether or not our highly esteemed preacher would accept the call to become our minister, I was, in the interval, instructed to write him and, accordingly, I informed him that, in case it seemed to him that an appointment for three years was too short a period and he would prefer to have it extended to five, the congregation would gladly enter into that stipulation. I consider it, therefore, only just for us to do as we promised and to extend the term of the appointment to five years. We may confirm the promised term unconcerned, for at last we have a man according to our wishes and needs; and in the choice of a conscientious and faithful teacher of our dear religion we could do no better.

With feelings of pride and of bliss, we saw at last the completion of our new cemetery, which we needed so badly, and in your name I express our thanks to those who furthered and hastened the completion of this excellent work.[34] This was accomplished by the effective efforts of the board of road surveyors of both societies and by the ample means provided them by the Emanuel and Eureka Societies, as well as by fellow members.

I take the liberty of further proposing that the post of delegate to the old board of supervisors of street-laying be abolished, with the remark that we are always ready and willing to pay our share of the expenses to keep the old cemetery in good order. By doing so, we only do our duty to our friends and relatives whose mortal remains are at rest there.

---

32. Benjamin stated that he received no money from Emanu-El. He did receive support from Sherith Israel, however (Benjamin, *Three Years in America*, vol. 1, 208).

33. Moroccan Jews fled across the Straits of Gibraltar in the wake of the Moroccan-Spanish wars.

34. The Emanu-El cemetery was located on Dolores Street between 18th and 19th Streets. Sherith Israel purchased land adjacent to the Emanu-El cemetery.

Now that I have presented all the points of our history for the past year worth mentioning and have recommended for your kind attention the proposals that I believe a successful guidance of the congregation requires, I cannot refrain, in conclusion, from expressing my gratitude to the board of officers for the effective and capable assistance that they gave me. They were punctual at their meetings and always ready to assist me in carrying out the duties of my office. By doing so, they contributed much to making my work easier.

I, likewise, take advantage of this opportunity to express my thanks to the members of the seating-committee. They performed their difficult task well during the holidays and we have to thank, in part, their effective and prudent management for the order and decorum that prevailed during services as well as their sound judgment that so great a sum was obtained for the seats.

My thanks also to the ladies who assisted so cheerfully and readily in the choir. I take the liberty of proposing that suitable presents be given them: they were always ready and zealous to assist us in glorifying our religious services and richly deserve our acknowledgment.

Finally, it gives me pleasure to be able to tell you that the harmony and concord that has so long prevailed among us was little disturbed. There was, it is true, a difference of opinion with respect to the laws and regulations as well as to the kind and manner of religious service as introduced among us a little while ago—a difference of opinion that has still not been resolved.[35] But there is no doubt that we, although under obligation to respect the wishes of the minority, for that very reason conscientiously have in view—and this is just what all friends of progress and reform demand—an impartial critical examination of the new kind of religious service and worship and an acquaintance with the manner of it and its success. And I am now convinced that after this has been attained nothing can further disturb the harmonious feelings which fraternal members cherish for each other. That this will be fulfilled is my deepest wish and most ardent desire as well as that Emanu-El may take a worthy place among the foremost sister congregations of the United States. Very truly yours, Heinrich Seligmann, president.

---

35. Because of the reforms, some members left to form Ohabai Shalome four years later.

21
"The Torah Be Read Entire"
Congregation Ohabai Shalome, 1864

Four years after Heinrich Seligman's address to the congregants of Emanu-El, there were still unresolved issues. Emanu-El had introduced a new prayerbook that included a German prayer, German hymns, and an emphasis on prayers read from the pulpit rather than by the congregation. Several congregants objected to the new *minhag* and the way it was adopted; they established a new congregation.

Although the founding of Ohabai Shalome was a reaction to the reforms at Emanu-El, its members had no intention of reverting to Orthodoxy. There was to be mixed family seating, as at Emanu-El, but a yearly reading of the complete Torah, not Emanu-El's recently adopted three-year cycle. Significantly, Ohabai Shalome's members, for the most part, shared a similar background with the members of Emanu-El. The majority were Bavarian born merchants; some drifted back and forth between the two congregations. Ohabai Shalome did not have a permanent building until 1895, when the impressive Bush Street Temple was built; it still stands today.[36]

Minerva Hall. Sunday Novbr 27th 1864

Meeting was called to order at 10 O'clock A.M.

President S. Wangenheim in the Chair.

The president stated the object of the Meeting to be the organization of a congregation; that a special Meeting of Congregation Emanu El had been called for the 24th inst, at which no satisfactory settlement could be had, to remove all strive and discord, in fact no overtures for peace was mooted by our opponents, who went even so far as consulting legal advice, as to granting us the boon of a special meeting and thus if possible to evade the plain Letter of the constitution, and deny us a hearing.

The first Business in order was the election of a vice President Pro Tem.

Mr B Hamburger was unanimously elected V.P. Pro Tem

Mr. Henry Greenberg[37] "   "   Treasurer "

Chas Greenberg   "   "   Collector "

SOURCE: Founding minutes, Congregation Ohabai Shalome, 1864, minute book. Western Jewish History Center of the Judah L. Magnes Museum, Berkeley, California.

36. The congregation disbanded in 1940. The building was designed by Moses J. Lyon and is important for its architecture, which uses Venetian and Moorish motifs.
37. Henry Greenberg, born in Bavaria, came to California in the 1850s. He worked as a merchant in Placerville before settling in San Francisco.

Mr S. Wand[38] stated that it would become necessary to appoint a committee on constitution and By Laws and in order that the committee could act understandingly, it would be necessary to find out the wishes of the Meeting as to the comingling of the Sexes, that having no choice or preferance in the matter, that the majority should rule, and declared that the choice of the Meeting would be his choice.

A Pledge to participate in the organization of the Congregation was read and all who were or are members of Congregation Emanu El came forward and signed the same.

The secretary was here instructed to draw up a Paper of the same import, for non members of Congregation Emanu El, but who wished to become members of the Congregation after its organization

Mr. L. Goldsmith moved that the Sexes may ["should" is crossed out] be seated together at our place of worship. the Roll was called from the List of Signers to the pledge to become Members of the Congregation with the following result. Total

number of votes		62.
number of voting	yes	55
" " "	no	3
excused from "		4.

the President declared the motion carried Mr B. Hamburger moved that the Torah be read entire every Sabath the same as in all orthodox congregations which motion was unanimously carried.

On motion each member was assessed Five Dollars or to give as much, as prompted by his liberality which motion was carried.

the following came foward and contributed the Sums sett opposite their names. [. . .]

Total $127.50

On motion the Secretary was empowered to purchase the necessary Books & co.

On motion the collector was allowed ten per Cent on all collections for the Congregation.

Mr L Goldsmith suggested *Ohef Sholom* as a proper name for the New Congregation, which being enioned [unclear] by several members, was on his motion unanimously chosen as our Title.

Mr S. Wand moved that a committee of five be appointed to draft a constitution & By Laws for this Congregation which motion was carried

---

38. Samuel Wand, a dry goods merchant, born in Bavaria, arrived in the United States at age fourteen. Traveling overland to California, he settled first in Sacramento and later in San Francisco. He had served Emanu-El as a trustee before helping to form Ohabai Shalome.

The Chair appointed the following as the Committee on Constitution and By Laws

Mess. S. Wand, L. Kullman, L Kahn

A Klein & Z. A Koenigsberger

On motion of S. Wand the Constitution and By Laws of Kahal [congregation] Emanu El adopted in 1856 shall govern this body, until the new constitution and By Laws are adopted. carried.

Mr. Wand stated that our temporary Laws provide for a financial as well as corresponding Secry on motion Mr M Waterman was honored with the unamious vote for the office of fin. Sec.

The following Gentlemen subscribed the sums opposide their name [. . .]

Mr. L Goldsmith moved that a committee of five be appointed to procure a temporary place of worship with full powers; the same committee is also instructed to enquire as to a suitable Lot for the building of a place of worship or to the purchase of a Synagogue but make their report to a meeting of this Congregation which motion was carried.

The Chair appointed as said Committee

B. Triest S. Wolf, B Adler,[39] S Koshland[40] & L Goldsmith,

On motion that Membership List as well as resignation List from Kahal Emanu El, be left at B Hamburgers place of Business, as being the most frequented and most Central, adopted.

Adjourned to meet at the call of the President

Sol Wangenheim, Pres. Protem.

M Waterman

Secretary Pro Tem

---

39. B. Adler was a kosher butcher.

40. Simon Koshland, born in Bavaria in 1825, settled in California in the 1850s, where he founded a wool business with family members. He later returned to Congregation Emanu-El.

22

"A Prophet with a Cigar in His Mouth"

Rabbi Aron J. Messing, 1870

Born in Posen in 1840, Rabbi Aron J. Messing left for the United States in 1866. After first settling in Chicago, he came to San Francisco in 1870 at the invitation of Sherith Israel. He returned to Chicago three years later, however, when he became reconciled to the fact that Sherith Israel would not return to Orthodox practices. In 1877 he again took a rabbinical post in San Francisco, this time serving as rabbi of the Orthodox Beth Israel until 1890. Messing regarded Rabbi Elkan Cohn of Emanu-El as his nemesis and as an enemy to Judaism. The following letter was written by Messing to his teacher, the rabbi of Greiditz in Poland.

Praise be God; Herein San Francisco, California, Sunday, during the weekly Torah reading Nitzavim, good tidings.

From the beginning of the year to the end of the year, may God remember you for good and inscribe you in the book for a blessed life. May He bestow blessings and holiness on you, for you are the messenger of the covenant that has been sent to the remnant of Israel to be their shield and bring honor and goodness to his people, and to stand in any breach in Israel and to strengthen truth and peace.

Who sits in the chair of the Rabbinate and who is the chief of the Rabbinical court of the holy congregation of Graditz.

May God lengthen his days and years for the sake of Israel, Amen.

My beloved master, teacher, rabbi and father:

Blessed be the Holy One that I have finally the privilege, most worthy and beloved father, to relay to you good and happy news, even though I am least worthy of all the blessings bestowed on me by God. My good, beloved, and praiseworthy teacher, I have especially during recent days, for a variety of reasons that are too complicated to relate, suffered a great deal. I would have to fill large reams of paper and spend my entire days to express what my heart feels. But why aggravate your fine and delicate sensibilities? It is enough to tell you that I was in reality at the point of denying the existence of the Creator, God forbid. An angry voice spoke to me in my mind, "Bless God and Die." I did not wish to live any longer. I asked myself, why does God persist in punishing me?

SOURCE: Rabbi Aron J. Messing to rabbi of Greiditz, 1870, in "Letters from America to the Rabbi of Greiditz (1868–1871)," ed. Zalman Reisen, American Branch of the Yiddish Scientific Institute. *Annual 2* (1939) [in Yiddish]: 191–218. Trans. from the Yiddish by Selig B. Weinstein.

Rabbi Aron Messing, Sherith Israel, 1870–73, Beth Israel 1877–90. From Messing, *A Farewell Gift to His Friends from Aron J. Messing* (San Francisco: Francis Valentine, 1890). Courtesy of the Bancroft Library (F869.S3C56), University of California, Berkeley.

Why? Why do these "people" make my life so bitter and unbearable? What was my crime? How did I sin? If that is the way you treat me, what need I of life?

The "Reformers" hate me and the Orthodox persecute me. Who will protect me? I have never knowingly insulted or hurt anyone. People who call themselves "Rabbis in Israel" and who have never seen me, make my life bitter. What have I done to them? Yet, God takes care of them who are persecuted. Yes, thanks to God the merciful one. He helped. Everything passes over.

Sunday, the 11th day of the month of Tamuz I was married. Previously on the 7th of Tamuz, I received a telegram from Poland from the messenger Naftali, that I was free according to the laws of Israel.[41]

My congregation celebrated my wedding at its own expense. (my father-in-law himself brought his daughter from Chicago, 3000 miles away) [. . .] So I am married now just three months and am convinced that God has favored me with a woman of valor and one who whole-heartedly fears God. Although young in years, she is the mistress of the house. And as she was raised by her mother to be observant (a situation seldom found here) she is perfect in every relationship.

I live in my house satisfied and happy to see how my wife loves my child, Zvi, and treats him as her own and raises him with love and to be observant. May God reward her for not running after the rich boys—for although she was poor, she could have married a rich man. But she would rather eat a piece of dry bread than be married to an ignoramus.

At any rate I have, thank God, a very honorable position here. It is not to be compared with Chicago. My congregation has 263 families, (in Chicago only about 100). Also here I do not need a cantor. My congregation Sherith Israel has built a school, which I consecrated 14 days ago. It was built for 75,000 dollars in gold, and did not need outside contributors. Its fame is known far and wide, but still I shall have much work to bring it back on the right path, religiously. They have strayed from the right path not from faithlessness and maliciousness. No. A false prophet by the name of Dr. Elkan Cohn (who was born in Kasten near Gretz), who is the rabbi of the reform Congregation Emanuel, who was until now the "Messiah," but due to our many sins has in 10 years made a Sodom out of the entire city. He rides on Saturday with a cigar in his mouth! and says, Moses and his generation have made up the story of the Torah and we have no part in it. Heaven forbid; and for that he receives $6000 a year. He is a rich man and therefore, answers impudently. From this you can infer that he is a bastard.

Now, with God's help that I have been here four months, I have his mask off his face. In the streets one hears now words about Torah and good deeds,

---

41. Messing and his first wife were divorced.

and Thanks to God, some hearts have returned to God completely and some wives have cleaned their homes and introduced Kashrut, and can say now a word to the wise is enough—that God has bestowed on me the force of words & language. And my words that come from the depth of my heart, have entered their hearts, and have made a deep impression. With God's help I am well received and admired. I enjoy great respect from all. Even the Christians call me in the newspapers. "The man of Deeds and Truth," for truth leads the way and falsehoods have no legs to stand on and no strength. [. . .]

And it is not in my nature to elevate myself by degrading others, heaven forbid. But for my sake I want you to know, that in my position I was a successful person, for God was with me at all times. I have a great deal of work to do. I am the superintendent of an eight grade day school and see to it that our children learn Torah, for that was my holy task for years. Also each Shabbat I preach for a large audience. Still I work with joy and diligence, for after all, it is holy work. Also, materially I am satisfied. I receive $3000 a year. [. . .]

For the present I must end. In these days I have much to do. Yet, God willing, after the holydays I shall write more. I would like to send you good wishes for the New Year, but I know that you will receive the letter much later. What shall I wish you? What can a pupil wish his honored & revered teacher, a son to his beloved father, except that I send you my best wishes from the depths of my heart.

Aron Yonathan

23
A Caustic Observer
Isidor Choynski, 1879

Isidor Choynski, born in 1835, emigrated with his parents from Graudenz, Prussia, to New Haven, Connecticut, in 1849, where he received a teaching certificate from Yale University before settling at the age of nineteen in San Francisco.[42] Choynski is best known as the caustic observer and critic of the Jewish elite of San Francisco and the first satirist of America's Jews. In his column for Cincinnati's national Jewish weekly, *American Israelite,* which he wrote under the name Maftir,[43] he made fun of the community's assimilationism and its Orthodoxy alike. But there was another side to Choynski. At the same time that he mocked his fellow Jews, he was an active member of San Francisco's burgeoning Jewish community. Owner of the Antiquarian Book Store, contributor to four California newspapers, and reporter and co-editor

Isidor Nathan Choynski, journalist, bookstore owner, and gold miner, ca. 1875.

---

42. Norton B. Stern, "Two Letters to Harriet Choynski: From Isidor N. Choynski and Julius Eckman," *Western States Jewish Historical Quarterly* 7:1 (1974): 45.

43. "Maftir," Choynski's pen name, is a section from prophetic writings recited on the Sabbath and at festivals.

of the *Weekly Gleaner,* Choynski also published his own newspapers, the *Antiquarian* and the *Public Opinion,* and was an officer of half a dozen Jewish organizations. In the following *American Israelite* column, Choynski offers a satirical look at the San Francisco Jewish community. Often quoted by other Jewish newspapers around the world, his columns helped shape American and worldwide impressions of California Jewry.

SAN FRANCISCO LETTER.

San Francisco, April 28, 1879.

TO THE EDITOR OF THE AMERICAN ISRAELITE.

AFTER THE APHIKOMEN

The Matzo-bakers have collected their bills, the crockery and tin shops have not been so fortunate yet, and as for the milliners, they must have *jahrzeit,* as our people always pay more promptly for their hash than their headgear.

Pesach has come and gone and so has grim old winter, and we are now ready for the smiling spring and the Feast of Weeks. For the matter of that, however, we are ever ready for feasts, even though they last for months, as this one of our failings, to be good to ourselves.

Preparations are being made, on extensive scale, in all our first-class synagogues, to show off the confirmation classes, and set questions and studied prayers will be the order of the day, not to mention the handsomest and wealthiest misses who will appear in silks and satins, loaded down with borrowed jewelry for the occasion, and shine for an hour as professors only. [. . .]

A SAD OUTLOOK.

Hard times have their blightening influence upon our congregations, as many old members cannot afford the tax, however much they dislike to divorce themselves from the synagogues which they were connected for years. The Jew pays more for his religion than any other denomination, owing, it is true, to the fact that not five per cent. of our people are members of congregations, and the expenses fall upon the few. Some of our wealthiest men never see the inside of a *shul,* and only mingle with their people when upon their death-bed.

The congregation Shearith Israel was obliged to cut down expenses in order to keep even; they reduced the salaries of teachers, janitors and stipendaries, and Dr. Vidaver very generously donated them fourteen hundred dollars, which while it speaks volumes for self abrogation of the Doctor, was very gratefully received by the Trustees, who acknowledged the donation in fitting terms.[44]

SOURCE: Isidor Choynski, *American Israelite,* May 9, 1879, 2.

44. Rabbi Henry Vidaver (1833–82), born in Warsaw, served as rabbi of Congregation Sherith Israel from 1874 until his death.

WANTED

We have no less than a dozen each of Rabbis, Doctors, Mohels, Cantors and Shochtim, and some of them take it upon themselves to combine all those offices in the first person, we would like to have a new invoice of fresh stock as we are tired of looking at the same familiar faces and, besides, those fellows are running such fearful opposition to each other, that I think half a dozen new Mohels with improved instruments and patent arrangements would sweep the field, provided they are familiar with anatomy; have an eye for the beautiful and mindful of coming events when they cast their shadows before.

What shall we do with all our reverends? The market is overstocked already, and if those immigrants from Roumania and those from the East come here—as I learn they will—all born rabbis, of course, there will be no dearth of music and of learning, and a "Kol Nidrai" for which our Mohelim Schochtim Rabbonim and other ecclesiastics were wont to charge two hundred dollars will be offered, I have no doubt for half price. I tell you this is a glorious country. [. . .]

MAFTIR

24

"Everyone Shall Enter the
Synagogue in a Respectful Manner"

Constitution, Beth Israel, 1878

Founded to serve an Orthodox congregation in 1860, Beth Israel, first located on Sutter street, rented larger quarters on Mission street in 1874 before building a new synagogue on Turk Street. During this period, Rabbi Aron Messing served the congregation of two hundred members of German and Polish origin. As in the other synagogues of the city, Beth Israel too emphasized decorum, as is evident in the 1878 constitution.

RULES AND REGULATIONS

I.—Gathering in front, or in the vestibule of the Synagogue will not be tolerated.

II.—Every one shall enter the Synagogue in a respectful manner, and take his seat.

III.—Any conversation, communication or other disturbances during the Divine service, and while entering or leaving the Synagogue is strictly prohibited.

IV.—None will be allowed either to enter or retire during sermons.

V.—It will be strictly enforced that the Congregation arise at the following passages, and remain standing until the President takes his seat:

At each opening of the Holy Ark.

At Borchu.

Silent Sh'mona Essra.

Kedusha.

Hallel.

At the prayer following the Sermon.

Olenu.

Kadish Yosem.

Boi Beshalom.

Kidush.

During the foregoing prayers, all entering shall not take their seats until the Congregation is seated.

SOURCE: Constitution, Beth Israel, 1878. Bancroft Library, University of California, Berkeley.

VI.—All prayers not read aloud by the Reader will be read in silence by
the Congregation, who are requested to abstain especially
From praying aloud.
From all manner of intonations.
VII.—The wearing of the Tallis over the head is not allowed; nor shall the
same be taken off until the services are closed.
VIII.—The Trustees and the Sexton of the Congregation are especially
charged to see that the foregoing regulations are strictly enforced.
Children under 6 years of age not admitted.

4
Caring for One's Own

TO SERVE THE GROWING COMMUNITY, JEWISH MEN AND WOMEN BEGAN building educational, cultural, and charitable associations that mirrored their members' regional and religious backgrounds. Most met local needs, but others, such as the Pacific Hebrew Orphan Asylum and Home Society, served the entire Pacific region.

In 1849 the First Hebrew Benevolent Association was founded by Polish and English pioneers of Sherith Israel. Soon the Eureka Benevolent Association was established by the primarily Bavarian pioneers of Congregation Emanu-El. Together these two societies bought and consecrated cemetery land on two lots running from Vallejo to Broadway and from Gough to Franklin Streets. Spurred by the 1850 cholera epidemic, the community formed a care and burial society for poor Jews. The *Daily Alta California* published the first community-wide plea for help, calling on the Jewish community to help Jews afflicted with cholera. The community's response was touted by the newspaper's editor as an example for others.

Women also organized mutual aid societies such as the Hebrew Ladies' Benevolent Association (1855), the Ladies' United Hebrew Benevolent Society (1855), and the First Hebrew Ladies' Mutual Benefit Association (1864), which provided support for poor women and for members in case of their husbands' death.

California Jews maintained ties with each other and with Jews in the East and in Europe through Jewish newspapers. One of the first of these, the *Gleaner,* edited by Rabbi Julius Eckman, had as its major goal the uniting of the community, an end it pursued by publishing news of and of interest to the Jewish community. Eckman also wanted to "amuse and instruct" every member of the community, men, women, and children alike.

Indeed, Eckman had an overriding interest in children and he founded and directed independent schools open to Jews rich and poor, where boys and girls were instructed in religious and secular subjects in German and English and girls were prepared for their roles as homemakers. Young men beyond school age formed the Hebrew Youths' Library and Debating Association. In the 1860s, they also established social clubs like the Concordia and the Alemannia where they played cards, relaxed, and dined together. Such men as Levi Strauss and Solomon Gump spent their evenings at such clubs.

Records of these associations and societies were placed in the cornerstone of Congregation Sherith Israel, and together they document the wide interests of the community. From the constitutions of the First Hebrew Benevolent Society and the Eureka Benevolent Society, to the Friends of Zion (Ohabai Zion), to newspapers from all of the countries of origin of San Francisco Jewry, this list provides a snapshot of the 1870 community.

Founded the same year that Sherith Israel buried its cornerstone, the Jewish Orphan Asylum and Home—later the Pacific Hebrew Orphan Asylum and Home Society—helped those in greatest need, the children and the elderly. As its founders were part of a new community lacking traditional ways of taking care of the young and old, they needed to establish novel charitable organizations in their new home so that Jews would not have to turn to public or Christian charities. The asylum was motivated in part by the fear that if Christians raised the orphans, they might be converted from the faith of their fathers. The asylum could not solve all the problems of the elderly and the orphans, however. There were questions about how to train girls so that they could support themselves in a way that was not demeaning. This was an issue of particular concern, as females outnumbered males in the community.

In 1876 Jewish women in San Francisco organized a fair to benefit the Orphan Asylum. An editorial in the *Fair Journal*, a newspaper that reported on the fair, noted that women who volunteered at the fair set an example for orphan girls by "working" outside the home. The girls needed training to support themselves, and the author believed that women working for pay should not be condemned by society. The author of this editorial may have been Hannah Marks Solomons, a teacher at the Orphan Asylum. The wife of a once prominent member of the community who had deserted his family, she worked to support her children by teaching in the public schools and at the asylum.

In the 1860s, Oakland's Jews founded the Hebrew Benevolent Society, which gave birth to the First Hebrew Congregation, later Temple Sinai. Located across the bay from San Francisco, Oakland's Jewish community maintained a close relationship with San Francisco Jewry. When the society gave a grand ball, all were invited, Oaklander and San Franciscan, Jew and Gentile alike. Often Masons and Odd Fellows joined the society at social occasions and burials.

25
The Cholera Epidemic
Daily Alta California, San Francisco, 1850

The cholera epidemic of 1850 affected 5 percent of San Francisco's population, 15 percent in Sacramento, and 10 percent in San Jose.[1] Although the majority of Jews living in San Francisco in November 1850 had been in California for less than a year, they already responded as a community, as can be seen in the announcement placed by Samuel I. Neustadt, owner of a jewelry business, in the *Daily Alta California.* Formerly of Birmingham, England, Neustadt was the first treasurer of Congregation Emanu-El.

This call, one of the first local newspaper reports of the Jewish community, generated a response by the editor of the *Daily Alta California* commending the "Israelites" for their vitality.

1

To the Hebrew Community of San Francisco. —In consequence of the fearful epidemic at present raging in this city, and more especially among the poorer classes of our people, who have not the means of procuring proper medical treatment and nurses, I beg to request the attendance of Israelites generally at a meeting to be held at my office, foot of Sacramento Street, this evening, at seven o'clock, to devise means of rendering assistance to those of our persuasion who may stand in need of it. Circulars have been issued to those whose addresses are known to me, and those who do not receive personal intimation are respectfully requested to accept this mode of apprising them of the meeting

San Francisco, 4th November, 1850.

S. I. Neustadt.

2

HEBREW SOCIETY.—By a reference to our advertising columns it will be perceived that the Israelites are called together for a very praiseworthy purpose. It is nothing more, however, than was to be expected from a people who have clung together so perseveringly and with so much fellow feeling during the scores of centuries throughout which the world has been to them an Ishmaelite world,

---

SOURCE: (1–2) *Daily Alta California,* San Francisco, Nov. 4, 1850, 2.

1. See Norton B. Stern, "Cholera in San Francisco in 1850," *Western States Jewish Historical Quarterly* 5:3 (1973): 200.

whose hands have been continually against them in all manner of oppressions, until the new light of freedom and toleration dawned. Their sympathies and benevolence are now called for and will find an appropriate echo, we doubt not. Now is the time for societies and friends and acquaintances to help those who claim their particular care, leaving to the city only such as are poor and friendless.

26
For the Benefit of the Jewish Poor
First Hebrew Benevolent Society, Constitution, 1862

Founded in 1849 by English and Polish Jews, the First Hebrew Benevolent Society's members would become founders of San Francisco's Congregation Sherith Israel. This was the first of many benevolent societies that would be established to care for its members and support the needs of the community.[2] Below is the earliest surviving copy of the society's constitution.

Adopted Oct. 4, 1862

Constitution.

Article I.

Society.

Section 1. The name of this Society shall be the "FIRST HEBREW BENEVOLENT SOCIETY," of San Francisco, California.

Sec. 2. This Society shall be incorporated under the above name; and all moneys, bonds, notes, mortgages, and other securities; lease-holds, reversions, real estate, property, and paraphernalia of any kind belonging to this Society shall be held in its own name, by the Trustees, for its sole benefit.

Sec. 3. Every public act of this Society shall be known by the seal of the Society and the signature of the President, Vice-President and Secretary.

Sec. 4. The seal of the Society shall be "a dial of a clock, in the centre of which, a figure and an hour-glass, and on the left a burning lantern— all surrounded by the words, FIRST HEBREW BENEVOLENT SOCIETY, San Francisco, California.["]

Article II.

Funds.

Sec. 1. The funds of this Society shall be appropriated to the relief of the indigent, the needy sick, and the burial of the poor, of the Jewish persuasion.

Sec. 2. Whenever the funds of the Society shall warrant such action, one or more institutions for the benefit of the poor, the indigent and the afflicted, may be established.

SOURCE: Constitution, First Hebrew Benevolent Society, 1862. Western Jewish History Center of the Judah L. Magnes Museum, Berkeley, California.

2. Other men's benevolent societies in San Francisco's first decades included Chevrah Bikkur Cholim Ukedusha (1857) and the Chebra B'rith Shalom Society (1861).

Sec. 3. The funds not immediately required shall be advantageously loaned by the Trustees, at such rates of interest and upon such securities as they deem proper.

Sec. 4. The Society shall celebrate its Anniversary in aid of the funds, on the feast of Purim, if practicable, in the manner determined upon at each annual meeting.

Article III.
Officers.

Sec. 1. The affairs of the Society shall be managed by a President, Vice-President, Treasurer, Secretary, and five Trustees, who shall be annually elected.

Sec. 2. The Trustees shall be elected by ballot separately. A member to be eligible for any office must have attained the age of majority, and have been a member to the Society for at least six months: and the President, Vice-President, Treasurer and Secretary, must have been members for one year.

Sec. 3. The Trustees shall be designated numerically, as First, Second, Third, Fourth and Fifth Trustee, in the order of their election. Any Trustee elected to fill an unexpired term, shall rank after those previously elected, who shall thereby be advanced in number for each vacancy.

Sec. 4. A collector shall be elected at each annual meeting.

Article IV.
Meetings.

Section 1. There shall be two general meetings of the Society in each year: an annual meeting on the first Sunday in January; a semi-annual meeting the first Sunday in July; or as near those days as practicable.

Sec. 2. The Trustees shall hold a regular meeting on the second Sunday in each month, or as near that as possible.

Sec. 3. Fifteen members shall constitute a quorum at all general meetings.

Sec. 4. The President may call special, general, or Trustee meetings whenever he shall deem the same necessary. Whenever nine members shall apply to him, in writing, stating the purport of such requisition, he shall direct the Secretary to convene the said meeting within one week thereafter. Whenever three Trustees shall apply to him in writing, a meeting of the said board shall be convened in like manner.

Sec. 5. Notices of meetings shall be in writing, delivered to each member by the Collector, signed by the Secretary, and shall state the purpose for which such meetings are called.

27

"This Shall Be Its Name Forever"

Constitution, Eureka Benevolent Society, 1860s, 1870s

By the late 1850s, the Eureka Benevolent Society [first known as the Eureka Benevolent Association], precursor of the Jewish Family and Children's Services, was the largest Jewish association in California, with three hundred members. Its founder, August Helbing, along with twelve others, primarily Bavarian Jews, believed that the organization was necessary because "[w]e had no suitable way of spending our evenings. Gambling resorts and theaters held no attraction. We passed the time in the back of our stores, disgusted and sick from loneliness."[3] Starting in 1850, the officers of the association "went out to the incoming ships in boats (there were no wharves then) and brought [the Jewish passengers] to the shore, the sick were taken to little chambers of the members who gave them a portion of their plain accommodations and plain fare. It was a God-sent blessing to the sick Israelite to be taken from the overcrowded ship and be met by his brothers in the faith and cared for."[4] The association also created a Widows and Orphans Fund in 1858. Helbing believed that "mere alms-giving is more likely to degrade than elevate the poor, while the advancing of a sufficient sum to enable those reduced to penury, to make a new start, imparts new hope and leaves the recipient his or her self-respect. Carrying out this policy, it was not uncommon to give large sums in single cases, as high even as $1000."[5] In 1861, the traveler I. J. Benjamin praised the society but noted two incidents where Jewish men were not helped because they were of Polish origin.[6]

Open only to men between the ages of eighteen and fifty, the association mandated that members pay dues as they would for an insurance policy guaranteeing health and death benefits. For at least its first twenty-five years, the Eureka Benevolent Society's business was conducted in German; English was allowed only upon request. By the mid-1870s it had become a more impersonal

---

SOURCE: Constitution, Eureka Benevolent Society, 1860s, 1870s. From I. J. Benjamin, *Three Years in America, 1859–1862,* trans. Charles Reznikoff (Philadelphia: Jewish Publication Society of America, 1956), vol. 1, 216–25. Eureka Benevolent Society Collection, Western Jewish History Center of the Judah L. Magnes Museum, Berkeley, California.

3. August Helbing, "How the Eureka Was Founded: A Reminiscent Sketch." Eureka Benevolent Society Collection, Western Jewish History Center. Founded as the Eureka Benevolent Association, by the late 1850s it became the Eureka Benevolent Society. See the Eureka Benevolent Society Collection, Western Jewish History Center.
4. August Helbing, "How the Eureka Was Founded."
5. August Helbing, "How the Eureka Was Founded."
6. Benjamin, *Three Years in America,* vol. 1, 212.

August Helbing, founder of the Eureka Benevolent Society. Courtesy of Jewish Family and Children's Services, San Francisco.

organization. No longer were members required to inform the president when a fellow member was sick, form a committee to care for a sick member, accompany the deceased member's body to the grave, or inform relatives abroad of his death.[7] The election process was also changed; officers were now chosen by a nomination committee rather than the general membership, and new members were no longer approved by the membership as a whole but by a special board. By around 1877, what had begun as a society of single men had become a society of family men with different needs.

The following 1860 constitution and by-laws were translated from the German by Charles Reznikoff.[8] The mid-1870s constitution omitted the sections that appear below in boldface.[9]

---

7. In the early years, most of the members were foreign-born and came to San Francisco alone, while by the mid-1870s families predominated.

8. Benjamin, *Three Years in America,* vol. 1, 216.

9. A copy of the constitution printed in German in 1870 is almost identical to the 1860 version printed here. Original copies of the 1870 and the ca. 1877 constitution are at the Western Jewish History Center.

Officers for 1861

August Helbing, President. Benjamin Schloss, Vice-President. L. B. Wertheimer, Treasurer. Julius Beer, Recording-Secretary. Trustees: M. Mayblum; Max Frankenthal; Leonard D. Heynemann; Moritz Meyer; Abraham Wolf. H. Greenbaum, Secretary. M. Steppacher, Collector.

Constitution

Article I

1. The Society shall be called "Eureka Benevolent Society" and this shall be its name forever.

Article II

1. The purpose of the Society shall be: *Aid for the needy; care for the sick; and burial for the dead.*

Article III

1. The administration of the Society shall be delegated to a board of nine members consisting of: a president, a vice-president, a recording-secretary, a treasurer and five trustees.
2. Election to the board shall be by ballot and requires a majority of the members present.
3. The board shall be elected for one year and the election shall take place in December.

Article IV

1. There shall be four general meetings annually; namely, on the first Sundays in March, June, September and December.
2. In urgent cases, the president has the right to call a special meeting.
3. The request of a member for a special general meeting must be supported by twenty members and must be accompanied by a written statement of the reasons for it addressed to the president. The president is then required to fix a date for such a meeting, which is to be held within ten days.
4. Special general meetings must be limited to the purpose for which they were called.
5. The society is authorized to frame by-laws; but in no case may these be contrary to the constitution.

Article V

1. The dissolution of the society may not be proposed as long as it has twenty members, and can only take place if three-fourths of the members vote in favor of dissolution.
2. In case of dissolution, the property on hand is to be applied to a charitable purpose in California. The majority is to designate the purpose.

205

Article VI

1. A proposal to change the constitution or amend it, presented in writing to the president, is only admissible at a regular general meeting. After it is read, it may not be discussed until the following regular general meeting. Its acceptance requires the consent of two-thirds of the members present.

By-Laws
Duties and Rights of the Board

1. The president presides at all meetings. He grants permission to speak and has the right to withdraw it. It is his duty to maintain the constitution and by-laws in all respects. At elections, he has the right to vote and is eligible for election. During debates, he may vote only if the members are equally divided. He signs all the minutes that have been accepted and particularly all documents authorized by the board or the society. He must resign his office in case he leaves the State for more than two months.

2. In the absence of the president, the vice-president has all his rights and duties. At the resignation or death of the president, the vice-president takes his place until the end of the term.

3. The recording-secretary is to take the minutes of the transactions of the society, as well as of the board, and after the minutes are accepted he shall certify that they are correct.

4. The treasurer is bound to furnish the board satisfactory security. He shall receive from the secretary, and give receipts for, the money of the society. He shall follow all instructions for the payment of money directed to him by the president in the name of the Society. He shall keep an accurate record of all income and expenditure, inform the board monthly of the financial condition of the Society, and likewise at the general meetings in June and December present an accurate report of income and expenditures with receipts for these. At these two general meetings, he shall have the cash-book in order for examination by a finance committee.

5. The trustees shall work for the good of the Society at the meetings of the board, together with the board-members named above.

   In the absence of the president and the vice-president, the trustee who was next elected shall take their place.

6a. The board is obliged to have monthly meetings at which five shall be a quorum. The president shall appoint from the members of the board the following committees: (1) a financial committee; (2) a committee for assisting the needy; (3) a committee for the care of the sick; (4) a committee for burying the dead; as well as other committees for extraordinary matters.

6b. The board is authorized to hire a salaried secretary, physician, and collector, as well as to discharge them.

6c. The secretary and collector must be members of the Society.

6d. The secretary shall not receive more than $300 annually.

6e. If a member of the board leaves the city for more than fourteen days, he shall notify the president of this so that the latter may transfer the duties of the board-member to someone else for the duration of such absence. Upon the absence of a board-member for more than two months his office shall be considered vacant.

6f. Whenever the board shall lack a member, it shall make up the full number.

6g. After its term of office is over, the board shall transfer to the newly elected board the complete inventory of the Society as, for example, its property, books and utensils.

Duties of the Secretary

7a. The secretary is required to furnish security satisfactory to the board.

7b. He shall keep a correct record of his accounts in a book; receive all monies and turn these over weekly to the treasurer; take receipts and prepare all bills as well as notices of general meetings and board meetings to be held and give them to the collector at the proper time. Within eight days after a new member has been accepted, he shall inform him of the fact and send him a copy of the constitution and by-laws by means of the collector. He shall, above all, attend to whatever writing the society or board may ask him to do.

Duties of the Collector

8a. The collector is required to furnish security satisfactory to the board.

8b. He shall collect all the monies due the Society and receive whatever payment the board shall decide.

8c. He shall carry all oral and written messages that the Society or board may ask him to.

Members

9a. Whoever wishes to join the Society must be at least eighteen and may not be more than fifty years of age.

9b. In all cases, petitions to be admitted as a member of the Society must be presented to the president in writing, must be sponsored by three members and must be accompanied by the initiation fee.

9c. At a meeting of the board, the president shall appoint an investigation committee of three. The committee shall report its finding with respect to the character of the applicant by the word "favorable" or "unfavorable" at the next general-meeting.

9d. Admission to membership is by ballot and requires the approval of four-fifths of the members voting.

9e. Within three months after admission, every new member is obliged to sign the constitution.

9f. Every member must attend the general meetings and vote, if asked to do so, whenever a vote is taken or an election held. A member will be excused from voting only with the consent of the meeting.

9g. It is the duty of a member who learns of the sickness of any other member to report it at once to the president.

Honorary Members

10a. The board, as well as every member, has the right to propose honorary members. The acceptance of such proposal requires the consent of four-fifths of the members present. Honorary members enjoy all the rights of members except that of voting on motions or at elections; but they are excused from any duties.

Life Members

11a. Members may become life members upon payment of $125. Of this sum, one hundred dollars is to go to the general fund and twenty-five dollars to the Widows and Orphans Fund.

11b. Life members shall be excused from any further payment, but they remain subject to all other duties of a member.

11c. Acceptance as a life member requires a separate vote by ballot.

Dues

12. Every member must pay ten dollars initiation fee and monthly dues of $1.25. Voluntary offerings shall be accepted and recorded in the minutes.

Capital on Hand

13a. The Society has agreed upon the sum of ten thousand dollars as capital on hand. This is to be used only in extraordinary circumstances and for this use the consent of two-thirds of the members present at a general-meeting is required.

13b. The management of the capital of the Society is to be left to the board.

13c. The Society is authorized to buy real estate and to sell it.

13d. Decisions with respect to the purchase or sale of real estate shall be taken at a general-meeting especially called for this purpose, and such decision shall require the consent of three-fourths of the members present.

13e. In the invitations to the meeting, the members shall be intrusted with the particulars of the proposal.

Purpose: Aid

14a. The president has the right to give a member, by way of assistance, for the first time, a sum not exceeding $25. A sum not exceeding $100 may be granted with the consent of the committee for assisting the needy. Assistance, beyond this sum, requires the consent of the board.

14b. The president is authorized to give one who is not a member, by way of assistance, for the first time, a sum not exceeding $10. Assistance, beyond this sum, requires the recommendation of a member and may then be granted, with the consent of the respective committee, but not in excess of the sum of $50. All larger amounts are to be decided upon by the board.

Care of Sick Members

14c. When the president is informed of the sickness of a member, he shall instruct the committee for the care of the sick to visit the sick man without delay, discuss the matter with the physician and put all necessary provision for the care and comfort of the sick man within his reach. If visits are desirable, the president shall take the necessary steps to provide them.

Assistance of the Sick Who Are Not Members

14d. If the president is asked to help a sick man who is not a member, his condition shall be investigated by a committee. The president with the assistance of the committee shall decide upon the manner and amount of help.

Burial of the Dead

14e. At the death of a member, the board shall see to his burial and, if necessary, defray the expense of it, provided this does not exceed the sum of one hundred dollars.

The president shall appoint at least twenty members to accompany the body to the grave and shall ask all members present in the city to take part in the funeral. If the grave of a dead member has not been provided with a grave-stone after eighteen months, the Society is obliged to erect one, but may not spend more than forty dollars for this purpose.

In case of the death of members who leave no relatives in this country, it is the duty of the board to notify their families by letter or notice in the Press. At the death of a member, it is desirable that the board watch over the property he has left.

Fines

15a. A member of the board who is absent from a meeting incurs a fine of two dollars.

15b. Members who participate in calling a special general-meeting and do not attend it themselves are subject to a fine of five dollars.

15c. Any member who leaves a meeting without the permission of the president is to pay a fine of one dollar.

15d. A member who leaves a meeting and thereby deprives it of a quorum shall be fined five dollars without the right of appeal.

15e. If in a meeting a member is called to order twice by the president without complying, he shall have to pay a fine of at least a dollar and not more than five dollars.

15f. A member who does not comply with his duties, according to Paragraph 14, section e, forfeits a fine of ten dollars.

Upon a satisfactory excuse, the president may remit a fine.

All fines collected shall go to the Widows and Orphans Fund.

Resignation

16. A member who wishes to resign must present his resignation in writing to the board. It shall accept the resignation provided the member in question is not in arrears.

Suspension

17a. The board is authorized to deprive, for a fixed time, members who have not paid their dues six months in succession, as well as those who refuse to pay fines imposed upon them in spite of repeated demands, of all rights and benefits of the Society without relieving them from their duties.

17b. If a member of the board fails to attend three meetings of the board in succession without satisfactory excuse, the majority of the board may deprive him of his office.

Loss of Membership

18. Members who have not paid their monthly dues for twelve months in succession as well as fines imposed, after repeated demands for payment, may be stricken from the list of members by two-thirds of the board and the board is without authority to receive them as members again until their arrears have been paid to-date.

Members who have been convicted of a crime are considered expelled.

Order of Business

19a. Twenty members shall constitute a quorum. The president shall take the chair at the exact time set for the meeting and call the meeting to order. All business shall be conducted in German. However upon request, the president shall permit discussion in English.[10]

The following order of business shall be observed:
(1) Reading of the minutes of the previous meeting. (If accepted, they are to be signed by the chairman and the recording secretary.)
(2) Reading of the minutes of the board.
(3) Introduction of new members.
(4) Reports of committees.

---

10. By the late 1870s English had become the first language and German the second.

(5) Agenda.

(6) Proposals.

19b. The president shall observe parliamentary rules and regulations during the meeting. He has the right to decide all points of order subject to appeal.

19c. At the request of the president or a member a proposal shall be committed to writing.

19d. Where the vote is in doubt the president may order a division. It shall also be ordered at the demand of five members.

19e. Every speaker shall confine himself to the question under discussion. No member may speak more than twice about one and the same matter unless the meeting consents.

19f. Committees shall be named by the president. The first named is always the chairman of the committee unless the meeting provides otherwise.

19g. If a decision has been reached about a proposal, a member who voted with the majority may move that the same subject be thrown open again for debate and a vote. If this does not take place at the same meeting, such notice must be given at the next meeting.

Amendment of By-Laws

20. A proposal to change the by-laws or amend them shall after it is read be tabled until the next meeting for discussion and a vote.

Such change or amendment requires the consent of two-thirds of the members present.

28

Gleanings from the Far West: A Prospectus

Weekly Gleaner, San Francisco, 1857

On founding the *Gleaner* in January 1857, Rabbi Julius Eckman set forth to inform, educate, and comment on the issues of the day as well as to write about the history and literature of the Jewish people. During its six years (1857–62), the newspaper was published as both the *Gleaner* and the *Weekly Gleaner.* It was not only popular in California but became one of the primary sources of information on western Jewish communal life for Jews living in the eastern United States and Europe. Although he did not succeed as a congregational rabbi, Eckman did have a great impact on California Jewry as a publisher and educator. Eckman's prospectus for the *Gleaner* reads as follows.

THE WEEKLY GLEANER

A FAMILY PERIODICAL,

DEVOTED TO RELIGION, EDUCATION, BIBLICAL AND GENERAL ANTIQUITIES, NATURAL CURIOSITIES, LITERATURE, DOMESTIC ECONOMY, DOMESTIC MEDICINE and GENERAL NEWS.

JULIUS ECKMAN,

Editor and Publisher....Office, 133 Clay Street, San Francisco.

TERMS OF SUBSCRIPTION,

$5.00 per Annum; $3.00 for Six Months; $1.50 for Three Months.

ADVERTISEMENTS at the usual Rates of other Weeklies.

THE GLEANER is too well known by this to require further recommendation. Perhaps no paper in the State has received such encomiums on its appearance as the *Gleaner.* The *Chronicle* of Saturday, Jan. 25th, 1857, pronounces it "complete in every department;" and again, "the *Gleaner* is a unique and valuable paper." The *Daily Alta California,* Jan. 17, 1857, says, "From the great variety of original and selected articles which it contains, it will, no doubt, prove a valuable acquisition to the family literature of both Hebrew and Gentile." The *Bulletin* of Jan. 16th, 1857, states, "such a paper will prove a valuable family companion to Christians as well as Jews." Want of space precludes us from quoting more.

Advertisement for the *Weekly Gleaner. San Francisco Directory for 1858.*

The *Measseph,* the *Gleaner,* Gatherer, Defender, for the original has all of these significations, is intended to be a religious and literary family paper, devoted to the general advocacy of whatever shall, in the opinion of its Editor, best be calculated to promote our material and moral welfare as a people.

Biblical and Jewish Antiquities.

As a repository of rare and varied information upon all matters relating to Jewish and Biblical Antiquities, we shall endeavor to make the *Gleaner* peculiarly valuable to all, whether Jew or Gentile, who are interested in the study of this important branch of human knowledge.

Eastern Travels.

Full and accurate descriptions of the classic localities of the land of our forefathers—localities that have been hallowed by the pen of inspiration, and that have witnessed the acting of some of the most important and extraordinary scenes in human history will form an important feature of our paper.

Illustrations.

Both the above mentioned Departments will be regularly illustrated every week with appropriate and tasteful wood-cuts.

Education.

Without directly encroaching upon the province of the teacher, the Press is, in this country at least, his best and most influential ally. The *Gleaner* will discuss all questions having a direct bearing upon the education and proper management of our children, whether in school or at home: always keeping in view the important fact that the training of the moral faculties, now in a measure neglected, should go hand in hand with that of the mental.

As the friend of the family, the *Gleaner* will also devote considerable space to articles calculated to promote the happiness and general welfare of every member of the household.

Juvenile Department.

An important and interesting feature of our paper will be the Juvenile Department—to the proper management of which we shall devote much care and thought. Our little readers will take up the *Gleaner* every week with the certainty of finding two or three of its columns especially devoted to their interests. To amuse and interest them will be with us a matter of no secondary importance; and the better to attain this two-fold end, we shall strive to convey our ideas to them in the simplest and plainest language we can employ.

Domestic Economy.

To the Department of Domestic Economy and Hygiene, we shall devote as much space as is consistent with our general plan, and shall in this connection

SOURCE: *Weekly Gleaner,* San Francisco, Jan. 16, 1857, 2.

publish regularly every week, a number of important rules and receipts for the household.

General News Regarding Our People and Interests.

Each number of this sheet will contain succinct and important summaries of foreign news in relation to our people and their interests, and we shall from time to time lay before our readers such interesting items of news from our brethren as may reach us from sources and countries hitherto little known to the general reader.

We shall endeavor to render the *Gleaner* a medium for the free interchange of thought from whatever source it may emanate—and its columns will always be open for the temperate discussion of all questions connected either with our own as with the public well being. Finally we shall spare no endeavors to render this sheet a welcome visitor at every fire-side, a credit to our people and an honor to our State. We shall strive so to blend the useful with the agreeable in our columns, in that no one, Jew or Gentile, can rise from the perusal of its pages without feeling that he has been at once amused and instructed.

In the momentous crisis through which our system of theology is now passing, we shall strive to pay due deference to the past, without however ignoring the requirements of the present, or failing to provide for our existence in the future.[11]

We thus send forth the *Gleaner* upon what we sincerely trust will prove a useful and blessed mission, and, however little temporary profit or advantage may accrue to us, we shall feel amply rewarded if in the end it shall be found to have advanced, however little, the cause of piety and the best interests of mankind upon earth.

---

11. There was much variety in synagogue worship, as traditional congregations were debating reforms.

29

Schooling with Hepzibah

Mary Goldsmith Prag and Rabbi Julius Eckman, 1860s

In addition to his work at the *Gleaner,* Rabbi Eckman, who had as rabbi of Emanu-El directed a religious school for its children and the community at large, continued after his dismissal to conduct a school as a private endeavor.[12] Tuition at Hepzibah [My Delight], as it was called, was free for those whose parents could not afford it. Rabbi Eckman composed prayers in English for the children and formed them into a junior congregation. At first, Hepzibah was an afternoon school, meeting every day after public school and on Saturdays and Sundays. Expanding in the 1860s, Eckman opened a day school and the Harmonia kindergarten. Stressing early childhood development, the schools followed the new educational methods developed in Germany.

Although there were other religious schools sponsored by Emanu-El and Sherith Israel, Rabbi Eckman's were the most comprehensive.[13] During the 1850s and 1860s, there must have been a substantial number of children present to support a school with more than one teacher, a multitude of subjects, and both full-day and after-school religious and cultural education.

The following two descriptions of the rabbi's schools represent different perspectives. Mary Goldsmith Prag was a student and then a teacher at the Hepzibah school.[14] Her account of the school, published in *The Chronicles of Emanu-El,* was probably written for what she believed was the fiftieth anniversary of Congregation Emanu-El, celebrated in 1900 (though in fact it was in its forty-ninth year). The second item is an advertisement placed by Eckman himself in his *Weekly Gleaner* in 1861.

SOURCE: (1) Jacob Voorsanger, *The Chronicles of Emanu-El* (San Francisco: Emanu-El, 1900), 133–35. (2) *Weekly Gleaner,* July 26, 1861, 5.

12. During the 1850s and 1860s, Daniel Levy (see chapter 1) worked with two schools that seem to have been in competition with Eckman. In 1857 the *Weekly Gleaner,* Eckman's newspaper, ran an advertisement for "Levy's Institute," which "taught [all classes offered] in elementary and high schools beside French, German and even Latin and Greek, if required" (*Weekly Gleaner,* July 4, 1857). In the 1860s Rabbi Elkan Cohn of Emanu-El organized another school, the Academic Seminary, where boys and girls were taught religion, Hebrew, French, German, and English by Rabbi Cohn and Daniel Levy.

13. In 1859, in appreciation of his abilities as a teacher, Eckman's students presented him with a gold-headed cane. *Weekly Gleaner,* Nov. 25, 1859, 5.

14. For more about Mary Goldsmith Prag, see chapter 3.

1
Mary Goldsmith Prag

Who can go back with me to my first recollection of the Sabbath school of the Temple Emanu-El? For my personal connection with that Sabbath school dates further back than merely twenty-eight years ago [when she began teaching at Emanu-El religious school].

Away back in the early fifties, I see myself, a little girl, going to my first Sabbath school—a Sabbath school which was the mother of the Religious school which is held in our magnificent Temple at present. That Sabbath school did not meet in a regular Synagogue, for in those days the Congregation had as yet no building of its own, but the services were held in what had been a private house on Green street, corner of Stockton. The upper rooms had been thrown into one, and were used as a place of worship in the morning and as a Sabbath schoolroom on Saturday afternoon. So, I see myself going there with my hand tightly clasped in that of him who had just been elected Rabbi of the Congregation [in 1854]. One of the gentlest, truest, noblest characters it has been my fate in life to meet. One whose every deed was Charity, and every thought was Mercy. One who left his impress upon the hearts and souls of all to whom was given the blessing of knowing him—Dr. Julius Eckman—the first Rabbi of the Temple Emanu-El.

The Sabbath school was under the direction and instruction of a corps of volunteer teachers, ladies and gentlemen of the Congregation. Mr. Labatt[15] was Superintendent, and among the most valued of the teachers was our dear departed friend, Leon L. Dennery, who later was for so many years the enthusiastic and earnest Chairman of the School Board of our present Religious school. In the meanwhile, the Congregation was busily engaged in the erection of its Synagogue on Broadway, above Powell, and when the Synagogue was dedicated the Sabbath school had its home in the basement. As long as Dr. Eckman remained Rabbi of the Congregation the Sabbath school was held there; on his severing his connection the greater number of the pupils (so had he endeared himself to the hearts of the children), went with him regardless of the fact that the fathers of many of them were the leading men of the Congregation.

Those children followed their dearly beloved teacher to the old "Portsmouth House," northeast of Clay and Dupont streets. In this building had been located the first post office in San Francisco, but when the post office was moved to its present location the old building was given over to other tenants. There was a drug store at the corner, while the upper rooms were rented out to

---

15. This was probably Abraham Labatt, the president of the congregation, or his son Henry, who was secretary of the congregation in the late 1850s. For more about Henry Labatt see chapters 3 and 5.

stray roomers. It was a ramshackle, weird old building, falling into decay; full of strange noises and haunted corners; its hall and stairways unswept, and decorated with cobwebs and dust. There we appeared every afternoon, after our daily school hours, for our Hebrew lessons, and on Saturday and Sunday mornings for religious instruction. How we waited for each other at the corner, how slowly we ascended the rickety old stairs, one holding on to the other, how we held our breath and shivered with fear as we heard the rats, the only occupants besides ourselves of the old building, scurrying across the rafters; how we finally made a rush for the door of the room, to be welcomed by our dear old friend; to forget all our fears and troubles in the charm of his presence and the magic of his instruction.

From the old Portsmouth House we followed our teacher to his editorial rooms. He was the editor and proprietor of the first Jewish periodical on this Coast, "The Gleaner." How we enjoyed our new quarters. What a sense of proprietorship we felt in every part of the establishment; how we watched the typesetters; what an interest we took in the hand printing press. What words of wisdom and of knowledge we gathered in his sanctum, which was now our schoolroom.

Soon our numbers outgrew these rooms and the little German church on Sutter street below Stockton having become vacant, the premises were rented for us through the generosity of some of the prominent men of the Temple Emanu-El whose interest and sympathy had followed us in all our wanderings; and so, at last, we had a permanent habitation and a name; thus was established the *Hepzibah* Religious School.

Oh the joy and pleasure of those dear old days! How we loved our school, how eagerly we hastened there every afternoon. How anxiously we looked forward to our Sabbath afternoon services which were regularly held there, and in which we officiated, where with all our souls we sang our "Shemah Yisroel" and "Enkelohenu," our dear Master seated at the organ, and then, how we enjoyed the feast of cake and fruit which was sure to follow if we had done well. No matinees for us; we had jollier times.

There, in that dear old school, I stepped from student to teacher, and became the voluntary assistant of our beloved Master. Gone is the old Sabbath school and at rest is the dear old Master. Sacred is his memory to us, his children, enshrined in our inmost hearts.

2
Advertisement placed by Rabbi Eckman

HARMONIA
Select
INFANT, DAY AND INDUSTRIAL
SCHOOL,

Sutter, near Stockton street; in the building formerly used as a City School, and originally as a church

---

THE DAY SCHOOL.

The undersigned has opened a regular Day-School, under his own management and that of a well known public school lady-teacher, and such assistance as the wants of the school may call for.

This school, in operation since the 1st of June, is an extension of the Hephtsi-bah (established July 1854), and is managed exactly like the public schools; with the difference that it aims at developing the moral faculties simultaneously with the intellectual powers: its efforts will be—as have been those of the Hephtsi-bah School these seven years—to afford children *an education besides instruction;* to supply a want very much felt in our system of education. We have too many "clever girls" and "smart boys"; we should like to see obedient children, and good men.

SEWING, CROCHETING, EMBROIDERY AND MUSIC.

These accomplishments, so necessary for the future housekeeper, are taught at the school as necessary branches of a common school education.

GERMAN AND FRENCH.—Pupils, already advanced in the elementary branches, will be taught French and German, if desired.

A number of German parents, wish their children early to learn to speak German. To satisfy this demand, provisions are made for the German to be read as a medium of instruction for those children, whose parents desire it.

MUSIC.—This ornamental branch, frequently so injudiciously taught, without regard to health; to talent, and to the probability of the student's being able to bring it to any perfection and of practising it when acquired—will also be taught as soon as there will be any appreciable demand for it.

THE INFANT SCHOOL

A School, after the model of Prussian Verwahrungeanstalten, under the management of ladies, whose gentleness, suavity of manners and deportment—the first requisites in the early training of youth—cannot fail to exert a healthy influence over the whole after life of the Pupils, is still a desideratum in this city.

The Harmonia School is making every effort to supply this want, and rejoices already in such a promising patronage, that the cooperation of a second lady was secured since the short time of its existence; so that ample justice can be done to the school.

Parents have the choice to have their children addressed in German or English.

The confinement of children at too early an age, and their premature intellectual development, is highly deprecable. Yet, many parents find it, as we see, acceptable to see their children guarded from street influence and (home) accidents, by placing them under the guardianship of ladies, who by a motherly treatment, will very early and especially cultivate in them the affectional and moral faculties; who will entertain them agreeably—partly by instruction, by stories, by play things and otherwise; and that, in a locality so large and lofty, that, while it keeps the young from the dangers and influences of the street, cannot be considered confinement.

The Harmonia (upper) School room measures 32 by 50, is 18 feet high, with a play ground of 10 by 70 feet for the girls, and another of the same dimensions for the boys; situated in one of the most healthy localities, with an appropriate internal arrangement and management, affording to pupils those rare accommodations.

Such a school ought to meet with that support which, similar establishments have met in Prussia and northern Germany; in which country, these Institutes, on account of their usefulness, are the special care and provision of Government.

The devotion of the undersigned to the cause of education is fully known, by his labors in this city since full seven years. He is determined to make the Harmonia School his special care; so that, while it is principally under the management of ladies—a great advantage for the young—he will, by his special care and superintendence, try to introduce into it that harmony and unity of action which is so necessary for the maintenance of a sound and healthy discipline.

Special care will be taken to see the children safely to and from school. Children living on the other side of the railroad will be sent for; particularly those who have to cross the Market street railroad-track.

Charges are those usual in other private schools in this city.

Apply at the School House daily from 9 A.M.; or at the "GLEANER" Office daily from 12 to 2 P.M. O' St; or 517 Clay st.

Independent Classes

in

NEEDLEWORK, EMBROIDERY, MUSIC, FRENCH AND GERMAN

Independent classes in the branches of this caption are in the process of forming for such pupils who visit the different city schools.

These classes will be in session from three o'clock [in] the afternoon; so they interfere not with the regular school hours.

JULIUS ECKMAN

30

Debating on the Second and Fourth Sunday

Hebrew Youths' Library and Debating Association, 1864

In answer to a letter printed in the *Hebrew* and signed "Truth," the members of the Hebrew Youths' Library and Debating Association (H.Y.L. & D.A.) made the following reply. "Truth" had asserted that there was no place for young Jewish men to gather, have discussions, and gain access to Jewish books and periodicals.[16] The association answered that such a place had existed for three years. This association was probably the same as the Union Debating Society that I. J. Benjamin states was formed in 1861, the same year as the H.Y.L.& D.A.[17]

San Francisco, Feb. 3, 1864

EDITORS HEBREW:—An article which appeared in your paper on January 22d, signed "Truth," is worthy of attention; and thinking it not amiss, we also make a few remarks in conjunction with that writer, and hope it will be of some benefit.

We were delighted to see that there was still some one who takes an interest in the spiritual welfare of the Hebrew young men of this city. We heartily agree with "Truth" that it would be the means of beneficial results if some benevolent persons would undertake to give them instructions in the faith, laws and customs of our forefathers. But where are those persons to be found?—as yet we have no examples here. The writer, in his advice, suggests the formation of an association for literary purposes, and by so doing strengthen the mind, improve the intellect, and connect the young men by more social ties. He is probably not aware that there exist[s] in this city an association of such aims, known as the "Hebrew Youths' Literary and Debating Association." This society has, by great exertion on behalf of its members, been upheld for more than three years, and during that period received no encouragement from the Hebrew

SOURCE: Hebrew Youths' Library and Debating Association, 1864. Western Jewish History Center of the Judah L. Magnes Museum, Berkeley, California.

16. "The Social Life of Our Young Men in this City—A Few Timely Suggestions," *Hebrew,* Jan. 17, 1863, Western Jewish History Center. (This clipping is misdated and in fact is from 1864.)

17. The Hebrew Youths' Library and Debating Association was probably the successor to the Hebrew Young Men's Literary Association, which was established in San Francisco in 1854 by members of Congregation Emanu-El.

community. We only ask aid intellectually—nothing more. We hope that some of our learned men will now come forward and give us their assistance.

Our Association numbers thirty-five members in good standing, who have done everything in their power to advance themselves in literature, especially that pertaining to our sacred faith. Through the energy of its members, the organization has obtained a good library, containing many very valuable books, which are eagerly perused by the members. There is also connected with the society, a Debating Club, where subjects are discussed every meeting. Our funds are in good condition.

We hope by these few remarks to awaken an interest in our behalf, and soon to see some movement taken that will better tend to assist us in our objects.

In the vestry rooms of the Synagogue Emanu-El, on Broadway street, the society holds its sessions. Meetings take place on the second and fourth Sunday of each month, on which occasions we will be pleased to see visitors.

MEMBERS OF H.Y.L.&D.A.

31
Clubs for the Elite
The Concordia and Alemannia Societies, 1865, 1866, 1879

In 1864 Jews of German origin who had joined with fellow Germans a decade earlier in founding *vereins,* or German clubs, formed the Concordia Club for Jewish men, in a room rented from the Odd Fellows at the corner of Bush and Kearny Streets. There young merchants of the city, including Levi Strauss, could play cards, eat, and socialize. A second club, the Alemannia, soon merged with the Corcordia and the united society moved to larger quarters. The second anniversary ball reported below was the Alemannia's last event.

1

The "CONCORDIA SOCIETY" filed its certificates of incorporation on the 10th inst. The objects of this society are the promoting of social intercourse, cultivating literary taste, and diffusing useful knowledge among the members thereof. Officers: Israel Steinhart, President; Levi Strauss, Vice President; Leon Ehrman, Treasurer; A. W. Michels, Recording Secretary; H. Herman, Corresponding Secretary; D. S. Bachman, S. Sachs, E. Mandel and Louis Strauss, Directors: Local Board; Wm. Mendersson, Louis Schlessinger and Joseph Rosenbaum.

2

THE CONCORDIA

The Concordia, the principal Jewish society of San Francisco, was established in 1864. The first President was Israel Steinhardt. The first rooms occupied were on the south-east corner of Bush and Kearny. In 1868, a change was made to rooms on Sutter street, between Kearny and Dupont. In 1873, the society took possession of the present commodious rooms in the army building at the corner of Stockton and O'Farrell, fitted up at a cost of $30,000. The membership is entirely Jewish, and chiefly composed of wholesale merchants. The rooms have the usual appliances for comfort and pleasant entertainment. There is a reading-room, furnished with magazines and newspapers; a library, with books of reference; a billiard-room, dining-hall, etc. The rooms are only open evenings and Sundays. The entertainments are monthly or bi-monthly parties, at which are seen the *élite* of the Hebrew residents of the city. The

---

SOURCE: The Concordia and Alemannia Societies. (1) *Hebrew,* Jan. 13, 1865, 4. (2) *Elite Directory for San Francisco and Oakland* (San Francisco: Argonaut Publishing, 1879), 8. (3) *Hebrew,* Oct. 5, 1866, 4.

officers are: M. Heller, President; E. Emanuel, Vice-President; J.H. Ackerman, Recording Secretary; P. Barth, Financial Secretary; M. Heynemann, Treasurer.

3

SECOND ANNIVERSARY OF THE ALEMANNIA.—We had the pleasure of attending the second anniversary subscription ball of the above named, and well known social club. The hall was neatly decorated with the national and German banners, and flowers. The band of music consisting of twenty-two pieces, discoursed most beautiful music; the ball room was graced with the élite of our Jewish community. The supper room being too small and inconvenient to seat all present, the main hall was partitioned off with banners so as to accommadate all: and Strauss who catered for the occasion, furnished a most excellent supper, such as is seldom given at balls. After the supper, dancing was again resumed; nearly two hundred couples enjoyed themselves to their heart's content, until an early hour in the morning. The executive committee deserve praise for the manner in which the entire affair passed off, and we hope to be present at many more such parties as was given by the Alemannia last Tuesday evening.

32
Buried in the Cornerstone
Congregation Sherith Israel, 1870

When Congregation Sherith Israel built a new synagogue at the corner of Post and Taylor Streets in 1870, the items listed below were placed in the cornerstone to be preserved for future generations. This wide assortment of newspapers, constitutions, and memorabilia documents the diversity of the community in 1870 and the importance members gave to their association with Jews in the eastern United States and Europe.[18]

1. Letter from Sir Moses Montefiore, Bart.
2. Historical sketch by Secretary Isaiah Cohn
3. Constitution and By-Laws Congregation Sherith Israel [1851]
4. Constitution and By-Laws Congregation Ohabai Shalome [1864]
5. Proceedings at Mass Meeting on the abduction of Mortara boy, of January 1859
6. Prayer Book Redelsheimer
7. Tsitsis
8. Mezuza
9. Kethuba, form of Marriage Contract
10. Rules of Giboth Olom Cemetery[19]
11. *Alta California,* newspaper of March 11, 1870
12. *Evening Bulletin,* newspaper of March 10, 1870
13. The *Examiner,* newspaper of March 11, 1870
14. The *Morning Call,* newspaper of March 11, 1870
15. The *Chronicle,* newspaper of March 11, 1870
16. The *Hasmonean* of December 9, 1853
17. The *Pacific Messenger* of October 5, 1861
18. The *Hamagid* of February 2, 1870
19. The *Archive d'Israelite,* Paris, of February 1, 1870
20. The *Jewish Chronicle,* London, of February 11, 1870
21. The *Hebrew Observer* of March 11, 1870
22. The *Hebrew* of March 11,1870

SOURCE: Congregation Sherith Israel Collection, Western Jewish History Center of the Judah L. Magnes Museum, Berkeley, California.

18. Today these objects are buried in the cornerstone of the temple on the corner of Webster and California. The founding dates of the associations listed, when known, are given in brackets.

19. This is the Sherith Israel cemetery, known in English as Hills of Eternity.

23. The *Hebrew Leader,* N.Y., of February 25,1870
24. Hebrew Calendar for 5630
25. The *Calomet,* periodical for Order of Red Men
26. *Der Sabbath,* a German pamphlet
27. By-Laws Eureka Benevolent Association [1850]
28. By-Laws First Hebrew Benevolent Society [1849]
29. By-Laws Ladies United Hebrew Benevolent Society [1855]
30. By-Laws Chevra Achim Rachmonim [1862]
31. By-Laws Chevra Bikur Cholim Ukedisha [1857]
32. By-Laws Chevra Berith Shalome [1860][20]
33. Constitution Independent Order B'nai B'rith
34. By-Laws Ophir Lodge No. 21 I.O.B.B. [1855]
35. General Laws I.O.B.B.
36. By-Laws Bricklayers Provident Association
37. Annual Report Young Men's Hebrew Benevolent F'nal Association of N.Y.
38. Constitution Kesher Shel Barzel
39. List of Officers Kesher Shel Barzel
40. By-Laws Har Hamoriah Lodge K.S.B.
41. By-Laws Friends of Zion
42. Fractional Currency of United States $1.95 with card of F. Toplitz
43. One Russian Coin with card of Abraham Magnus
44. Seventeen (17) Silver and Copper Coins of the United States
45. Twenty-three (23) Silver and Copper Coins of Foreign Nations

---

20. According to Benjamin, in 1861 this mutual assistance association had 105 members and a treasury of $1,000; I. N. Choynski was its president (*Three Years in America,* vol. 1, 228).

33
"To Protect the Poor and Fatherless"
Pacific Hebrew Orphan Asylum, 1870–1879

The founding fathers of the Pacific Hebrew Orphan Asylum and Home Society were the members of the B'nai B'rith District Lodge 4. This was a statewide endeavor, however, as members came from all over the Pacific region, from Los Angeles to Portland, San Francisco to Reno. It was common for religious groups to take care of orphans, and as the community grew, the care of orphans became an increasingly urgent matter.[21] B'nai B'rith also sought to take care of elderly members of the Jewish community, who as immigrants may have been isolated from family members.

The documents below illustrate four stories of the early history of the asylum: the first fund-raising appeal; the call for support of the new institution; excerpts from the *Fair Journal,* a fund-raising tool; and an annual report at the close of the asylum's eighth year. The annual report highlights the Jewish education given all youngsters and the special problem of finding proper work for girls.

1

APPEAL
in behalf of the
orphan asylum and home!
*Protect the poor and fatherless, do justice
to the afflicted and needy.*
[written in Hebrew, followed by English]
Psalm LXXXII, 3.

ISRAELITES OF THE PACIFIC!

The time has at length arrived to put into effective being the hopes and wishes which have long been cherished in your hearts.

SOURCE: (1) Constitution, Jewish Orphan Asylum and Home, District 4, Independent Order of B'nai B'rith (San Francisco: M. Weiss Oriental Printing House, 1870). Bancroft Library, University of California, Berkeley; (2) Congregation Sherith Israel, Collection, Western Jewish History Center; (3) *Fair Journal* 1:1 (1877): 4, Pacific Hebrew Orphan Asylum and Home Society Collection, Western Jewish History Center; (4) annual report to the board of directors, Pacific Hebrew Orphan Asylum and Home Society, 1878. Bancroft Library, University of California, Berkeley.

21. For more information on Jewish orphanages in general, see Reena Sigman Friedman, *These Are Our Children: Jewish Orphanages in the United States, 1880–1925* (Hanover, N.H.: University Press of New England for Brandeis University Press, 1994).

Of the many communities of Israel in America, none have proved their claim to the promptings and deeds of charity more than those dwelling on the shores of this Western Ocean.

The acts of mercy, benevolence, and humanity, performed by you in past years, give assurance that you hail with joy the early practicable realization of a permanent institution of charity, which shall be immediate in its blessings and far reaching in its influence. Experience has proven, that in the associated efforts of philanthropists lie the true sources and most effective means of doing good.

The existence of a JEWISH ORPHAN ASYLUM AND A HOME, for aged and infirm Israelites, is demanded by the accumulating necessities of our rapidly growing population, and the desire, actuating every true Jewish heart of affording the same means of protection and relief, bestowed by other denominations, upon the unfortunate of their faith.

The I. O. B. B. have carefully matured plans and already contributed the sum of $23.000[22] towards the objects herein set forth.

The institution is designed:

1st.—*a*) To take care of and protect Jewish children of both sexes, deprived of either or both parents and without adequate means of support.

—*b*) Children under the care of the Asylum, will be provided with a home, food, clothing, education and medical attendance, and when necessity arises, legal guardianship.

2d.—To give shelter and a home to aged and infirm Israelites worthy of protection, and whose declining years render them incapable of self-support, or whose physical condition make them objects of charity and amelioration.

3d.—The benefits to be extended to Jewish Orphans, irrespective of being children or not of members of the B'nai B'rith, and to Israelites irrespectively.

The design is to secure one or more blocks of land,—comprising from three to five acres,—situate in the most healthful quarter of the city, (on its borders perhaps,) a location which shall give childhood happy thoughts and pleasing impressions, and to erect thereon an ORPHAN ASYLUM; and in the immediate vicinity, a commodious building for the HOME.

ISRAELITES! in this work, in which we ask you to participate by your membership or contribution, there is all which should inspire the most laudable emulation.

It is a work of charity in the loftiest acceptation of that word, so often quoted, so frequently misunderstood.

---

22. This sum may be $230 or $23,000.

It is that charity which concerns the helplessness of innocent childhood, of hapless and helpless infirmity and age.

It is that charity which has no selfish aim, which looks with a pitying eye upon the misfortunes liable to our common humanity, and seeks to mitigate and restore the losses which death and the reverses of life involve.

In this work all Jews alike may join without reference to nationality, or differences of dogmatical belief.

We need—we must have—in San Francisco—for the benefit of the Pacific States, a JEWISH ORPHAN ASYLUM AND HOME.

We claim no originality in the thought which shall give birth to this Institution. We only ask that you unite with us to make it a reality.

While in other lands our brethren are groaning under the yoke of despotism and oppression; denied civil liberty and political freedom; suffering anguish and misery; we, Israelites of America, are blessed with unlimited opportunity, and have all avenues open to secure material prosperity.

We owe a debt of gratitude to the *genius of liberty* and the *spirit of Charity,* to see that no Orphan child of Judah, no helpless brother of the house of Israel, become inmate of eleemosynary institution, denominational or public.

Nay, this debt is due to our holy religion which especially commands us to provide for the poor and fatherless, to protect the afflicted and needy.

ISRAELITES! believing you will share these sentiments and be anxious to associate your efforts with ours in the consummation of this noble work, we direct to you this appeal, that its early triumph may be secured, and the name of ISRAEL be universally honored and respected.

EXECUTIVE COMMITTEE,
I. O. B. B
San Francisco, July 1870.

2

Pacific Hebrew
Orphan Asylum
and Home

San Francisco, September 30th 1872,
To the President and Officers of the Congregation Sherith Israel
Gentlemen,

By order of the Board, I have the honor to notify you, that the filling-up of the Pacific Hebrew Orphan Asylum (on Mason St., between Broadway & Vallejo St) has been completed; that the doors of the Institution are open for reception of orphans and that several of them have found there a paternal home.

Inviting you to inspect the premise and being convinced, that you will be pleased with the results of our united efforts thus far. I beg to convey to you the thanks of this Society to the members of your Congregation to accomplish the charitable object.

Finally, it is left to your wise judgement to select the best means to always and everywhere enliven the sympathies and to solicit patronage, necessary to the support of the Asylum.

Respectfully
Leo Eloesser
Secr

3

THE HEBREW ORPHANS' FAIR

A.

Publication office in front of the art gallery

All communications referring to this journal to be addressed to the Editors of THE FAIR JOURNAL.

Notice

——The Fair will be open daily from 1 to 5 o'clock P.M. and from 7 to 11 o'clock P.M. Friday evening and Saturday afternoon excepted. Saturday evening, from 7 to 11 o'clock.[23]

B.

The Fair Journal
December 5th, 1876,
A SIDE ISSUE.

We are tempted to somewhat swerve from the discussion of the charitable cause to which we particularly devote ourselves. The Fair and some of its incidents afford an opportunity for reflection and food for thought, which, though perhaps not directly affecting our Orphan Asylum, still bears some relation to the ulterior wisdom, that is to guide its wards and certainly concerns many earnest and well-meaning workers, at present engaged in their behalf.

We refer to the impression produced upon our minds by the spectacle of a few hundred young ladies, busily occupied with the duties assigned to them at Horticulture Hall. We observe them selling their wares, furnishing refreshments, absorbed in attending to the department allotted to them, making themselves so thoroughly useful, and withal, in so graceful and refined a manner that, somehow, we ask ourselves, why should all this find such ready tolerance merely under these extraordinary conditions? How does it come that such

---

23. For a report of the fair, see California Newsprint Collection, American Jewish Archives, Cincinnati, Ohio.

pursuits, open equally to both sexes, are shunned by so many young ladies, as if a taint were attaching to labor of this kind? What is becoming and commendable in a case involving charity, why not likewise in the great Fair of the world—a world made for work? Let our words not be mis-construed. We do not put ourselves forward as moral preceptors. If we were, these columns are not given to grave discussions. But may we not be permitted to here and there step aside, and, even in our humble capacity, draw attention to matters well worth serious consideration? It affects, to a certain extent, those tender children for whom we are now all striving to do our best. If we are not allowed to suggest an argument of this nature to many of the excellent young ladies, now full of activity at our Hall, might it not prove a source of strength to our orphan girls, who, on reaching the age of womanhood may readily avail themselves of every honorable opportunity, to do useful work, lessening poverty and privation and emancipating themselves and their sisterhood from the arbitrary edicts, society chooses to impose?

A truth, no matter where uttered, still remains a truth; and why should we hesitate to enter upon so interesting a field, merely because our readers might be unprepared for it? The gay assemblage, the glittering light, all the fun and gaiety of the Fair will pass; and may we not broach this most important subject for an after thought? We see a large number of the most respected ladies of our denomination, working harmoniously together and putting their stamp of approbation upon an employment, so willingly and pleasantly performed by hundreds of their younger sisters. Why, we ask ourselves, might not this patronage be extended? To wider fields of usefulness? Where the hard realities of life confront us, where many a brave woman, shrinking before that idle phantom "what the world might say" could be induced, to perceive the folly of such fear and—encouraged by those of position in society—lend a helping hand in amelioration their own condition and that of many of their sex.

4

Eighth Annual report of the Pacific Orphan Asylum and Home, 1878

PRESIDENT'S REPORT.

To the Patrons and Members of the Pacific
Hebrew Orphan Asylum and Home Society:
LADIES AND GENTLEMEN—I have the honor to submit to you the annual report of the Society for the fiscal year 1878–79.

This being the only opportunity of which I can avail myself to address our members, I hope to be excused for repeating some subjects and dwelling thereon, which I have already presented in former annual reports and at previous annual meetings.

I here specially refer to a complaint, which, with me, has nearly become chronic, and in view of the prosperity of our institution and its sound financial standing, might appear unjustifiable, viz.: That our membership is not at all in proportion to the number of Israelites on this Coast, and consequently our regular monthly income from that source is not in proportion to their ability to contribute the trifle represented by the dues, which is but fifty cents per month.

With the consciousness that your Board of Trustees have done their duty, and the cheerfulness with which each one of its members participated in our labors, I believe to be justified in the demand that every Israelite on this Coast should do likewise, and only be too glad to share in our work and prove his sympathy with our cause by at least joining the Society.

Although the charitable spirit that characterizes our co-religionists is a guarantee that our institution will never be endangered, or even financially embarrassed, and although we may bear the loss of material benefits involved in the loss of, or non-increase of membership, we, nevertheless, cannot afford to do without the full sympathy of the many Israelites who are not enrolled, as evidenced by the following facts:

In the course of the fiscal year which terminated on the 31st of August, 1879, the Society accepted 52 members, and lost 175; of the latter number, we have to deplore 10 whom we lost by death. By resignation, the Society lost 71; and 94 were stricken from the roll for non-payment of dues. At present, there are enrolled 1,570 members, classified as follows: 79 life members, 35 patrons, 11 life patrons, and 1445 ordinary members.

These figures are telling enough, and it is needless to further justify my urgent solicitation for every member to awaken his friends and acquaintances to their duties, and enlist them in our cause.

From this unpleasant subject I beg to turn to a more pleasing view of our field of action.

The number of orphans at present under the care of the institution is 61, viz.: 28 boys and 33 girls; of whom 55 are under the roof of the Asylum, and three boys and three girls board outside.

During the fiscal year over which this report extends, viz.: from September, 1878, to the same date of the current year, nine children were admitted, one died, and four were discharged. One of the latter, after having learned the printer's trade, found good employment in Sacramento, and is doing exceedingly well. Of others who are not apprenticed at different trades, they all give good promise of finishing their respective trades, so as to share the same good fortune.

The mental training of the orphans, under the supervision of the Committee on Education, has been in public schools, as heretofore; and at home the children are guided and assisted in their studies by their teachers, Mrs. Seixas

Solomons[24] and Mr. Jaffe. I am glad to state that they compare favorably with their classmates in the public schools.

Most of the members present will, I am sure, cheerfully remember an exhibition of the pupils, given as a sample of their abilities, under the auspices of the Chairman of the above named committee, Mr. Alfred P. Elfelt, and conducted by him and the teachers of the institution.

It is not my intention to conceal that, although in general there is good cause to be satisfied with the behavior of the orphans, nevertheless we had a fair sprinkling of an element which required a stern hand to be governed, and the Board exercised the same upon such characters as were necessary to be thus treated.

In regard to the health of the children, it is gratifying to state that although the institution has not altogether escaped serious visitations by sickness, yet, thanks to the Almighty, under the careful treatment of our volunteer staff of physicians, Doctors L. J. Henry, Henry Gibbons, Jr., and Joseph O. Hirschfelder, our sick were spared with one exception, and I can not refrain from repeating again and again how great an obligation the Society owes to the above named benefactors who untiringly and cheerfully respond to each call of the Matron, and attend to each case with as much promptness and care as they extend to any patient of whom they expect remunerations other than blessings and thanks. Whilst bestowing the tributes of our unbounded thanks to the before-mentioned physicians, I also tender them to Doctors Schmidt and Sichel, who, as heretofore, are always ready to serve whenever solicited.

Now, it seems incumbent upon me to make a few remarks more general than special, concerning the most difficult duties of your Board.

The first problem to be solved by them is how to comply with the laws of the State concerning the orphan asylums, and at the same time admit to our institution unfortunate children abandoned by their parents, who are not considered orphans in the legal sense, but viewed from the stand-point of humanity, and in the interest of the community, must be rescued and fitted for useful membership of this commonwealth. In most of such cases the Board assumed the responsibility, and accepted these children. But broad as is the basis on which the rules of your institution rest, there is no room for such an interpretation as allows the *unlimited* acceptance of these helpless children, who, as your Board experienced, are abandoned for the purpose solely of forcing them upon this Society. In such cases the Board, although in full sympathy

---

24. Hannah Marks Solomons was the sister of Bernhard Marks and was raised by her aunt and uncle, Judith and David Solis-Cohen in Philadelphia. She traveled to California in 1853. Refusing to enter a loveless arranged marriage, she began teaching at Temple Emanu-El and at a public elementary school and became the youngest and only woman principal in San Francisco. In 1862, Hannah married Seixas Solomons; see chapter 7.

with these poor children, and in favor of giving them the benefit of any possible doubt, yet cannot always gratify personal feelings, and when refusing admission into the Asylum, is sure to act conformably with the approval of the members generally.

A second problem, still harder to solve, presents itself in the question: how to provide for the orphans, especially girls, after they have reached the age when their future life has to be molded, and when they have to be prepared to earn a livelihood?

The aim of your Board has been, and unceasingly is, to apprentice the boys to any trade or calling they may choose, and have the girls brought up as good housekeepers; but the difficulty is to find suitable places for the latter—places where the employers take more interest in the physical welfare and moral culture of our ward than is bestowed upon domestics generally.

And here is the province where the co-operation of *all* the members is wanted and urgently solicited. Whenever, ladies and gentlemen, an opportunity offers to place one of said wards in a good home, or to procure a situation for our boys, remember the same and communicate with this Board, who will always be thankful for your exertions. [. . .]

I herewith tender the grateful thanks of the Society to the Matron and her husband, Mr. and Mrs. G. Braham, for the affectionate manner they treat the children under their care, and the interest the Matron takes in teaching the girls to become good housekeepers; to Messrs. Naphtaly, Freidenrich and Ackerman, attorneys for the Society; to Mr. C. D. Evers, foreman for Mr. I. Gutte; Korn and McCarthy, Adolph Pollack, and Englander & Son, for continuous service in hauling supplies to the Asylum without fee or reward; to the Secretary, Collector, and all employees of the Society, for their efficient and faithful manner in the discharge of their duties, and particularly to that small band of noble women, known as the "Ladies' Visiting Committee," who are always on duty, and in a great measure sacrifice their own comfort and means in their service of the poor waifs under our care; to the ladies who assisted in sewing, and to all persons who have in any manner contributed to the success of our charity. My personal thanks are due to every member of the Boards of Directors, who are always ready and willing to aid and assist me in my duties as executive officer of your Society.

Respectfully,

S. W. LEVY, President.

San Francisco, September 1879

233

34
"The Terror of Death"
First Hebrew Ladies' Mutual Benefit Association, 1879

Founded on January 10, 1864, the First Hebrew Ladies' Mutual Benefit Association provided mutual assistance, medical care and medicine, weekly sick benefits, and death benefits to its members.[25] In this letter, the association joins Rebecca Harris in mourning the death of her husband Isaac. In 1851, Ricka Brodek (Rebecca Harris) married Isaac Harris in London. Soon afterward, Isaac left for San Francisco and was followed by Rebecca, who traveled across the Isthmus of Panama with their infant daughter, who did not survive the trip. The owner of a tailor shop, Isaac Harris was killed after completing a sale of property in the Red Light District of San Francisco. At the time of his death, he was forty-six years old and the father of six children.

First Hebrew Ladies Mutual Benefit Association
San Francisco May 11th 1879.
To the President Officers & Members of the
FHLMB Association
Ladies & Gentlemen
Your Comittee appointed at the Special meeting held April 27th to draft suitable Resolutions of Condolence to the familie of the deceased Gentleman
Isaac Harris
whose Lady is a member of the above Association beg leave to Report as followes.

Source: Lipman-Harris Family Collection, Western Jewish History Center of the Judah L. Magnes Museum, Berkeley, California.

25. Ruth Kelson Rafael, *Continuum: A Selective History of San Francisco Eastern European Jewish Life, 1880–1940* (Berkeley: Judah L. Magnes Memorial Museum, 1977), 45. There were many associations in San Francisco that cared for Jewish women. The first was the Israelitishe Frauen Verein, usually translated as the Hebrew Ladies' Benevolent Association. This association was started by the women of congregation Emanu-El, while the second, the Ladies' United Hebrew Benevolent Society, was connected with Congregation Sherith Israel. The constitutions and by-laws of these associations were very similar to those of the Eureka Benevolent Association. Benjamin commented that in 1861 there were few claims on these societies' monies because there were few poor Jewish women in San Francisco (*Three Years in America,* vol. 1, 229).

Four generations of Harris women: Mrs. Isaac Harris with her daughter, granddaughter, and great-granddaughter, ca. 1912. Courtesy of the Western Jewish History Center, Judah L. Magnes Museum, Lipman-Harris Collection.

Whereas! It has pleased an *Allwise Providence* to remove from this *Sphere* of *usefulness* the *beloved Husband* and *dear Father* of the familie of our Sister R Harris who was stricken down suddenly by the Terror of Death and

Whereas! We are called upon to mourn the Loss of such a usefull Man who by the infinite wisdom of the Creator of all beings has taken from this earthly *Labor* and *Toil,* it is hereby.

Resolved! That the *First Hebrew Ladies Mutual Benefit Association* deeply deplore the Great Loss of Mr Isaac Harris and that we bow down with submission to the will of God who has so suddenly demanded of us this great Sacrifice

Resolved That we hereby tender our Earnest and heartfelt Sympaties to the familie of the deceased Isaac Harris in this sad Hour of their sorrow and beravement in the Loss of a loving and devoted Husband & Father

Resolved That this Resolution be spread upon our Record, a Copy thereof be transmitted to the familie of the deceased
Isaac Harris
We have the Honor
to remain Yours
Louis Licht
Louis Salomon
F Seligman[26]
Committee

---

26. Although the letter refers to "our sister," it was signed by men, for men commonly served as officers of female organizations at this time.

35
Benevolence across the Bay
Oakland Hebrew Benevolent Society, 1862–1880

During the 1860s there were approximately thirty Jewish families in the Oakland area.[27] When the Oakland Hebrew Benevolent Society was founded in 1862, its members were small shopkeepers. Its first president, Samuel Hirshberg, a native of Prussia who received a Jewish education and had taught Classics at the University of Edinburgh, arrived in California in 1852.[28] Unlike other small communities where benevolent societies expired when a synagogue was founded, the Oakland Hebrew Benevolent Society remained active for some years after the founding of the First Hebrew Congregation (later Temple Sinai) in 1875.

The following address was given when the society was consolidated with the First Hebrew Congregation on November 16, 1881.

October 5, 1862–November 16, 1881

The Committee of arrangement have appointed me, to give a history of the Oakland Hebrew Benevolent Society, which I have accepted, but to my regret, I will not be able, to give the subject the justice which it deserved, because on account of sickness and other causes—I could not pay that attention to the matter, as I first intended.—My friends will therefore pardon me, for only giving a brief Sketch of that noble institution, which stood since October 5, 1862, and is therefore of the age of 19 years and 6 weeks, and if I may predict, it will live and do more good, until time will be no more.

On Sunday October 5th 1862, some of the leading Jewish Citizens of Oakland numbering 14 persons, met in Convention, for the purpose of establishing a benevolent institution for Israelites in this City. After an temporary organization was accomplished, it was resolved; to name it the Oakland Hebrew Benevolent Society. Then the meeting proceeded to the election of regular officers, which resulted as follows: S. Hirshberg President, S[olomon] Adler Vice

SOURCE: Oakland Hebrew Benevolent Society, 1862–80. Typescript, Alameda-Contra Costa County Collection, Western Jewish History Center of the Judah L. Magnes Museum, Berkeley, California.

27. Rosenbaum, *Free to Choose: The Making of a Jewish Community in the American West* (Berkeley: The Judah L. Magnes Memorial Museum, 1976), 2.
28. Rosenbaum, *Free to Choose,* 3.

President, R Heiman Treasuror S Shultz, Secretary—S[olomon] Beel, J[acob] Letter and S. Mayer Trustees.[29]

A Committee to draft a Constitution and By Laws were then appointed, consisting of Vogelsdorf, Lissner and Davidson.

On January 1th 1863, Two months later the membership had increased to 26.

The most prominent among the members at this time, it affords me great pleasure to mention the names of S Adler, S Beel and R Heiman the latter two of which have preceded me into that undiscovered Country from whose borne no traveler returns. The former now a resident of San Francisco and although at present no more a member of the Society, he yet feels deeply interested in its prosperety.

On April the 5th, 1863

being the Constitutional General Election the former officers were reelected for One year.

On May 30th 1863

The first grand Ball was given in aid of the Society funds, Tickets to which were sold at 5.00 a piece and resultest, as the grandest success on the Pacific Coast at that time. The aristocracy of both Jews and gentiles from this City and San Francisco took the greatest interest and assisted in the good cause

The expenditure to the Society were about 600.00 and the proceeds amounted to 1130. thus realizing 530.00 net profit.

On August 2th 1863 the society were incorporated.

On September 5, 1863 the Society received a Sephar Ha Torah and a Shophar from Europe and on the 18th of the same month the same was Consecrated to its holy use, with great pomp and Ceremony, at which time 255.00 was donated to the Society by its members. Mr. Jacob Meyer then a member and who has since been gatherd to his forfathers donated 3 times 18.00 $54.00 R Heyman & S Adler also donated liberally

September 27 1863

The General election of Officers, resulted in the reelection of the same officers the third time.

On that day the Charity Committee reported of having paid out for Charity purposes 752.50 during that year

On October 1, 1865

The Hebrew Benevolent Society purchased 2 Acres of land from the Mountain View Cemetery Association at the price of 400.00 for a Jewish Cemetery.

---

29. Rosenbaum, *Free to Choose*, 3. Rosenbaum notes that Jacob Letter, Solomon Beel, and Solomon Adler were in the clothing business.

and on April 1, 1866 R Heyman, H. Ash and S. Hirshberg were elected the first board of Supervisors of the said Cemetery.

On June 24 1866

The Society sustained a graite loss, being no less than the death of one of its very best members and Citizens in the Community, namely R. Heyman the then President of the Society and Exoficio President of the board of Supervisors of Cemetery.

The funeral took place on a Sunday and was the largest ever witnessed, being under the Auspices of the Masons Oddfellows and H. B. Society the latter haven taken the greatest part in the Ceremonys—on account of the Consecration of the Cemetery, which took place on that day and were conducted by Rev. Mr Eck- man of San Francisco who named the ground "Beth Sholom"—Home of peace.

After the demise of President R Heyman S Beel succeeded him to fill the vacancy and at the General Election of September 23, 1866, he was reelected, and during the period of his office, the Society was very much prosperous, under his administration a fence was built round the Cemetery at a cost of 350.00

On October 9 1867.

The Election of Officers terminated of S Hirshberg being chosen President and S Adler Vice President

On September 27 1868.

S. Adler became President.

On September 19 1869.

J Letter was chosen the leader of the Society and October 9, 1870, he succeeded himself.

On October 1th 1871.

H Ash was the Choice of the Society to the presidency and on October 13th 1872 he was reelected as second term, under his two years administration the Society was starteled On October 26 1872 by the announcement of the death of the wife of a fellow member and Ex President S Beel, whereupon suitable resolutions were offered and the Society in a body attended the funeral. And on December 15 the same year again the Society was grieved by the announcement of the demise of a very worthy and Charitable member Daniel Eisner, whose funeral took place in the City of San Francisco under the auspicous of the Society, and one year later on the day of the setting his grave stone, the Wife of the deceased Daniel Eisner presented the Society with Silver Yad (pointer) as a recognition of her appreciation for the Society, and in return the Society passed a resolution: to have El Mollay Rachamim made for the repose of his Soule during the existence of the Society.

On the General Election

October 5 1873.

Mr J Marcus was elected President and on September 27 1874 he was reelected by the Society.

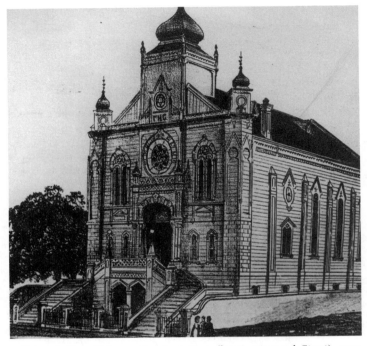

The traditional First Hebrew Congregation (later renamed Sinai), was incorporated in 1875. At a cost of $8,000 the congregation built a wooden synagogue capable of seating five hundred, which was dedicated on August 15, 1878, at 12th Street near West, Oakland. In 1881 the Congregation merged with the Hebrew Benevolent Society. Courtesy of the Oakland Public Library, Oakland History Room.

Under his administration on August 24 1875, a petition was send to the Grand Lodge of the Independent Order Bnai Brith for the granting of a Charter to form a Lodge in this City which was granted.

On the General Meeting
October 10, 1875.

A Barrett was the choice of the Society for President and October 12th 1876 he was reelected for another term.

Under the administration of Mr. A Barrett on December 5, 1875 a Conferrence Committee was upon motion appointed by the Society to meet with a similar Committee of Citizens to devise ways and means to establish a Schul in this place, and to offer $300.00 as a starter.

On February 26

The messenger of death again summoned one of our best members into the other world and another Expresident had to leave us hurriedly, while yet in the prime of life, it was my old friend Solomon Beel.

The funeral was attended by the Society in a body with J Marcus and Max Greenhood as Pallbearers

On September 24 1877.

D S Hirshberg[30] took charge of the Hebrew Benevolent Society, he was reelected on October 17 1878 reelected on October 10th 1879 [and] was again elected on October 10th 1880 and again reelected on October 1881, and is thus President of the Hebrew Benevolent Society at the present time.

Under his administration on July 2th 1879, a Conferrence Committee, consisting of D S Hirshberg J Samuels and S Hirshberg were appointed, to meet a Similar Committee from the first Hebrew Congregation for the purpose of bringing about a harmonious compromise between the two institutions, in order to strengthen both.

And on October 30th 1881, the Society passed a unanimous Resolution, donating, all the property belonging to them, unto the first Hebrew Congregation and ordering the President and Secretary to Execute a bargain and Sale Deed for the same which has been Consummated to day.

---

30. The son of Samuel Hirshberg, David Hirshberg was the undersheriff of Alameda County in the 1890s and a president of the First Hebrew Congregation.

III
Personal Struggles

5
Earning a Living

THE LEGENDS OF THE GOLD RUSH BUSINESS COMMUNITY ARE WELL
known. Perhaps the most famous myth is that a '49er named Levi Strauss
singlehandedly invented denim jeans. In fact, Strauss was a typical Jewish
merchant of the era, but atypical in his success. He arrived in California in
1853 and became a peddler before making a fortune, patenting metal-riveted
denim work pants with Jacob Davis, a Nevada tailor. Anthony Zellerbach, the
founding father of the Crown-Zellerbach paper company, followed a similar
path. More characteristic were the small shopkeepers, both men and women,
who often lost their shops and everything in them to the many natural and
man-made disasters that plagued the cities and towns. While some managed
to become part of the middle-class Jewish community, others failed and went
elsewhere to try again or returned to Europe. The only surviving traces we
have of some of them are found in city directories, invoices, advertisements,
and letters.

Business and social life were very much intertwined during California's first
decades. Young men fresh off ships, trying to sell their wares, often wrote of
their loneliness and financial despair. Alexander Mayer chronicled the ups and
downs of the San Francisco economy, the lives of his friends, the relations
between ethnic groups, and the city's gambling houses. The daily influx of
people and products to San Francisco created a climate where uncertainty was
the rule. The major decision facing most new arrivals was whether to peddle
their merchandise or rent a store. These stores, many of them mere tents, also
often served as homes, which left their inhabitants vulnerable to the fires that
devastated the city and took many lives.

A friend to many immigrant merchants, the American-born Sephardic
lawyer Henry J. Labatt chronicled the importance of Jewish businessmen to
the community in an 1856 article in the *Voice of Israel.* Labatt wrote in the

voice of an outsider; his exuberant description of Jews in commerce could have been written by a philo-Semitic Christian of the time.

Labatt should have included women in his assessment, for Caroline Tannenwald of Placerville owned one of many dry goods stores established by Jews throughout the mining country. Tannenwald operated the store under her own name, as California law, unlike that of many eastern states, guaranteed married women this right. Tannenwald's Merchant Intent Record demonstrates that both men and women bought, sold, and traded clothes, dry goods, and gold dust. The Round Tent Store that Tannenwald operated changed hands many times, as was common among Jewish merchants as they moved about the gold country.

Moving with the flow of Gold Rush prosperity was a typical pattern for merchants. Samuel Oscar Alexander moved from a mining town to a supply town and finally to the economically more stable city of San Francisco. There his history and options were recorded in an interview by the staff of Hubert Howe Bancroft, for already historians were aware that there would be interest in the foundations of the new California.

Advertisements and business records also tell the story of these small shop owners. Levy and Wolf were butchers who used Hebrew script to advertise a wide assortment of kosher meats in local papers. However, most shopkeepers were importers from the East Coast, selling clothes, knives, perfume, playing cards, and other merchandise—in Levi Strauss's case, Panama hats. Mark Levinsky of Jackson and Philip Schwartz of Columbia were typical merchants of the time. Both emphasized in their advertisements the volume of merchandise they made available. By naming his store the New York Dry Goods Store, Schwartz equated his merchandise with that which could be found in the nation's greatest city, while Mark Levinsky's advertisements stressed that his merchandise came directly from San Francisco, the port for all supplies coming from the eastern United States. Both merchants' stores were stocked with a wide array of goods. More unusual was the advertisement by a dentist, Dr. Levason of Nevada City. While there were many Jewish professionals in the larger cities, few risked settling in the unstable Gold Rush towns.

By the 1870s, some Gold Rush merchants had become substantial businessmen. Louis Sloss, Lewis Gerstle, and their associates founded the Alaska Commercial Company, which did business in the West as well as in Europe and Asia, supplying furs from Alaskan waters that were in demand throughout the world.

A different type of business was operated by the Stone family, whose dairy supplied milk to San Francisco families. Active members of the Jewish community, the Stones and the Koshlands (Mrs. Stone's family) were pioneers who had come to California for the Gold Rush and became an important part of the Jewish and secular communities, supporting religious institutions and fulfilling wider communal needs through their businesses. An observation of their day-to-day activities, recorded by Rabbi Max Lilienthal, documents the family's business and social life.

Through their knowledge of merchandise and salesmanship, and their ability to transport goods to the developing cities as well as small gold camps of the region, Jews became an integral part of the California economy.

36

Send No More Goods

Alexander Mayer, 1850–1852

There are many questions about the life of the Alexander Mayer whose letters appear below. Whether he was the Alexander Mayer who became president of a congregation and benevolent society in Sacramento, or even if he remained in California, is not known. What is known about the man who wrote these letters is that he was born in Germany, immigrated to Philadelphia, and in 1850 was sent to California by his uncle, Lazarus Mayer, to sell merchandise. Between 1850 and 1852, he wrote no fewer than twenty-seven letters to his uncle and to his friend, Edwin Bomeisler, in Philadelphia. During this time he tried to sell dry goods, primarily fabrics, clothing, and shoes. Written in a garbled medley of German and broken English, his letters suggest that he had difficulty writing in either language.[1] The letters convey the ups and downs of doing business in California during the early 1850s.[2] The most telling lines are those in which Mayer describes his state of mind after six months in San Francisco. "My wish is only to bring back Again whate I brought Here there fore it is impossible for me to tell when I go back again. You may really Belive me Since I left Philadelphia I look ten years Older. In all my Days alife I have not been so down Hearted as I have been for the Last 6 weeks."[3]

One of Mayer's setbacks occurred on May 4, 1851, when a fire destroyed most of San Francisco. Mayer lost close friends to the flames and experienced an overwhelming sense of despair. He knew the Greenebaum family from Philadelphia and the four men, ranging in age from twenty-four to thirty-one, who went back into their store to try and save the merchandise. The store, probably brick, was considered fireproof, but because of the fire's intensity the metal doors expanded and could not be opened, trapping the men inside. Their bones were found lying in a pile two days later.[4]

SOURCE: (1) Alexander Mayer to Lazarus Mayer, 1850, box 1, folder 2; (2) Alexander Mayer to Edwin Bomeisler, May 12, 1851, box 1, folder 1. Alexander Mayer Letters, American Jewish Historical Society, Waltham, Mass., and New York.

1. These letters were edited with the assistance of Ruth Steiner of the Western Jewish History Center.
2. The letters of Alexander Mayer were first published in Albert M. Friendenberg, "Letters of a California Pioneer," *Publications of the American Jewish Historical Society* 31 (1928): 135–71.
3. Friendenberg, "Letters of a California Pioneer," 158.
4. Gerstle Mack, *Lewis and Hannah Gerstle* (San Francisco: privately printed, 1953).

San Francisco fire, 1851. Etching, 1862. Courtesy of the Bancroft Library (1963.2.7-A), University of California, Berkeley.

1

SAN FRANCISCO 30th 1850.

Dear Unkle.

I arived here the 23rd Febr. we have been very long on the Road.[5] But Still we are too soon Yet, I tell You it looks bad about Buisness, it is right Flat. Plendy Goods are in the Market. There is no use to Offer any Goods at Presents, I really belive there are More Cassi Pants here. Than you can find in hole Philad[A] they do Sell from $42. to 60 Dollars.a/dz. Cassinet Pants fetch better prices from $36 to 50 a/dz. and even on those prices You can not Sell any. I am really Surprised. And Cord Royes Sell from $18. to 36—for 36 the best in the Market. Vest hardly no sale. and Comforts will fetch about the frait from 1[50] to $1 1/2 If they bring so much they will bring Good deal. Silk Mantillas not much sale Plenty in the Market. Silk Hkfs are a great Many in the Market Peaple in the North have got no Idea, for Instant. Boots & Shoes do sell at Auction for $1.1/2 what cost in Philad[A] $2 1/2. and another thing of every description of Dry Goods You Cant

---

5. It took Mayer almost three months to reach San Francisco from Philadelphia, traveling by way of the Isthmus of Panama.

find here. there is not a thing to be Mantioned, and Brown Domastics sell here from 8 to 10 cts. Prints cheap. every Iear they had rain here and this fall non. As dry as Can be.

I am in hopes that You have not Sent me any More Goods. at present. till I write for. —I advice You not to sell any Goods to Califor and don't discont any Notes who is Interested in the California Buisness I think there will be a Great Many failures here and in the North. A Great many Goods are stored up. in Philad[A] they make all Fortunes If they taulk about Buisness. in California I don't belive that Sternberger & K have not made a damn cents. and they been here in the Good times and there is a Great many others I shall ask. Marcus and Jonas Jacobs for the Money But I don't I get any. Jonas has left the City wentt to the Contry I have ask him before he left he said money I can't spair any But I pay Mayer soon. they are very Friendly towards me. invited me often to Dinner. I took supper with them they have got very large House belongs to them. and have got a Vinager Manf. there Building there Backery at present. the Note will be due from the 30th/2nd Febr I shall have the note protested any how then I see what I do. 0. I think that debt is perfectly safe. You will best send Friedlander's Notes out Sigmund Meyer told me that you get sure 50 per cent. of him But he says he would not settle without he gets. B. Einstein & C[o] Claim. I have got some damaged Goods for about 3 to 400 doll. I wish they were all damaged by the next Steamer I shall send you the papers I could not send them by this Steamer. I only got my Goods Yesterday they have been in the Custom House o/account them Bales they are Mighty Perticuler in the Custom House; San Francisco is quit a large City a Great many Gambling Houses You have Got no Idea what Saloons they have. You can not See any like it in Philad[A] I think the place is putty Healthy. but a great many Ratts every wheres. I am very well. But I have been very sick from Panama to S. Fran about 12 days long nothing But Fever. —I hope Buisness will be better after while there is enough Goods for the next 12 or 18 Months what is here and on the Road. And on Mexican Drad I don't Bilive much on it The Americans Have treated the Mexicans bad and have driven them out off the Mines there fore they will stay away. I don't know what I am gone to do till next week wether I take Store or not. You can't Sell any think in wholeSale at present not much no How. a little Store will cost me bout $200 a Months, and to Retail I have not got assortment enough and to Peddle in City is not much there are too Many. running. There were some Comforts at auction belonged Julies Jacobs first cost $6.00 sold $1 1/2 I shall keep my Comf. In Months of November in Course of 4 days the arrivals of Vessels were 139 from foreign Ports what you think of that. there is only one Vessell came in the white Squaw she brought Goods for 800. Consigners Buisness is down entirely at present And another thing the Creted Buisness is coming in Fashion too here. It cant be otherwise every body wants to sell Julius Jacobs has left in time from here. I don't know anything more to write. I hope this letter finds you and your family in good health. Regards to your wife and children. Again don't send any merchandise, also no coats and vest, there are enough here.

Cordial Greetings
Your nephew
Alexander Mayer
Fried Edwin

Please tell Your Mother I Saw your Cousin John & Jack they are all very well and send there best respects to Your whole Family and I have told them every think whate Your Ma told me Give my best respects to your Father Mother Eveline &c. &c.

I remain
Yours truely friend
Alex Mayer

2

San Francisco May 12th/51.

Dear Edwin

I take the liberty to write a few lines to you. This very minute I come from the Funeral. the Bones which we found Here Have been burried this Day. Dear Edwin the Losses which we had in this dreadfull Fire in the City of San Francisco Only Consider this four Lives, which have been lossed in this Fiere, Mr Greenebaum Baker Nusbaum and his Cousin Rosenthal. we have barried this four Friends their remains of Bones in One Coffin this afternoon. Now Dear Edwin You always told me when ever I write you to come, You would do so. I think surely we cun make enough. Now. britty much every one Cannot sent any more Goods t[o] this Marked. The losses have been to Heavy. Perticular amongst the Jehudem [Jews]. Dear Edwin I had britty Heavy Losses in this Fire. from 4 to 5000 But Edwin I am not afraid to make up again this Summer yust as much as I have lossed My Domastics I have got was offered 12 1/2¢ But I want to wait till the Market is settled. Edwin try that Leser sents Goods enough around the Cape Horne with a fast Clipper Try Yourself and come here, if your Parents let you go. I think we can make money. You & Me.

I remain Your
Truely Friend
A. Mayer

37
"Thinking of Home"
Salaman Bachman, 1854

In 1854, Salaman Bachman traveled to California by steamer, crossing the Isthmus at Nicaragua. He fit a well-established pattern of having a family member in the East send him merchandise by boat to sell in the West. Translated from the German, these letters describe his life in San Francisco.

San Fransisco, May 14th 1854

Dear Brothers, Sisters, and Brother-in-law,

With this letter I am glad to be able to let you know that after a 29-day journey I have arrived here safely and, thank God, feel quite well, which I also hope for you; I am only very sorry that I only arrived on May 4 and therefore had to defer letting you know my safe arrival until today. [. . .]

Now to the main subject [. . .] one can't sell much at present. Since I have been here, we had a few days when we sold more than $1,000 worth per day, and 20% remains; however that is nothing, and I hope that it will get better. Otherwise life is agreeable; for example, we sleep in the store on a mattress and blanket where the fleas don't let me sleep. In the morning I take breakfast with a German where I receive coffee and cake for 25¢. At [unclear] o'clock I take lunch where one can eat and drink what one wants for 25¢. [. . .] I have dinner with a Jew where it costs me 25¢ [. . .] at which time we close up and play or take a walk. In the morning it is warm. [. . .] Among acquaintances that I meet is also Dinkelspiel[6] [. . .] is still as before, but is worth money [. . .]

San Francisco in itself is not beautiful but will in time become an important city. Wherever one goes, one has to go uphill, since it is located on a mountain; however that matters very little to me. I like it quite well; However it is doubtful whether I and [unclear] can get along. Should that not be the case, then I will come back again next spring, which also doesn't matter to me very much, since I see so much that my calculation, as we made it often at home was correct. However I can only say very little about it. [., . .]

How is your business? Hopefully good, and I wish that you are content together. Should that not be the case, I would rather give $1,000 if I wasn't away,

SOURCE: Salaman Bachman to his family, 1854. Van Praag Collection, American Jewish Archives. Translated by Hank Hoexter. Western Jewish History Center, Judah L. Magnes Museum.

6. This was probably Lazarus Dinkelspiel, who arrived in San Francisco in 1853. A dry goods merchant, he was an officer of Congregation Emanu-El.

but I hope that you have enough sense to get along with each other; especially Hermann and Heinrich, the former shouldn't imagine that he has more to say than the latter even though he has a share in the business and even though he can sell a little more. I hope to see in your letters only contentment about it. You see that I am also in a strange business, and you probably know that I don't have to put myself back because of business knowledge; yet I have to give in and have to swallow much. But this is all for a short time [. . .] to keep my admonitions in mind, since you know that I don't presume anything improper of you, and should you do it, which I don't doubt, it will be for our best [unclear] which you will find out in time.

With your purchases I hope that you are making good progress and only buy good merchandise. This letter will reach you about June 12, when you will have made your most important purchases for the season, and I hope that those were only the best and most seasonable items; how does Hermann purchase? It is my view that it would be very good if you would take H. Clement with you to New York for a few days next winter, since he knows what sells well and will go for merchandise and best colors; however you will act according to your best judgment.

How is it going with my outstanding accounts? I hope that you will take an interest in them and get everything in, particularly the Caralers account and Abraham Williams account, which you can find out by Easter [unclear] and then several others; Clement should do his best to get them.

Should you not be able to sell the blue clothes, send them to E. A. Stern, and he should pack them along with (other items); I believe that I can sell them here. Also send me the silk fringes, these without hatting, that is the light blue, green with hatting brown, dark blue but no remnants; send those to Stern, and he shall ship them across the Isthmus, that is if you can't sell them, also the drab: but the cloth, if you want to ship it, must go around the Cape. [. . .]

Now what is new in Newberryport? Who sells the most merchandise? How well do silks, shawls, etc., sell? I hope you won't let yourselves be put back and not have too much. What is Bernhard doing? His brother is here and doesn't have anything to do and is unhappy about his life. He couldn't even get a job as a clerk, and the same thing happens to many. To David Steinhauser I have written; he wrote me that he wants to visit me soon, and I hope that I can sell him some goods.

Some gorgeous shawls are sold here at auction and bring $50 to 60 apiece. Should I be able to buy one, I will send it to you for the show [. . .] but black with colors embroidered, brown with white embroidery [. . .] here every day, and what is sold does not bring the original cost which makes business poor, but what is sold privately brings a nice profit.

Enclosed you will find letters from our dear Parents, and I will send them off with the first steamer; should you receive a letter, you will send it to me immediately but answer it first. I expect a letter from you with every steamer which leaves on the 5th and 20th of every month (Sundays excepted). [Following in English]: Give my best respect to Henry Clement, Sarah Clement especially and all the rest. I hope they enjoy the best health, which I can assure them from me and all who enquire about me, which I think can be easily counted.

This day is Sunday and am not much engaged except in writing, with which I amuse myself very much, as everything comes in my mind by thinking of home.

I remain your brother

Salomon Bachman.

[Postscript in German]

You may also send the drab silk fringes, also those with hatting if they don't sell well.[7]

---

7. These letters were written in a mixture of German and English.

38
"The Commercial Position of the Jews in California"
Henry J. Labatt, 1856

Lawyer and journalist Henry J. Labatt was, with his father, Abraham Labatt, one of the leaders of early San Francisco Jewry.[8] A member and officer of Congregation Emanu-El, the American-born Sephardic Jew was able to describe the mostly immigrant Jewish community in the voice of an outsider. Labatt believed that once these newcomers established themselves, they would reduce the prejudice against Jews by achieving wealth and behaving with dignity.

THE COMMERCIAL POSITION OF THE
JEWS IN CALIFORNIA—1856
By Henry J. Labatt

On a first arrival in our city, it becomes a matter of astonishment to all who see the large number of mercantile houses conducted by Israelites, being much greater, in proportion to the commerce, than in any other city in America. Every line of business is engaged in by them, with credit to themselves and honor to the community.

Among the largest importers, rank foremost many Jewish firms, the prosperity of whose engagements is evident in the large returns which are made on every steamer day.

The influence they command upon the trade in the State, the weight of their transactions, and the generality of their mercantile callings, may well class them among the most useful, beneficial and respectable merchants.

Each mining town and city had a large representation, and everywhere you hear of their success and prosperity, which in turn they devote to the improvement of the place by erecting substantial buildings and warehouses for the increase of their business, caused by industry, economy and attention.

In all the great fires which have devastated the settlements of California, they have been great sufferers. Year after year, have they seen the hard earnings of their labor swept away by ruthless conflagration, and yet, with the indomitable energy of their race, have they toiled on to regain what they thus were deprived of by misfortune. Often, indeed, would they not only lose what they had accumulated, but become reduced by being brought into debt by the destruction of

---

SOURCE: Henry J. Labatt, *Voice of Israel,* 1856. First printed in 1856 by the *Voice of Israel*, this article was reprinted in the *Asmonean,* Dec. 10, 1856, 76; by the *True Pacific Messenger,* May 24, 1861; and again by the *Jewish Messenger,* July 12, 1861.

8. For information about Henry J. Labatt, see chapter 3.

their stock. Even this would not deter them. The previous character which prudence and honesty had stamped upon them created unmistakable confidence and sympathy, and they soon rose above these accidents.

Everywhere they seemed anxious to guard against their great affliction of our country, and, by erecting substantial tenements, avoid another calamity.

In all commercial enterprise they keep pace with the marked improvements of the day, and, as merchants, are courted, admired—nay, even sometimes envied.

The almost universal success of the Jews as merchants, in California, must be attributed to some peculiar reasons; for while many of all nations have succeeded in this State, yet as a general thing, no class of people who began with so small a capital have accumulated the same amount of fortune. Any close observer will find that their individual industry dispenses with the necessity for extra clerks, who, at the exorbitant rates necessary for support, soon make sad inroads upon monthly profit. They seldom pay unwarrantable rents, being willing to submit to many inconveniences rather than indulge in extravagance. They eschew all display of brilliant fixtures or other unnecessary expenses, but study economy in every department of their business. Yet, after years of success, when they are conscious of their ability to display their wares and merchandise, then you may find a few who will indulge in such outlays.

Their method of conducting business is also worthy of consideration. They seem anxious to dispose of their stock in a short time and at little profit, and you will generally find, throughout the country, that their stores are known as the "cheap stores." This is a great secret of trade; and when once the reputation is acquired, the customer will seek that store. For the most part, they first seek this enviable notoriety for their establishment, and then, by courtesy and a determination to give satisfaction, success seems inevitable; and what is thereby gained economy secures.

Their quick perception gives them insight into the requirements of every branch of trade, and when they once embark in it they are determined to call to their assistance every available faculty; and the natural sympathy of, and connected with, the other members of their faith, incite them to an emulation, the result of which is a high commercial position in the community.

Merchandise, from the time it is freighted on the clipper ships until it is consumed, passes principally through the hands of the Jewish merchants. As importers, jobbers, and retailers, they seem to monopolize most of the trade, and our business streets are thickly studded with their warehouses, stores and shops. Their commercial position is high indeed, and without them now, trade would almost become stagnated in the State. The express companies of the interior depend mainly upon them for support, and the freight and packet lists continually abound with their names. This position they have not acquired without great attention, honesty, industry and personal sacrifice, and by unremitting prudence and civility; and they seem determined to add to it dignity and wealth.

This has had much influence in banishing the shameful prejudices otherwise existing against the Israelites as a sordid and cunning race. Practice and experience in California have taught our neighbors the falsity of these opinions. Nowhere in America is the Jew so well understood and so readily appreciated as in this State; and nowhere does he more deserve the respect and esteem of his fellow-citizens. May it always be so. May this abandonment of those prejudices be as lasting as it is just; and the Jew, as he is just and honest, ever merit that esteem and regard which has been so long withheld from his nation, and which always the liberty of America and the honesty of California, is willing to accord to his enterprise, economy, civility, forbearance, and capability.

39

A Woman of Business

Caroline Tannenwald, 1856

Caroline Tannenwald was one of a succession of Jewish owners of the Round Tent Store in Placerville. In fact, she owned the store on two occasions, once in 1853 and again in 1856. Several owners of the clothing, dry goods, and gold dust store, including Tannenwald, had been members of the Cincinnati Jewish community. Caroline and her husband, Lazarus Tannenwald, acquired various properties in Placerville before leaving California and returning to Cincinnati. In 1856, after a fire destroyed the Round Tent Store, a wood and canvas frame building, it was rebuilt with brick.[9] An 1852 California statute allowed Caroline Tannenwald, as a married woman, to operate her own business; by the 1849

Lazarus and Caroline Tannenwald, owners of the Round Tent Store, Placerville, ca. 1860. Courtesy of Betsy Klein Schwartz.

Source: El Dorado County merchant intent records, 1856, County Records, Placerville.

9. This may be the fire described by Bernhard Marks in chapter 7.

California Constitution, married women could own property in their own name. In nearby Tuolumne County, of the 131 documents recording sole ownership of property between January 1852 and November 1870, 11 were filed by wives of Jewish merchants.[10]

C. Tannenwald

Be it known that I Caroline Tannenwald of the city of Placerville Wife of L. Tannenwald do hereby declare my intention to carry on in my own name and on my own account the business of buying and selling and trading in Clothings dry goods and gold dust and of trading gennarlly under and by virtue of the statute Entitled and met to authorize Married women to transact business in their own name as sole traders passed 12th April 1852 and I further declare that the amount originally invested by me in said business does not exceed the sum of Five Thousand dollars.

Witnes my hand this 17 March 1856.

Caroline Tannenwald

---

10. Levinson, *Jews in the California Gold Rush* (Berkeley: Commission for the Preservation of Pioneer Jewish Cemeteries and Landmarks of the Judah L. Magnes Museum, 1994), 51.

40

A Businessman's Story

Samuel Oscar Alexander, ca. 1880

Samuel Oscar Alexander arrived in California in 1852 and became a naturalized citizen in Stockton. Before settling in San Francisco in 1858, Alexander briefly returned to Europe to visit his family. Like other Jewish merchants, Alexander was in the clothing business with family members. In the 1880s, his son-in-law, Isaac Hoffman, became a partner in his business. Alexander, a life member of Congregation Sherith Israel, died in 1894 in Merced, California.[11] This interview was made for the Hubert Howe Bancroft series.

Q. What is your name in full?

A. Samuel Oscar Alexander

Q. When and where were you born

A. I was born in Nakel in Prussia in 1836 Aug the 19

Q. What was your fathers name?

A. Oscar Alexander.

Q. And your mothers?

A. My mothers name was Dora Samuels; My father and mother were both Jews and my wife is a Polish Jew.

Q. Where was your father born?

A. My father and mother were both born in Nakel, he was a retail dry goods merchant there, he died soon after I was born and my mother took charge of the business.

Q. What kind of place is Nakel

A. Nakel is a small commercial place of about 4,000 people

Q. Where [were] there any other children?

A. Yes nine, I was the youngest.

Q. Where and for how long did you go to school?

A. I went to a private school in Nakel for five years, from eight to age thirteen. There was no public schools in those days they have only had them since '49.

Q. What induced you to come to California?

A. Well I was apprenticed to a brother in law of mine in the tailoring business, but my mother died, and a brother of mine in St. Louis wrote for me to come

---

Source: Interview with Samuel Oscar Alexander, ca. 1880. Bancroft Dictation, BANC MSS C-D 810.4, Bancroft Library, University of California, Berkeley.

11. Jacob Rader Marcus, "Samuel Oscar Alexander," *American Jewish Archives* 7:1 (1955): 85.

out because he thought there was more chance for me in this country; so my brother-in-law let me leave the tailoring business, I went from Nakel to Radling [Radolin] from there to Hamburg and from there to New York; I arrived in New York on the fourth of July 1849 and thought the boys with the [fire]crackers would kill me. I had never seen them before

Q. And then?

A. From New York I went to St. Louis, I was there for some time in business with my brother, then another brother of mine who was in Stockton wrote me to come to him and I agreed to go, I started on the steamship California a very small steamer but it was a very long trip, we had not been able to get a through ticket so we had to wait in Panama for almost a month while those who had through tickets went along; at last I got a ticket from a man who had died, I paid $100 for it, and arrived here in July 52 going at once to Stockton to my brother who was a merchant tailor I stayed there some time and then went into partnership with a man named Freeland the two of us buying out my brothers business.

Q. Yes, and how long did you stay there?

A. I stayed there until 57, I had got a little money and so thought I would like to go back to the old country but I could not stop there I did not like the country any more, so I came back reaching here once more in 58.

Q. What did you do then?

A. I opened a small store here on Clay and Montgomery but did not make a success of it; so I moved to the corner of Dupont and Jackson where I did very well.

Q. That was right in the heart of Chinatown?

A. It was not Chinatown in those days

Q. How long did you stay there?

A. I stayed there until the war ended which was in 66 or 67 then I went into the importing business, I opened a small store in a basement on California Street and did very well

Q. You had to send all your stuff by ship in those days

A. Yes, we had no railroads then, I had a man in New York who used to manufacture the goods for me and ship them from there

Q. How long did you stop there?

A. Well I could not have stayed there very long because I have been here for seventeen years, right in this building Since two years ago I have gotten into business with my son in law Isaac Hoffman

Q. And what are your ideas about politics

A. Well I have always been a strong Democrat

Q. Why?

A. Well I don't exactly know. I was always very much attached to the South, in local politics I have no choice.

Q. And you are still of the same religion

A. Yes I am an orthodox Jew and belong to a church on the corner of Post St[12]

Q. And you hold office in that church I suppose.

A. No I never hold office in either churches or politics I have enough to do to attend to my business

Q. How many children have you

A. I have three boys and two girls, two of the boys are with me in the store, and one girl is married

Q. And whom did you marry

A. I was married in 1860 to a Miss Simons in Stockton Street church,[13] her parents came from Poland, she was born in this country and educated in New York.

Q. And you have a very nice home I suppose.

A. Yes I have a very nice home on Van Ness Avenue, I used to live in a house of my own on O'Farrel Street but it was so much in town that I was obliged to leave it (children were born there.)

Q. And your children, do they go to school here?

A. Yes my children all went through the public schools

Q. And are they all Jews?

A. Yes they are all Jews although I never restricted them, after they got to a certain age I always allowed them to believe in what they liked I am sort of freethinker, you know.

Q. And do you think California is still going ahead?

A. Yes I think it is steadily improving and that it will continue to do so, but what we want is more immigration I dont mean Chinamen, although I think they are a necessary evil.

Q. How would you stop them

A. Well that is more than I can tell you

Q. And do you think that a boom does good or harm

A. Well I think that a boom does a certain amount of good

Q. And what is your idea on the tariff question?[14]

A. Well I think that most people have a wrong idea about tariff, I think a high tariff should be put on luxuries and taken off necessities

Q. And do you think wine is a luxury?

A. Yes, I dont think wine is a necessity.

Q. Do you think then that the tariff should be high on wine?

A. No I think if the tariff was reduced on wine we should be able to compete with other places. [B]ut it is hard to decide.

---

12. Sherith Israel was located at Post and Taylor from 1870 until 1904.

13. This was the location of Sherith Israel from 1854 to 1870.

14. In the 1880s a national debate raged between the Democratic and the Republican Parties over which American commodities needed protective tariffs.

Q. And you think San Francisco is improving?

A. Yes I think there is a steady improvement, there is no boom or excitement but I think it is going ahead, outside property is a good investment and is going up in price

Q. What do you think the population will be say in about twenty years?

A. Well I think it ought to be close on a million.

41

From New York to You
Advertisements and Invoices, 1850s–1880s

This section includes advertisements and invoices from the Jewish communities of San Francisco and the foothill towns. Some merchants, like Levi Strauss, formed world-famous companies, but most were small shopkeepers who served local needs. These advertisements and invoices show the types of products they carried. Gold was often the currency of choice.

San Francisco:
Advertisements and Invoices

1
Haas and Rosenfeld: Dry Goods Store

Born in Bavaria in 1817, Soloman Haas emigrated to the United States in 1844. After peddling in the Midwest and establishing stores in Alabama and Mississippi, Haas made his way to the mining town of Sonora in 1850. After a short stay there, he moved on to the more urban Stockton and by 1853 was living in San Francisco. There Haas married Julia Rosenfeld and started a dry goods business with his brother-in-law, Julius Rosenfeld. Active in the Jewish community, Haas belonged to the Eureka Benevolent Association and was a treasurer of Temple Emanu-El.

SOURCE: (1) Haas and Rosenfeld advertisement, *Weekly Gleaner*, Mar. 14, 1858; Haas and Rosenfeld invoice, Western Jewish History Center; (2) Levy and Wolf advertisement, *Weekly Gleaner*, Oct. 3, 1857; (3) Mrs. E. Blochman advertisement, *Weekly Gleaner*, Oct. 21, 1864; (4) Mr. E. Blochman advertisement, *Weekly Gleaner*, Oct. 21, 1864; (5) Levi Strauss invoice, Levi Strauss and Co. Archive; (6) Glazier Cigar Store invoice, Western Jewish History Center; (7) Dr. Levason, advertisement, *Nevada Democrat*, Feb. 1, 1860, 2; (8) Philip Schwartz advertisement, *Columbia Weekly Times*, Aug. 8, 1861, 3; (9) M. Levinsky Dry and Fancy Goods advertisement, *Jackson Amador Dispatch*, Oct. 24, 1868, 2.

HAAS & ROSENFELD

Wholesale Dealers in
Yankee Notions, Fancy Goods, Playing
Cards, Cutlery, Perfumery, Gold Dust
Rags, Gent's Furnishing Goods, &c.,
No. 96 California Street between Samsome
and Battery

Constantly on hand an assortment of
*MART'S, COHEN'S, DOUGHERTY'S,
CREHORE'S and FUK'S* Playing Cards.
S. Haas
J. Rosenfeld

2
Levy and Wolf: Butchers

Isaac Goldsmith, the *shochet* for Levy and Wolf, was the father of Mary Goldsmith Prag and a member of Sherith Israel.[15]

בשׂר

S. LEVY & D. WOLF.
SUCCESSORS TO
M. SELIG;
Second St. between Mission and Minnie Streets.

HAVE ALWAYS ON HAND A LARGE AND excellent assortment of

BEEF, MUTTON, AND VEAL,
OF a quality that cannot fail to recommend them to those who once honored them with their confidence.

They also have on hand home cured *SMOKED AND SALT BEEF, TONGUES, AND SAUSAGES* of all kinds.

☛ They employ MR. ISAAC GOLDSMITH.

N.B. Orders to any parts of the city will be most punctually attended to on the shortest notice.

---

15. In the late 1850s a controversy was carried on in the pages of the *Weekly Gleaner* regarding the abilities of some of the *shochetim*. Several times, lists signed by leading members of the community, including Rabbi Eckman, publicly attested to the competence of Goldsmith's work. Moses Selig served as president of Congregation Emanu-El, 1871–80.

3
Mrs. E. Blochman: Milliner

Nanette (Yettel) Conrad, born in Bavaria in 1830, emigrated with her parents to New York and later to San Francisco. There she opened her first millinery store on Stockton near Vallejo. After marrying Emanuel Blochman in the mid-1850s, Mrs. E. Blochman Millinery moved several times and was often the sole support of the family.[16] Occasionally the Blochmans and their five children lived above the store. As they were Orthodox Jews, the family observed *kashrut* and the store was always closed on Saturday.

Nanette Blochman, ca. 1880. Courtesy of Mary R. Hoexter.

---

16. The Blochmans' son's memoir is included in chapter 6.

4

Mr. E. Blochman

Born in Alsace-Lorraine in 1827, Emanuel Blochman arrived in California in 1851 after crossing the Isthmus of Panama. Active in the Jewish community, Blochman started a Torah school for children in 1864. Like his wife, a trained milliner, he worked for a time alongside his wife in a hat shop before turning to matzoth baking, dairy farming, and wine making. Blochman edited the *Weekly Gleaner* when Rabbi Julius Eckman was in Portland. He belonged to the Eureka Benevolent Society, served as the secretary of the Society for the Relief of the Jews of Palestine, and was a member of Congregation Ohabai Shalom.[17]

Emanuel Blochman, ca. 1880. Courtesy of Mary R. Hoexter.

---

17. The Emanuel Blochman Collection, containing some eighty items, is at the Western Jewish History Center.

5
Levi Strauss: Importer of Clothing, Dry Goods, Fancy Goods & C.

Levi Strauss was a dry goods merchant before he started to manufacture denim pants.[18] Born in Bavaria in 1829, Strauss emigrated to New York in 1847 and moved to San Francisco in 1853. He opened his first wholesale dry goods store soon after his arrival. In 1872 he received a letter from Jacob Davis, a tailor in Nevada who was making denim pants stronger with metal rivets. Together they patented the famous Levis® jeans. Soon Jacob Davis was supervising San Francisco production.

---

18. For more about Levi Strauss, see Lynn Downey, "Levi Strauss Invented Western Work Clothes for Miners, Cowboys, and Engineers," in *The American Frontier*, ed. Mary Ellen Jones (San Diego: Greenhaven, 1994), 272–76.

Levi Strauss, ca. 1860. Courtesy of the Levi Strauss Archives.

Small Towns:
Business Advertisements, 1856–1868
6
Glazier Cigar Store

In 1851 the Austrian-born Isaac Glazier settled with his brother Simon in Marysville, California, where the two established a thriving cigar store. In 1861 they decided to move to San Francisco, where they gave up merchandising and joined the San Francisco stock exchange with William Seligsberg. Simon Glazier married Clara May, and Isaac married Bertha Kohn.[19]

---

19. A large collection of Glazier family materials is housed at the Western Jewish History Center.

7
Dr. Levason

A dentist originally from England, Dr. Lewis Levason arrived in Nevada City in 1860 at age sixty-six. An editorial in the *Nevada Democrat* noted that Dr. Levason "speaks every sort of language and that he knows how to fit the mouth to pronounce equally well the liquid Italian and the convulsive Chinese."[20] After four years in Nevada City he planned to retire in San Francisco, but bad investments forced him to resume his dental practice.

TEETH! TEETH!! TEETH!!!

After forty years of practice in all parts of the world
Doctor Levason

By the advice of his friends, intends residing permanently in Nevada City. He has by him a large assortment of artificial teeth of French, German, English and American make, besides some of the most beautiful manufactured by himself, composed principally of California Quartz!!

Those requiring the dentist, will find the benefit of visiting the doctor, he being a thorough mechanic, they will have the advantage of watching their cases during the construction, and the years of experience in allaying the pain of a toothache by Galvanism, or if necessary, extraction with facility, with all operations of scaling, cleaning, plugging & stoping, will at once prove the advantage the ladies and gentlemen of this and adjoining counties will derive by visiting at his office, upstairs, over Block & Co's store, corner of Pine and Com. Sts., Nevada City, Cal.

---

20. Norton B. Stern, "A Dentist in a Gold Rush Town," *Western States Jewish Historical Quarterly* 19:2 (1987): 134–35.

8
Philip Schwartz, New York Dry Goods

In Columbia, Schwartz, in addition to owning and operating a store, was a
bonded collector for foreign miners' licenses.

PHILIP SCHWARTZ, of the New York Dry Goods Store,
on Main street, is one of the most enterprising business
men in the country. He appears to be
    determined, that no other store in his business shall
get ahead of him, in the way of keeping up his stock—
for he has got—
    All manner of things that a woman can put
    On the crown of her head or the sole of her foot,
    Or wrap round her shoulders, or fit round her waist,
    Or that can be sewed on, or pinned on, or laced,
    Or tied with a string, or stitched on with a bow,
    In front or behind, above or below;
    For bonnets, mantillas, caps, collars and shawls;
    Dresses for breakfasts, and dinners, and balls;
    Dresses to sit in, and stand in, and walk in;
    Dresses to dance in, and flirt in, and talk in;
    Dresses in which to do nothing at all;
    Dresses for winter, spring, summer and fall;
    All of them different in color and pattern,
    Silk, muslin, and lace, crape [sic], velvet and satin,
    Brocade and broadcloth, and other material
    Quite as expensive and much more ethereal;
    In short for all things that could ever be thought of
    Or milliner, or modiste, or tradesman be bought of.

9
M. Levinsky, Dry and Fancy Goods

Mark Levinsky of Jackson had come to California from Exin, Prussia, with his brother John in 1849, and was followed soon after by a third brother, Louis, and a sister Lena, who married a local merchant.[21] The brothers owned "Levinsky's Brothers" store until the late 1860s. After Louis and John left Jackson, Mark continued to operate the store, closing on the Rosh Hashanah and Yom Kippur

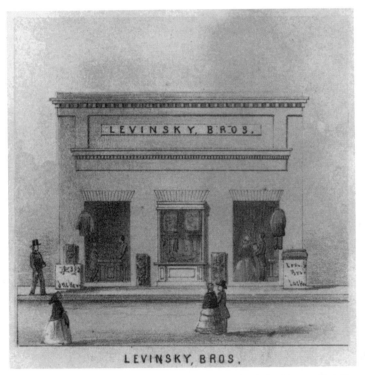

Levinsky Brothers Store, Jackson, 1857. Courtesy of the Bancroft Library (1963.2.905-C), University of California, Berkeley.

---

21. Louis Levinsky's granddaughter was Alice B. Toklas. John Levinsky was an officer of B'nai Israel and active in the community. Two of John Levinsky's children were buried in the Jewish cemetery in Jackson. See Levinson, *Jews in the California Gold Rush.*

holidays. Active in Jackson's Jewish community, he was an officer and a trustee of the Jackson Hebrew congregation and a Mason.[22] In 1869 the Jackson Hebrew Benevolent Society was organized in his home. Mark and his wife Fanny had five children, of whom three died in infancy and were buried in the Jewish cemetery in Jackson.[23]

Great Excitement!!

IT IS A MISTAKE THAT THE

SAN FRANCISCO EARTHQUAKE

Causes the excitement now reigning in Jackson and vicinity.

Reliable authorities assert that it sprang solely from the immense stock of Goods just brought up from the Bay by M. LEVINSKY, for the fall and winter trade.

In his store you can find now a choice and large variety of latest styles of

DRY AND FANCY GOODS, Clothing and Furnishing Goods, Boots & Shoes, Hats, (new fashion,) Groceries, (the best the market affords,) Furniture and Bedding,

And a great many other articles too numerous to mention.

Call and see him; it is a pleasure for him to show his goods.

---

22. *Gleaner,* Oct. 21, 1864.
23. The gravestone of Rachel Levinsky, the stillborn first child of Mark and Fanny Levinsky, is decorated with a rose bush with a fallen rose and is intended to represent a flower being cut from the family tree. See William M. Kramer, "Tree Art in Western Jewish Cemeteries," *Western States Jewish Historical Quarterly* 2:2 (1970): 91–100.

42

The Alaska Seal Business

Lewis Gerstle, 1870

Like so many of San Francisco's Jewish elite, Lewis Gerstle was born in Bavaria (1824–1902) and journeyed to California via Louisville in the wake of the Gold Rush. He first settled in Sacramento, where he met Louis Sloss (1823–1902), a fellow Bavarian who had traveled overland in 1849 and who joined him in operating a general store.[24] In Sacramento, Sloss and Gerstle met two other Jewish merchants, the Greenebaum brothers, who introduced them to their sisters, Sarah and Hannah of Philadelphia, whom they soon wed.[25] After several years in Sacramento, tired of the yearly flooding, the two families moved to San Francisco, where, in 1868, one year after the purchase of Alaska by the American government, Sloss and Gerstle and their associates established the Alaska Commercial Company.[26] This would make San Francisco the headquarters of the emerging fur, fishing, canning, and shipping empire on the West Coast. As the following letter demonstrates, Sloss and his vice president, Gerstle, were no longer small merchants but leaders of a trading company that conducted business on a global scale.[27] John F. Miller became president of the Alaska Commercial Company in January of 1870.[28]

---

24. For more about Louis Sloss and his trip west, see chapter 2.

25. Mack, *Lewis and Hannah Gerstle,* 24–29.

26. Of the seven original partners, four were Jewish. See Matthew J. Eisenberg, "The Last Frontier: Jewish Pioneers in Alaska," *Western States Jewish History* 24:1 (1991): 51–73. (In October 1983 the *Western States Jewish Historical Quarterly* was renamed *Western States Jewish History*.)

27. For more information on Jews in Alaska, see Rudolf Glanz, *The Jews in American Alaska 1867–1880* (New York: F. Maliniak, 1953).

28. Miller, a former Civil War general, went immediately to Washington, D.C., after his election to president of the company. He replaced Louis Sloss as the negotiator with the secretary of the treasury for the right to buy the first twenty-year lease for the sealing concession in Alaska. By August he had succeeded. Sloss believed that he was having trouble securing the contract because he was a Jew and that a non-Jew would have an easier time (Eisenberg, "The Last Frontier," 53).

Gustave Niebaum, Lewis Gerstle, and Louis Sloss in the Alaska Commercial Building, 1871. Courtesy of the Western Jewish History Center, Judah L. Magnes Museum, Ernest Lilienthal Collection.

Office of Alaska Commercial Company
No. 310 Sansome Street.
San Francisco, Sept'b 18th, 1870
Genl. John F. Miller.
care C. M. Hampson & co.
London.
Dear General;
    Not hearing anything from Hampson for some considerable length of time, we naturally supposed, that the Sealskin business had assumed a satisfactory basis, hence fully justified in the prediction, from the character of skins forwarded this season, that our next sale would show a considerable advance from prices realized at the last sale, we now fear however that we shall be disappointed in our anticipations and strongly suspect, that this branch of our business has not received timely attention on the part of Messrs Hampson &

SOURCE: Lewis Gerstle to John F. Miller, Sept. 18, 1870. Alaska Commercial Company Collection, BANC MSS folder 81/106 C-D, Bancroft Library, University of California, Berkeley.

Company to prevent results above indicated. Heretofore the trouble was with the unhairers the successful efforts on the part of Messrs [Emil] Teichmann[29] and Company however gave us reasonable hopes that no further troubles need to be apprehended in the future so that with the increased force of laborers the trade could be supplied promptly as warrant conclusions of a continued & active demand for sealskins in Europe as well as in America. We deem it most fortunate for the future interest of this company, that you have gone to London at this critical moment and confidently hope, that your combined efforts will have a tendency of arranging matters on a more permanent basis, than what has been the case in the past year.

Messrs Hampson & Company under date of August 29 reports to us as follows:

"The change we made about the dressing was none too soon to prevent the article going out of fashion. At the present moment the new men are turning out some 2000 skins a week & having surmounted this difficulty a month ago, we felt quite happy about the trade, but it now turns out that the dyers can only do about one half the quantity of skins that are required in time for this years trade, they have now on hand about 50,000 dressed skins, one half of which will not be finished until it is too late for this years consumption and our furriers are so unable to supply their customers, that they are beginning to recommend other articles. We have been obliged to interfere with this branch of the business & see our way clear to get it into shape three months hence and our furriers both here and in America will be encouraged to hold on to the article under the promise, that next year they shall have their skins in good time."

When we consider that three years ago something like 400 thousand skins came in market during one season, with no apparent difficulty for dressing facilities, it is somewhat strange, that the limited quantity coming forward at present should be subject to so much delay; we cannot expect the article to remain in fashion in the face of constant disappointment to the trade. Already in March last we wrote for 300 dress skins for Millers & Company as yet however we have no advances of their shipment and the chances are, that we will get them so late in the season, that they cannot dispose of them this year, the result is so precisely what the London furriers recommend to their customers, namely the introduction of other articles. If Hampson & Company have been able to interfere with this branch of the business so as to get it in shape 3 months hence, why have they not looked to it already 3 months ago securing thereby a full supply of dressed skins for this years consumption and warrant an active demand for the fresh skins coming forward at this time? If the unhairing and

_____

29. Emil Teichmann was a non-Jewish fur agent for the large Jewish firm of Oppenheim and Company.

dressing facilities can be increased to a sufficient capacity to finish dressed skins promptly and in proper season, no cause for a decline on the raw skins need be apprehended. It is most evident that with proper energy on the part of Messrs Hampson & Company the necessary remedy can be brought about, enabling us to conduct our business on a permanent & profitable basis; we are exceedingly anxious to hear from you in reference to this subject and feel hopeful at the result.

In view of the facts herein alluded to it seems quite probable, that the next sealskin sale will not take place as soon as we had anticipated and consequently we deem it best not to make any disbursement of the company funds for the present simply drawing against consignment to pay Merchandise creditors & Government tax, which doubtless meets your approval.

Should you be able to succeed in arranging matters satisfactory to the trade and give new life to this important branch of our business, we have every reason to expect fair & remunerative rates for the cyane cargo of skins, if on the other hand however, the season is too far advanced to permit any decided improvement in the manufacturing interest for this years consumption, it may be policy to offer but a limited number at the first sale and should there be any disposition on the part of the buyers to lower rates, we would suggest to purchase and have the same dressed for the Company's Account, in order to keep up prices.

We make this simply as a suggestion & shall be satisfied with anything that you may deem proper in the matter.

The decline of Seaotters was rather unexpected & it is impossible to surmise the object of the Russian Buyers to sell at a loss, the 410 we sent by Express were mostly selected skins and the prices realized show a decline of fully 30%. Our collection for this year will be more, than what we first expected and the stock on hand, with those yet to come forward from Alaska will probably give us from 1800 to 2000 for the next March sale at which time we hope the demand will justify the expectation of an advance.

From the Japan fisheries only about 30 skins have so far arrived in this market, which Louis Sloss & Co. have bought we have yet been unable to ascertain the probable amount of this years catch from that source, in the course of about two months or so we will be able to form a proper estimate, and some conclusion might be reached in respect to a probable advance or further decline of that article.

Trusting that you had a safe and pleasant journey and that yourself and family are enjoying good health, we remain

Yours very truly,

Gerstle

Vice President Alaska Commercial Co.

43

A Dairy

Rabbi Max Lilienthal, 1879

On returning to Cincinnati after the wedding of his son Theodore Max Lilienthal to Sophie Gerstle in San Francisco, Rabbi Max Lilienthal of Congregation Bene Israel wrote to the editor of the *Jewish Record* of Philadelphia describing his visit to Stone's dairy.[30] The dairy business was founded by Isaac Stone, who came to the United States in the 1850s. Stone married Hannah Koshland, who had come to California with her brothers from Bavaria in the wake of the Gold Rush.

A WEALTHY JEWISH DAIRYMAN

The dairy is situated about two miles from the city. After a pleasant drive we arrived at a stately house in front of which blooms a nice little garden, adorned with those rich flowers for which California is known.

Father and mother were out, which they afterwards sincerely regretted, but we were cordially received by son and daughter. After having rested in the parlor, we were led into the stables. One hundred and seventy-five cows were here fed and milked by four Swiss men. It was a beautiful sight, indeed; perfect order and cleanliness showed that Mr. Stone thoroughly understands his business. The old stable had been lately burnt down, but had at once been replaced by a new one with better and more ample accommodations.

From the cowstable we were led into a second one, built for the eighteen horses; to which were added fine accommodations for the milkwagons, the hay and the implements. Nearby is a blacksmith shop, an excellent well, and a diminutive gasworks (for lighting), all belonging to the dairy of Mr. Stone. The sons, who with the servants drive the milkwagons, showed us everything in detail, and though hardworkers, are perfect gentlemen, and look like health itself.

They told us that they had formerly lived in Sacramento; that the flood had swept away all their property, and left them penniless. But being known, both he and his good lady as hardworking, industrious people, the Israelites in San Francisco advanced them a small capital, with which they began to work; and Stone's family is now not only in good circumstances, but has amassed a nice

---

SOURCE: Rabbi Max Lilienthal, *Jewish Record*, Philadelphia, Oct. 3, 1879, 3.

30. This letter and information about the Stone family was printed in Norton B. Stern, "The Jewish Dairyman of San Francisco," *Western States Jewish Historical Quarterly* 14:2 (1982): 167–74. For more about Rabbi Max Lilienthal, see chapters 2 and 12.

little fortune. Many of our Jewish paupers may remember this example, which teaches that honesty, industry and economy will always yield a rich, golden harvest.

A few days after this visit, Mr. Stone and lady celebrated their silver wedding (anniversary). We drove out to the dairy again, and found there the best Jewish families, offering their congratulations, and their costly silver presents. The dairyman and his lady, adorned with silver emblems, received us in style; and their sons and daughters entertained the company to their heart's content.

The family of course, was invited to my son's wedding. I was pleased to see the dairyman's daughters in their silk dresses and lace shawls, and his sons in frock coats, white vests, cravats, and kid gloves, dancing with the millionaires' daughters. But after two o'clock in the morning the sons took leave, the milkwagons waited for the drivers. God bless these good folks; they are an honor to themselves and the Jewish community of San Francisco.

6
Family Life

AS THE COMMUNITY PROSPERED, MEN MOVED OUT OF THEIR BOARDING houses and stores, wives and children joined their husbands and fathers, and young men returned to their former homes to seek brides or married the sisters and daughters of fellow migrants. From a society that had been overwhelmingly male in the 1850s there emerged an increasingly family-oriented community in the 1860s and 1870s. Through letters, memoirs, and newspaper reports, this chapter portrays the patterns of marriage, childbirth, family life, and the ambiance of the Jewish home.

The birth of children brought new joys as well as new heartaches. The high infant and child mortality rates of the era were reflected in the proportion of cemetery headstones memorializing the passing not of the old but of the very young. With few relatives nearby to share in good times as well as bad, letter writing to relatives in the East and in Europe became a major family activity. The documents below range from M. Morris's spirited letter to his brother in Cincinnati describing his future wife, to a newspaper report of Annie White's conversion to Judaism and traditional marriage ceremony with Morris Frederick. The letters of William and Rebecca Mack tell of the birth of children, the difficulty of finding a wet nurse, and the celebration of a bris. With the extended family absent, traditional family relationships were no longer possible. Friends, fellow lodge members, and local dignitaries regularly took their place at major family events. In Nevada City in 1857, a gentile reporter witnessed the circumcision of a Jewish child. While the ceremony was a novelty for the reporter, it not only signified the birth of a child but testified to the growth of family life in the smaller communities.

One dramatic event was the circumcision of triplets in 1867 at a ceremony attended by San Francisco's Jewish elite. With a theatrical air, formal invitations were issued to this unusual event, which included a festive banquet and presentation of gifts. The *Hebrew Observer's* brief report disapproved of the participation of women in the ceremony, while the *San Francisco Evening Bulletin* mistakenly described the event as a "christening."

Another child of Gold Rush San Francisco, L. [Lazar] E. Blochman grew up during the Jewish community's first decades and describes his rearing in a middle-class Orthodox Jewish home. Carrie Goldwater enjoyed a more elite upbringing. When she married in 1876, her father, Michael, an immigrant merchant who built a department-store empire, arranged an opulent wedding. This type of grand party became part of the lifestyle of the families of newly wealthy Jewish merchants and businessmen.

A newcomer to the west, Rebekah Kohut experienced a different type of family life. The daughter of a rabbi, Kohut's memoirs paint an intimate portrait of Jewish family life—of the family's religious observances, the Sabbath dinner, her reaction to the San Francisco Jewish community and to the important men who visited her home and the city.

Like business life, family life depended on the regional economy. As men could afford to marry, they did, thus establishing families whose children became part of California's first native-born Jewish community.

44

Love in the Air

M. Morris, 1858

Written in 1858 from San Francisco, the following letter sent to Cincinnati notes the arrival of many women in San Francisco. The city was becoming more genteel and men were coming in from the mining areas to look for wives. Morris's wife-to-be was born in Europe and, after spending time in New York, traveled to California with her parents. As families were often far away in the East or in Europe, advice for one's business or love life was often sought by letter.

S.F., 11-18-58

Friend Isidor;

I think, my boy, that it is time to let you have a few lines, since I have already received two letters and have not answered any to date. The cause, my boy, is unfortunately love. [. . .] Have made the acquaintance of a young girl, but, my boy, you know only for fun (but it is so nice to have fun with young girls) [. . .] She arrived in New York and has been in S.F. with her parents for six months. [. . .] Even dear friend Sam Levy from Jackson is with the other sister; the one I have chosen is the oldest but, my boy, beautiful . . . the other, passable. Now I ask you for advice, since you can speak from more experience. As friend and brother you will stand at one side and give us good advice—isn't that so, my friend—I'm speaking with you openly, you know my taste, that it is all right with personality. I don't need to give you a description of her, since you know me exactly, lively, wild and very agreeable. You know that I like to flatter myself—but my friends were always glad to see me. You will find this letter quite ridiculous; but what aren't we men when we are in love? . . . but what good does it do? Nature has created us so, and it won't change. Show this letter to your dear wife, and she will say it is true.

I hope you are happy with her, and wish that in your marriage (a beautiful word) you won't encounter any dark hours, and every dark cloud, wich might fill the happy hours, be desolved—nothing more beautiful than contentment in marriage.

Regarding business, it's not a good topic with some one in love, but I can inform you it's still the same. California, one still makes one's little share, and if one is contented, it's good. Alexander has taken a store on Clay St. and is

---

Source: M. Morris to friend Isidor, 1858. Friendlander Collection, American Jewish Archives, Hebrew Union College.

expecting his brother by Nov. 29, since he had a letter from his from New York where his indicated that he would arrive in S.F. by that steamer. I can't say at all how it will work out in future; but I am very satisfied with you since I believe you have taken better care for yourself than he. Only be content, if you don't like it at home, California is open to you, which I don't want to wish. As I see from your letters, thank God you are doing well and you have a life companion who will share everything with you. But I am surprised that your dear wife has not answered my few lines, not because of courtesy but because of your friendship to me, to give proof that the same has also been transferred to the better half.

Now keep well and be greeted from the bottom of my heart; don't wait as long as I with your answer and remember me to your dear wife.

Most sincerely, Yours

M. Morris[1]

---

1. Translated from the German by Ruth Steiner, volunteer, Western Jewish History Center.

45

An Intermarriage: Annie Becomes Hannah

Daily Alta California, San Francisco, 1859

In 1859, in a ceremony that made news across the country, Rabbi Henry A. Henry of Sherith Israel performed the wedding ceremony of Anne White, a convert to Judaism, to Morris Frederick.[2] The following report was of such interest in the East that it was reprinted by the *American Israelite* in Cincinnati.

A very interesting ceremony of marriage was performed yesterday by the Reverend Dr. [Henry A.] Henry, at the Synagogue "Shearith Israel" (House of Israel,) Stockton Street, near Broadway, being no less than the nuptials of a descendant of the Children of Abraham with a young lady who had left the faith of her forefathers and espoused that of Israel. The intermarriages of Jews and Gentiles is by no means uncommon in the United States, though few proportionately, of the number enter the pale of the church. In California, within the past few years, some four or five Christian females have abjured their faith in taking Jewish husbands. The Synagogue was, of course, filled with spectators, among whom we noted a large proportion of Christians, drawn thither by the novelty of the marriage. The bride, whose Christian name was Annie White, with the consent of her parents, some days since voluntarily professed the Jewish religion and was admitted a daughter of Israel.

The instruction necessary to such a step was conferred by Mr. Henry, of this city, and consisted of both religious and secular studies, for the Jewish religion clothes even the daily business of providing food, ablution, &c., with ceremonial forms. These in a great measure are of Rabbinical origin, called Din. A knowledge of the Mosaic creed is absolutely necessary, and the Pentateuch, it will be found, contains a list of rules and regulations that ordinarily nowadays, would not be considered absolutely religious, although their observance certainly entitles them to that distinction. A knowledge of the Hebrew tongue is not absolutely required, for it is a portion of the creed that woman is an irresponsible party and the onus of her sins falls to the burden of the broader and more stalwart shoulders of the man and husband. No greater or more beautiful tribute was ever paid the sex, and the serenity and happiness which form such marked features of the Jewish connubial state, are doubtless owing to this fact,

---

SOURCE: *Daily Alta California*, San Francisco, Sept. 13, 1859; reprinted in *American Israelite*, Oct. 28, 1859.

2. For more about Rabbi Henry A. Henry, see chapter 1.

for the wife, like a true woman, looks up to her husband and relies on his judgment and support.

The lady in question, on leaving the Catholic Church, that of her birth, and entering into the Jewish, was named Annie, becoming Hannah Abrams, adopting that of the patriarch. The bridal party was attended to the Synagogue by the usual number of bridesmaids and groomsmen, and the different members of the bride's family were present. The party entered the Synagogue about half past eleven and proceeded to the reader's desk in the centre thereof, over which a crimson canopy was spread. The young couple were seated with their faces to the east, whilst the preliminaries of the ceremony were gone through with, such as signing and witnessing the marriage contract.

Dr. Henry then in a brief address in English spoke particularly of the peculiarity of the ceremony he was to perform, and asked the bride if she was persistent in her avowal of her new religious belief, which, of course, she was. He then in a very elegant strain admonished both groom and bride on the importance of the act they were about to perform, and the responsibilities they were to undertake and closed with a prayer for their future happiness in Hebrew, which he rendered into English as he progressed. No more beautiful, poetic, touching or applicable appeal to Divine Grace have we ever heard. On the conclusion, the hymns of the ceremony were chanted by him, the marriage contract read in Hebrew and English, the invocations and blessings said, the wine tasted and the fragile glass broken, and the twain were pronounced one; and Annie White, now Hannah Abrams, became Mrs. Morris Frederick. The usual salutes were exchanged, father, mother, sisters, brothers, and acquaintances bestowed the nuptial kisses in plenty, the whole auditory seemed infused with pleasurable emotions and peace, happiness and prosperity, as far as human wishes, sincere ones too, were showered on the youthful couple, and the company separated.

Both bride and groom are young—both possessed of more than the allotted share of human beauty, and we can only trust that their future life may prove the realization of their fondest hopes. That she will make a good wife we rest assured, for, like Ruth, she said, "Where thou shalt dwell, I will dwell; thy people shall be my people, and thy God my God."

After the ceremony, the bridal party received their friends at Pickwick Hall, where a splendid entertainment was spread. Toasts were drank, speeches made, and general conviviality prevailed until about two o'clock, when the company separated until evening; at the same place. At 8 o'clock, a large number of the lady and gentlemen friends of the bride and groom assembled, and a fine band of music being in attendance, dancing was the order of the evening. Until a late hour, the numerous company tripped the light fantastic toe, and enjoyed themselves to the fullest extent.

46
Sweet Child Rest in Peace
Rabbi Henry A. Henry, 1864

This gravestone inscription or funeral oratory for two-year-old Melville Greenberg is typical of the many tributes and epitaphs that Rabbi Henry A. Henry wrote for children. The child's father, Henry Greenberg, born in Bavaria, first settled in Placerville in 1854. With his wife, the former Marie Bergtheil of Bavaria, he moved to San Francisco, where he entered the wholesale clothing business. Both Marie and Henry Greenberg, the parents of six children, were members of Ohabai Shalome and active in the Jewish community.

Child of Henry Greenberg. S. Francisco
np
Sacred to the memory of Melville, the beloved and affectionate child of Henry and Mary [Marie] Greenberg. Born Nov 10th 5622–1861—died May 14th 5624–1864 May his Soul rest in Peace
Sweet Child, once your parents' hope and joy, Till Cruel death did their bliss annoy.
and tho' to Heaven's glorious bright abode Your happy spirit wings its destin'd way Your parents weep, while travelling life's dull road.
Your blossoms Cropped in early day.

Source: Rabbi Henry A. Henry, 1864, day book (including sermons and other writings), American Jewish Archives, Hebrew Union College.

47

Babies Are Born

Rebecca and William Mack, 1865, 1868

Rebecca and William Mack, the parents of eleven children, wrote family members in Cincinnati of the birth and infancy of their first child, Henry and their third-born, Hila. Rebecca, born in 1844 in Louisville, Kentucky, traveled to San Francisco across the Isthmus with her parents, Fanny and Abraham Tandler, and her two sisters, arriving in San Francisco twenty-eight days later in 1853. William, born in Bavaria in 1836, came to the United States with his brother Max and younger sister Lottie, both of whom settled in Cincinnati. William went on to San Francisco, where he married Rebecca Tandler in 1864, was active in the Jewish community, and served as president of the Young Men's Hebrew Literary Association.

1

San Francisco July 16th 1865

Dear Max, Lotte, Jette, Wieber, Alex and Remike

We received your dear letter of June 8th last week, and were pleased to hear of your good health. We are all quite well with the exception of myself; I am still troubled with sore breast, although it is not as bad as it was. The day before we received your letter, we received those things for the baby; for which, dear Lotte I thank you very much. They are really beautiful, those little shirts particularly, and I think it must have taken you quite a time to make them, as they are sewed very fine.

Dear Max, we are much obliged for your photographs and they all think it is taken very good; of course I cannot judge, not knowing you personally.

Since we have the wet nurse, our dear Harry is improving rapidly, and as Max says he is so smart.[3] Of course he is. He laughs and plays with anyone and begins to notice things already. We received a letter of congratulations from our dear Parents the same day we received your letter. They wrote a beautiful letter telling us of their joy and happiness on receiving the news that they were Grand Parents. We intend to write today to them.

SOURCE: (1–2) Rebecca and William Mack to family, 1865, 1868. William Mack Collection, American Jewish Archives, Hebrew Union College.

3. The use of a wet nurse was not unusual, but only family members usually discussed "women's problems."

I know of no news to write that would interest you. Hoping to hear from you soon.

I remain Your Sister

Beckie

My Parents and Sisters send their regards and thanks for Photograph.

[letter continues]

Dear Max, Lotte, Jette, Weiber, Alex and Emilie

This being Sunday and weather stormy outside I concluded to stay at home and devote the day to writing letters, the first of which is to you—We were glad to learn of your good health and can assure you that matters with us are thanks to God also improving. Beckie has been suffering with sore breast for 7 weeks and is not over it yet although improving—Owing to her sickness, her milk was bad and about 3 weeks ago the boy took sick and was soon reduced to such a state of weakness that we almost despaired. I was lucky however in getting a strong, healthy Irish Wetnurse, at once and in a week he had entirely recovered. He is now perfectly well, growing fatter every day and doing nothing but drinking, sleeping and laughing. As for his looks, neither our family nor my wife's can pride themselves on Beauty and the highest compliment can pay him therefore, is to assure you of the fact that he resembles his father most. You can easily imagine how much trouble and expense it has been; besides our regular expenses which are no trifle, it has cost me over 600 Dollars for Doctor, Medicine, Wet and dry nurse, Bris Milah and etc., etc, etc.; still neither Max nor Lotte need to be frightened, as the joy and happiness now that everything is progressing smoothly, is worth more than a thousand times the cost and trouble.—

Being on the subject, I might as well ask both Max and Lotte, what our dear mother would gladly ask in every letter, if she was not afraid. Is nothing in the wind yet! Now that the war [Civil War] is over, the only excuse Max has had is vanishing and I can earnestly hope, that you will think of marrying, and go to work seriously.— My expenses for the last 2 years were so great and my profits so small that my finances have not improved a bit, but if I should have luck in the next two years and a half, you need not be surprised to see me coming to Cincti, for I think of it and wish it, most seriously. For those baby thing dear Lotte we thank you and hope sometime to be able to reciprocate. How little we needed them you can imagine when I tell you that besides money and fine things her sisters made for her, my wife spend over 100 dollars for Baby clothes and this is far less than a great many others spend

From fathers letter I perceive that he expected money from me, which I was unable to send, except 100 Doll[ars] for their Bath expenses, and hope that you have send some as I spoke of it to you in some of my former letters.—You might send him all my interest on Bonds being gold, and thereby save exchange.—As soon as Beckie is well we hope to send you our photographs; thanks for yours. Answer soon.

My love to all Friends Yours,
William

2

San Francisco August 14th 1868

Dear Max and Jennie

It gives me pleasure to be able to inform you that my dear Beckie was confined with a girl on the morning of the 12th and both are doing well and getting along first-rate. It passed off about as quick as with Julian [the second child] and we can indeed consider ourselves fortunate in that respect.—At 20 minutes to 7 she woke me some and at 20 minutes past 7, it was all over—The doctor happened to live in the neighborhood, otherwise he would not have been able to reach the house in time.

I wanted to write to you at once but was too busy, and even to-day have only time to add my hearty congratulations to the new year [Rosh Hashanah].—May Heavens choicest blessings be yours to a good old age—have to write today to our parents and Lotte, consequently must close. Yours William

My love to Jette Weiber Isaac uncle Alex and Emilie, etc. etc. and excuse me to them for not informing them direct—but I really have not the time WJM

Beckie sends her love to you all, and wishes me to congratulate for her the approaching new Year.

48

A Family Ceremony

Nevada City Journal, 1857

The following selection celebrates the first rite of Jewish passage and witnesses the growth of family life in the Gold Rush communities. The article illustrates the survival of Jewish ceremony and the respect given the community by the gentile press, even if the reporter did not know a rabbi from a priest.

Local Affairs.

Circumcision.—We were induced to witness the rite of circumcision at the house of a Jewish friend, on Wednesday. The officiating priest was the Rev. Mr. Laski of San Francisco.[4] The ceremony consisted of first lighting a couple of candles, putting on of hats by the whole company present, procuring a glass or two of wine, and reading a portion of Hebrew. Second, introduction of the child, nipping in the bud, and a short ceremony of reading. Third, partaking of hospitalities, more reading which was all Hebrew to us, and adjournment. Those curious in such matters are advised to obtain further information by seeing for themselves, or consulting a rare old book a part of which is said to have been written by Moses.[5]

SOURCE: *Nevada City Journal,* Dec. 11, 1857, 2.

4. Samuel M. Laski of San Francisco was also a *shochet* who traveled to Nevada City to ritually slaughter animals for Passover (Norton B. Stern and William M. Kramer, "Early Nevada City Jewry: A Picture Story," *Western States Jewish History* 16:2 [1984]: 160).

5. For more about circumcisions in mining communities, see Levinson, *Jews in the California Gold Rush,* 118.

49

Triplets Circumcised for All the World to See

Hebrew Observer and *San Francisco Evening Bulletin,* 1867

On Saturday, June 15, 1867, triplets were born to Mr. and Mrs. Henry Danziger in San Francisco.[6] The boys' father, a pawnbroker born in Poland in 1830, had come to the United States in the early 1850s. Three months after their birth, rather than on the customary eighth day, the boys were circumcised in a public ceremony at Congregation Ohabai Shalome. The event was by invitation only. Those invited included the leaders of Emanu-El, Sherith Israel, and the benevolent and fraternal societies, as well as prominent military and public officials. When the triplets were a year old, a grand fund-raising ball held at Platt's Hall helped the family with the expenses of raising the boys. Two of the three triplets lived long lives: Abraham Lincoln Danziger died at age eighty-two and Jacob John Conness Danziger at age sixty-five. Isaac Andrew Johnson Danziger did not survive boyhood. The details of the circumcision ceremony were reported by both the Jewish and the gentile press.

1

Hebrew Observer

Circumcision of Triplets.

We mentioned in these columns some time ago, that the wife of our co-religionist, Mr. Henry Danziger, was delivered of three sons at a single birth, and that steps were taken by the societies of which Mr. Danziger is a member to have the ceremony of circumcision performed in an auspicious manner.

Accordingly, on Sunday morning last, the Synagogue "Ohabai Shalome" on Mason street, was thronged by men of all creeds and nationalities, by the representative men of our city and State, who were there by invitation, and who seemed to take a lively interest in this, to them altogether novel ceremony.

The ceremony of the rite of circumcision is one with which all of our readers are familiar, and though the secular press of this city gave it full attention, we merely make mention of it from the fact that it was extraordinary in its character, since triplets, boys, were not circumcised to our knowledge, anywhere, in this century, and inasmuch as such men as H. H. Haight, Governor

---

SOURCE: (1) *Hebrew Observer*, San Francisco, Sept. 20, 1867, 4. (2) *San Francisco Evening Bulletin,* San Francisco, Sept. 16, 1867, 3.

6. Norton B. Stern, "The First Triplets Born in the West—1867," *Western States Jewish History* 19:4 (1987): 299.

elect of this State, John Conness, U.S. Senator, and Maj. Gen. McDowell, stood as sponsors for the infants.

Mr. Galland, in his capacity as *Mohel* acquitted himself in a manner worthy of the best surgeons of the day. The triplets were presented from Progress Lodge, No. 125, F. & A.M., of which Lodge, Mr. Danziger is a member, though their secretary Mr. L Kaplan, with three gold medals bearing inscriptions of a Jewish and Masonic nature as also their name, being respectively, Abraham Isaac and Jacob, to which were added those of Lincoln, Conness and Andrew Johnson; they were also recipients of three silver goblets presented by Mr. Louis Ehrlich, President of Achim Rachmonim Benevolent Society, of which Mr. Danziger is also a member.[7] Other presents from various quarters; some very costly were made, and the Presidents of our congregations, acting as *Sandiks,* while our Rabbies and distinguished guests delivered short addresses at the sumptuous table spread, after the ceremony in the basement of the synagogue.

We may be pardoned in saying in conclusion that, while we do not entirely object to such a display on such a rare occasion, we are decidedly opposed to such a gathering of females, both old and young, on similar demonstrations. It strikes us as altogether out of taste for ladies to bend over the galleries to witness what modesty forbids. At all events we have never seen ladies in Europe, taking such undue interest in ceremonies like these, and we hope they will in future do as their mothers have done before them.

2
San Francisco Bulletin

SACRED HEBREW RITE AT THE SYNAGOGUE OHABAI SHALOME—CIRCUMCISION OF JEWISH TRIPLETS

During a portion of last week special invitations were circulated among the friends of Henry Danziger, to distinguished military and civic personages, and to the representatives of the press, to attend at the Synagogue Ohaibai [*sic*] Shalome, on the corner of Geary and Mason streets, and witness the ceremony of circumcising his three infant sons, products of a single birth. The hour for the performance of the ancient and solemn rite was fixed at 11 A.M. yesterday.

Before the hour appointed arrived, there was a large throng of people in waiting about the doors of the Synagogue, but none were allowed to enter who did not present the cards of invitation. At an early hour the building was crowded to excess and a large number of the ladies occupied the galleries. Gen. McDowell and Hon. John Conners were present, as was also Gov. Henry H.

---

7. Abraham Galland had served as a *mohel* and rabbi in Sacramento in the 1850s. One of the silver goblets is in the collection of the Judah L. Magnes Museum.

Haight, but he was obliged by another engagement to leave before the ceremony was finished. The various Jewish religious and benevolent associations were fully represented as follows:

Of religious—Emanu-El, by Isaac F. Block acting President Sherith-Israel. C. Meyer. President Ohabai Shalome. A. N. L. Dias, Vice President of the First Hebrew Benevolent Society—Wm. Stewart, President of the Hebrew Benevolent Society, J. M. Mariln, President of the First Hebrew Benevolent Society, and Joseph Bien, G.N.A. of the Independent Order of B'Na. [B'nai B'rith] were also present on the occasion; furthermore, the Chebra Achim Rachmonim had its representative in the person of its worthy President, Louis Ehrlich. The altar was occupied by Rev. Dr. H. A. Henry, Rabbi of Sherith-Israel; Rev. Dr. Elken [Elkan] Cohn of Emanu-El; Jacob Frankel, Reader; and A. Galland Surgeon in attendance.

Surrounding these persons were tables on which were placed goblets and medals of beautiful design, gifts to the triplets, glasses of choice wine, etc

At about the hour of noon Mr. Galland advanced to the front of the altar and exclaimed in the Hebrew tongue, "Boruch Habo," which translated signifies "Blessed be the comer." Upon this the doors of the Synagogue were opened and three ladies, wives of Presidents of Hebrew Churches bearing each one of the Babes came down the aisles and delivered them at the altar to the Godfathers selected for the ceremony. The infants were arrayed in elegantly ornamented dresses and caps. They were named respectively Abraham Lincoln Danziger, Isaac Andrew Johnson Danziger and Jacob John Conness Danziger—Major General Irwin McDowell held Abraham in his arms. Mr. Wasserman for Mr. Haight held Andrew Johnson and Hon. John Conness supported John Conness in his arms. A few preliminaries were had, and then the appointed surgeons performed the ceremony of circumcision. While it was in process each Rabbi christened each babe as he held it in his arms and placed a medal of gold about its neck. The infants were then handed to their nurses in attendence [sic] at the side of the altar. The medals were of solid gold and were inscribed as follows:

1st. On the one side pillar of strength, with the inscription (name of child Abraham Lincoln) and on the reverse, "Abraham offering up his son."

2d. Same design, name, (Isaac Andrew Johnson), and on reverse, "Isaac's blessing to Jacob"

3d. Same design, name. (Jacob John Conness); and reverse. Jacob sleeping and the angels ascending and descending the ladder.

These gold medals were presented by Progress Lodge. No 125, F. and A.M., through their Secretary, Louis Kaplan, Esq., Their value is at least $150.

THE BANQUET,

After the ceremony was concluded the invited guests repaired to the basement of the Synagogue and partook of a sumptuous banquet, at which Rabbi Henry presided, where appropriate speeches were made by Rev. Dr. Henry, General McDowell, Senator Conness, Rev. Dr. Cohn, and Jacob Benjamin.

297

Three successive goblets were then presented to the children by Louis Ehrlich. President of Chebra Achim Rachmonim, who accompanied the presentation with a fitting speech, to which the father feelingly responded. The goblets were inscribed with the words—

"Presented by the members of the Chebra Achim Rachmonim, San Francisco, September, 1867–5627."

On the reverse side the names of the children were each engraved in Hebrew letters.

The festivities finally closed with grace by Rev. Dr. Cohn.

50

Hats and Cows

L (Lazar). E. Blochman, 1870s

Written by a member of an Orthodox family and the son of a woman who owned and operated a variety of businesses, this memoir documents both family and business experiences. L. E. Blochman, born in San Francisco to Nanette (Yettel) Conrad Blochman and Emanuel Blochman, was the eldest of five children. His mother was born in Bavaria in 1830 and came with her parents to San Francisco, where she married Emanuel Blochman in the early 1850s. Emanuel Blochman became a businessman who operated a variety of shops and farms.[8] Observing kosher laws and keeping the Sabbath, the Blochmans always closed the millinery store on Saturdays. As an adult, L. E. Blochman moved to Santa Maria, where he worked as a clerk, started a high school, and eventually entered the oil business.

In addition to describing the childhood of a native San Franciscan, the following memoir demonstrates that women owned and operated businesses in early California while adhering to traditional Jewish law.

BIBLIOGRAPHICAL MEMOIRS with passages from diary
by L. E. Blochman

I was born in San Francisco in 1856. The one-story house I was born in, was located on the west side of Stockton close to Vallejo Street. [. . .]

My mother opened a Millinery shop near the part of town where I was born and was going quite well as she told me, but father's restlessness saw big money in the milk business and induced her, after about two years, to give up her shop and move to a leased place in the second Potrero of San Francisco called Hunter's Point. He remained there only about a year and then moved out probably in 1860 to the hills about a mile west of Mission Dolores. There was excellent grass there but not a house in sight west of the Mission. I remember once as a four year old boy I hiked some distance up to the top of the hill and beheld the San Francisco Bay towards Golden Gate, and was wondrously struck by the marvelous scenery, in contrast, I suppose, with the monotonous grazing lands about us. I was a lonely child then with no companions. Father

---

SOURCE: L. E. Blochman, biographical memoirs, ca. 1870. BANC MSS C-D 5123, Bancroft Library, University of California, Berkeley.

8. For more information on the Blochmans, see chapter 5; Mary R. Hoexter, "Emanuel Blochman: French-Born Orthodox Activist of San Francisco," *Western States Jewish Historical Quarterly* 20:2 (1988): 99–108.

then had a partner in his milk business and they delivered milk daily over a city route. It did not pay well, so I was told, so they gave up the business and father moved out to San Mateo County to do some farming on land close to where the cemeteries are now [Colma]. There the great flood year of 1861–62 swamped us out of house and home and we had to leave our house until that heavy January rain subsided. Records show that 24 1/2 inches of rain fell that month, the greatest flood year in a 100 year record.

Mother, who had come from Germany before she was married, located with her parents in New York where she had earned a living and better as a Milliner. She now thought that if she had an opportunity she could go into the millinery business again in San Francisco, but my father had no money so my uncle Abe came to the rescue. He helped her out and we moved into the city where we located on 4th Street near Mission for some time. Gradually the business improved and Mother made a fair living for us all with several milliner hands in her shop as I recollect.

I was then, when we moved in to the city, a little over 6 years old. I was sent to school at once and was interested in my work as I grew older. We must have remained in the 4th Street store with living rooms in back for about 5 years, a respite from the previous 4 or 5 years wanderings. I remember well the great San Francisco earthquake of 1865. We lived in this 3 story brick building and the building was badly cracked in places but did not topple down. But I can recollect having seen several brick buildings badly wrecked elsewhere. There was, however, no fires as an aftermath because there was no electric wiring in those days, nor even any gas stoves.

Our next move was in about 1867 to a one story store at 3d and Market, exactly where the entrance to the Examiner building is now. Mother evidently wanted to enlarge her business so that she sought this better location, where we remained for several years. I certainly must admire my mother's incessant work in business, as well as raising a family of 5 children. I was the eldest, next came my sister Hannah, then Herman, Bertha, nine years younger than I and the youngest, Rachel. Mother was a strict adherent to the Jewish faith and so kept her business closed every Saturday as well as on Jewish holidays. Her Jewish customers knew this, but she lost much of the transient trade of that day. [. . .]

My father, seeing mother's business progress, decided to go into the whole-sale millinery business, with the help of several excellent millinery workers. He did quite well for about 3 years when his restlessness and venturesomeness led him to invest in a flour purchase on account of the Franco-Prussian war of 1870 and the rising prices. But the war did not last as long as he expected and he held too long and sold at quite a loss which affected the stability of his business, which he was obliged to discontinue. Father stood for the Alsatian French side and Mother for the Germans. I was neutral so we did not agree about the war affair.

We had moved to a house on Everett Street near 3d, as we could not afford to live separately from the store. I went to the Cosmopolitan school on Natoma near 1st, where it had its beginning. I do not remember much about the school at that time, only that it moved the next year to the old South Cosmopolitan school building on Post Street (North side) below Stockton, where they taught either German or French or both, in its intermediate grades. [. . .]

My Mother's next move was to Kearney [Kearny] Street, close to Sutter—a good business center. Here she remained for several years, and in spite of Saturday closings, built up a good trade. She, with her well trained milliners established a reputation as a fancy milliner and had a wide scope of customers. I helped a little by delivering hats and also by attending to small purchases—all after school hours.

Now as to my schooling—I was neither a dull pupil nor a bright one—just an average pupil. When I was 13 1/2 or 14 I entered the San Francisco boys High School and seemed to take much more interest in my work. At the age of 13, Jewish lads of orthodox parents became communicants of the faith or ordained as members of the synagogue. They read a portion of the Hebrew scroll and occasionally make a brief speech—which I remember doing at the time. My Jewish and moral training by my father stood me in good stead on the virtuous side of life in the immoral atmosphere at the time.

In the fall of 1876 my Mother decided to move from Kearney [Kearny] Street to a new location on Larkin near Sutter where, through a building and loan she was enabled to build a store and two stories above for dwellings. Gradually the business profits paid for it and she owned store and house, free of rent. She kept on in business there for many years.

301

51
The Elegant Goldwater Wedding
San Francisco Chronicle, 1876

When Carrie Goldwater married P. N. Aronson in 1876, Congregation Sherith Israel was twenty-five years old, occupied an opulent building at Post and Taylor, and was led by Rabbi Henry Vidaver.[9]

Born in Poland, Carrie's father, Michael Goldwater, immigrated to London, where he married Sarah Nathan in 1850. Going to California later that year, they settled in San Francisco. After two years, they left for Sonora, where he became a merchant and a leader in the small Jewish community. He was a member of the Hebrew Benevolent Society and served as its founding vice president. Probably due to his business reversals, his wife Sarah established a tailoring and merchandise business in Sonora in her own name in 1855. Although Goldwater later became a successful businessman in Arizona, San Francisco remained the permanent family home. Sarah Goldwater never joined her husband there. Michael Goldwater, grandfather of Senator Barry Goldwater of Arizona, was a several-term vice president of Sherith Israel, and an officer in San Francisco's First Hebrew Benevolent Society. The following article is a San Francisco reporter's account of his daughter's wedding.[10]

AN ELEGANT WEDDING.

THE MARRIAGE AT THE JEWISH SYNAGOGUE YESTERDAY

NUMEROUS COSTLY PRESENTS—A GRAND WEDDING FEAST

AT THE PALACE HOTEL. AND A BRILLIANT DRESS HALL.

One of the most fashionable and elegant weddings that has ever taken place among the Jewish community on this coast was celebrated yesterday afternoon, at the synagogue at the corner of Taylor and Post Streets [Sherith Israel]. The contracting parties were Miss Carrie Goldwater, the beautiful and accomplished daughter of M. Goldwater, a prominent merchant and contractor of Arizona, and P. N. Aronson of Jacinto, Colusa County.

The synagogue was beautifully decorated, and the altar and pulpit being covered with a profusion of flowers. At 5:30 the bridal party arrived at the

---

SOURCE: *San Francisco Chronicle*, Sept. 14, 1876, 3.

9. See Morris B. Margolies, "The American Career of Rabbi Henry Vidaver," *Western States Jewish Historical Quarterly* 16:1 (1983): 41.

10. For more information about the Goldwater family, see William M. Kramer and Norton B. Stern, "Early California Associations of Michel Goldwater and His Family," *Western States Jewish Historical Quarterly* 4:2 (1972): 173–96.

synagogue and entered. The way was led by Miss Phenie Miller, who was tastefully attired in a white tulle and silk, trimmed with flowers; Miss Annie Goldwater, a sister of the bride, dressed in the same manner; Baron Goldwater, Teresa and George Goldwater. Next came the bride leaning upon the arm of her father. She was elegantly dressed in a white gross-grain silk, en train, profusely trimmed with lily-of-the-valley fringe and white fuchsias, and customary white wreath and veil; her jewels were diamonds. Next came the groom, attired in a customary suit of solemn black, who escorted the bride's mother.

The bridal party were

SUPPORTED BY EIGHT BRIDESMAIDS.

escorted by as many groomsmen. The groomsmen were David Bloom, S Goldwater, M. Tash, M. Hyman of Sacramento, P. Nathan of Colusa, S. Bromberg, E. Nathan, and James M. Ellis. The bridesmaids were Miss Lizzie Goldwater, sister of the bride, a lovely demi-blonde, beautifully dressed in an ecru silk en train, trimmed with fringe and flowers, jewels, pearls and cameos: Miss Rose Aronson, sister to the groom, tastefully attired in a white grenadine, en train, trimmed with white satin and fringe—jewels, pearls; Miss Rebecca Miller, a charming demi-blonde, who wore a flesh-colored silk, en train, trimmed with white tulle—jewels of onyx and pearls; Miss R. Lewis, in a white tulle, en train— jewels of amethyst and gold; Miss L. Greenbaum, in ecru silk, en train—jewels, pearls and gold; Miss R. Lewis, in white tulle, with ornaments of cameo and gold; Miss Josie E. Lande, in a lovely white silk, en train, covered with crepe delisse and white silk, with a garland of pink roses—jewels, pearls; Miss R. Mendelssohn, in crepe delisse trimmed with silk fringe and flowers, with jewels of pearls.

The main body of the synagogue was reserved for invited guests, and the gallery for other spectators. The entire building was crowded. The ceremony was performed by Rev. Dr. Vidaver, assisted by Dr. Wise. The services were very simple, opening with a prayer and followed with a song.

"May God Protect Us."

The sermon occupied about fifteen minutes, and was directed principally to the contracting parties. After the usual formalities the bridegroom delivered the solemn charge to the bride—"Thou art wedded unto me according to the Law of Moses and Israel," when the ceremony was concluded, and the bridal party retired. The presents, which were displayed at the residence of the bride's parents, were very numerous and costly, embracing one pair solitaire earrings, one point-lace handkerchief, one point-lace bob, about 200 cases of silver, and flowers, vases, bronzes and pictures in great numbers. After the ceremony the bride's father made a present to the Jewish Orphan Asylum of $100.

In the evening a costly and elegant supper was given to about 200 invited guests at the Palace Hotel. The *menu* embraced every delicacy tempting the eye and taste, and was gotten up in Mr. (Warren) Leland's finest style. Several toasts were drunk to the health of the newly-married couple, and one by

Rev. Dr. Vidaver to their health and happiness was concluded by three rousing cheers for them by the entire company. While at the repast a band of music discoursed sweet strains to those present. At half-past nine the guests retired to the main parlors of the hotel where a band of music was stationed, and

DANCING WAS INDULGED IN

Until an early hour this morning. An elaborate refreshment table was also spread in an adjacent room, covered with everything that could appeal to the appetites of those present. The toilette of the ladies present was very beautiful and costly, and silks, satins, diamonds and pearls were profusely displayed.

Among the many present a *CHRONICLE* reporter noted Secretary of State Beck, E. Wertheimer, L. Sachs, L. Wertheimer, D. Bloom, P. Anspacher, Mr. Coghill, C. Coleman, B. D. Wolf, H. Levy, Mr. Tobrina, and M. Tash. The whole affair was exceedingly *recherche,* and everything passed off pleasantly, nothing occurring to mar the happiness of anyone present.

52

A Rabbi's Daughter

Rebekah Kohut, 1875–1880

Rebekah Bettelheim Kohut (1864–1951) was born in Hungary, the daughter of Rabbi Albert (Aaron) Bettelheim. She and her family traveled west by train from Richmond, Virginia, when her father became the spiritual leader of Ohabai Shalome, the third largest congregation in San Francisco, in 1875.[11] Rabbi Aaron Bettelheim was one of the first rabbis of the Historical School (later Conservative Judaism) to serve in the city.[12]

After graduating from a California normal school with a teaching certificate, Rebekah moved to New York and married Rabbi Alexander Kohut, a scholar and the father of eight children by a previous marriage. When Rabbi Kohut died seven years later, Rebekah established the Kohut College Preparatory School for Girls, a New York boarding and day school for Jewish girls, to support herself and the children. She later became the first president of the New York chapter of the National Council of Jewish Women, a trustee on the board of the Jewish Institute of Religion, and a published author.[13] In the following pages she describes her girlhood in San Francisco, the visit of Isaac Mayer Wise, and her perspective on the city's Jewish community.

The state of California was at its period of greatest romantic appeal, and the glamour of the Golden Gate, radiating over the entire country, touched my father, too. The West allured with the many tales of the land flowing with milk and honey. To be a pioneer, or almost a pioneer, was a pleasing thought. He

SOURCE: Rebekah Kohut, *My Portion (An Autobiography)* (New York: Thomas Seltzer, 1925), 37–55.

11. Ohabai Shalome had 125 members in 1877. Born in Hungary, Bettelheim came from a family where firstborn sons became both rabbis and doctors. He upheld this tradition but never actually practiced medicine. Leaving Hungary in 1867, in part because of his non-Orthodox beliefs, he immigrated to the United States, where he served congregations in Philadelphia and Richmond before going west. In addition to his congregational duties, Bettelheim was a co-editor of the *Jewish Times* of San Francisco, published an array of articles, and worked for social issues, including revision of the California penal code (William M. Kramer, ed., *The Western Journal of Isaac Mayer Wise, 1877* [Berkeley: Western Jewish History Center, Judah L. Magnes Museum, 1974], 58).

12. Moshe Davis, *The Emergence of Conservative Judaism* (Philadelphia: Jewish Publication Society, 1963), 329.

13. Kohut's published works include *My Portion* (1925); *As I Know Them: Jews and a Few Gentiles* (1929); *His Father's House: The Story of George Alexander Kohut* (1938); and *More Yesterdays* (1950).

saw as his own duty in such a world not the hewing of roads and the building of houses for people to dwell in, but the building of a spiritual house in which souls might dwell. His thoughts of California were induced by a venturesome spirit rather than by a restless nature. So, when simultaneous calls came from congregations in Hartford and San Francisco, he chose the latter. After seven years in the dear old city of Richmond, he pulled up stakes and with high hopes turned his face west. He left several months in advance of the rest of the family to prepare our new home for us.

In the early autumn of 1875 we bade farewell to Richmond. At that time it took ten days to cross the continent—ten days in a railroad train! Our party almost filled one coach, as we were accompanied by a bridal couple and two boys whose parent had entrusted them to our custody. These was no dining-car service, so we were obliged to carry along our own food. The members of the congregation had donated huge hampers filled with foodstuffs, and at each stop we hurried off the train for hot coffee. How we ever escaped spells of indigestion is a mystery.

The journey was enlivened by our anticipations and fears. In the imaginations of the boys and girls of that decade the place of the "movies" was taken by harrowing tales of Indian warfare. The tribes were resentful over the many new railway lines that cut through their stamping-grounds. It was a year before the Custer massacre. As our train left the East, my brothers, at each curve of the track, expected to see Indians. As a matter of fact their apprehensions came true; on two different occasions Indians discharged arrows at the train— probably a gesture of resentment rather than a desire to do definite harm. Yet the act had its effect upon us. I was convinced that the Indians were as ferocious as I had been told. Later my notions were upset in a distressing manner. I was left without my perfected design of the universe when we found other Indians peacefully selling beads at Cheyenne and other stations.

The little house on Larkin Street, which had been furnished us by the congregation, seemed palatial. In delight and wonder we began our acquaintance with the city which only a few years before had been El Dorado.

San Francisco afforded the most vivid contrasts. Half of the city was still sand-hills; other districts gave all the appearance of a well-built city, conscious of itself and anxious to appear to good advantage. It was the most cosmopolitan city of America. One could see members of almost every nationality on the streets. It presented the curious anomaly of crudity and sophistication, of rough free-handedness and an attempt at culture. Chinatown was squalid and Barbary Coast sinister but San Franciscans preferred that attention be given their art-galleries and libraries, their flourishing social and literary clubs, and their public school system, which ranked third in the United States. [. . .]

Our home was the gathering place of an interesting group. All sorts of people came to us, among them many striking personalities. Michael Reese, who had been a resident of Richmond and later left $200,000 for the construction of the Michael Reese Hospital in Chicago, was a frequent visitor, though he had the reputation in his lifetime of being a recluse. Mrs. Apponyi, a California member of the famous Hungarian family of that name, exchanged memories of Hungary with us. John Swett, superintendent of public schools and one of the original Forty-Niners, became a dear family friend. Toby E. Rosenthal, afterward one of the most distinguished Californian painters, received at our home encouragement which was instrumental in making possible his first trip to the studios of Europe. Adolph Sutro was frequently in the Larkin Street house. Sutro was a name to conjure with in San Francisco in the seventies and eighties. Who did not know of Sutro, of Sutro's Gardens and Sutro's Baths, of "Mount Parnassus" and the famous Cliff House? He collected a magnificent library of rare books and precious manuscripts and decided to donate the library to the city and provide a building to house it. His visits to our home were for the purpose of consulting my father about various Oriental and Semitic manuscripts. [. . .][14]

Shortly after our arrival in San Francisco, Isaac M. Wise came to the city in behalf of the Union of American Hebrew Congregations. He became not only our guest but my father's inseparable companion during his stay, and we children got to adore him. [. . .]

The remarkable thing about the relation between Isaac M. Wise and my father was that they remained close friends in spite of the differences in their attitude towards Reform and Orthodox Judaism. [. . .]

Almost everybody except ourselves seemed to be enjoying wealth. [. . .] Although our poverty and shabbiness made no difference socially, since we were the Rabbi's children, yet my sisters and I were really unhappy. We blamed the congregation. We felt it stood between us and contentment. There was such a marked contrast between what, to our mind, was a rare human being and the compensation that was granted him. The root of the trouble was that San Francisco had too many congregations, and none of them thrived. This also had a bad spiritual effect. On account of the unhealthy rivalry among the congregations, they were more concerned with membership drives than with higher values. My father, so much a man of warm human contacts, was sickened by the petty competition, and chose lay associates rather than the company of local rabbis.

My brother and I often spoke of the situation, and in our adolescent way we expressed very decided views not only as to Jews and Judaism but as to rabbis as well. We did not see the other side of the picture. These groups were having their own struggles. Only inherent love for the faith kept the congregations alive. We did not realize, either, the common tendency of the heterogeneous groups— among Jews as well as among Christians—to consort with others of their own

---

14. For more about Toby Rosenthal and Adolph Sutro, see chapter 10.

temperament and identity of origin. Just as in Richmond there were the Polish, Sephardic (Spanish Jewish) and Ashkenazic (German-Jewish) congregations among the Jews, so in San Francisco, to an even larger extent, people divided themselves into groups according to their European backgrounds. [. . .]

Father's study was in the basement of the house. On pine shelving from ceiling to floor fitted against each wall stood his books in Hebrew, German, English, Sanskrit, Persian, Arabic, books on all subjects, medical as well, arranged in orderly rows like captains, corporals and privates, standing at attention. The long table was piled with newspapers and open volumes, evidence of the owner's constant association with literary and scientific research. My father did not require the quiet of the cloister for his studies; he could concentrate upon his work with a half a dozen of us about, and he allowed us to use his room for our study room also. He encouraged us, in fact, to browse there all we liked, and never labeled certain books as forbidden fruit. Excellent modern psychology that for one of his generation.

We soon learned how to use the reference books, but always supplemented our information by interrogating Father, who was glad to help us. His methods of teaching, however, were often at variance with current school methods. Nevertheless our teachers had great respect for us because there was someone at home who took such pains to prepare us for our school work.

And the preparation of our school lessons was a joy, certainly by contrast with our practicing on the piano. For despite our limited means, we were given musical instruction, the belief having then prevailed—does it exist to-day?—that no young woman could be considered cultivated and refined unless she could play the piano. Tedium, thy name is piano practice. I, for one, absorbed this sort of refinement under protest.

The library became the meeting-place of the family. For me it served the purpose of the drawing-room in a mansion. It was the one place to which I brought my friends, as it was the one place where poverty was not in evidence. One might judge from it that we were both rich and wise. I enjoyed the snobbery of it.

It was not long after we were established in San Francisco that I began to broaden my worldly knowledge by eagerly reading the periodicals, dailies, weeklies, monthlies, religious and secular. But my reading had all to be saved up for Saturday and Sunday, the week-days being taken up with school studies. So how to get the most out of Saturdays and Sundays became a problem. I had to appear at the temple Saturday mornings; then I was pressed into service to teach religious school, at which pupils were only one or two years younger than myself. And there was so much that I wanted to read, so many things about town that I wanted to see. For instance, there was the sensation of the moment, Dennis Kearney, the sand-lot agitator, the demagogic spouter who sought prominence by, among other things, pronouncing himself the friend of the workingman and inveighing in thunderous tones against the Chinese. Every speech of his closed with "The Chinese must go," a slogan suggested to him by a newspaper acquaintance.[15] My brother and I, having heard of the crowds that packed his tent to cheer his war-cry and curious to know what it was all about, went to his meetings on Saturday mornings before attending the Sabbath services. My father, strongly against such appeals as Kearney's to the baser passions of the mob, would have rebuked us sternly had he learned of our presence at the sand-lot meetings.

It was my dissatisfaction with the congregation and my duties toward it that brought me, by not altogether pleasant ways, more leisure to read and improve my knowledge. During divine service on the Sabbath, instead of following the prayers, I read the Bible, and at Sunday-school instead of teaching catechism, I used what I liked from the Bible as the subject-matter for instruction. The catechism was the only teaching manual allowed Sunday-school teachers in those days, and one morning, when the chairman of the school-board visited the classroom he was surprised to hear me telling the story of Ruth.

"Why are you not teaching the catechism?" he demanded.

Hotly, disrespectfully, I replied: "I teach what I please."

When he left the room I realized that my father might be an innocent sufferer from my outburst, and went home heavy-hearted. Surely enough, he was called to account for neglect of the Sabbath-school, and I was dismissed. Of course, I was fearfully sorry and repentant that my father should have been involved. Yet the bit of leisure was a great joy, and one of the direct results was an enlarged knowledge of American history, in some respects also revised knowledge; for San Francisco's version of the Civil War differed widely from Richmond's. Between the two influences, the Union finally dominated in my receptive mind, despite my mother's continued bitterness.[16] The San Francisco schools and a performance of *Uncle Tom's Cabin* made me an ardent believer in the righteousness of the Union cause. [. . .]

Friday nights at home were devoted to singing and story-telling. Forgotten were the little cares of the week. My father would have us be like a guild of singers, with himself as choirmaster. There was nothing he liked better than to direct the chorus and hear the hearty outpouring of our voices. He himself contributed a baritone of considerable volume, and among the girls it was the rich contralto of my sister Minnie that sounded best. After the singing my father's talents as a story-teller were called into play. He never failed to delight us, and we could listen to the same thing over and over again. Several of the tales he told us were published in *The Argonaut* and received high commendation for their interesting subject matter and charming style. Our favorite was the one he called *The Man With The Marble Heart*.

---

15. Denis Kearney (1847–1907), labor agitator and president of the Workingmen's Party, led protests against San Francisco capitalists, political parties, and Chinese workers.

16. This was her stepmother, who was from the South.

It must not be imagined that we were a closed family circle on Friday evenings and Saturdays. On the contrary. My father, with his big, expansive nature, believed in sociability, and wanted us to broaden our outlook through having many friends. The family's meager purse did not prevent our entertaining a great many people. My father would have been unhappy had he not been able to act as host. Every year, at the Passover festival, he had us invite our friends and teachers to our home for the first two evenings of celebration, the Seder services, they are called. They were memorable evenings. Usually there were about forty or fifty guests, a great many of whom were Christians.

Once I asked my father why he invited Christians.

"To let people see that we have no secrets," was his reply. "You can be made to believe fantastic things about people when you do not know them. But when you know, you cannot be misled. So many lies are manufactured about us—especially in regard to Passover—and they gain credence among the unthinking and the ignorant. But those who know us will see that these are lies. Throw open the doors and let people view us as we are. In this way we dissolve antipathies and make friendships, and when efforts are made to defame us, we will have friends who will champion the truth."

IV
Gold Rush Country

7
The Mining Towns

IN 1852 THE EIGHT GOLD RUSH COUNTIES OF SIERRA, TUOLUMNE, Calaveras, Amador, El Dorado, Placer, Nevada, and Mariposa accounted for half of California's population. In order to organize religious services, Jews in mining towns often rented halls from the Masons or Odd Fellows, for only in Jackson and Placerville were synagogues built, and only a few Torah scrolls were available. Known for its elaborate social functions for both men and women, Nevada City in particular became a social and religious center for the smaller mining communities. As was common throughout the United States, the Jewish community of Nevada City welcomed prominent non-Jews to their services. Founded in 1849, when gold was discovered buried in its river beds and under its hills, Nevada City had a population of six thousand by the fall of 1850. There more than elsewhere Jewish families observed religious tradition by placing *mezuzoth* on their door frames, holding Jewish ceremonies, closing their stores on the Sabbath and religious holidays, and keeping the dietary laws. In an 1852 letter to Isaac Leeser, editor of the *Occident and American Jewish Advocate*, A. Rosenheim described one of the first Yom Kippur services in the foothills.

A merchant in several mining communities, Henry Cohn learned what services miners needed, and how to purchase, transport and sell what they required. Cohn's writings paint a vivid picture of the symbiotic relationships that developed between miners and merchants. Bernhard Marks, a Jew who tried to earn a living as a miner, wrote from Spanish Camp and Placerville (then also known as Hangtown) about his day-to-day life.[1] Marks's letters illustrate

---

1. Placerville was one of the first destinations for '49ers. Incorporated in 1854 during the Gold Rush years, the town was for a few years the third most populated city in the state. It was the end of the Overland Trail as well as a stop for the Pony Express.

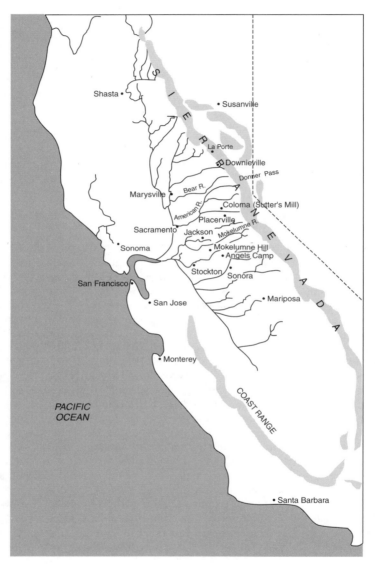

Gold in California

the uncertainty of life in the mines and in the towns, where a mine collapse, fire, or severe weather could quickly destroy weeks, months, or years of work.

Men also traveled to the cities to seek wives. Emanuel Linoberg, a prosperous businessman in Sonora, courted and married Pauline Meyers of San Francisco in 1851. Linoberg's mule train transported supplies from larger cities and river towns to his store in Sonora and hauled his produce to market. Twelve stagecoaches passed by his ranch every day, an indication of the large number of people traveling in the area. A letter from San Francisco printed in the *Asmonean* of New York took note of his wedding and especially of the arrival of women in the city. Linoberg's letter to Rabbi Wise, strongly advocating Reform Judaism, points to the level of thought given to Jewish practice in the mining towns, and to the communication of new ideas to remote communities. Linoberg's estimate of the number of Jews is high and includes those living in outlying areas as well. As a leader in the Sonora Jewish community, Linoberg offered his home as a gathering place for other Jews. Four years after he and Pauline were married, their home served as the site for the wedding of Hannah Barlow and Elias Gumpert.

While it is difficult to know much about the lives of women in the mining towns, the documents in this chapter reveal a few of the facts. In their *Ketubah,* Gumpert promises to take care of Hannah and provide her with a traditional Jewish home. Sadly, Hannah died twelve years later. Her obituary shows that the whole community, men and women, Jews and Gentiles, mourned her death.

The members of the Sonora and Columbia Hebrew Benevolent Society, in addition to participating in their local communities, demonstrated that they wanted to be counted as part of American Jewry. In 1861 Henry Stroup, secretary of the society, answered a survey sent to Jewish communities by the Board of Delegates of American Israelites. Though it lacked a formal congregation, the city of Sonora served as a site for Jewish holidays and a burial place for many Jews who settled in the southern foothills. By participating in the survey, Sonora affirmed its connection with other Jewish communities. Many of the town's Jewish merchants closed their businesses for Passover and the High Holidays.[2] But not all of Sonora's merchants were happy and successful. Store owner Selig Ritzwoller committed suicide in his store, probably because of financial problems. In his suicide note he expressed his hope that a Hebrew benevolent society in San Francisco would take care of his wife and children.

Men whose homes and families were in the larger cities often journeyed alone or in company to the goldfields. Isidor Choynski, whom we encountered in chapter 3, ventured into the countryside with his father-in-law in search of gold. They encountered hardship and illness but returned safely to San

---

2. *Sonora Union Democrat,* Apr. 11, 1868, Sept. 28, 1872.

Francisco. Not so fortunate was young Isaac Lurch, who died in Lancha Plana and was buried in Mokelumne Hill in 1859. At the height of the Gold Rush, Mokelumne Hill had a population of nearly ten thousand and boasted an active Jewish community that included a Hebrew benevolent society for men and a separate society for women.

Placerville to the north, a local center for many mining camps, had a substantial Jewish community, with a synagogue building, several fraternal organizations, and a consecrated cemetery. It was during the High Holiday observance that bar mitzvot were celebrated in Gold Rush communities. In most towns it was difficult for boys to obtain a religious education; teachers for most bar mitzvah boys were their fathers or close relatives. The lack of Jewish education for children was often noted by visitors and in documents of the day.[3] The movement toward reform Judaism may have been an additional reason for the small number of bar mitzvot. Nathan Kohn and Samuel Louis celebrated their bar mitzvot on Rosh Hashanah in Placerville in 1867. Their fathers were active in the Jewish community, as becomes clear in Julius Goldner's descriptive letter to Isaac Mayer Wise, written six years after the bar mitzvot in 1873, when the community was already in decline. Henry Raphael, a local businessman, describes his visits to non-Jewish families and his dislike of intermarriage. His letter, like most of the letters and documents from the mining towns, incorporates business and personal values as well as a longing for Jewish traditions, family and friends.

Located in Amador County between Sutter Creek and the Mokelumne River, Jackson was a good stopping off point for miners because of its spring. By 1859 agriculture had become more important than mining to the economy of the community. The Jackson Jewish community built a synagogue in a central place to serve their local community as well as the surrounding towns and gold camps. The constitution of the congregation had several interesting features. Usually a congregation held elections in the spring or on Rosh Hashanah, not after a fast day, but the election of officers in Jackson took place on Yom Kippur night—probably because this was the only day of the year that the entire membership came together. Intermarriage was discouraged by prohibiting synagogue membership to Jews who were married to non-Jews. In addition, one could lose one's membership for doing business on the High Holidays, if not on other holidays, though the fines were low compared to those assessed by the 1851 constitution of San Francisco's Sherith Israel.

In most foothill communities, Jewish worship ended in the late 1870s and 1880s, when congregations disbanded as their members left. Some had intermarried and others had left Judaism altogether, but most had moved to San Francisco, Sacramento, and other larger cities.

---

3. Benjamin, *Three Years in America,* 28.

53
The Day of Atonement in Nevada City
A. Rosenheim, 1852

Aaron Rosenheim was a merchant, a trustee of the Nevada Hebrew Society, an amateur actor, and a member of the Nevada Rifles, an association that sponsored military and civic balls. Men like Rosenheim often wrote descriptions of their lives and communities to the editor of the *Occident and Jewish American Advocate,* Isaac Leeser, and offered their services as agents for the newspaper. Leeser published excerpts from Rosenheim's letter, one of the first accounts of High Holiday services in a mining community.[4] By the 1870s Rosenheim, like many others, had left for San Francisco.[5]

Nevada City, California, Dec. 28, 1852
Mr. Isaac Leeser.
Dear Sir:
Having lately become a subscriber to your invaluable journal, The Occident, the third Number of which I have received and read with interest and satisfaction. I am under the impression that a few words from this distant land for our cause may not be uninteresting. I will therefore give you a short history of the advancement of our principles in this part of the world. Two years ago when I first arrived in this place it was but a small mining village, there were but about 5 o[r] 6 Jews in the place, but the place having grown to some importance, many of our Jewish brethren have wended their way hither, and there are now no less than 30 Jews here the most of whom are willing to close their stores and suspend business on our great holidays as was shown on last Rosh Hashoneh and Yom Kippur. We all assembled at a place to arrange things for the above named days. We appointed a committee to obtain a Hall. The Masonic fraternity of this place having been made acquainted with our request very generously tendered us the free use of their spacious Hall, the room was appropriately furnished and the Ceremonies conducted with dignity and ability, the Room was crowded with Visitors, who were anxious to visit our ceremonies. Among the visitors were the first Citizens of the place, the Judges of Courts, &c, and

SOURCE: A. Rosenheim to Isaac Leeser, 1852. Isaac Leeser Collection, Center for Judaic Studies Library, University of Pennsylvania. Microfilm courtesy of Hebrew Union College.

4. Excerpts from the letter were published in the *Occident and American Jewish Advocate,* May 1853, 124.
5. Stern and Kramer, "Early Nevada City Jewry," 158, 166.

all expressed their entire satisfaction at our ancient and holy ceremonies and proceedings which were conducted with profound respect. Our Hasan for the occasion was Mr. Leo of New York, a man of considerable ability, but of course there were others who took their respective parts and conducted themselves with credit, the whole passed off finely and to the satisfaction of all.[6] So much for us of this new land. Dear sir, I am not in the habit of communicating except with my Relatives at home, which is done in the German language principally, but on this the first occasion, I felt it a pleasure to do so. I will try to obtain as many subscribers for the Occident as possible, and if you wish me to act as your agent I will act for you cheerfully.

in the meantime
I remain Truly Yours
A. Rosenheim.
To Rev. Isaac Leeser, Philada.

---

6. The *Nevada City Journal,* Sept. 17, 1852, printed a thank-you note from the congregation to the Masons for the use of their hall on that occasion. One of the signatories was A. Rosenheim (Levinson, *Jews in the California Gold Rush,* 92).

54
A Merchant of Poker Flat and Saint Louis
Henry Cohn, ca. 1856

This account continues Henry Cohn's chronicle from his arrival in California, recorded in chapter 2, through his life as a merchant in Saint Louis and Poker Flat during the Gold Rush and his decision to return to Europe.[7]

I knew that a cousin of mine, Jacob Heimann, together with H. Mendelsohn, also a relative, operated a business in Saint Louis, Sierra County, in the gold-mining country, I wrote asking them whether they could advise me to come there. In spite of the discouraging reply of bad times and poor opportunities, I set out for the place, first by taking the steamer from San Francisco to Marysville, from there by walking approximately fifty miles into the mountains to La Porte,[8] and finally five miles up to Saint Louis.[9] My relatives were of course very surprised at my sudden arrival but soon discovered that I made myself very useful in their business.

Saint Louis was a very lively gold-mining village, consisting of from twenty to twenty-five wooden houses among which were three good merchandise stores, a cigar store, a bank, Wells Fargo & Co., a fine French restaurant and hotel, a butcher, a baker, an American and a German doctor, a livery stable, etc. The place was really populated only on Saturdays and Sundays when the miners showed up to sell their gold and buy the things they needed for the following week. Numerous gamblers and card players appeared simultaneously with them. The gold miners sold their gold to the bank or to the storekeepers; the price paid for the gold varied according to its quality and origin and averaged about $18.00 per ounce. The crude gold was then melted and purified. By Sunday night, little of the money which the miners had received for their gold remained in their hands; most of it was carried away by the gamblers. In this manner life proceeded from early spring until late fall, at least as long as the mining continued to be so productive. The mining activity practically ceased

SOURCE: "Saint Louis and Poker Flat in the Fifties and Sixties from the Jugenderinnerungen of Henry Cohn," ed. Fritz Ludwig Cohn, *California Historical Society Quarterly* 19:4 (1940): 289–98.

7. For more about Henry Cohn see chapter 2. Fritz Cohn is a grandson of Henry Cohn. A version of this narrative was published by Fritz L. Cohn as "Poker Flat: A Journey in the New World," *International Quarterly* 5:2 (1941): 33–36, 61.
8. Named in 1857 after La Porte, Indiana.
9. Founded in 1852 by Missourians, Saint Louis was destroyed by fire in 1857 and rebuilt in the 1860s for hydraulic mining.

LA PORTE, SIERRA COUNTY, CAL.,
(MAIN STREET.)

Published by **Dr. E. L. Willard**, *dealer in*

BOOKS AND MEDICINES, LA PORTE.

ESTABLISHED IN 1858.

This prettily-located mountain mining town is situated on the bank of Rabbit Creek, after which it was formerly named, and on the dividing ridge between Yuba and Feather rivers, at an altitude of 4500 feet above the sea. From Marysville it is sixty-one miles, and from Downieville twenty miles. Gold was discovered here and at the head of Little Grass Valley in the fall of 1850, by Hamilton Ward and Brother and Jas. Murray. Siller's water ditch was completed in 1851 Hydraulic diggings were commenced in 1852, when Foster's ditch was finished. In 1854 a number of new buildings were erected, forming the Main Street. In 1855 the "Martindale" ditch, which is now known as the "Geeslin Ditch," was finished, which is the greatest ditch running into this place at the present day, furnishing about 1200 inches of water, which sells for fifty cents an inch per day, which was at first sold for one dollar per inch a day. Fuller & Buel were the first in Sierra County to build a brick building here, being fire-proof, and others were soon after built. At a public meeting in 1857, the name of the town was altered to La Porte, its present name. Bald Mountain, 1000 feet above the town, one-half mile distant to the northeast, is a *high old* prospecting place for the citizens to view the surrounding country, as far as the eye can reach on the horizon. In 1858 a fine spring of water was brought in to the town in wooden pipes by B. W. Barnes, the present proprietor, who, through lead pipes and cocks, delivers it to the families pure as melted ice can well be. An excellent weekly newspaper, devoted to the interest of patrons, called the *Mountain Messenger*, was started in 1855. A sweeping fire carried away the whole of the business part of the town, with three exceptions, destroying a hundred and fifty thousand dollars worth of property, and only thirty thousand insured. The town has been rebuilt, with great improvements, there now being thirteen fire-proof stores and brick buildings, and the business firms are becoming more permanent, and the mines are being worked to a much greater advantage than in former years, and the miners not to travel, nt. since this county has the wealth and men to turn out more treasure than any other county in the State, however large others may be, which fact has been proven for many years past. There is a Methodist and a Catholic Church in the town, and a Social Hall; also a Masonic Lodge and Odd Fellows' Hall, both of which are in a flourishing condition, and show plainly their influence in the town over society generally for sobriety and morality, and, in fact, every thing which makes society in a small town agreeable and pleasant. Quartz mining in gold and silver are now attracting miners and capitalists to this vicinity, and will greatly enhance the property of this locality.

Henry Cohn's La Porte, 1858. Courtesy of the Bancroft Library (1963.2.681/2.A), University of California, Berkeley.

at the end of every October and did not begin again until March, since the deep snow, often reaching the roofs of the houses, made working impossible.

For a short period after my arrival I peddled my merchandise, visiting the towns of La Porte, Pine Grove, Downieville, etc. Although my "loyal" mule was of valuable assistance on my travels in this mountainous region, this kind of occupation was very cumbersome. Moreover, very few women, who were my best customers, lived in this gold-mining region.

The business of my relatives, Mendelsohn & Co., consisted of a main store in Saint Louis and a branch in Poker Flat, about four miles from Saint Louis. It was a prosperous undertaking, and I found plenty of work for myself. All our buying was done either in Marysville or directly in San Francisco. For the transportation of our goods from Marysville into the mountains we employed our own pack-train of forty mules, otherwise one had to pay from $50.00 to $60.00 per hundred pounds from San Francisco to Poker Flat.

In the spring of 1857 H. Mendelsohn and Jacob Heimann decided to return to Europe and sold their business shares to Jacob Alexander, a relative of mine who mainly took care of the business in Poker Flat, to my cousin, Jacob Engler, who had arrived from Thorn in 1856, and to myself, and left for Europe. After that I was in charge of all the buying and transportation of our goods. For this purpose I went to Marysville every other week and every five or six weeks to San Francisco. In between I spent much time in Poker Flat. This town, as its name indicates, was a gambling place. It consisted of our store, that of M. Armer & Bros., a butcher shop, a bakery, and about fifteen taverns and gambling houses. It was located in a very deep ravine along a creek which yielded considerable quantities of gold. The miners lived in their cabins next to their stakes by the creek where they worked successfully throughout the summer. Here, as in Saint Louis, Saturdays and Sundays were our best business days. On week ends the miners came to buy new outfits at our store, discarding their old ones in our place. They ordered food and mining equipment which were sent to them during the week. They took only the most essential things with them. Among our customers there were no women. It was very seldom that a woman would enter the place. Our prices were of course very high due to lack of competition; for in 1858 we bought out the business of M. Armer & Bros., the other supply store in Poker Flat. When the older of the Armer brothers returned to Kempen, Germany, his younger brother Morris entered our business as a clerk.

As in Saint Louis, crowds of gamblers came to town during the week end. In Poker Flat, often gambling took place in the open street. I must, however, admit that these people acted quietly, seldom causing disturbances. They withdrew on Sunday night, and the little town was once again deserted for the following week.

One summer day in 1858, Poker Flat experienced feverish excitement. A rumor of discovery of rich claims in the near-by mountain region had been reported. After a number of people moved to this spot from Poker Flat, we decided to open a branch store in this locality. I took along a carpenter, but instead of finding a newly arising settlement I arrived at a spot where a few men prospected in a primeval forest. Although I was reluctant to stay I was finally persuaded to open a store, and as lumber was plentiful, a log cabin was ready within three weeks. Shelves were put up, an iron stove for cooking was procured, and merchandise was brought from a long distance. Yet the customers failed to appear. Winter was not far off and, as I knew that the deep snow would make digging impossible, I thought I might have to wait until spring for the mining activity to begin. Nevertheless, a rich claim discovered by four Irishmen attracted more people who settled down in their quickly built cabins before the winter set in. Ready to spend the long winter in this isolated region, they seemed to have plenty of money. To kill time, these ten or fifteen men assembled nightly in my store and played card games until morning. On the tables they found two or three packs of cards as well as whisky and other drinks, their special favorite being peaches in liqueur. My friend and helper, a husky miner by the name of Darr, and myself, did not have to stay up, as the gamblers behaved absolutely quietly throughout the night. For every game they put one dollar, and for every drink a quarter or half a dollar, in a money box. This money was my principal income during the winter months. Upon arising in the morning I found the gamblers had disappeared and all I had to do was to collect the money which these honest people had left.

A number of people finally arrived in spring and staked their claims but were disappointed to find very little gold. My store was by that time almost depleted, and I was compelled to send for more supplies from La Porte, from which place the goods had to be carried to my store-cabin by Chinese. For the transportation alone I had to pay half a dollar per pound. Because of the departure of most of the miners I closed my business and bade farewell to my lonely cabin. The result of this interlude in the mountains was nevertheless a net profit of several thousand dollars. In this connection I ought to relate an episode which dated back from this winter in the mountains. Among the gamblers who spent the nights in my house were four miners who, after having bought merchandise on credit, disappeared without paying their bill of about $600.00. A long time afterwards, when I had almost forgotten the loss, I was passing through Pine Grove on my usual ride from Saint Louis to Poker Flat when someone shouted to me to halt. At first I paid no attention as I carried a considerable amount of money on me. The man begged me to stop and, upon my asking him what he wanted, he said that I had once done him the favor of lending him money. He now wanted to take this opportunity to pay the old bill.

The store in Saint Louis as well as that in Poker Flat continued to prosper. Also the pack-train was a steady source of income. In 1858 we built an annex in which we opened a plumbing shop to satisfy the demand for sheet metal and pipes for the miners. During the summer of the same year a conflagration consumed the entire town of Saint Louis with the exception of the bank and of our store. Upon the outbreak of the fire, several miners who had deposited gold in our iron safe came running to us, demanding the return of their deposits. I refused resolutely, telling them to stay instead and to help extinguish the fire. Realizing that I would not open the safe during this critical situation, they turned to give assistance to the fire fighters. Fire insurance was of course out of the question because the risk was too great. I personally was so upset after the fire that I suffered from constant nightmares, shouting "Fire!" in my sleep. I felt life too unsafe unless we had a fire-proof building. Hence we decided to begin immediately its construction. The building progressed rapidly, as we found stones in the neighborhood which seemed as if hewn for ready use. Iron doors were brought up from Marysville and in a few months we were able to move into the new, fire-proof building.

In 1859 I participated in the construction of a long ditch, together with two Germans, Charles Hendel and Christian Berg. This flume was to catch the water from the near-by gold diggings. It was constructed of wooden boards, twelve to fourteen inches wide and equally high, while cross boards were nailed to the bottom at intervals of six feet. The channel was then laid out with stones and quicksilver was strewn near the cross boards. Every other Saturday and Sunday when the washing in the mines above ceased, the stones were removed and the quicksilver and the gold were carefully taken out. However, as we were not experts in mining, the result was rather unsatisfactory.

In the spring of 1861, I noticed a general slowing up of business as a result of reduced yields in the mines. I availed myself of this opportunity to take a trip to Europe to visit my parents. By this time the railroad across the Isthmus of Panama was of course completed and I had a fast and pleasant trip, via Panama and New York, to Hamburg. On the return trip, I arrived in New York on May 20, 1862. After five days of sightseeing I continued in the usual way and was back in San Francisco on June 15. Upon my arrival in Saint Louis I discovered that our business as well as the whole situation had suffered greatly during my absence. Many miners had left their claims since the outbreak of the Civil War and the production of gold had decreased. In addition to all this, a disastrous fire broke out again in the spring of 1863, consuming the entire town with the exception of the two fire-proof houses.

While I was in Europe, our pack-train had suffered serious losses as a result of a flood. It might be of interest to learn how such a train was composed. A fairly decent train consisted ordinarily of twenty-five to forty pack- and riding animals. Ours was usually comprised of thirty-five mules of which six were riding animals, while the rest carried freight. Besides, every train had a white mare with a bell around her neck to lead the train. The crew consisted of the proprietor, the *cargador* (supervisor and manager), four *arrieros* (packers and drivers), and a cook. Mexicans seemed to be best fitted for this occupation. The cook on his white mare, the *yegua,* rode ahead, followed by an animal carrying cooking utensils so that he could begin preparing the meals as soon as a stop was

Mule train, as used by Henry Cohn and Emanuel Linoberg, 1903. Courtesy of Amador County Archives.

made. The *cargador*'s business included the distribution of the freight among the individual animals, the supervision of his crew, and the maintenance of the harnesses. According to their ability to carry, the mules were packed at the starting point for a four day trip with 300 to 425 pounds each, including 50 pounds of fodder. The distance covered in a day averaged about sixteen to eighteen miles. During the winter period, when snow lay too deep, the train was taken to the lowlands in Yuba County for grazing. Once every summer a rest period of from four to six weeks was inserted during which the animals grazed at a mountain meadow and the equipment was overhauled. Carrying on the transportation by mules in winter was a difficult and strenuous undertaking. We often had to start at two o'clock at night when the snow crust was still hard and had to halt at eight o'clock when the sun came out. At one time, in the fall, a very severe snow storm took us by surprise, and despite our most arduous efforts we were forced to stop and unload the animals and to stay there throughout the night. Worn out by the hard work, I fell asleep. When I woke up at two o'clock in the morning, I was covered by a blanket of several inches of snow. After a wagon road had been laid out to Saint Louis, our pack-train became unnecessary and we sold the animals at an average price of $120.00. The departure of my two loyal Mexicans, the packer and *arriero,* Pedro, and the *cargador,* Juan, was a moving episode.

On the whole, it looked pretty desolate in the mountains, and I made up my mind to leave the country for good. I sold my business share to a German, Jake Smal, but did not insist upon payment in gold. Thus I received greenbacks which at that time had a value of 65% and which I, moreover, later sold in New York at 43%.

During the middle of August 1863, I left Saint Louis and the Sierra Nevada after a sentimental farewell scene, escorted by ten friends as far as the "American House." They had borrowed every available horse in Saint Louis, otherwise more friends would have come to bid me farewell. After a touching "Good bye, boys," I went by stage to Marysville where I stayed a few days, and from there by steamer to San Francisco. On September 4 I sailed by the steamer *Sacramento* to Panama and continued to New York where I arrived on the 26th. The journey along the Atlantic seacoast was very dangerous at that time. Several Confederate ships, including the notorious *Alabama,* impeded navigation, for which reason we had to proceed completely blacked out for several nights. From New York I continued to Liverpool, arriving there in twelve days. I visited London and Paris and returned to Germany in October 1863.

So much is now being written about America that I cannot think of adding anything of general interest except that during the eleven years I lived in that country I never met a single uniformed policeman or soldier, except in New York on my trip home during the Civil War.

55

A Miner in Spanish Hill and Placerville

Bernhard Marks, 1855–1856

Born in Poland, Marks came to the United States as a child and settled with his family in New Bedford, Massachusetts, where he worked as an errand boy and bookkeeper. In 1852, at age nineteen, he left for San Francisco by way of the Isthmus of Panama, and worked there as a peddler and a clerk before going to the gold country. Written in 1855 and 1856, the following letters provide a firsthand account of a miner's life in Spanish Hill and Placerville. They were selected from the eighteen letters that Marks wrote to his cousin, Dr. Jacob Solis-Cohen of Philadelphia, over a four-year period.

Marks later opened a school with his wife in Columbia, but after losing an election for a position in the public schools in which his Jewish origin became an issue, Marks left for San Francisco, where he became a teacher and school principal.[10] He later entered the real estate business, living in Fresno and Marin counties.

1

Spanish Hill, January, 1855

Dear Cousin:

At last, after a longer silence than any I have maintained since the incipiency of our correspondence, I once again take heart to write. Although, in the interval, I have written frequently to Hannah,[11] she is still ignorant of the fact that for the past three months I have been very sick. My attending physician tells me that it was a species of fever peculiar to the climate and brought about by sudden exposure from an excessively warm atmosphere to the chilly night air. Continual inspiration of vitiated air also contributed. And as sorrows never come as single spies but in battalions, the lady of the wheel gave it a sudden jerk in the wrong way for someone and that happened to be me. A piece of work which we were doing and cost us near five thousand dollars caved in one night,

---

SOURCE: (1–2) Bernhard Marks to Dr. Jacob Solis-Cohen, 1855, 1856. *Publication of the American Jewish Historical Society*, Sept. 1954, 53–56. For original letter see the Solis Family Papers, box 1, folder "Jacob da Silva Solis Cohen": Correspondence from Bernhard Marks, 1850–1857, American Jewish Historical Society, Waltham, Mass., and New York.

10. Marks may not have been a practicing Jew at this time; he had married a non-Jewish woman in 1859.
11. For more about Hannah, Bernhard's sister, see Hebrew Orphan Asylum, chapter 4.

a total loss, one fifth of this I have to bear, which added to full five hundred more for labour, physician's fees, and commitants make a very serious drawback to my success. We have already started from another direction to reach our best or richest ground and hope to compass it in about six or eight months. In the meantime, our pay will be moderate, so that I shall not be able to return to the East as soon as I expected. I think, however, that it will not make more than a few months difference. It may be that I shall have to stay here this year, but certain it is that unless I lose what I have remaining I shall not spend another year in the country. We had sunk a shaft one hundred and eighty feet deep, seventy feet through hard rock, and started a drift or tunnel from the bottom to a distant part of our mine. In doing so, we wished to run to a certain spot which we had reason to believe to be extremely rich and about the title to which there was, and is a dispute between my company, "The Golden Gate," and another in the opposite side of the hill called the "Humbug Tunnelling Co." They were running a drift to get there first, as according to our peculiar mining laws, the first who got possession could hold by priority. As they were making their way there very leisurely, we desired to get there first by running all night as well as day. It would not do to allow any hired hands to work in it, as we wished to keep our destinations a profound secret, the whole work then devolved on us five proprietors. Our drift was four feet wide and five and a half high or just large enough to allow a man to work. We worked two at a time, that is, one stands up and works with all his might as long as he can stand it, generally from 8 to 10 minutes, he then lays down and the next goes through the same operation by which time the other is recruited. In this way many thousands of feet are dug through the hills of California. After we had gone about two hundred, the air by continual respiration had become so vitiated that it would not support two men and two candles. We were obliged to dispense with one and even that would scarcely burn for want of Oxygen. We had just reached ground which paid over four dollars to the bucket, or as our machinery is arranged, about four thousand dollars every eleven working days when owing to some water which came through an old shaft the whole concern caved. Fortunately, no one was hurt. Such bad air and violent exertion soon wet us to the skin. Indeed, I never thought of leaving the drift, when relieved, without wringing out my shirt. And although I took precaution to have a pair of heavy blankets ready to wrap myself in when leaving the diggings, I still caught a very bad cold from which resulted a three month's spell of sickness. I am now, however, as well and robust as ever. I intend never again to exert myself so violently or expose my health to such an extent. I can scarcely assume the assurance to reprove your dilatoriness in writing when I am or rather have been so negligent myself, but still, don't you think I have a little the best excuse? We were visited by a young tornado about ten days since which took my cabin with stove, bed, books, desk and in short all it contained down hill. I recovered some of my books but lost all my papers, among which were several sketches of California characters and scenes which I intended to have sent you. And by the way, I regret exceedingly the unavoidable and sudden interruption in my journal, and, from the fact of your not having mentioned it in any of your letters I take for granted that it is a matter of indifference to you wether I continue or discontinue it. Indeed, the latter would be my choice were it not that I entertain so great an aversion to leaving anything unfinished. I cannot promise to resume next mail, because I have neglected all my correspondents lately, excepting Hannah, and must make up in part at least, the deficiency. But when I do I will make a summary of my disposition of my itinerant descriptions and give you as I at first proposed, sketches of the peculiar characters of this country.

Why will not Aunt write? I have not forgotten her promise to do so. My love to her, to uncle, Leon and their cousins. Remember me kindly to Miss Solis and all enquiring friends.

Your ever affectionate cousin

B. Marks

2

Placerville, July 18, [18]56

Dear Cousin:

How often must I chronicle disaster? Placerville is again ashes. This time however the devastation is complete. Three houses only mark the place where Placerville stood. Some have lost all, many heavily and others slightly. Among the latter I class myself, for having nothing invested in the city I lost nothing but my wardrobe and what few books were left me from the last fire. Two hundred dollars will replace my loss entire, less if I recover my watch which I hope to do.

I presume that you have ere this heard of the fate of Sam Rosenthall. He left his place of business, Chips Flat, on a mare having a young colt following her. He had in his saddle bags near $4,000. in coin and gold bullion which he was carrying to Sacramento. At night the mare without saddle or bridle and her colt were found estray in the road near Auburn. He was last seen by a party of miners not far from where his mare was found in company with another man who is not known and of whom nothing has since been seen or heard. The first intimation that I received of it was from a stranger who was passing through the city and who could give me no particulars. I immediately armed myself and mounting my pony started off for Mormon Island, distant from here about forty miles determined to ride all night and reach it before morning. But I had gone only about eight miles when I met a particular pedlar direct from Auburn who informed that it had occurred 3 days previous, that search had been made everywhere by parties perfectly familiar with the country, that the Masonic fraternity had put forth the uttermost exertions to find his remains, if as is doubtless the case he has been murdered for the sake of the money he had about him. That everything in fact that could be done, was attended to and that Sam Hyman with whom I believe he had some business relations had returned and was settling his affairs. Thinking it should be useless to proceed under the circumstances I returned at once and wrote for information. The answer elicited by my letter gave me no further particulars. If Elsie his wife has not heard of it by last mail she will by this. The poor woman would deserve commiseration, even under the most favourable circumstances, as it is, with a family of 6 or 7 children and his means limited when he met his fate she is indeed to be pitied. I do not believe he was worth more than about 3,000 as about a year ago when I saw him last, he said that he wished to go into a business on the American River which would require 3,000. that he had 2,000 and desired me to lend him 1,000 more. I agreed to let him have it in 30 days but as my mine caved in the same week I was prevented from doing it, having need for all the money I could raise myself. He could not have made less than 1,000 since then and if he loses, as I expect he does, half of the $4,000. which was lost at his death, 1,000 only will remain, and that before it reaches his family may be diminished greatly. The mail arrived this afternoon but I receive no letters from either you or Hannah. I am writing this on a flour barrel and even this miserable accommodation is waited for by others.

I must close abruptly.

My love to Aunt, Uncle and Cousins and respects to Miss Esther Solis and all others.

Your affectionate cousin

B. Marks

56

The Tiende Mexicano, Steam Baths, and Little Prejudice

Emanuel Linoberg and Pauline Meyers, 1851–1857

One of Sonora's first settlers, Emanuel Linoberg came to the Sierra Nevada from his native Poland in 1849 at age thirty-one. Among Sonora's leading citizens, he served on the first town council and participated in the political, business, and religious affairs of the new town. The enterprising Linoberg operated the Tiende Mexicano, a large store on the corner of Sonora's main street, Washington, and Linoberg Street, as well as a mule train to bring in supplies from Stockton, an entertainment hall, a gold mine, and the Russian Steam Baths described below. Recorded in September of 1850, his brand "44" was the first recorded in the county.[12]

With a large number of people in attendance, at 2:00 P.M. on December 30, 1851, Linoberg married Pauline Meyers in San Francisco, an event recorded in the minutes of Congregation Sherith Israel,[13] and they had two children. He became president of the Hebrew Congregation of Sonora, a leader of the Jewish community, and a founding member of the Masonic Lodge. Linoberg died suddenly of a stroke at the age of forty. "His funeral was attended by the Masonic Fraternity, the Fire Department, the Hebrew Benevolent Society and a large number of citizens."[14] He was buried in the Sonora Jewish cemetery. His epitaph states in Hebrew that he was a "man of a good name."[15] His gravestone is decorated with the image of a mourning wife and child.[16] After Emanuel's death, his widow married Emanuel's brother, Louis Linoberg, who had settled in San Jose, and she established a millinery store there. In the following property deed, similar to a traditional *ketubah* and witnessed by two officers of Sherith Israel, Linoberg bequeaths to his wife-to-be his property in Sonora.

SOURCE: (1) Deed, Recorder, Tuolumne County, Sonora, Separate Property of Wife, vol. 8, 1. (2) "B." [probably Herman Bein], "An Interesting Letter from San Francisco," *Asmonean* 5:16, Feb. 6, 1852, 141. (3) Advertisement, *Sonora Union Democrat,* Oct. 13, 1855, 4. (4) Emanuel Linoberg to the *American Israelite,* Nov. 13, 1857, 145.

12. Levinson, *Jews in the California Gold Rush,* 42. Sonora, the county seat of Tuolumne, was the Queen of the Southern Mines. Founded by Mexicans from the state of Sonora in 1848, it was incorporated by American settlers in 1851 after the foreign miners' tax pushed the Mexicans off their claims.
13. This minutebook is at the Western Jewish History Center.
14. *Gleaner,* May 21, 1858, 8.
15. The death of Emanuel Linoberg was noted in a letter from Sam Marks of Stockton to Isidor Friedlander, probably in Cincinnati. The letter appears in chapter 8.
16. For explanations of gravestone symbols see Kramer, "Tree Art," 91–100.

1

State of California, County San Francisco, Know all men by these presents, that I Emanuel Linoberg of the Town of Sonora, in the County of Tuolumne, and state afore said, for, and in consideration of the love and affection which I have for Poline [Pauline] Meyer[s] of the City of San Francisco, and state aforesaid, and also of the contemplated marriage between me and the said Pauline Meyer[s], and also the promise made by the said Pauline to marry me, and also the sum of one dollar, the receipt whereof is hearby acknowledged, by these presents do give, grant, alien and confirm into the said Pauline Meyer[s], her heirs and assigns, to, and for her sole and separate use, and benefit, not subject in any way to the debts contracted, of any husband she may have. All the lands, tenements and hereditaments, situate in the Town of Sonora, in the County of Tuolumne, and state aforesaid, and known as lots, number one hundred and twenty three (123) and one hundred and twenty four (124) on the

Sonora, California, 1852. This is the Sonora to which Emanuel Linoberg brought his new wife, Pauline, after their San Francisco marriage. Lithograph, Courtesy of the Bancroft Library (1963.002:0221-C), University of California, Berkeley.

map of said town, said lots being located on the corner of South Washington and Linoberg streets, fronting seventy four (74) feet on Washington street, and having a depth of one hundred (100) feet, together with the premises and appurtenances to the same belonging or appertaining and also all my right, title and interest, in, and to said premises, and every part and parcel thereof. To have and to hold, all and singular the said premises unto the said P—— Meyer[s], her heirs, and assigns, to her, and their use, benefit, and behoof, sole, and separate, forever. In witness whereof, I have hereunto set my hand and seal to this 29th Dec. 1851.

 Emanuel Linoberg—Seal

 Signed, sealed and delivered in presence of Meier Rehfisch—A.A. Joseph.

 State of California, County of San Francisco, on this thirtieth day of December, A.D. 1851, personally appeared before me, Alexander Campbell County Judge of the County of San Francisco, Emanuel Linoberg, satisfactorily proved to me to be the person described in and [. . .] competent and [. . .] that he executed the same.

2

 Socially.—We have been more than usually gay, and the large and constant influx of the fair sex have tended to foster and promote that gaiety. Our people anticipate the pleasure of witnessing tomorrow, a matrimonial ceremony, among the members of the Congregation, "Shearith Israel." The affianced parties are Mr. E. Linaberg [sic] of Sonora, and Miss Pauline Myer [sic]; both natives of Germany. I shall make a point of being present, for happiness I am told is contagious, and who knows, I may be infected. [. . .]

B.

3

RUSSIAN STEAM BATHS.

T HE undersigned respectfully informs the public that he has just erected at his ranch, within half a mile of Sonora, under the direction of Dr. ELWERT, capacious and convenient Russian Baths, universally recommended by the medical faculty to be beneficial and in fact a panacea in the eradication of some of the most stubborn diseases—such as Rheumatism, Gout, Contractions, Seretula, Chronic, Nervous and Pulmonic diseases, &c.

A person will be in attendance to administer baths, and physicians sending patients are requested to prescribe the manner in which they are to receive them. Price $3.00

Every facility is offered to reach the premises— the Stockton and Jamestown stages passing twelve times a day.

Prices of passage—From Sonora 25 cents; from Jamestown 75 cents.

E. LINOBERG

Dr. Elwert can be found at his office corner Washington and Linoberg streets, from 8 o'clock A.M., to 4 P.M.

Sonora, Sept. 1., 1855.

4

Linoberg's Ranch
October 2, 1857

Mr. Editor. [Isaac Mayer Wise]

A tiller of the soil, during the hours of recreation, I have written a few lines.

We are here in the mountains, near the Sierra Nevada, which ten years ago was a wilderness; but, with American progressive spirit, has changed to a civilized, populous mining district—none superior in the State. The Israelites in this county number about 250 to 300, in Sonora about 100; all are doing well. The tax list of this county mentioned their names to a considerable extent, with credit to their industry. There is very little prejudice known here toward us as Jews; in social intercourse with our fellow-citizens, no distinction is made between Christians and Jews; in fact there is no persuasion more esteemed for moral conduct than the Jews.

I fully approve your advocacy of Reform. Orthodoxy suited times past, but reform suits times of progress; be not discouraged; *steadily advance,* and sound the trumpet of reform constantly; the elevation of our position in society from day to day is caused by the system of religious reform. Orthodoxy would have kept us 500 years back in our position, whereas reform steadily advances our position—socially, morally, and religiously—and the will of God will be accomplished.

I remain, Yours truly,

E. Linoberg

57
A Woman's Life Cut Short
Hannah Gumpert, 1855, 1867

It is extremely difficult to learn about the lives of Jewish women who settled in California's Gold Rush communities. Unless a woman became a public figure or owned a business, or her personal letters or diaries were collected, she would leave a paper trail of at most six documents to attest to her life: a birth certificate, visa, or travel document from her place of birth, a naturalization certificate, a wedding invitation, a *ketubah* or marriage certificate, a published obituary, and an inscription on her gravestone.

A *ketubah*, obituary, and gravestone inscription alone survive to document the life of Hannah Barlow Gumpert. The wife of a merchant, Gumpert led a life similar to that of many women who resided in the mining towns. The *ketubah* and obituary notice make it possible to learn more about her social and economic situation than is the case for other women.

Born in Wittkowo, near the Prussian border with Russia, Hannah, like many young Jewish women, sought a new life in California's mining towns. She may have come to the United States with her brother in 1850 at the height of the Gold Rush or been sent for by him after he established himself as a boot and shoe merchant in Sonora. It is also possible that she was sent for to be betrothed to Elias Gumpert, a merchant and an officer of the Sonora Hebrew Benevolent Society.[17]

As the children of a rabbi in a small eastern European town with a large Jewish population, the Barlows were well versed in traditional Judaism. Hannah's brother, Abraham Barlow (1825–1916), became active in the pioneer Jewish community, conducting community Passover celebrations at his home. Because single people predominated in the early years of the Gold Rush, the whole community often celebrated family-centered holidays together.[18]

Hannah's wedding, a community event, took place at the home of Emanuel and Pauline Linoberg, Emanuel by that time having become the founding president of the short-lived Sonora Hebrew Congregation.

---

17. Sometime after the death of Hannah Gumpert, Elias Gumpert moved to Stockton, where he joined Congregation Ryhim Ahoovim (today Temple Israel) and remarried.

18. A photograph of Abraham Barlow and an engraved emblem are in the Abraham Barlow Collection, Western Jewish History Center.

1

Elias Gompert [sic] To Hannah Barlow
On the third day of the Week the nineteenth day Sivan Ano Munde, Five
Thousand six Hundred and fifteen corresponding with the fifth day of June A D
1855, as we number here in the City of Sonora, Tuolumne
County State of California
I Elias the Son of Wolf Gumpert, do say to this spinster Hana daughter of
Baruch Abraham. Be thou to me a Wife agreeable to the laws of Moses and
Israel, and I will honor, cherish, nourish, maintain and sustain thee according
to the customs of Hebrew men, who are bound to honor, maintain, Sustain,
cherish and nourish their wives in respect, and thy marriage portion shall be thy
maintainance, habilaments, and thy time, as is the Custom of mankind and this
all will I perform unto this Spinster to whom I take to me to wife from her fathers
house, and will supply therefore, with Clothing Bed and habitation. and I, Elias,
the Bridegroom do appoint the Said Spinster, Hana from my own personal
Estate all the above recitals, and therefore do acknowledge and ve[r]ify by this
said Marriage Contract, that I will secure to her from my personal Estates as
her portion thereof, the Sum of Five Thousand Dollars, and which I now do take
on me to Secure her from my Stock, property and possessions, and personal
effects which I may or do hold in the presence of Heaven now and for the
future, and which I may hereafter add to my present personal estates, property
or possession during my life, and by this do Secure her, her Share at my death if
I Shall Still continue to hold the same property, and this do I the Said Elias, the
Bridegroom undertake by virtue of the Marriage Contract and these conditions
do promise to fulfill as is customary in all Marriage Contracts performed among
the daughters of Israel and which is acknowledged and allowed by the Order
of our Sages May they be remembered in a blessing and this I the Bridegroom
promise to perform all which the Contract doth contain to this Spinster Hana,
Either in the Writing, Meaning and construction of this document, and I hereby
vouch it all to be earnest, just, firm and binding. Dated this fifth day of June
A.D. 1855 according to the vulgar [common] Era, and corresponding with the
nineteenth day of Sivan in the year of the creation Five Thousand Six Hundred
and fifteen anno mundi.
Elias Gompert [sic]
[Emanuel] Linoberg
President of the Hebrew Cong[regation]

Source: (1) Hannah Gumpert's *ketubah,* vols. 1–4 of Marriages, Tuolumne County
Recorder, Tuolumne County, Sonora, 38–40. (2) Hannah Gumpert's obituary, *Hebrew*,
Nov. 29, 1867, 4. (3) Hannah Gumpert's gravestone in the Sonora Jewish Cemetery.

Sonora California
attest
M. Seeligsohn[19]
Secretary of the Hebrew Congregation
Sonora California
State of California
Tuolumne County On the 5th day of June A.D. 1855 personally appeared before me L. Quint County Judge in & for the aforesaid County Elias Gumpert known to me to be the person described in the foregoing instrument who acknowledged to me that he executed the Same freely and voluntarily for the uses & purposes therein mentioned Witness my hand & the Seal of the aforesaid County Court the day & date last above in this certificate written

L. Quint
County Judge
Tuolumne County cal
State of California
Tuolumne County I hereby certify that on the 5th day of June A D 1855 at [the] house of E Linoberg in said County & State aforesaid Elias Gumpert & Hannah Barlow both of Sonora County & State aforesaid were with their mutual Consent lawfully joined together in the bonds of holy matrimony which was duly solemnized in the presence of Emanuel Linoberg & M Seeligsohn & others attesting witnesses & I do further certify that the Said Elias Gumpert & Hannah Barlow are Known to me to be the persons described in ths Certificate; That the Said parties were of sufficient age to contract the Same; & further that there appeared no lawful impedament to the Solemnization of said marriage, Given under my hand this the 5th day of June A D 1855

Leander Quint
County Judge
Tuolumne County Cal
Recorded June 9th A D
1855 at 2 P.M.

2

SONORA, November 26, 1867

EDITOR HEBREW:—The painful duty devolves upon me to announce the death of Mrs. Hannah Gumpert, wife of Mr. Elias Gumpert, of the town, at the age of

---

19. M. Seeligsohn was the founding secretary of the Sonora Hebrew Benevolent Society in 1856.

thirty-two years. For many years afflicted with an incurable nervous disorder, she at last succumbed under its blighting effects on Saturday evening, the 23rd instant. Her funeral took place on Sunday last, and, notwithstanding the inclemency of the weather, was attended by a vast number of citizens, amongst whom we noticed also the members of Odd Fellows' Lodge and many ladies, who by this act of courtesy wished to testify their regard for the deceased. Her domestic virtues, her kindheartedness, and her amiable disposition, which withstood the souring influence of a chronic affection, had endeared her to the hearts of all her acquaintances, and the annexed resolutions, passed by the Sonora and Columbia Hebrew Benevolent Society, express the universal sentiment in this community. Mrs. Gumpert leaves a husband and three interesting young children to mourn their irretrievable loss.

At a special meeting of the S.& C.H.B. Society, the Committee appointed offered the following resolutions, which were unanimously adopted:

WHEREAS, The Almighty Father has seen fit to remove from this earth our much esteemed sister in faith, Mrs. Hannah Gumpert, and, whereas, we deeply feel the loss which her family and friends have sustained; be it

Resolved, That our heartfelt sympathy is extended to the bereft husband, children and brother of the deceased lady, and may their grief be tempered by the thought that their beloved relative is now released from her severe sufferings, and has departed to a better sphere, to reap the reward that awaits the just and virtuous.

Resolved, That these resolutions be spread upon our minutes, and be published in the San Francisco HEBREW[20] and Sonora Democrat, and that a copy of them be transmitted to Mr. Gumpert.

H. JOSEPH,
A. M. LEVI, COMMITTEE
M. REEB,[21]
TUOLUMNE

3

Here is buried
the important woman
Hannah the daughter of our teacher and rabbi

20. A weekly in English and German published in San Francisco from 1863 to 1887.
21. H. Joseph may be related to A. J. Joseph, who is listed with Elias Gumpert as a founding officer of the Hebrew Benevolent Society of Sonora. A. M. Levy (sometimes with an "i" and other times with a "y"), is listed as a Sonoran and as a Rabbi who officiated at a marriage. Moses Reeb sold boots, shoes, and gaiters in 1863 Sonora (Levinson, Jews in the California Gold Rush, 175, 182, 47).

Rabbi Baruch
from the city Wittkowo
who died on the day of Holy Sabbath
the twenty-fifth of Mar Heshvan
and was buried on the
twenty-sixth of Mar Heshvan in the year 5628.
[Translated from the Hebrew][22]
In memory of
Hannah,
Wife of
E. Gumpert.
Born in Wittkowo
Prussia
Died Nov. 23, 1867.
Aged 33 Years.
Peace to her Ashes.

---

22. Translated by Tova Gazit, Librarian, Judah L. Magnes Memorial Museum, and
Rabbi Steven Chester, Temple Sinai, Oakland, California.

Invitation to the wedding of Rachel Hoffman and Abraham Haines at the home of Rachel Hoffman's sister, 1865. Courtesy of Mrs. Robert Guggenheim and Susan Smith Morris.

Rachel Hoffman Haines died three years after her marriage and was buried in the Goldner family plot in Jackson. Photograph by Ira Nowinski. Courtesy of the Western Jewish History Center, Judah L. Magnes Museum.

A Gold Rush Wedding, Jackson, 1865 (also seen on facing page).

The bride, Rachel Hoffman, left Prussia to join her sister, Rosalia Hoffman Goldner, in Jackson, 1865. Courtesy of Mrs. Robert Guggenheim and Susan Smith Morris.

The groom, Abraham Haines, was a merchant in El Dorado active in the Jewish community, 1865. Courtesy of Mrs. Robert Guggenheim and Susan Smith Morris.

58

Sonora Reports to the Board of
Delegates of American Israelites

Henry Stroup, 1861

In 1859 the Board of Delegates of American Israelites, the first national Jewish organization in the United States, had as one of its goals the gathering of congregational statistics. The following letter is a response to that survey by the Sonora Benevolent Society. In 1853 Sonora's Jews acquired land for a cemetery and three years later established the Sonora Hebrew Benevolent Society. Four years later the Jewish community of nearby Columbia joined them, and together they established the Sonora and Columbia Hebrew Benevolent Society.

Sonora March 5th 1861

To the Board of Delegates of Am. Israelites N. York.

Enclosed I hand you the schedule you sent our Congr. 2 months ago with my excuses for keeping it so long but I expected to leave California before this and bring it myself but as I am not yet ready I must write to you an explanation to the Schedule. Our Society does not exactly exist of Sonorian & Columbian only as the name would lead you to believe, but it has besides these a few stragglers from all the surrounding camps, nor is it a criterion of the population. From Sonora there are 20 members in the Society of whom 9 are married whilst there are 15 Israelites amongst whom are 2 married who do not belong to our Society. The Ladies do not belong to the Society strictly speaking, i.e. they are not recorded in the books. Our Society is as its name implies a Benevolent Society for Israelites, but has nothing to do with Prayer Meetings, though we have regular Service at which nearly all the Israelites of Sonora and surrounding Camps partake on every Rosh hashona & Yom Kippor. Our Society was first organized in 1851. These books have been burnt on the 17th June 1852 from which time our present records date. Its Laws were not followed though so that it was reorganized with nine Bye Laws on Dec. 3 1857.

Yours obedt
Henry Stroup
Secretary.

SOURCE: Henry Stroup to the Board of Delegates of American Israelites, Mar. 5, 1861, box 4, folder "Congregations and Organizations" (by city), S–W, Board of Delegates of American Israelites Records, American Jewish Historical Society, Waltham, Mass., and New York.

59

A Sonora Suicide

Sonora Union Democrat, 1869

The unknown Selig Ritzwoller's life and death register the struggles of Jewish merchants in the Gold Rush era. Why he believed that a San Francisco Hebrew benevolent society would take care of his family, we do not know. Nor do we know where he was buried. Because he committed suicide, it is unlikely that he was interned in the Jewish cemetery.

Last Sunday evening about nine o'clock the body of Selig Ritzwoller a dry goods dealer of this place, was found in his store hanging by the neck, to a rope which was fastened to one of the uprights supporting the shelves. His wife and children upon returning from an evening visit to one of the neighbors, found the store securely fastened, after calling to her husband for sometime, receiving no answer, and not being able to get in the house, she returned to her neighbor's, and told them that something must have happened, as the doors were all locked, that she had knocked, called her husband's name, and could get no answer. Mr. Pinto then went to the Store with her, knocked and called to Ritzwoller, getting no answer, he went for Mr. Kaufman. Not being able to open the iron doors they dug a hole through the back wall of the building large enough to gain an entrance. Upon entering the store his body was found suspended, still warm. Dr. Walker cut the rope and upon examination found that life was extinct. [. . .] He was a native of Prussia, his name was Selig Ritzwoller, and his wife told me to-day that he was aged between 43 and 44 years. I went after the Coroner and when I came back I found Mr. Kaufman reading a paper which he, Kaufman said was written by deceased, I am quite positive he came to his death by his own hand as he was in the house alone.

M. Kaufman sworn. I keep a store in town and was acquainted with deceased, I heard the statement of Mr. Pinto the same is correct with the exception that upon entering the house I went to the back door first after discovering deceased, and then went and opened the front door and admitted Doctor Walker and others. I think that trouble in his business matters led to depression of spirits, and was the cause of his taking his life by his own hand. This letter I found lying on the counter and is the handwriting of deceased with which I am well acquainted, it is written in German and translated is as follows:

> "Dear God pardon and forgive me—my poor wife and poor children, pardon and forgive me—my heart is broken—the Hebrew

---

SOURCE: *Sonora Union Democrat*, Mar. 20, 1869, 2.

Benevolent Society in San Francisco take pity on my poor wife and children—do not let them starve—to my kind brothers in law Rosener I owe a great deal, of money—Dear God into thy hands I recommend my soul amen—Joel Levy and Kaufman take care of my wife and children."[23]

---

23. Adolph Pinto and Joel Levy were merchants who officiated at Jewish services for the community. Pinto was also an early member of Sherith Israel in San Francisco (Levinson, *Jews in the California Gold Rush,* 181).

60

Dear Harriet

Isidor Choynski, 1863

A year after marrying Harriet Ashim, Isidor Choynski, the satirist, editor, bookstore owner, and author of the "San Francisco Letter" (reproduced in chapter 3), became a gold miner. In the following letter to his wife, written while Choynski and his father-in-law Morris B. Ashim were seeking to strike it rich in a recently discovered goldfield on the California-Nevada border, he describes the hardships of camp life. Ashim, born in Posen, had come overland to San Francisco in 1850 from Kentucky, where he had been living when his daughter Harriet was born. Harriet, a teacher in Rabbi Julius Eckman's school, married Choynski in 1862, and together they raised five children.[24] Choynski sought through letters to stay in touch with the day-to-day life of his family while he mined for gold unsuccessfully in the hills.

Aurora, May 17, 1863.

My dearly beloved wife,

Have just received your affectionate epistle, together with the cartes de visite[25] which please me much, especially the one without the bonnet. Ducky, I too have been sick, and only left my bed this afternoon; the chills, stomach and headache have played the very deuce with me for the last three days, but I am now on a par with most men in this camp. It is rather unhealthy here this season on account of the draught, and very many are suffering. Dad is doing very well, but the sudden change from a high life in the city, to one in a rude mountain camp has nearly prostrated me, but thanks to a wise Providence and my strong frame I shall be all right again in a day or two.

The weather is hot and the grub bad. Golinsky has not got his boarding house open yet and I have to pay $12 per week, though I can eat nothing, and if I could the fare in the restaurants here consists chiefly of pork and beans and my palate rebels against such unwholesome food. I fared much better here last winter, but I must be content as I am making a living here for you and my boy [the Choynskis' infant son Herbert]. So the little fellow crys at you! Well, well, he is showing his colors rather early.

SOURCE: Isidor Choynski to his wife, May 17, 1863. "Two Letters to Harriet Choynski," *Western States Jewish Historical Quarterly* 7:1 (1974): 46–47.

24. Stern, "Two Letters to Harriet Choynski," 44.
25. Card-sized photographic portraits.

Ducky, warm steam baths may be had at North Beach, you know the place. Do not neglect to follow the precepts of Dr. Bruns and try to be well as soon as possible. Buy 25 express envelopes at Wells Fargo & Co. for $2.25 and so you will have them handy.

When will you be through sewing those invincible short dresses? Had an invitation, while in bed, to dine with Mrs. Hitchison, but poor I was unable to concede her request. Harriet, I wish you would send me a pinch of my tea in two or three of your letters; I only want enough to last me for about a month. I don't use much of it, and you can well put a trifle in a couple of letters.

Falk has the key to the post office, and he will bring you my letters. Should you see him ask if there is anything for me. Dad sends love. My love to the family.

Your affectionately,

Isidor

P.S. Dad says that as soon as he will strike a rich claim he will come home, no sooner.

61
Burial at Mokelumne Hill
Isaac Lurch, 1860

More is known about the death of Isaac Lurch in Lancha Plana, and his burial a few miles north in Mokelumne Hill, than is known of his life. Lurch's was the first of thirteen burials in the consecrated Jewish cemetery adjacent to the Protestant cemetery. On the gravestone are inscriptions indicating that Lurch was a Mason. The symbol of a broken column on the gravestone denotes that he died in the prime of life.[26]

Died at Lancha Plana, on December 28, 1859, Isaac Lurch, a native of Upper Rhenish, Bavaria, formerly of Wilmington, N.C. Deceased has during his residence in this section of the country, for the last five years, really deserves that a few words may accompany the spirit that has left its earthly toils.

In the bloom of life, at the age of twenty-eight years, he was called by that All Wise Providence, to pay that unavoidable debt, which with his call only, must meet with obedience. He has left a circle of friends, that have administered all in their power for his comfort during his last sickness; and no pains nor expense were spared, to afford his relief. But, alas, it was beyond the power of any mortal being; and as it has pleased that just Ruler to relieve him from his earthly troubles, and take him nearer under his care.

It will take years to heal the wound that his untimely death caused to those, that really appreciated his friendship. But his friends and relations feel consoled, when trusting to the just sentence that his spirit will repose in one of the "lanes of Eden," where in peace may it rest.

He was brought to this town, and buried on *kavar Yisroel* [Jewish burial] with the honor of the Masonic and Odd Fellows' orders besides. He was followed by the Lancha Plana Fire Company and a large number of citizens, and it would not be exaggerating to call it the largest funeral ever witnessed in a mining town.

Since the above was set in type we received a well written communication from Mr. Herzog, of Campo Seco, from which, for the consolation of a bereaved mother and sisters of so worthy a young man as was the deceased, we beg the indulgence of our readers for copying the following:

"He departed this life last Wednesday morning, Dec. 28, 1859. His death was not anticipated; as the doctors reported him, but the day before, quite

---

SOURCE: *Weekly Gleaner*, Jan. 6, 1860, 5.

26. For a discussion of Jewish cemetery symbols, see Kramer, "Tree Art," 91–100.

improving; announcement of his decease therefore, struck chill to every heart, and tears dropped from many a manly eye, who but seldome wept before.

"His reputation and standing, when living, were such, as few men of his age enjoy. He was possessed of sterling quality and virtues, and was a strong enemy to everything that was mingled with vice.

"He was buried last Friday morning, Dec. 30, at Mokelumne Hill, in the Jewish burying ground. His remains were accompanied by the Masonic and Oddfellow's fraternities of Amador and Calaveras counties, also by the firemen of Lancha Plana. The funeral procession which was headed by a band of music, ordered by the Masonic members, numbered over 500 persons, among whom the Jewish ladies of Mokelumne Hill, was the largest that ever took place in this part of the country.

"The deceased leaves an aged mother, and two sisters, whose sole support he was, to mourn his loss."

62
Bnei Mitzvah in Placerville on the Jewish New Year
Placerville Mountain Democrat, 1867

Henry Louis, known as the rabbi of Placerville, operated the Orleans Hotel and assisted in Jewish ceremonies in the mining towns. He was probably the father of Samuel Louis, one of the bar mitzvah boys. The second boy, Nathan Kohn, made his school's honor roll in 1868 with his sister Sarah. Nathan and Sarah's father, Jacob Kohn (1818–1902), came to Placerville from Hungary in 1849 in the wake of the failure of the rebellion against Austria in which he fought. In Placerville he worked as a miner and later became a merchant. Coon Hallow Road was named after him. Both Jacob Kohn and Henry Louis were officers of the Placerville Hebrew Benevolent Association. The Placerville synagogue located on Cottage Street was built in 1861, and was destroyed by a hurricane in 1878.[27]

JEWISH NEW YEAR.— Monday last the 5628th anniversary of the Jewish New Year, was celebrated by our Jewish fellow-citizens at their Synagogue in this city, with accustomed religious ceremonies. Masters Samuel Louis and Nathan Kohn, being of the age of 13 years, were at the same time confirmed according to Jewish custom in such cases.

SOURCE: *Placerville Mountain Democrat,* Oct. 5, 1867, 2.

27. Levinson, *Jews in the California Gold Rush,* 112, 118, 154, 168, 140. Kohn married Thersa Cohn (1830–92); both are buried in the Placerville Jewish Cemetery. See Susan Morris, *A Traveler's Guide to Pioneer Jewish Cemeteries of the California Gold Rush* (Berkeley: Commission for the Preservation of Pioneer Jewish Cemeteries and Landmarks, Judah L. Magnes Museum, 1996), 45. When Kohn died, the local newspaper reported, "His funeral under the auspices of Placerville Lodge I.O.O.F. [International Order of Odd Fellows], of which he was a charter member, was conducted by Dr. Bernard Kaplan, Rabbi of Sacramento. The Hebrew ritual was impressively rendered with prayers in the original language" (*Placerville Mountain Democrat,* Nov. 8, 1902, 4).

63

We Have a Hebrew Society

Julius Goldner, 1873

Known for his Hebrew and biblical knowledge, Julius Goldner was a merchant and a farmer, as well as a leader of Placerville's Jewish community.[28] Goldner Street in Placerville was named in his honor. The community maintained strong connections with Cincinnati and its institutions; Isaac Mayer Wise, editor of the *American Israelite*, published the following letter to inform his readers about life in the mining towns. By 1873 many of Placerville's Jewish residents had moved on, as silver had been discovered in Nevada, which became the new boom area.

Placerville, El Dorado Co. [California].

To the editor of *The Israelite*.

Every time I read in your paper a communication coming from some distant inland town, where but a few Jews reside, I seem to hear the question asked, in a reproachful tone: Why don't some one in this town take the trouble to inform the editor of THE ISRAELITE that we also have an existence as a Hebrew society? So often has this question recurred to me that I can no longer ignore it, and therefore proceed to act upon its suggestion, at the risk of doing it but once, as ours is a "routine" life.

We have in this town a "Hebrew Benevolent Society," or what is left of it, consisting of eleven members, all told. The society was first organized in 1854, flourished till about 1862, when the discoveries of extensive silver deposits in what is now known under the name of the "State of Nevada" began to excite the people of this part of the country. Miners and storekeepers rushed over the Sierras into the silver land, the Jews furnishing their proportion. Thus has this society been losing one member after another until reduced to the number already stated, and comprising all but two Jews residing here. Out of this number we choose our officers yearly. Our last election, held on the first of June last, resulted in the choice of:

Augustus Mierson, President.

Jacob Kohn, Vice President.

M. Simon, Treasurer.

J. Goldner, Secretary.

SOURCE: Julius Goldner to the *American Israelite,* July 25, 1873, 6.

28. Levinson, *Jews in the California Gold Rush,* 182.

H. Louis, E. Cohn, and J. Goldner, trustees, who were duly installed the sixth of July.

Our regular meetings are held on the first Sunday of every month. Our business seldom surpasses the importance of paying dues and the issuing of orders on the treasury for money in relief of some stranger who may happen to apply.

On Rosh Hashanah and Yom Kippur, we manage to have services at the synagogue, conducted by some volunteer chasan and reader from our midst. We have no preaching, yet have these exercises generally the effect of healing all dissensions that may have arisen through politics, for, in the matter of politics, our Jews are not so united.

Our Jewish children have no other opportunity for religious instruction than such as each parent may afford at their respective homes; but they are more favorably situated with regard to receiving a good English education, as we have one primary, one intermediate, and one high school—free to all—besides which we have one private academy (Mr. F. B. Conklin, Principal); also one private institution for writing, drawing, and painting (Professor Richard Dreise's); all of which are liberally patronized by our Jews and I guarantee that our Jewish children will compare favorably with those of other denominations. And while I mention this in praise of the parents for their liberality, and of the children for their usual aptness, let me also pay due homage to the liberality of the citizens of this town generally, to whose endeavors we owe the very existence of these public and private schools (for the other denominations combined outnumber us about seventy-five to one), and such is their freedom from religious bias that in the face of such a preponderance of pupils of other denominations in our public schools, the Citizens' committee selected a Jewish maiden of fourteen summers [Celia Alsberg] to read the Declaration of Independence at the public celebration held here on the 4th of July last; and to show you how well she acquitted herself, I enclose one copy of each of our town papers, wherein you will find expressed the opinions of the editors representing both political parties, and in this particular case the whole public opinion. You will also find the compliment passed her by the orator of the day, Hon. Geo. M. Pinney.

Before closing this communication I'll state, that the citizens of Placerville have voted to tax themselves $2000 for school building purposes, beside which numerous contrivances in the shape of picnics, balls, etc., have been invented, all of which have proved successful, and will nearly double the original amount. Yours, etc., J.G.

64

Sunday Visiting

Henry Raphael, 1871

Henry Raphael, was one of many migrants from Cincinnati who created a familial atmosphere for themselves in Placerville, often forming business partnerships and buying and selling property with fellow Cincinnatians. An officer in the Masons, Raphael served as a delegate to a county Democratic convention and was a trial juror in district court. In 1864 he entered into a business partnership with P. Silbermann. Henry Raphael and his business partner were described as "well-known and devilish good fellows [with an] exhaustless supply of perseverance and energy."[29] The following letter shows the more personal side of Raphael.

Placerville Cal
May 14th 1871
Dear Mother

Your usual very interesting letter and general remarks came duly to hand [I] was pleased to learn of the welfare & good health of all likewise of my sick friend Dormer would occasionally like to change place with Dormer & Dan & have Moses take a Hangtown Meal and give me some of your best. You can imagine I would try with my utmost endeavors to enjoy the same, and could do it. Still with a balance of climate in our favor rather prefer the healthy good Pacific to the warm sultry Ohio.

Have just returned from visiting several families and have so far spent a pleasant afternoon. Have had my laughs & jokes & any amount of fun, still going around in Christian families is but poor work to one who cares but little for them. There is such a broad distinction in their actions in comparison with good Jewish company, that the dividing line favors us Jews to such an extent, that I can hardly discern how a full fledged Israelite can in common reason but draw a big line in our form as a chosen people as superior. Such being the case, a man must be blind not to see it & those who believe in intermarriage outside of our faith are both fools & knaves.

This is getting on to a religions strain somewhat, of course being noted for my piety. I can thus discern matters without undue bias & prejudice, and you now

---

SOURCE: Henry Raphael to his mother, May 14, 1871, Henry Raphael Collection, American Jewish Archives, Hebrew Union College.

29. *Placerville Mountain Democrat,* Sept. 3, 1864; Levinson, *Jews in the California Gold Rush,* 163, 158.

have my opinion conclusively. Did not as you imagined contract any marriage relations in San Fran. visited some Jewish families, still without any intent of marriage. Mother I dont See why you want to get rid of Dan & me by sending us from blesed Singleness to a Martyrdom of Matrimony. If Dan will only take the Leap I might follow, at present I am not settled enough to make the start, Jerhop you have some one in view for us if so let Dan write me full particulars & have him select for both giving me the loveliest. Laying nonsense [to] one side I am well, and was glad of such good tidening from you all. May you ever be thus and may Heaven bles & prosper all. Have enjoyed myself well during the week and business good With a shower of blesings from Above to all of our family I trusting that a kind Providence will guard you all I remain

Your Son

Henry

Regards to Grandmother at Leons

Mr & Mrs Cohen & aunt & other friends

Raphael

65

Annual Elections on Yom Kippur Night in Jackson

Constitution and By-Laws, Congregation B'nai Israel, 1873

The first known High Holiday announcement in Jackson appeared in the *Volcano Weekly Ledger* in 1856. "Notice. We the Hebrew congregation of Jackson, take this method of notifying our Hebrew brethren, that a Synagogue will be held, in this place on the 30th of September, and on the 1st day of October,—that being their regular New Years day."[30] In 1857 the Jewish community built a synagogue and again held High Holiday services. From 1859 to 1873, the honor of conducting these services fell to at least sixteen different men from the neighboring communities as well as two from San Francisco.[31] I. J. Benjamin noted in 1860, "there are thirty-five Jews here. [. . .] But they have no Scroll of the Torah and must borrow one every year from San Francisco for the high holidays. The synagogue is closed and deserted the rest of the year."[32] By then, sixteen members of Jackson's female Jewish community had organized a Ladies' Benevolent Society.[33]

CONSTITUTION

OF

CONGREGATION B'NAI ISRAEL.

ARTICLE I.

NAME.

The name of this Congregation shall be "B'NAI ISRAEL."

ARTICLE II.

FORM OF WORSHIP

The religious service in the Synagogue of this Congregation shall be according to Minhag Polen.[34]

[. . .]

SOURCE: Constitution and By-Laws of Congregation B'nai Israel (San Francisco: M. Weiss Oriental Printing House, 1873), F869.S3.4.S175 no. 6, Bancroft Library, University of California, Berkeley.

30. Levinson, *Jews in the California Gold Rush,* 103.

31. Levinson, *Jews in the California Gold Rush,* 113. The men from San Francisco were invited by the congregation to conduct services.

32. Benjamin, *Three Years in America,* vol. 2, 96.

33. For more about Jackson, see Harold I. Sharfman, *Nothing Left to Commemorate—The Story of the Pioneer Jews of Jackson Amador County, California* (Glendale: Arthur H. Clark, 1969).

34. The Jackson community and Sherith Israel in San Francisco used the same style of Polish prayer and name for their cemeteries.

ARTICLE V.

Elections

Section 1. The election of all officers named in Article IV, shall be held annually on Yom Kippur night, and the officers then elected shall enter upon their duties immediately. [. . .]

ARTICLE VI.

Duties and Powers of the Board of Officers.

[. . .]

SEC. 2. They shall have the entire management of the Cemetery, [Givat Olam, written in Hebrew] (Giboth Olem)—Hills of Eternity—and adopt such rules and regulations for its government as they may from time to time deem necessary. [. . .]

ARTICLE VII.

DUTIES OF THE PRESIDENT

[. . .]

SEC. 5. It shall be his [the president's] duty to superintend all religious ceremonies in the Synagogue, and to distribute the Mitzvahs, and he shall present a hiyuv [obligation, in Hebrew] with at least one [Mitzvah, written in Hebrew].

[. . .]

ARTICLE XI.

MEMBERS

SECTION 1. Any Israelite desirous of becoming a member of this Congregation, shall apply in writing to the Board of Officers, occompanying the napplication with an admission fee of three dollars ($3), at tee Annual meeting of the Congregation, the application shall be acted upon; and if the majority of the votes favor the acceptance, the applicant shall be declared duly elected to membership.

SEC. 2. No Israelite shall be considered qualified for membership who is united in marriage contrary to the laws and ordinances of our religion nor any Israelite who has not attained the age of eighteen (18) years.

SEC. 3. Every new elected member must sign the Constitution and By-Laws, and after complying with these duties, he shall be entitled to the rights and privileges of membership.

SEC. 4. No member shall be eligible to office, unless he has been a member for twelve months previous to the election.

SEC. 5. An applicant for membership being rejected, his initiation fee shall be refunded to him, but he may appeal to the Congregation at a regular meeting, when two thirds of the votes of the members present shall be required to elect him.

SEC. 6. Any member who shall marry contrary to the laws and ordinances of our religion, who shall renounce Judaism, shall forfeit his membership.

SEC. 7. Any member wishing to resign shall signify the same in writing, addressed to the President and Board of Officers, who shall, if he is not in arrears accept the same, and he shall forfeit all rights and privileges and interest as a member of this Congregation.

SEC. 8. Sons of members shall enjoy the privileges of members; childern until the age of eighteen, and daughters until they are married.

SEC. 9. A widow, whose husband was at the time of his demise a member of this Congregation, shall enjoy the same privileges as a member's wife; the children of such members as members' children—that is: the widow, while she remains unmarried; sons, until they attain the age of eighteen; and daughters, until they are married, provided the arrears of such members be paid.

SEC. 10. Sons of members of this Congregation, who have attained the age of eighteen years, shall, upon application, be entitled to become members without paying the admission fee; subject, however, to all other laws provided for applicants for membership.

SEC. 11. Any member in arrears for dues, assessments, or offerings, or otherwise indebted to the Congregation over twelve months, shall not vote at any meeting, nor take part in any proceedings; neither shall he be eligible to any office until such arrears are paid.

SEC. 12. Any member who may refuse to conform to the rules and regulations for order and decorum during Divine Service, after being notified by an officer of the Congregation, shall be liable to a fine, suspension or expulsion, at the discretion of the Board of Officers; but an appeal may be taken to the Congregation against the penalty of expulsion.

SEC. 13. Any member of this Congregation who shall keep, or cause to be kept open his usual place of business on [Rosh Hashanah, written in Hebrew] (Rash Hashanah) and [Yom Kippur, written in Hebrew] (Yom Kipur) for the purpose of transacting buisness, shall be stricken from the Roll of membership.

[By Laws]

ARTICLE V

FINES.

SECTION 1. Any member of the Board of Officers not attending a meeting of the Board, if notified, shall be subject to a fine of two dollars ($2).

SEC. 2. Any member not attending a regular meeting of the Congregation, if duly notified, shall pay a fine of fifty cents (50 cts.).

SEC. 3. Any member signing a petition for a special meeting, or preferring charges and not attending, shall pay a fine of five dollars ($5).

SEC. 4. Any member leaving a meeting without the permission of the presiding officers, shall be subject to a fine of one dollar ($1). Any member leaving a meeting so as to destroy a quorum shall be subject to a fine of five dollars ($5).

SEC. 5. Any member not attending to his duty, when appointed on a committee, shall be subject to a fine of five dollars ($5).

SEC. 6. The presiding officer shall have the power to fine members for disorderly conduct at a meeting with any sum not exceeding two dollars ($2).

8

The River Supply Towns

BECAUSE THEY SUPPLIED GOODS FOR THE MOTHER LODE AND THE northern mines, the river towns of Sacramento, Stockton, and Marysville were more stable than the mining camps. With steamers docking regularly, they became centers of communication where people from far and wide could exchange gossip and business news. As regional hubs and farming towns, their economic viability was not completely dependent on gold strikes, but when the weather was poor or mining fell off, they suffered. Because they were port towns, they were also prone to disastrous flooding, which often destroyed their business districts. The business enterprises in supply towns were similar to those of mining towns, but they were more diverse and catered to a larger market. This market declined with the end of the Gold Rush and the coming of the railroad, which superseded the waterways.

A Jewish community structure evolved in supply towns as it did in other towns, with the establishment of benevolent societies, cemeteries, congregations, and social and fraternal organizations. Stockton's Jewish cemetery stood as evidence of the care residents took in burying their own. A synagogue building dedicated in 1855 was in use until 1861, when it was inundated by flood waters and had to be moved to higher ground.[1] The congregation followed the Polish *minhag* and functioned as both a *minyan* and a benevolent society for many years. In 1868 the community built a Sunday school to educate its children. An indication of the increasing number of women and families in

---

1. The building was moved once again in the twentieth century and converted into an apartment house. It was designated a historical landmark, the oldest surviving building in California of Jewish provenance.

California is found in Sam Marks's description of weddings and schools. In the spring of 1858, at least two couples were married within a short period of time in Stockton. This was the wedding season, when travel between the eastern and western United States, as well as between the mining and supply towns, became easier after the winter rains subsided, and couples and their families could be reunited. Weddings were held at close intervals so that families could share the expense of bringing a rabbi from San Francisco.

While Stockton supplied the Mother Lode, Marysville became a supply center for the northern mines. Named for Mary Murphy Clovillaud, a survivor of the Donner Party and the wife of the town's principal land owner, Marysville was founded in 1842 near the Feather and Yuba Rivers on property formerly belonging to John Sutter. The Jews of Marysville did not have a rabbi at their first religious services in 1853 and had to borrow a Torah from Sacramento. The leader of the service, A. M. Englander, identified himself in a letter to Isaac Leeser as a follower of traditional Judaism. A recent arrival, Englander may have prompted the Hebrew Benevolent Society to organize the services. Three years later, seventy couples gathered in Marysville for a charity ball sponsored by the benevolent society. The balls provided rare social entertainment and are evidence of the growing presence of women in the supply towns.

The increased number of families also created a need for cemetery ground. Headstones in the Marysville Jewish cemetery record the deaths of many young children and mothers, as well as of men who came to a violent end. These gravestones often provide the only evidence of the former vitality of Jewish life in the supply towns.

Most of these men and women at some time visited or lived in Sacramento. Because of its intermediate location, its Jewish community was always changing, with miners and merchants moving between Sacramento, San Francisco, and the mining country. In 1850 there were approximately two hundred Jews in the city.[2] By 1851 there was a flourishing benevolent society and about twenty Jewish firms in the clothing business, a larger number than existed in San Francisco.[3] A decade later, many of these merchants, most notably Louis Sloss and Lewis Gerstle, would become prominent in the San Francisco Jewish community. Selling men's, women's, and children's clothing, David Lubin's one-price store was an innovation, as it offered merchandise for a set price and ended the traditional practices of haggling and discounting for favored

---

2. Rudolf Glanz, *The Jews of California: From the Discovery of Gold until 1880* (New York: Southern California Jewish Historical Society, 1960), 45.

3. Iser, *Almanac*. The Benevolent Society grew slowly; by 1857 it had about seventy members and by 1860 eighty members. It raised funds for the Jews of Morocco and Prussia, as well as for Marysville when much of the town was destroyed by fire (Glanz, *Jews of California*, 45, 47).

customers. This small store grew into Weinstock's Department Store, one of the largest Jewish-owned chain stores in the West. Not as well known, but equally important at the time to the families of the mining and supply towns, were the services offered by Moses Hyman, who announced that, as a *mohel,* he was "ready to initiate children into the Covenant of Abraham."[4]

Lacking rabbis, congregations relied on their knowledgeable members to lead services. They could also count on visiting rabbis from San Francisco to dedicate synagogues and school buildings, perform weddings and other life-cycle events, and augment Jewish community life on religious holidays. Rabbi Henry A. Henry of Sherith Israel traveled by boat from San Francisco to Sacramento in 1858 to lecture, officiate at a funeral, and visit friends. In a letter describing the trip to Samuel Myer Isaacs, editor of the *Jewish Messenger,* he took pleasure in the presence of a strong Jewish community in Sacramento and refuted the common belief that the search for wealth in California's interior would deter Jews from religious observance.

---

4. *Weekly Gleaner,* Nov. 27, 1857, 358.

66
Stockton's First Fenced Cemetery
San Joaquin Republican, 1851

In 1851 a Jewish Benevolent Society held regular worship services and social gatherings in Stockton and consecrated a fenced cemetery that drew the attention of the local press. The land was donated by Captain Weber, the city's founder, and was first used for the burial of Solomon Friedlander, formerly of St. Louis, who died at age eighty-six in Sonora,[5] where there would not be a Jewish cemetery until 1853.

JEWISH CEMETERY. The Jews have stolen a march on the Christians. They have provided a cemetery for their dead, which is enclosed with a strong, solid fence, and is in every way a credit and an honor to them. It is situated near the Calaveras. We are told that *our* cemetery is unenclosed and that the swine root up interred bodies. Jesus!

SOURCE: *San Joaquin Republican,* Nov. 19, 1851, 2.

5. *San Joaquin Republican,* Oct. 18, 1851; Levinson, *Jews in the California Gold Rush,* 94, 174.

67

A Synagogue for Stockton

Occident and American Jewish Advocate, Philadelphia, 1856

Word of the founding of a new Jewish community reached all the way to Philadelphia. In 1855, when lumber for the synagogue was shipped from the East Coast around the Horn, members of the congregation met the ship at the river front and hauled the lumber by horse and wagon to the synagogue site.

STOCKTON, CALIFORNIA.—[. . .] After considerable debate, [they] formed themselves into a congregation under the name of Rayim Ahubim [also written in Hebrew]. "Beloved Friends" [. . .] The members were but few when the society was started; but at the date of the letter before us (October) they amounted to forty-three, many of whom live within thirty miles from the city. At this meeting it was resolved to rent a suitable room, and to fit it up for a Synagogue. A committee was appointed to carry this resolution into effect, who at the subsequent meeting reported on the cost of renting and fitting up a room. Several members having made some suggestions regarding the report, it was resolved, after considerable debate, to build a place of public worship, and a subscription was opened to raise the requisite amount of funds. A lot of ground one hundred feet square, in the best locality of the city, was generously presented to the congregation by CHARLES M. WEBBER, [*sic*] Esq., and it was resolved to erect the Synagogue thereon. The officers made a contract for a structure of wood, on a solid brick foundation of 50 by 35 feet, for $2650, and it was already completed on the 28th of August; and on the first Friday of September the building was dedicated to the worship of God by the Rev. Dr. Julius Eckman, of San Francisco, in pretty much the usual manner observed on these occasions. Liberal offerings were made after the Sepharim had been placed on the desk; Dr. Eckman then delivered an address, and the whole was concluded by an hallelujah sung by the choir. In accordance with the constitution, an election was held for officers [. . . thus] we have a new organization of Israelites in the distant West, and we trust to hear many good reports from the members, and that peace and happiness may attend them at home and abroad.

SOURCE: *Occident and American Jewish Advocate*, Philadelphia, Feb. 1856, 561.

68

"Having Nothing to Do the Knight"

Sam Marks, 1858

Communication between supply town residents and their friends and relatives in the East revolved around the comings and goings of the mail steamers. In the following letter, Sam Marks tells of weddings in Stockton, family activities, and the death of his friend Emanuel Linoberg.[6]

Stockton March 20 1858

Friend Friedlander

Having Nothing to Do the Knight I make the time usfull to Drop to you these few Lines, the mail Steamer from the States Cam in last knight to San fr[ancisco] We Will gitt her[e] the Mail up in morning, Shall I gid a Letter from you to morrow I will ancer it. [. . .] To marrow is Sunday, and we will have a Wedding I. Mitchell with Miss. Pyser, N. Mitchell with Miss Jacobs will be before long. Sister Rahle and children are here in good health—She will go up in a few Days, Rose will stay hir we [encouraged] her to go to the Ladis Cemenery for 5 monts. She is a smart child. She is going thir no[w] 2 weeks. [. . .] Business has been slow for the last few Days, but We Expect it better in a few Days 3 Brl. of the Cario Dimond and the Black Julius have left by the last steamer, I will send to you the steamer after to morrow, I hope to recieve Letters from you. Monthly if no more. I have written to you in my last letter that I will let you know more in my next, but I left San francisco sooner an I Expect, and was not able to find out. Last friday a Dispatger cam down to San francisco that E Linoberg was sick a few Hours and Departed for ever. Jacob Cohn Cam down this evening and on we[dnesday] the mail the Steamer will stay here entill to morrow so he stop here with us the Knight.

Good morning. This Sunday morning the Mail Cam up but no Letter from you I am in Hopes to hear from you by the next Steamer. Nothing more now of importance

Remembering yours Truly

my kind regards to your Bro Sister and family

Sam Marks

[note added by Jacob Cohn] I send my Regard to you also to all my Friends[,] your Friend Jacob Cohn.

SOURCE: Sam Marks to friend Friedlander, 1858. Friedlander Collection, American Jewish Archives, Hebrew Union College.

6. For more about the life of Emanuel Linoberg, see chapter 7.

69
Charity Balls: A Feature of the Season
Weekly California Express, Marysville, 1856

Like its counterparts, the Hebrew Benevolent Society of Marysville was dedicated to raising funds for "relief to the poor, needy, sick, and the burial of the dead of the Jewish persuasion in Marysville and vicinity."[7] Meeting on the first Sunday of the month, either in the city hall, rented rooms, or their own rooms in a brick building in central Marysville, the society acquired land for a cemetery and through the 1860s sponsored public events, like the ball described below, to raise money to support their efforts.

First annual ball of the Hebrew Benevolent Society.—The Ball of Wednesday evening, given by the Hebrews of this city, for the benefit of their benevolent association, was the feature of the season. The Hall—it was held in the City Hall—was tastefully and appropriately decorated. We cannot do justice to the detail, and will, therefore, not attempt it; but cannot omit a notice of the two portraits of the Father of his country, that were placed vis a vis.

There were present about seventy couples of beautiful women and brave men. We dare not attempt a description of the beauty, elegance and good taste of the former, the latter we will take the liberty of congratulating on their good fortune in being in such fair company.

The music was exquisite, the managers all attention. Here we must pause to pay a well merited compliment. Never has there been a Ball in our city, where so much pain was taken, and with so much success, to make each feel that he was a favored guest. Strangers were introduced and provided with partners, the very best order was preserved, and the wants and desires of all cared for.

The supper was served at the Haun House by that prince of caterers, Videau, and we need not add that everything was *au fait.* Our old time friend Henry has to make his first mistake.

After supper, the dance was continued until the wee small hours were increasing in their number, so much as to admonish all of the propriety of breaking up, but all seemed loath to separate- but at length, good-bye was said and the pleasant reunion was broken up. It will long be remembered with pleasure by those who were so fortunate as to be participants.

SOURCE: *Weekly California Express*, Marysville, Oct. 25, 1856, 4.

7. Article Two of the constitution of Marysville's Hebrew Benevolent Society, as quoted in *History of Yuba County California with Illustrations descriptive of its Scenery, Residences, Public Buildings, Fine Blocks and Manufactories* (Oakland, Calif.: Thompson and West, 1879), 62.

70

The Religious Views of a Marysville Farmer

A. M. Englander, 1857

A farmer and supporter of traditional Judaism, A. M. Englander wrote to Isaac Leeser about the battle between proponents of Orthodox and Reform Judaism in Marysville. Three months later an article appeared in San Francisco's *Weekly Gleaner* noting that men gathered "in the rooms of the M. H. Benevolent Society, and organized a Congregation by the name of, 'Bnei Beris' whose principal object it is, to maintain our holy Religion, and the erection of a Synagogue."[8] Mr. Englander was listed as the secretary of the congregation.

Rev. Isaac Leeser Philadelphia

Marysville Yuba County Cal. Aug. 2th 1857.

Rev. Sir! Although not having the pleasure of being personally acquainted with you, yet my name will not be quite strange among some of your correspondents, say in the years [18]46–47, and in reference to this I take this opportunity congratulating you most heartily to your present appointment as Minister of the Portuguese Congregation in Philadelphia; a better choice Sir, could said Congregation not have, and in no way could she have shown that its members Know to appreciate your talents as well as your merits in behalf of the true Judaism and our holy Religion. May the Almighty heavenly father grant you a long long life with uninterrupted health, that you may be the pride of our nation, the true religious guide of your beloved Congregation, for an unlimited time of years yet, and that you may henceforth be the defender of our ancient faith, when attacked by but a very few.

Believe me Sir, the great mass is with you, the enlightened is with you, the old and the rising generation are with you. We do not want any reform, because, we are reformed, more than we ought to be, we proclaim Torat Moshe Emet [Hebrew script: the Torah of Moses is true] and shall never allow *one* or *two* individuals to profane that what is sacred to every Israelite, and therefore every Israelite who has the maintenance of our Religion at heart will sustain you, in that cause you have taken and which I hope you'll pursue, Et laasot la-Adonay heferu Toratan [It is time for the Lord to work; They have made void Thy law (Psalm 119: 126)]. I would have written to you sooner, had my situation not

---

SOURCE: A. M. Englander to Isaac Leeser, Aug. 2, 1857. Isaac Leeser Collection, Center for Judaic Studies Library, University of Pennsylvania. Microfilm courtesy of Hebrew Union College.

8. *Gleaner,* Nov. 9, 1857.

been the cause of not doing so. I am now four years in this country and have devoted myself since that time to the agriculture business, I am a farmer, have a Ranch of my own about 2 1/2 miles from Marysville, where I live with my family, till and work the soil with my own hands, and thank God I can say, I met till now, with success, all what grieves me, is the impossibility of living according to our Religion, but I entertain the joyful hope, that times is not far off when I am able to do it. Speaking of my situation which is in my way of not writing to you oftener, that is to say, that I am so continually engaged in my farm, that I always like to see the evening come, on account of seeing the hours of Rest.

The affairs of the Israelites here are progressing slowly, there exists a Benevolent Society, of which I am a member, counting some 40 more, and having a fund of about 700 dollars, a beautiful burying ground with a little brick building on it, as a *mtahara* house [Hebrew script: *metaher*, house where Jews purified and washed the bodies]. A great deal of money is always expendet in the way of charity, and although we live in the so called Golden country, yet there is scarcely a week where we are not called to exercise our charity. About a year ago I started the Idea of erecting a Synagogue, but met with some resistance by a mister A. Tuska[9] a son of Rev. Mr. Tuska of Rochester, an adherer to the reformed party of Mr. Wise, it caused some unpleasant newspapers artikels, between Mr. T. and myself and then I dropped the idea, being satisfactorily convinced that the majority of our co-religionists in Marysville, have neither the religious feeling, not the energy for such a work.

I repeat my congratulation, and remain Rev. Sir
your humble servant
A. Englander

---

9. A. Tuska, a subscription agent for Rabbi Wise's *American Israelite,* was a merchant and an officer of Marysville's Hebrew Benevolent Association (Kramer and Stern, "Letters of 1852 to 1864 Sent to Rabbi Isaac Leeser," 43–59).

71
If the Stones Could Talk
Marysville Cemetery Stones, 1859–1869

Acquired in 1855 by the Marysville Hebrew Benevolent Society, Marysville's Hebrew Cemetery has more than forty-six grave sites. Purchased for fifty dollars from the estate of Robert Buchanan, the cemetery land located at the southeast corner of the City Cemetery was one block square, with a high fence and a small building for preparing the dead for burial. There are several family plots, the last burial having taken place in 1945. Except for the California-born children, many of whom died in infancy, most of the gravestones list Prussia and Germany as places of birth.[10] Many of the stones have Hebrew as well as English text.

Simon Glucksman

Simon Glucksman died August 26, 1859, at the age of twenty-four. Born in Kempen, Prussia, he was murdered on the road between La Porte and St. Louis, mining towns just north of Marysville. The stone shows a broken tree limb, symbolizing that Glucksman died in the prime of his life.

SOURCE: Marysville Cemetery Stones, 1859–69. Photograph of Hanchen Hirschfelder's stone by Bram Goodwin. Photographs of Simon Glucksman's and Eddy Armer's stones by editor.

10. For more information on the Marysville cemetery, see Susan Morris, *A Traveler's Guide to Pioneer Jewish Cemeteries.*

366

Hanchen Meyer Hirschfelder

After an initial trip to California,[11] Emanuel Hirschfelder had returned to his home city of Karlsruhe, Germany, to marry Hanchen [Meyer] and return with her to California. In 1856 they settled northeast of Marysville in Downieville. There he operated a furnishing and variety store in a brick building and advertised in the local newspapers. The Hirschfelders had three children. After Hanchen's death, the children, still quite young, were raised by relatives and family friends. Emanuel later settled in Ventura in southern California, where he remarried and became the father of two additional children.

---

11. For Hanchen Meyer Hirschfelder's account of her trip west, see chapter 2.

Eddy Armer

Eddy, the son of Max and Dorothea Armer, died in 1861 at the age of two. His German-born father, Max Armer, was a merchant and member of the B'nai B'rith and the Yuba Engine Company. He died in San Francisco in 1904.

72

The Sacramento *Mohel*

Moses Hyman, 1858

Tradition has it that Moses Hyman, a Sacramento storekeeper and *mohel,* used the profits from his work to purchase property for a Jewish community cemetery.[12] It was in the back room of Hyman's store that the first Jewish religious services took place during the High Holidays of 1849. Born in Poland in 1810, Hyman came to the United States in the 1840s, settling in Sacramento, where he became a founder of congregation B'nai Israel and the community's Hebrew Benevolent Society. In 1851 Hyman married Rosina Goldstein, a widow whose husband had drowned in the Sacramento River. Hyman adopted his wife's child, and they had three sons of their own. Moses and Rosina Hyman are buried in the Sacramento Jewish cemetery, where Moses's gravestone reads: "The Pioneer of California Judaism. The true friend of the poor. Beloved by

Notice to Israelites.

THE undersigned brings to the notice of his numerous friends in Sacramento and elsewhere that he is ready to initiate children into the convenant of Abraham. He shall be happy to attend most punctually on those who wish to honor him with their confidence,

Sacramento City, Cor. 6th and N sts   M. HYMAN.

☞ Parties who come to Sacramento for the occasion, can be accommodated with rooms free of charge.

NOTICE.—Parties who desire to have letters writen for נצרח or Synagogues need but apply to me and they will be accommodated at moderate charges. Samples of my Hebrew writing may be seen in both synagogues here.

SOURCE: Advertisement, *Weekly Gleaner*, Jan. 8, 1858, 409.

12. Harold F. Reinhart, *Diamond Jubilee: The Seventy-Fifth Anniversary of the Consecration of the First Synagogue Building in the West 1852–1927*, Temple B'nai Israel (Sacramento: Temple B'nai Israel, 1927), 8; Marlene S. Gaines, "The Early Sacramento Jewish Community," *Western States Jewish Historical Quarterly* 3:2 (1971): 69. Hyman is buried in this cemetery, Home of Peace.

God and man."[13] According to the advertisement there were two synagogues in Sacramento at the time; one is believed to have followed the German *minhag* and the other the Polish *minhag*.

13. For more information about Moses Hyman, see Norton B. Stern, "The Pioneer of Sacramento Jewry," *Western States Jewish History* 21:4 (1989): 345–49.

Sacramento flood, 1850. Etching 1852. Courtesy of the Bancroft Library (FF861.C245V3:7BIC), University of California, Berkeley.

73
A Rabbi Visits the Garden City
Rabbi Henry A. Henry, 1858

Rabbi Henry A. Henry of San Francisco's Congregation Sherith Israel (1857–69) often traveled to California's interior and especially to Sacramento to visit and perform religious ceremonies,[14] as is evident in his letter to Rabbi Samuel Myer Isaacs of New York, editor of the *Jewish Messenger*. An author of a number of books on Jewish practice and prayer, Henry also regularly contributed articles to journals and newspapers. When the following article was written, Sacramento did not yet have a permanent rabbi.

San Francisco, August 17, 1858.

Rev. S[amuel] M[yer] Isaacs:

Dear Sir—I take pleasure in acknowledging the receipt of your *Messenger* and to express my humble opinion of the marked improvement visible in it, since I have left your empire city. I have no doubt if it shall continue progressing in the same ratio, you will have the gratification of seeing the child you have so carefully fostered in infancy, realise all your fondest expectations, for the benefit and improvement of its readers. I am happy to find on a perusal of its pages, that you avoid all controversy and party-feeling—I think such a course is the most prudent, and better calculated to ensure a wide circulation of any periodical, especially among us Israelites who (though we may differ on certain minor points), should always bear in mind, that we have but one object at heart and that is the diffusion of knowledge and learning, and the promulgation of the principles of our Holy Law and religion, as practised by our forefathers of old—all that I want is unity—for where unity reigns, happiness exists, and success ensues.

I am led to make these few remarks, having but just returned from a visit to Sacramento, the garden city of our land of gold, where I had the happiness of meeting many old friends and acquaintances, who greeted my arrival among them in a manner I shall never forget. It was really delightful to see how they welcomed one whom they knew in infancy, and from whom they had received the germs of an education, which reminded them even on the distant shores of the broad Pacific, that they are the descendants of Israel, the favorite and chosen people of God.

SOURCE: Rabbi Henry A. Henry to Rev. Samuel Meyer Isaacs, *Jewish Messenger*, Sept. 24, 1858.

14. For more about Rabbi Henry A. Henry, see chapter 6.

As a proof of the desire which is now prevalent among our nation for religious instruction, immediately on my arrival an invitation was extended to me to preach in the synagogue on Saturday, which I did, to a very respectable auditory for so small a number of Israelites in the city. It was gratifying to me to behold how attentively all listened—and the satisfaction they all expressed in hearing the Word of God expounded in a language which they understood.

On the next day, Sunday, the congregation *en masse* repaired to the burial ground to witness the ceremony of placing a *matzevah* [monument] over the grave of the late Mr. Julius S. Winehill, of that city, of whom the tongue of good report has resounded wherever his name is mentioned. I learned while there that in life he was beloved, in death regretted and lamented; and having been requested to perform the ceremony, I took the opportunity of preaching a funeral sermon which elicited that spark of a religious feeling which no other circumstance in life can produce, as the death bed scene, and the depositing of the lifeless clay in the cold, cold grave.

On our return to the city, the remaining part of the day was spent by most of our friends in thinking as to which mode should be adopted among them in order to ensure a more rigid observance of the Sabbath, and a better attendance at the synagogue; and also, to promote the cause of Judaism. And they did me the favor publicly to declare that I had succeeded in awakening among them that feeling for our holy faith, and a zealous enthusiasm to walk humbly before their God.

What greater reward could I have anticipated? I assure you, my dear sir, that the impression it made on me will never be obliterated from my mind. This, in addition, to the kindness extended to me by all around, will at all times prove the most powerful incentive to apply my humble talent to further the spiritual interest of my people, wherever fate may destine my lot to be cast.

Having declared my intention to depart for my home on Tuesday, I was honored by a deputation composed of the president and trustees of the congregation to favor them with another address previous to my departure, to which I readily consented, as such request was highly flattering to me and an encouragement to disseminate the Word of God, and reminded me of the recommendation of our sages: "If thou art living in a generation who show a desire to have the law expounded to them, encourage them by your teachings and spread the law widely among them."

Accordingly on Tuesday evening, the lecture having been announced in the public press, the house of God was crowded at an early hour; the evening service having been read as usual, I ascended the pulpit and addressed the people for upwards of an hour on the beauties of our holy religion, and the duties imposed on all Israelites by that religion. Tracing our origin up to the present period and pointing out all the privations our nation has endured, and the persecutions to which we have been subjected, and still by Divine Providence we are yet a people, a visible sign of the peculiar favor of the Great Architect of the Universe—and in conclusion exhorted them not to neglect the education of their children, both morally, and spiritually. Apparently I had made some impression on my hearers, if I am to judge from the expressions offered me at the close of the services.

On Wednesday morning, the day of my departure, the president and trustees waited on me in the name of the congregation, to tender their united and heartfelt thanks for the lectures I had delivered, expressing at the same time their wishes that I should soon return among them, and that they would take an early opportunity of publicly expressing their sentiments through the press. My response was brief, but soul-stirring, for I felt so delighted that the God of Israel had so far inspired a feeble mortal like myself to preach His Holy Word, and that it should have so successfully gained the hearts of my coreligionists as to induce them to follow Judaism as commanded by its Divine Author.

Having finished this part of their duty, the vice president, who was appointed chairman on the occasion, in behalf of my friends tendered me a purse containing a verified token of their feelings, and in the kindest manner requesting my acceptance of the same as a substantial proof of their gratitude and good wishes towards me. This pleasing task being fulfilled, we all repaired to the boat and left the garden city for the bay amid the greetings and well wishes of all my friends among whom I had spent a week so happily and comfortably.

It may not appear invidiously to the rest of my friends in thus publicly eschewing my best thanks to Mrs. Aronson and family, to whose hospitality I am considerably indebted for the many pleasant hours I enjoyed during my short stay in their happy domicile. My trip down the Sacramento River was really delightful as it was accompanied by so many pleasing reminiscences of present and past days, and which pleasantly gliding on the pearly stream in the floating saloon of the *Queen City.* I thought of the friends I had left behind, and in behalf of them and all their associates I invoked the blessing of Him who sits on high, praying that the coming years may prove a season of joy and gladness, a life of happiness and concord both to them and all Israel. Amen.

Should you think this communication worthy a place in your journal, I shall be happy in having had the opportunity through your kindness, to publish to the world that in the far distant land of California, the Jew, notwithstanding his desire for wealth, does not forget the God that made him, nor the religion which has at all times been the rock of his support through all his tribulations. As I shall have an opportunity shortly to address you on interesting subjects, I shall conclude with my best wishes and kind regards.

Yours faithfully,

H. A. Henry

74
The One-Price Store
of David Lubin and Harris Weinstock
Mechanics' Store Advertisements, 1876

Founded by Sacramento merchant David Lubin and his half-brother Harris Weinstock and known for its single-price policy, the One-Price Store first opened its doors in 1874. Born in Poland, Lubin arrived in San Francisco in the 1850s and traveled throughout the country before settling in Sacramento. A year after the store opened, it was renamed the Mechanics' Store, then the Weinstock-Lubin Company, and finally Weinstock's. Born in London, Weinstock arrived in California in 1869. Known for his public service, Weinstock was a member of the U.S. Industrial Relations Commission, as well as of many civic and Jewish organizations.

David Lubin had a deep interest in agriculture and was a founder of the California Fruit Growers' Union, the International Society for the Colonization of Russian Jews, and the International Institute of Agriculture, a precursor to the United Nations Food and Agriculture Organization. Lubin encouraged Jews to become farmers rather than merchants, and he promoted good employee relations, cooperative marketing, and agricultural reform.

David Lubin and Harris Weinstock, Sacramento, ca. 1880. Courtesy of the Western Jewish History Center, Judah L. Magnes Museum, Lubin and Weinstock Collections.

The Mechanics' Store, ca. 1878. Courtesy of the Sacramento Archives and Museum Collection Center. Weinstock-Lubin Collections.

YE TROD ON THE TAIL OF ME COAT!

CRY THE GRABBERS!

WE HAVE DETERMINED TO PROTECT THE POCKETS OF the hard-working toilers from the claws of the Grabbers, and WE WILL DO SO. We shall fight the combined army of Grabbers, singly and alone, as we have been doing. The people are watching the fight with interest, and are backing us to a man.

The Grabbers say that One Price is a Humbug. The People of Sacramento say THEY LIE.

The Grabbers copy and imitate our advertisements, having no brains of their own. All can see that they are without principle. They not alone steal and rob the money from their customers, but also the thoughts of their competitors. The copying, however, is so clumsy, and the lies they advertise so barefaced, that even the dullest mind cannot fail to see its true worth at a glance.

The Grabbers claim to do justice to their beswindled customers. Their unfortunate patrons and the People of Sacramento unite in saying that **They Lie.**

The GRABBER-IN-CHIEF has Reformed, or at least claims to have done so, as he now advertises that he has One Price. The People of Sacramento all unite in saying **He Lies.**

Grabbers, crawl back to your holes of oblivion, and don't put your dishonest faces before the public in such a conspicuous manner that honest people will have to stare at you.

Grabbers, howl as you will, your last dodge and struggle for the mastery avails you nothing, for WE HAVE ON OUR SIDE **Truth, Justice, Square Dealing,** and the solid support of the Sacramento public, while YOU HAVE ON YOUR SIDE **Lies, Injustice and Robbery.** Advertise as you will, you are doomed, as the people know you lie and dread to go near you.

Grabbers, lie all you can about the **Mechanics' Store.** We give you this privilege heartily, as it is an advertisement for us free of charge, as every man, woman and child in Sacramento knows that the **Mechanics' Store Sells only at One Price, that All Our Goods are Marked in Plain Figures, that no Goods are Misrepresented, that WE AIM to do Justice to One and All.** We assert that if a Storekeeper takes but 5 cents more from one customer than he does from another for a similar article, that he robs that customer of the 5 cents.

We do not make our prices according to the appearance of the customer, but **Have All Our Goods Marked in Plain Figures,** the inexperienced not paying one penny more than the sharpest and closest buyers.

☞ **To Strangers who have never been in the Mechanics, Store,** and have never traded with us, and wish to know if we do our business as we advertise, we would refer them to any person who has ever been in our Store or who has ever traded with us. There is no occasion for any one to hunt very hard to find people who have traded at the **Mechanics' Store,** as they are thickly scattered around throughout the States of California and Nevada.

We Publish a PRICE LIST, and also a Story Paper, which will be mailed Free to any address.

Send all Communications to the

MECHANICS' STORE,
100 K STREET,
SACRAMENTO.

m20-1m4p

SOURCE: Mechanics' Store advertisements, 1876. Lubin Collection, Western Jewish History Center of the Judah L. Magnes Museum, Berkeley, California.

Why Does
—THE—
MECHANICS' STORE
DISPOSE OF SUCH LARGE QUANTITIES
—OF—
MEN'S AND BOYS' UNDERWEAR?

SIMPLY,
BECAUSE THEY SELL A GOOD ARTICLE
FOR A LOW PRICE!

NO JUDGMENT REQUIRED
TO BUY GOODS
—AT THE—
MECHANICS' STORE!
CHILDREN RECEIVE THE SAME VALUE FOR THEIR MONEY AS GROWN PERSONS!

ONE PRICE TO RICH OR POOR,
—AT THE—
. MECHANICS' STORE!

Inquire for the BLACK HERMIT HAT at the Mechanics' Store.

It is Astonishing to see at what low prices Boys' and Youths' Suits are sold for at the Mechanics' Store.

The Aim of the Mechanics' Store is to hold the Grabbers in check, and to see that a hard-working Mechanic receives a Dollar's worth for a Dollar.

V
Group Relations

9
The "Mythical Jew" and the "Jew Next Door"

CALIFORNIA'S FIRST DECADES WERE A TIME FOR THE MEETING OF peoples who had barely if ever encountered so many strangers before, strangers whom they stereotyped, Jews among them. All brought with them historical and cultural memories, as well as ideas and expectations of what America should be. In this chapter's documents, Jews are seen both as individuals and as members of a problematic group occupying a pivotal niche in the Christian mind. They are depicted positively and negatively, in terms that are colored with both philo-Semitic and anti-Semitic terms. As Jonathan Sarna has astutely put it, gentiles attempted "to reconcile" their conceptions of "the 'mythical Jew,' found in the Bible, recalled in church, and discussed in stereotypical fashion, with the 'Jew next door' who seemed altogether different."[1]

During its first decades of statehood, California attracted a host of visitors eager to broadcast their experiences to a greater public. Among them were James H. Carson, J. D. Borthwick, and Charles Peters, who, like most mid-nineteenth-century writers, stereotyped Jews.[2] It was a common belief that Jews in Gold Rush California did not become miners, though in fact, as we have

---

1. Sarna, "The 'Mythical Jew' and the 'Jew Next Door,' in Nineteenth-Century America," in *Anti-Semitism in American History,* ed. David A. Gerber (Urbana: University of Illinois Press, 1986), 58.

2. The Tuolumne County Historical Society used Borthwick's descriptions of most ethnic groups in the county for its article "The Ethnic Argonauts," by Carlo M. De Ferrari. But Robert Levinson's description of the Jews was used in that article because, as Ferrari noted, "It is difficult to acquire an impartial picture of the Jews in the Gold Rush, for the prejudice of centuries weighed heavily upon the pens of those who wrote of them" (*Chispa: The Quarterly of the Tuolumne County Historical Society* [January/March 1978]: 591).

seen in the letters of Bernhard Marks and Isidor Choynski, a number of Jews did test their mettle in the mines, however fleetingly and unsuccessfully.[3] Peters's report of the role of Jewish merchants in the mining region takes account of their disproportionately heavy business losses in repeated fires. Like other writers, Peters admired Jewish merchants. In an era when physical assault in the mining regions was common, a Sonora Jewish merchant became a legend celebrated for his physical prowess, as the courageous "Israelite" thrashed an "Ammonite" bully.

Similarly, an 1860 Marysville newspaper report emphasized Jews' decorum in worship and invited non-Jews to attend services. An editorial several years later portrayed the Jews of Marysville as Jews of the Bible who had become Americans and should not be confused with European Jews, who were typically depicted in negative terms. It may be that the ugly turn taken in the legislative debate of the Sunday Laws in 1855 prompted that spirited rejoinder by the Marysville paper. In discussions of the Sunday Laws, Jews were often accused of not participating in the local economy but of sending their money elsewhere.

Quite the opposite was often the case, however. Jewish businessmen in San Francisco comprised such an important segment in the business community that in 1858 the Pacific Mail Steamer delayed its departure so that Jewish merchants could post their letters and packages after the close of the Yom Kippur fast. The *Daily Alta California* explained the holiday to its readers and used the occasion to celebrate the integration of Jews into California life.

In the tense atmosphere that preceded the Civil War, Jews were both reproved and courted as a voting bloc by both political parties in elections that would decide California's role in the North-South struggle. Newspaper editors both Jewish and gentile used Jewish history and culture to underscore Jewish patriotism or to argue Jewish disloyalty to the Union. As evidence of such disloyalty, Unionists cited Rabbi Julius Eckman's editorials in the *Gleaner,* which not only failed to support the Republican war effort but claimed that American culture was corrupt.[4] Eckman was viewed by many gentiles as the voice of the Jewish community. He was countered by Philo Jacoby, however, whose rival *Hebrew* strongly supported the Union.

Occasionally Jews and gentiles developed close and long-lasting professional and personal relationships. Frank Lecouvreur, writing of his association with his Jewish employer, pointed to the advantages accruing to gentiles from such ties. The deep friendship between Rabbi Julius Eckman and Rev. O. P. Fitzgerald, a

---

3. See chapter 7 for more about Marks and Choynski.
4. Robert J. Chandler, "Some Political and Cultural Pressures on the Jewish Image in Civil War San Francisco," *Western States Jewish History* 20:2 (1988): 154.

Methodist minister, was movingly portrayed by Fitzgerald's tribute to Eckman in *California Sketches.*

But perhaps the most thoughtful statement on the relations between Jews and gentiles in those years came from the pen of Henry Sienkiewicz, the noted Polish novelist who marveled over the adaptability of Polish Jewish immigrants to the California scene. In this he detected an object lesson for Poles, whose failures, he insisted, to recognize the great merits of their Jewish compatriots in Poland created a bogus "Jewish question."

75
Dutch John
James H. Carson, 1852

James H. Carson, a writer for the *San Joaquin Republican* in Stockton, described the different ethnic groups he encountered in Gold Rush country, portraying the Jew, "Dutch John," in stereotypical terms.[5] First published as a serial to accompany the steamer edition of the *San Joaquin Republican,* Carson's sixty-four-page pamphlet won high praise from California historian Hubert H. Bancroft.[6]

A JEW IN THE MINES.

Amongst our population of that golden day, we had one *Jew.* The old miners will ever remember Dutch John. When I arrived in the diggings, old friends hailed from every side, and an invitation was soon given all hands to go down to Dutch John's and take a *big drink.* As John's store was about a fair sample of the trading establishments of the day, a short description may not be uninteresting:

The *building,* like all others then used, consisted of brush cut from the closest trees; his stock of goods, two boxes of crackers, a few boxes of sardines, a few knives, (samples of every pattern ever made,) a half box of tobacco, and two barrels of the youngest whiskey I had ever tasted. The counter was the head of an empty barrel, set off with a broken tumbler, tin cup, and a junk bottle of the ardent. Scales and weights were not much then in use, and John's store had none. A drink was paid for by his taking a *pinch* of gold dust with his thumb and fore-finger from the miner's bag, or sorting out a lump the size and value of a dollar, according to Jewish ideas of such things.[7] Before taking the pinch from the bag, John's finger and thumb could be seen sliding down his throat (as far as the balance of the hand would permit) for the purpose of covering them with saliva, to make the gold stick, and he then thrust it into the miners *pile.* The amount of such a pinch was from four to eight dollars! "Got und Himmel," John: if we have accounts to settle in the next world, wont the clerks have a time of it with yours! This mode of settling was looked upon rather as a source of fun for the miners, than as an imposition.

SOURCE: James H. Carson, *Early Recollections of the Mines, San Joaquin Republican,* Jan. 17, 1852, bound copy at Bancroft Library, University of California, Berkeley.

5. "John" was a name used for all ethnic groups. Chinese were known as "Chinese John." "Dutch" comes from a misunderstanding of the German word "Deutsch," which translates to "German."

6. Erwin G. Gudde, *California Gold Camps* (Berkeley: University of California Press, 1975), 390.

7. A "pinch of gold" was considered a common form of payment before scales were available.

76
The Jew Slop Shops
J. D. Borthwick, 1857

J. D. Borthwick, an affluent Scottish artist, toured the California gold country from 1851 to 1855, eagerly observing, sketching, and writing about every ethnic group he met, including the Jews of Hangtown (Placerville). Although Borthwick wrote negatively about the Jews, he had quite positive things to say about the Chinese, which was uncommon among those in California during this era.

The clothing trade was almost entirely in the hands of the Jews, who are very numerous in California, and devote their time and energies exclusively to supplying their Christian brethren with the necessary articles of wearing apparel.

In traveling through the mines from one end to the other, I never saw a Jew lift a pick or shovel to do a single stroke of work, or, in fact, occupy himself in any other way than in selling slops. While men of all classes and of every nation showed such versatility in betaking themselves to whatever business or occupation appeared at the time to be most advisable, without reference to their antecedents, and in a country where no man, to whatever class of society he belonged, was in the least degree ashamed to roll up his sleeves and dig in the mines for gold, or to engage in any other kind of manual labour, it was a very remarkable fact that the Jews were the only people among whom this was not observable.

They were very numerous—so much so, that the business to which they confined themselves could hardly have yielded to every individual a fair average California rate of remuneration. But they seemed to be proof against all temptation to move out of their own limited sphere of industry, and of course, concentrated upon one point as their energies were, they kept pace with the go-ahead spirit of the times. Clothing of all sorts could be bought in any part of the mines more cheaply than in San Francisco, where rents were so very high that retail prices of everything were most exorbitant; and scarcely did twenty or thirty miners collect in any out-of-the-way place, upon newly discovered diggings, before the inevitable Jew slop-seller also made his appearance, to play his allotted part in the newly-formed community.[8]

Source: J. D. Borthwick, *Three Years in California* (Edinburgh and London: William Blackwood, 1857), 116–18.

8. The term "Jew slop-shop" was sometimes used to describe non-Jewish stores.

The Jew slop-shops were generally rattletrap erections about the size of a bathing-machine, so small that one half of the stock had to be displayed suspended from projecting sticks outside. They were filled with red and blue flannel shirts, thick boots, and other articles suited to the wants of the miners, along with Colt's revolvers and bowie-knives, brass jewelry, and diamonds like young Koh-i-Noors.

Almost every man, after a short residence in California, became changed to a certain extent in his outward appearance. In the mines especially, to the great majority of men, the usual style of dress was one to which they had never been accustomed; and those to whom it might have been supposed such a costume was not so strange, or who were even wearing the old clothes they had brought with them to the country, acquired a certain California air, which would have made them remarkable in whatever part of the world they came from, had they been suddenly transplanted there. But to this rule the Jews formed a very striking exception. In their appearance there was nothing whatever at all suggestive of California; they were exactly the same unwashed-looking, slobbery, slipshod individuals that one sees in every seaport town.

77

"The Most Expert Gold Dust Buyers"

Charles Peters, 1850s

Carlo Pedre Deogo Laudier De Andreiado (Charles Peters) was born in 1825 on the island of Fiol off the western coast of Portugal. Leaving Fiol as a cabin boy, Peters landed in San Francisco just in time for the Gold Rush. In this reminiscence he narrates tales, tall and otherwise, of Jews he met. A peddler with a heavy backpack was Peters's stereotype of a Jew.

GOOD LUCK FOR JEWS

The descendants of Abraham came to California in large numbers from every part of the globe in the '50s. They do not appear to have done any prospecting;

A JEW PEDDLER OF THE '50s

His Four Degrees of Business
1st.   Mit a pack on his back
2nd.   Mit a horse and wagon
3rd.   Mit a store
4th.   Mit a bank or bankrupt

138

A Jewish Peddler, 1850s. From Peters, *Autobiography of Charles Peters* (Sacramento: La Grave, 1915).

any pioneering; made any discoveries or worked any placers,[9] but they were there with the goods as fast as new channels of trade were opened.

A well known showman of that time was used to often remark, he could easily gauge the prosperity of a mining town by the number of Jewish storekeepers it maintained and the size of its Chinatown.

It is stated that on hearing of a rush to a new mining excitement in the interior, a Jewish merchant in San Francisco sent a relative to view the prospect and advise on the proposition of opening a store. A few days afterward he received a telegram from his relative, sent from a telegraph office, the nearest to the new diggings, reading: "Come. It was richness." Such was the way they kept in touch with the movements of the mining population and they were soon on the spot with the necessary goods to feed, clothe and supply the heedless rushers.

Many of the Jews amassed wealth and with their investments and their backing of experienced miners, gave material aid in developing the mining industry of the State. Many more would have gathered wealth had it not been for the frequency that the hastily built business sections of the mining towns were swept away by fire. The names of the Jewish merchants were always amongst those of the heaviest losers.

Numbers of these people soon developed into the most expert gold dust buyers in the State. It was seldom a rogue attempted to fool one of them with bogus dust. They could tell at sight from the color of the gold, its fineness and value per ounce, and besides that, they could invariably name the locality where it had been dug. To this fact was due the following incident: The Iowa Hill express office was robbed one night of a large quantity of gold dust. Officers investigating the robbery were unable to obtain a clew and after a few days' search concluded the robbers had departed and might sell the gold dust elsewhere. Circulars were sent out all over the State giving particulars of the robbery.

A short time after this a communication was received from an El Dorado County gold dust buyer stating that a miner, claiming to be working in a ravine in El Dorado County, was selling small quantities of Iowa Hill gold dust mixed with that he mined in El Dorado County. The buyer knew it was Iowa Hill gold dust from its characteristics and fineness, and at the times he had bought it, he did not know of the robbery. This information led to the robber being traced, located and arrested.

SOURCE: Charles Peters, *The Autobiography of Charles Peters* (Sacramento: La Grave, 1915), 137–40.

9. Placer refers to a type of surface gold mining in which water pressure is applied to gravel that contains gold ore.

A Jew gold dust buyer in one of the mountain mining towns, from the frequency which stages were being held up and robbed, surmised that it would not be long before the route by which he expressed his sack of gold dust, weekly, to the mint, would receive an unwelcome visit. He, therefore, instead of agreeing to share the heavy expense of sending armed guards with the express, figured out a plan of his own to save himself from loss. He sent to San Francisco for several hundred pounds of lead bars. He held his gold dust shipments back for a month, then melted the quantity over a furnace and made it into a bar. This he incased in melted lead until it made an ingot, when cooled, that weighed over two hundred pounds. He placed it in an oilcloth pouch without any handles or straps. As he anticipated, the stage was stopped by two robbers and the express box rifled, but when it came to this bar, there was loud profanity. It could not be lifted, and as the men of the road had neither tools nor conveyance to handle it, they were compelled to leave it.

78
Some of Our Best Citizens
Daily Evening Herald, Marysville, 1853

First organized in 1853, the Marysville Jewish community came to support several fraternal organizations, including a Hebrew Benevolent Society, B'nai B'rith, and Kesher Shel Barzel, which also had a women's affiliate. In this report of the dedication of a synagogue in 1853, Marysville's *Daily Evening Herald* probably referred to a room set aside for worship services by the Hebrew Benevolent Society.

The Israelites of Marysville, comprising a large class of our best citizens, have established a synagogue in this city, as a place of worship.

It was dedicated yesterday; a large number of adherents of that church being present. The ceremonies were imposing, and withal beautiful. The Synagogue is in the new brick building on C. st., between 1st and 2nd, east side, up stairs.

Services were held in the synagogue this morning, and will be again, this evening at 6 o'clock. They are now engaged in celebrating one of their feasts [Rosh Hashanah], an account of which can be found in Leviticus, chapter 23, from 23d to 32d verses, inclusive.

Services will also be held to-morrow forenoon; and on Wednesday next, they will hold service in the synagogue, in commemoration of the day of atonement. The services will commence on the evening of the 11th and continue until the evening of the 12th.

For the perfection of this, to them, Holyday, they procured from Sacramento, the holy writings which have been handed down from the days of the Patriarchs. The ceremonies will be held with regularity and decorum, and to those who have never witnessed the mode of worship of these "chosen people," will, no doubt, be exceedingly interesting.

An invitation is extended to the citizens of Marysville, and all others who desire, to attend the services at the synagogue. A. M. Englander officiates for the present, as the leader of ceremonies.

SOURCE: *Daily Evening Herald*, Marysville, Oct. 3, 1853, 3.

79
Sons of Israel Do Not Beg
Marysville Appeal, 1860

The character of the American Jew in general, and of Marysville's Jews in particular, was attributed by the *Marysville Appeal* to the Jewish tradition of *Tzedakah,* or charity.

Marysville Hebrew Benevolent Association.

Did any of our readers ever see a son of Israel begging? We think not, for although there are mendicant Jews in some portions of Europe, in America the Hebrew is better circumstanced, and is too loving and proud of his race to let a brother ask charity of the gentile. One of the means by which this is prevented may be found in the organization of Hebrew Benevolent Associations in every town where a score or two of the ancient people have taken up residence. Such an organization was organized in Marysville July 22, 1855, and now numbers 31 members. The whole basis of the Society is found in the scriptural precept: "If there be among you a poor man of thy Brethren within any of thy gates in the land which the Lord thy God giveth thee, thou shalt not harden thy heart, nor shut thy hands from thy poor Brothers." The payment of monthly dues of one dollar each, with some aid from festival gatherings and donations, affords the Marysville Hebrews a fund which is sufficient not only to carry out this precept from day to day, but to leave in their joint treasury a handsome capital for investment against future exigencies. They now have almost $1100 out on interest at 2 1/2 per cent per month and some $250 in hand. They have purchased and improved a Hebrew Cemetery an acre of ground wherein repose the ashes of twenty-two persons buried by them, mostly children. Several marble monuments have been erected in this God's acre, to use the good old Saxon phrase, and a brick edifice has been erected wherein to wash and prepare the dead for burial, after the Hebrew custom. The demands upon the Society for charity have not been numerous, a fact which is accounted for by the temperance and frugality of American Jews, and by the no less creditable fact they privately help one another. The amount charitably expended last year, not including money paid for interments was only $85. The receipts were about as follow: From fees and dues, $405; interest on money invested $128; net receipts from Anniversary ball, $84; donations $10; burial collections $16; total $643. After deducting rent and expenses a respectable amount was left for the permanent fund; so it will be seen this excellent society is in a prosperous and healthy condition.

Source: *Marysville Appeal,* Dec. 5, 1860.

80

Steamer Day Postponed on This Day of Atonement

Daily Alta California, San Francisco, 1858

In 1858, in deference to the Jewish mercantile community, the Pacific Mail Steamship Company postponed the departure of its steamer for three days to give Jewish merchants sufficient time to complete their correspondence after their work had been interrupted and their businesses closed during their observance of the Yom Kippur fast. The following editorial sees Pacific Mail's decision as an indication of widespread acceptance of Jews as an integral part of the California community and economy.

The Day of Atonement

The remnants of God's chosen people, the children of Israel, bow their heads to the ground, to-day, in sorrow and humiliation, for it is with them the most solemn of all the holy days ordained in the Pentateuch; a day of fasting and affliction of souls for the ills of the past, and grace to enter upon the future. It is a day cherished by strict observance wherever an Israelite sets his foot, and where they are not, for they have carried their altar—their faith—to all climes and among all nations, and with that consistency which their nationality alone evinces through the vista of the past, they offer up to the throne of grace their humble supplications in the same tongue which Moses, and all the hosts of great and good names—prophets and kings, used even at the day of their ingathering. It is a day on which even those of the faith who, throughout the year, are lax in their religious observances, feel it incumbent to join again with their brethren, and humble themselves with a contrite heart before the Almighty. Where can history point a parallel? The mighty nations which controlled the world before the advent of Christianity have been swept from existence. Their great cities are a heap of ruins, sublimely grand even in their decay. None live to tell of their faded greatness, save the Jews, who are "a cloud by day, and a pillar of fire by night" to the people of the present age. They still live, in the mercy of the Almighty, a nation without nationality, deprived of power, of country, of everything which they hold dear, save their faith. To this they cling with an earnestness of purpose which cannot fail but elicit the admiration of all liberal minds.

The ordination of this fast is found in 23d chapter of Leviticus, and reads as follows:

Source: "The Day of Atonement," *Daily Alta California*, San Francisco, Sept. 18, 1858, 2.

392

Steamer Day in San Francisco, 1866. Courtesy of Wells Fargo Bank.

Upon the tenth day of this seventh month shall be the day of atonement; it shall be most solemn, and shall be called holy, and you shall afflict your souls on that day and shall offer a holocaust to the Lord.

You shall do no servile work in the time of this day, because it is a day of propitiation that the Lord your God may be merciful unto you.

Every soul that is not afflicted on the day shall perish from among his people, and any soul that will do any work, the same will I destroy from among his people.

You shall do no work therefore on that day; it shall be an everlasting ordinance unto you in all your generations and dwellings.

In conformity with the above, from last eve at sun-down to this eve at sun-down, neither meat nor drink is taken, and with many the whole time is passed in prayer. The public services last evening in the synagogues, five in number, concluded at half-past eight o'clock, but in all watchers passed the night. The ceremonies to-day occupy the whole thereof, and are of most impressive character.

The Jewish portion of the citizens of California constitute a very important element of our inhabitants, more numerous than would be generally believed. They exercise considerable influence, and never has that influence been perverted. As a class, they have built up for themselves a name they can justly pride themselves on. They have adopted California as their home; their families around their "own vine and fig tree," and a future generation is growing up in our midst. They are Californians, for they abide with us. At the bar, in the forum, on the commercial mart, the press, medicine, agriculture, mechanics, and the fine arts, they occupy prominent positions, and have won the respect and esteem of all. A marked example of this consists in the fact that in consequence of those in the mercantile world, not being able to transact business to-day, which in the usual course of affairs would have been steamer-day, the Postmaster and the agents of the Pacific Mail Steamship Company, with that courtesy and defference [sic] they have always paid, postponed the sailing of the steamer until the 21st.

No other part of the world can instance a similar act of liberality. This, taken in conjunction with the fact that the Jew has but lately accorded his political rights in England, after years of endeavor affords a striking example of the workings of the peculiar institutions of our government.

81

Jews Will Support the Union

San Francisco Evening Bulletin, 1861

In the 1861 elections, Californians supported the Union by a two-thirds majority. The *San Francisco Evening Bulletin,* a pro-Union newspaper, highlighted the patriotism of Jews on the eve of the election.[10]

THE HEBREWS AND THE SECESSIONISTS

The Secessionists boast that they are sure of getting all the votes of our Hebrew fellow citizens for their candidate for Governor. When asked upon what ground they base their opinion as to the politics of this large class, they say, knowingly, "Oh! the Jews don't like to pay taxes: they go for 'peace, 'cause itch de sheepest.'" We have no doubt that some of the McConnellites really believe this.[11] The Hebrews are an industrious and thrifty class, beyond dispute. They love to earn and accumulate money—and in this they do not differ much from their neighbors, be they Southerners or Yankees. But to say that their love of money predominates over all their other feelings and principles, is a base slander. The unity of the race, after near two thousand years of dispersion and persecution proves that there is *something* in this people which the noblest races might well be envious of. No class have been truer to the calls of patriotism in this country than the Jews. In war and peace their blood and treasure has never been stated. We have no fear, therefore, that in the present peril of the nation, which is by far the greatest it has ever known, the Hebrews will allow mean parsimony to betray them into the basest ingratitude and treason. Time will show that the necessary taxation to support the measures of the Administration will be as cheerfully borne by the Hebrews as any other class in the community.

Truly, if any being in the world should do battle against the traitors who are warring against the American Government and the Constitution, it is the Jew. The inspired men who framed the imperishable charter of our liberties were the first to recognize the perfect political equality of that persecuted race,

---

SOURCE: "The Hebrew and the Secessionists," *San Francisco Evening Bulletin*, Aug. 30, 1861, 2.

10. See Chandler, "Some Political and Cultural Pressures," 145–70.

11. Supporters of John R. McConnell, a '49er from Kentucky who was a prominent lawyer and politician. He served as attorney general of California from 1853 to 1856 and in 1861 sought the governorship as a Democratic candidate on a peace platform but was defeated by Leland Stanford. His followers argued that California should not take sides in the Civil War.

and to establish their rights on an immovable basis—thus setting an example to the world. This country has been the refuge of hundreds of thousands of Hebrews, who have fled from the persecutions of other and less generous lands. Here, wealth, consideration, political position, and distinction of every kind, have been freely opened to them. They have occupied the highest posts in the Government, in the army and in the navy. Under our institutions, the prejudice of nearly nineteen centuries have been almost eradicated in less than one. What monstrous, what beastly ingratitude it would be, then, for a Hebrew to raise his impious hand against that Constitution and Government! Let others do as they list, but we cannot believe that the Jews of California will collude with the Secessionists, or pander to their scheme by voting for McConnell. Better pay their last dime in taxes than be guilty of such depravity.

82

Israelite Over Ammonite in Sonora

American Flag, Sonora, 1863

Local newspapers often associated Jews in the gold country with the Hebrews of the Bible. In this philo-Semitic article, a local merchant is identified with the city of Jerusalem and his victorious bout with an assailant is equated with the triumph of the Israelite over the Ammonite.

Jerusalem on Top!—A great, two fisted Irishman, intending to buy a pair of kid gloves of our Hebraic friend, Mr. Fridenberg, insisted on first trying them on! The merchant objected to the magnitude of the glove-stretchers, where at the fellow called him a Jewish son of a bitch. He was ordered out, and when outside he dared the merchant to come out and get licked. Mr. Fridenberg, who is some on the shoulder, went out, and then the Irishman shot at him. It was then that Israel went up against the Ammonite, prevailed mightily, threw him down, took the pistol away from him, and was about to take the top of his head off, when others interfered and let the fellow off.

"That is the third pistol which that unoffending and worthy citizen has forcibly taken from ruffians who had shot at him."

SOURCE: *American Flag*, Sonora, Oct. 8, 1863. American Jewish Archives, Hebrew Union College.

83

"Kosher Food Is Good for Gentiles"

Frank Lecouvreur, 1866

Frank Lecouvreur was born in Ortelsburg, Prussia, in 1829 to a Prussian mother and French father. Trained as a civil engineer and linguist, he set off for California at the age of twenty-three, settling first in Los Angeles and then in San Francisco. In Los Angeles he worked as deputy county clerk, served two terms as a county surveyor, laying out many of the downtown streets, and later became a director of the Farmers' and Merchants' Bank. While living in Los Angeles, he became acquainted with Harris Newmark and other members of the Los Angeles Jewish community. For reasons of health, Lecouvreur's doctor suggested that he relocate to the cooler climate of San Francisco.

This journal entry provides insight not only into the workings of Jewish businesses but also into the close relationships that often developed between Jews and gentiles.

January–December, 1866.

The new year brought disagreeable weather but then I had been spoiled in Los Angeles. All went well with me except that E. Boettcher and I agreed to disagree. Among those who surprised me with their visit were my former employer, P. Banning, W. H. Peterson and John Lazzarovitch. Schubnell and I took daily walks.

Through J. P. Newmark (brother of my former employer) I obtained a position as bookkeeper at E. Wertheimer's, who agrees to pay me one hundred and fifty dollars a month. As I arranged to begin work by the fifteenth of February, there was time for a flying business trip to Los Angeles, which I enjoyed on board of the "Orizaba," Capt. Butters, though wind and weather were in a wintry mood.

Three days in Los Angeles sufficed to settle all matters and bid good by to my many staunch friends and acquaintances. The "Orizaba" took me safely back to San Francisco, where I entered my position on the appointed date. And here I am at the end of the year.

From the beginning I have boarded at the St. Nicholas Hotel—a Jewish hostelry well kept by Levy Hess—where I also took rooms after June the first,

---

Source: Frank Lecouvreur, *From East Prussia to the Golden Gate* (New York and Los Angeles: Angelina Book Concern, 1906), 318–19.

upon leaving Dr. Zeile's place.[12] Hess charges me fifty dollars a month and treats me well. "Kosher food" is good for Gentiles.

As our business, like all Jewish mercantile houses, closes on Saturdays at one o'clock, I find ample time for excursions. The Contra Costa ferry lines and the railroad connection to San José offer many a wholesome outing. During the spring, however, most of my Sunday trips were directed to Oakland where my friend Schubnell had found a home at Conrad Zimmermann's. These visits gave me at first considerable pleasure, as I sincerely enjoyed the company of the plain honest hearts who met under the green foliage of the pretty little garden. But alas! Simon Schubnell's health grew poorer and poorer, so that we had to stay in his little room and cheer him, while our hearts were aching. I tried to be more punctual in my visits than ever. At last the end came on June 21st a.c. As my Los Angeles friend, Dr. Wollweber, happened to be in the city, he too took part in the Masonic rites, which distinguished the otherwise simple funeral.

At the beginning of September the Jewish holidays gave me a chance to pay my friend, Henry Jackson (Grünhagen of old), a short visit at his place in Watsonville, but as I did not arrive until seven o'clock in the evening, we had only the night for a friendly chat, as the stage left at six o'clock the next morning. This mountain trip did me a great deal of good and the scenery is truly magnificent.

As my genial landlord has sold his "St. Nicholas" and installed himself in new quarters at the corner of Market and Third streets, I followed him hither and occupy now a room on the fifth floor, with a magnificent view of the bay, for which I have to pay ten dollars more than at the old place. But I get my money's worth and the board is excellent. The new year finds me in the same position and home comforts as heretofore. My employers are gentlemen.

---

12. Meetings and other events of the Jewish community were often held at the St. Nicholas Hotel.

84

Rabbi Eckman as Viewed by a Friend

O. P. Fitzgerald, ca. 1874

A Methodist minister and editor of both the *Pacific Methodist* and the *Christian Spectator,* Oscar Penn Fitzgerald arrived in California in 1855 from his native North Carolina. In addition to pursuing clerical and journalistic careers, Fitzgerald served as state superintendent of public education from 1867 to 1871. He shared his interests in religion, journalism, and education with Rabbi Julius Eckman, a fixture among a small group of clergy in San Francisco. Fitzgerald, who knew Eckman as a close friend, may have understood him better than did most members of the Jewish community.

THE RABBI

Seated in his library, enveloped in a faded figured gown, a black velvet cap on his massive head, there was an Oriental look about him that arrested your attention at once. Power and gentleness, child-like simplicity, and scholarliness, were curiously mingled in this man. His library was a reflex of its owner. In it were books that the great public libraries of the world could not match—black letter folios that were almost as old as the printing art, illuminated volumes that were once the pride and joy of men who had been in their graves many generations, rabbinical lore, theology, magic, and great volumes of Hebrew literature that looked, when placed beside a modern book, like an old ducal palace along-side a gingerbread cottage of to-day. I do not think he ever felt at home amid the hurry and rush of San Francisco. He could not adjust himself to the people. He was devout, and they were intensely worldly. He thundered this sentence from the teacher's desk in the synagogue one morning: "O ye Jews of San Francisco, you have so fully given up yourselves to material things that you are losing the very instinct of immortality. Your only idea of religion is to acquire the Hebrew language, *and you don't know that!*" His port and voice were like those one of the old Hebrew prophets. Elijah himself was not more fearless. Yet, how deep was his love for his race! Jeremiah was not more tender when he wept for the slain of the daughter of his people. His reproofs were resented, and he had a taste of persecution; but the Jews of San Francisco understood him at last. The poor and little children knew him from the start. He lived mostly among his books, and in his school for poor children, whom he taught without charge. His habits were so simple and his bodily wants so few

SOURCE: O. P. Fitzgerald, *California Sketches* (Nashville: Southern Methodist Publishing House, 1881), 153–60.

that it cost him but a trifle to live. When the synagogue frowned on him, he was as independent as Elijah at the brook Cherith. It is hard to starve a man to whom crackers and water are a royal feast.

His belief in God and in the supernatural was startlingly vivid. The Voice that spoke from Sinai was still audible to him, and the Arm that delivered Israel he saw still stretched out over the nations. The miracles of the Old Testament were as real to him as the premiership of Disraeli, or the financing of the Rothschilds. There was, at the same time, a vein of rationalism that ran through his thought and speech. We were speaking one day on the subject of miracles, and, with his usual energy of manner, he said:

"There was no need of any literal angel to shut the mouths of the lions to save Daniel: *the awful holiness of the prophet was enough.* There was so much of God in him that the savage creatures submitted to him as they did to unsinning Adam. Man's dominion over nature was broken by sin, but in the golden age to come it will be restored. A man in full communion with God wields a divine power in every sphere that he touches."

His face glowed as he spoke, and his voice was subdued into a solemnity of tone that told how his reverent and adoring soul was thrilled with this vision of the coming glory of redeemed humanity.

He knew the New Testament by heart, as well as the Old. The sayings of Jesus were often on his lips.

One day, in a musing, half-soliloquizing way, I heard him say:

"It is wonderful, wonderful! a Hebrew peasant from the hills of Galilee, without learning, noble birth, or power, subverts all the philosophies of the world, and makes himself the central figure of all history. It is wonderful!"

He half whispered the words, and his eyes had the introspective look of a man who is thinking deeply.

He came to see me at our cottage on Post street one morning before breakfast. In grading a street, a house in which I had lived and had the ill luck to own, on Pine street, had been undermined, and toppled over into the street below, falling on the slate-roof and breaking all to pieces. He came to tell me of it, and to extend his sympathy.

"I thought I would come first, so you might get the bad news from a friend rather than a stranger. You have lost a house, but it is a small matter. Your little boy there might have put out his eye with a pair of scissors, or he might have swallowed a pin and lost his life. There are many things constantly taking place that are harder to bear than the loss of a house."

Many other wise words did the Rabbi speak, and before he left I felt that a house was indeed a small thing to grieve over.

He spoke with charming freedom and candor of all sorts of people.

"Of Christians, the Unitarians have the best heads, and the Methodists the best hearts. The Roman Catholics hold the masses, because they give their people plenty of form. The masses will never receive truth in its simple essence;

they must have it in a way that will make it digestible and assimilable, just as their stomachs demand bread, and meats and fruits, not their extracts or distilled essences, for daily food. As to Judaism, it is on the eve of great changes. What these changes will be I know not, except that I am sure the God of our fathers will fulfill his promise to Israel. This generation will probably see great things."

"Do you mean the literal restoration of the Jews to Palestine?"

He looked at me with an intense gaze, and hastened not to answer. At last he spoke slowly:

"When the perturbed elements of religious thought crystallize into clearness and enduring forms, the chosen people will be one of the chief factors in reaching that final solution of the problems which convulse this age."

He was one of the speakers at the great Mortara indignation-meeting in San Francisco. [. . .] The Rabbi made a speech, and it was the speech of a man who had come from his books and prayers. He made a tender appeal for the mother and father of the abducted Jewish boy, and argued the question as calmly, and in as sweet a spirit, as if he had been talking over an abstract question in his study. The vast crowd looked upon that strange figure with a sort of pleased wonder, and the Rabbi seemed almost unconscious of their presence. He was as free from self-consciousness as a little child, and many a Gentile heart warmed that night to the simple-hearted sage who stood before them pleading for the rights of human nature.

The old man was often very sad. In such moods he would come round to our cottage on Post street, and sit with us until late at night, unburdening his aching heart, and relaxing by degrees into a playfulness that was charming from its very awkwardness. He would bring little picture-books for the children, put them on their heads, and praise them. They were always glad to see him, and would nestle round him lovingly. We all loved him, and felt glad in the thought that he left our little circle lighter at heart. He lived alone. Once, when I playfully spoke to him of matrimony, he laughed quietly, and said:

"No, no—my books and my poor school—children are enough for me."

He died suddenly and alone. He had been out one windy night visiting the poor, came home sick, and before morning was in that world of spirits which was so real to his faith, and for which he longed. He left his little fortune of a few thousand dollars to the poor of his native village of Posen, in Poland. And thus passed from California-life, Dr. Julius Eckman, the Rabbi.

85

Reflections of a Polish Nobel Laureate

Henry Sienkiewicz, 1877

The Polish novelist and later Nobel laureate Henry Sienkiewicz traveled the United States from 1876 to 1878. After the demise of a short-lived utopian agricultural colony in southern California, which he established with other Polish intellectuals, he visited San Francisco. In this letter to an unknown friend, Sienkiewicz presents his view of California's Jews and the "Jewish question."

San Francisco
September 9, 1877

MY dear!

I should have answered your last letter long ago. I was a little angry with you for printing my previous letter since neither in form nor style was it suitable for publication. Furthermore, your editorial explanations in some places altered or generalized the meaning of my words. From the conclusion readers may get an impression that I have nothing but jeers for the Jews, whereas in reality I have a lot of respect for them.

It was only here that I became convinced what an energetic and enterprising people they are. It is less surprising in Poland that the Jews have gained control of commerce and, in part, of industry, but here where the population is extremely industrious, where competition is especially keen and the struggle for survival is conducted ruthlessly, the real commercial abilities of the Jews become fully evident. In trade and commerce the Polish Jews hold their own against Yankee competition, and if need be, could do so against the devil himself. They come here in most instances without a cent, without a knowledge of the language or conditions, in other words, with only their two hands and a good head on their shoulders. The day after their arrival each one of them opens a business. If anyone tries to cheat them, he is himself cheated. In commercial transactions they are no less honest than other businessmen. I do not know a single Jew who, after a year's residence, is still in poverty. Each of them has money; each, as the Americans say, "is making a living"; and after a while each "is worth" such and such a sum of money. Some of them manage to make millions. But be that as it may. More important is the fact that the Jews from

SOURCE: *Portrait of America: Letters of Henry Sienkiewicz,* ed. and trans. Charles Morley (New York: Columbia University Press, 1959), 219–20. Reprinted with the permission of the publisher.

the kingdom of Poland do not forget whence they have come and where lie the bones of their forefathers, whereas those from Austrian and Prussian Poland tend to identify themselves with the Germans. It cannot be denied that the Jews are a hardy race. This element in our population should not be discounted, for the Jews possess exactly those traits which we Poles lack and which, added to our own, would make for a strong nation.

Such is my frank opinion. Anyone who looks down upon the Jews as being of inferior birth and ancestry is an imbecile. I do not advocate that we court them with special favors. When they do wrong, they should be punished like anybody else. But under no circumstances can we exclude them from the orbit of our lives. So much for the Jewish question.

10
The Wider Community

JEWS WERE SOMETIMES COMPELLED TO VIGOROUSLY ASSERT THEIR claim to religious equality, especially when laws defied the cherished American principle of the separation of church and state. Sunday Laws in particular, which mandated that places of business be closed on the Christian Sabbath, affected Jews adversely. At one time or another Sunday Laws became an issue most places in the United States. In 1855, when William W. Stow, the speaker of the California Assembly and a proponent of the Sunday Laws, charged that Jews were depriving Christian shop owners of customers by staying open on the Christian Sabbath, the Jewish community was forced to act. Observant Jews were unfairly penalized by these laws, since Christians were able to stay open on Saturday, the Jewish Sabbath, while Jews were forced by law to close on Sunday. Supporters of the Sunday Laws argued that they were enacted to show the civility and moral order of the time. Stow even accused Jews of being foreigners who did not contribute to the state. Henry Labatt, the America-born lawyer and community leader, reacted with outrage to such charges. He was not alone; a resolution passed at a meeting of the Jewish community in Sacramento reaffirmed Jews' commitment to good citizenship and accused Assembly Speaker Stow of slander.[1] The newly enacted Sunday Laws were contested in court in 1858 by defense lawyers, Solomon Heydenfeldt, a Jew, and Daniel Webster Welty, a Christian. The judges found the laws unconstitutional and overturned them. They were reenacted in 1861, however, and not finally abolished until 1883.

---

1. *American Israelite*, May 11, 1855: 1–2.

The place of religion in the public schools was also a perennial issue. In 1875, like Henry Labatt and Solomon Heydenfeldt before him, Joseph Brandon stood up for Jewish rights and for the separation of church and state in a religiously diverse society.

More generally, misunderstandings were based on ignorance of Jewish religious practices, as the case of *David Spiegel vs. John Ellis* demonstrated. In 1862 Spiegel's possessions were confiscated by Sheriff Ellis for payment of debt. Spiegel petitioned the court for the return of kitchen utensils and plates on the grounds that they were religious objects used in the observance of Jewish holidays and therefore necessary family furniture and exempt from seizure. The case was decided in Spiegel's favor, and the court ruling recognized Judaism as a respected religion and precursor to Christianity.

California Jews' response to Lincoln's assassination was a dramatic demonstration of their full incorporation into American life. San Francisco's District Grand Lodge Number 4 of the B'nai B'rith identified Lincoln with the "Patriarch Abraham" and with the spirit of the United States, which welcomed men of all creeds.[2]

Some Jews became as well known outside the Jewish community as they were within it. More than any other single individual, Philo Jacoby assumed the role of interreligious statesman in the German-American world. In publishing the *Almanach für Californien* for the German-speaking community, Jews, Protestants, and Catholics alike were provided with a weekly listing of Protestant, Catholic, and Jewish holidays, along with information about the growing economy of California. As German Jews often felt a stronger identification with German culture and other Germans than they did with Jews of non-German origin, the almanac doubtlessly attracted a wide readership outside California. Jacoby, an award-winning marksman and strongman as well as a journalist and editor, became a larger-than-life character, respected by Jews and gentiles alike

---

2. The District Grand Lodge of the B'nai B'rith passed a resolution requiring that subordinate lodges "drape their Halls and Charters in mourning, for the period of thirty (30) days, as a mark of respect and esteem (*Hebrew,* Apr. 21, 5625 [1865]: 5). A complete copy of the resolution can be found in the B'nai B'rith Collection, Western Jewish History Center. According to I. J. Ascheim, Jacob Mayer, a San Francisco merchant, had read about B'nai B'rith in the Jewish press and suggested to fellow Jewish Masons that they form a chapter of the Jewish fraternal association (Jacob Voorsanger, *The Chronicles of Emanu-El* [San Francisco: Temple Emanu-El, 1900], 36); William M. Kramer, "They Killed Our Man But Not Our Cause: The California Jewish Mourners of Abraham Lincoln," *Western States Jewish Historical Quarterly* 2:4 (1970): 200. By the time of Lincoln's death there were four B'nai B'rith lodges in San Francisco alone, with a combined membership of 390. Six lodges petitioned their district lodge for permission to form their own district. The petition was granted, and district 4 was founded in 1863. For a copy of the petition see Seymour Fromer, "B'nai B'rith Centennial Convention: District Grand Lodge Number Four," at the Western Jewish History Center.

and identified around the world with the American West and especially with San Francisco.

Others who gained high visibility in these years were David Belasco, the theater producer who first emerged as a fledgling director at Maguire's Opera House; poet and actress Adah Isaacs Manken;[3] Julius Kahn, who was later elected to Congress; and Salmi Morse (Sammy Moss), author of an extravagantly produced Passion play. Toby Rosenthal, a painter who spent most of his later life in Germany, grew up in San Francisco, where his talents were first discovered and nurtured. Adolph Sutro, who came to San Francisco as a merchant, became wealthy because of his mining ingenuity and concluded his career as mayor of the city. A name more synonymous with San Francisco is that of Emperor Norton (Joshua Abraham Norton), whose business disaster led to the delusions of grandeur that drove him to reinvent himself as the Emperor of the United States and the Protector of Mexico.

San Francisco was also home to the greatest Chinese colony in the United States in the mid-nineteenth century. The city's Chinatown aroused the attention of San Francisco Jews and the greater American Jewish community. In the final document of this chapter, Rabbi Isaac Mayer Wise chronicles the depression of the 1870s, nationally as well as locally, and the deplorable attacks on the Chinese.

---

3. Adah Isaacs Menken (1835–68), poet and star of outrageous melodramas, was a international celebrity who traveled extensively, especially in the western United States. She was known for her adherence to Judaism and refused to perform on Jewish holidays. See Paul Lewis, *Queen of the Plaza: A Biography of Adah Isaacs Menken* (New York: Funk and Wagnalls, 1964).

86
The Bible and Sunday Laws
Occident and American Jewish Advocate, Philadelphia, 1855

During a debate on a Sunday Closing Law in the California legislature on March 16, 1855, Speaker of the Assembly William W. Stow of Santa Cruz charged Jews with being undesirable citizens. Stow outraged Jews and non-Jews alike, most notably Assemblyman E. G. Buffum, who had many Jewish constituents in his San Francisco district.[4] The report of the debate makes evident that Stow's Sunday Closing Law was intended not only to discipline an unruly frontier society but to keep Jews out of the state by imposing a special head tax on them.[5]

Sacramento Democratic State Journal:

The Speaker [Stow] was in favor of the bill, and had no sympathy with the Jews, who ought to respect the laws and opinions of the majority. They were a class of people who only came here to make money, and leave as soon as they had effected their object. They did not invest their money in the country or cities. They all intended or hoped to settle in their "New Jerusalem." He was in favor of inflicting such a tax upon them as would act as a prohibition to their residence amongst us. The Bible lay at the foundation of our institutions, and its ordinances ought to be covered and adhered to in legislating for the state.

Mr. [E. G.] Buffum [of San Francisco] contended that the bill would act more for the protection of certain merchants of Santa Cruz and Santa Clara, who found their trade interfered with, because the Jew merchants saw fit to open their shops on a Sunday. He was astonished to hear the gentleman who last spoke, and whom he had regarded as the exponent of liberal principles, express such sentiments as he had done in favor of inflicting such a tax on Jews as would amount to a prohibition of their residences amongst us. In San Francisco they had built some of the finest edifices the city could boast, and their wealth, influence, and enterprise were as conspicuous there as they were throughout the whole civilized world.

SOURCE: *Occident and American Jewish Advocate,* Philadelphia, vol. 13, 1855, 124.

4. Stow was born in 1824 in Binghamton, New York, and died in San Francisco on February 11, 1895. Elected to the state legislature in 1853 and 1854, he became Speaker in 1855. Edward Gould Buffum (1820–67) was also from New York and came to California in 1847 with Stevenson's Regiment. He became an editor of the *Alta California* before returning to New York to work on the *Herald.*

5. For reports of the Sunday Laws in the *Allgemeine Zeitung des Judentums,* see chapter 1.

87

"Saturday Is the Sabbath of the Bible"

Henry Labatt, 1855

As an American-born Jew living in a city in which most Jews were immigrants, Henry Labatt often served as spokesman for the Jewish community.[6] In the following article, first published in a local newspaper and then reprinted in a national Jewish weekly, Labatt responded vigorously to the accusations of House Speaker William W. Stow. Stow's name is misspelled throughout the article.

THE JEWS OF SAN FRANCISCO AND MR. STOWE

Mr. Speaker Stowe:—With much astonishment I perused in the Sacramento journals, what purports to be a report of the proceedings of the Legislature, and certain remarks of yourself and other leading men of the lower House, relative to the Jews of this State, in the discussion of the Sunday Trading Bill. The Jews of San Francisco are in favor of a Sunday Bill.

Perhaps Sir, you are a medium and the English House of Lords, in the migratory spirit of rappers, visited you. If so, more is the pity that they only communicated their opinions on the "Jewish Disability" feeling, and left you, tranquil in the free enjoyment of your profound ignorance and the false knowledge of facts and recreant regard of truth.

Mr. Buffum shall receive the warm gratitude of my co-religionists for the course he has taken in this matter.

Mr. Speaker: occupying the position you do as the head of the House of Representatives, you should be loath to disgrace our Legislature and our State by flagrant and malicious falsehood; for to say you are ignorant of the real facts and open truths, would be to insult the body which elected you their Speaker, although you are an ignorant man, nevertheless, to assert and advocate measures which are directly opposed to the wishes of your constituents.

You say, "They come here to make money, and leave as soon as this object is effected." This bears upon its face unwarrantable falsity. Are you ignorant of the number of families arriving [on] every steamer, and of the Jewish faith, to make California their home? Are you ignorant of the brick synagogues erecting in our large cities for family worship? Are you ignorant of the permanent benevolent

---

Source: Henry Labatt, *Occident and American Jewish Advocate,* vol. 13, 1855, 125–27.

6. See Labatt's profile of the Jewish business community in chapter 5 and his letters to Isaac Leeser in chapter 3.

societies, which extend the hand of charity to their bereaved brethren, and relieve the state, county, and city of taxes for almshouses, hospitals, asylums, etc.? If you are ignorant of these acts, then you are basely ignorant; if not, you have greatly misrepresented facts, and you are a disgrace to the House over which you have the dishonor to preside. You may choose between this dilemma.

You say, "They do not invest their money in the country nor erect any fine stores." This is another equally great falsehood. Examine the tax-books of any county in the State, and the names of Jews are found thick upon their pages.

I will produce twenty names of Jewish citizens of my county who pay taxes on over two millions of property.

This fact you know and have misrepresented to the injury of a large body of respectable citizens, or else you were grossly ignorant of important facts connected with your position as Speaker of the House, which constitutes you unworthy of your position.

Mr. Speaker: You would prohibit their residence here. How have they harmed you at all, and in what respect?

Have the Jews squatted on your lands? If so, I have yet to learn who; the Jews are not squatters.

Have they built grog-shops to poison the people? Surely not; the Jews are not rum-sellers. Have they filled your jails or taxed the state with criminal trials? Surely not; they are not robbers, murderers, or leading politicians.

Have their females prostituted the morals of young men? Surely not; they are noted for the virtue of their mothers and the chastity of their daughters.

Yet I claim no superiority for this unfortunate people; but I do claim Mr. Speaker Stowe, that they are good citizens, and better than you; and that they are worthy men and worthier than you; and that they would scorn to vilify the Gentiles as you have grossly and falsely vilified them, knowing it to be false.

Then why cry out against them? There's the rub! They are numerous, but yet of the right stripe. Unfortunately, they are too wise to be ignorant, and *know nothing* of their rights. Speaker Stowe, you are right on that question. Whoever has a heart to think for himself, and a voice to speak and cry out against the evil influence of that party which would undermine all religions but that of Quaker-hanging Puritanism, must be taxed so as to prohibit their residence among your numbers.

You cannot convince them of the great evil they inherited from their mother, because she was not on American soil at the hour of their birth, or because they are not of the Puritan religion, nor can you ameliorate their condition; therefore they must be exterminated.

Pray, on whom will you commence? In the Supreme Court where sits on the bench of three Judges, one Jew?[7] What tax will you place on that bench to exclude the Jew? What will you do in the halls of legislation or public offices, the bar, and medical fraternity? Surely Jews fill or have filled these positions in our State, and without the like disgrace and profound ignorance that hovers over yourself! Every trade, profession or employment (excepting begging, and there are no Jew beggars) has been filled honorably by Jews.

But it is not, Speaker Stowe, upon the basis of the Bible and Sunday laws. The former belongs to the Jew, and God gave it him. It is not Christian's Bible alone, and the Bible is silent upon rest on *Sunday*. Saturday is the Sabbath of the Bible. But this question I leave to divines, as you, Speaker Stowe, in your profound ignorance and falsehood could not comprehend the argument, or would vilify the facts in the Bible scarcely less palpable than those you have denied in your statement in that House you have disgraced.

It is well, Speaker Stowe, you have shown the colors of your order. Many Jews have slumbered in ignorance of the fact, that when they *know nothing* their religion and their people are in danger. It is well your ignorance has opened their eyes and your falsehood has given them inspiration that arouses them to a knowledge of the truth.

A large and numerous body of voters of this State will remember these facts, and I trust every Jew will bear in mind many a long day, for you cannot expel them from this State. For myself, I shall use every endeavor to keep it constantly before them.

I am yours firm in Judaism,
Henry J. Labatt,
151 Clay Street.

---

7. Solomon Heydenfeldt served on the court 1852–57.

88
Testing the Christian Sabbath Law
Sacramento Daily Union, 1858

The "Act for the Better Observance of the Sabbath," known as the Sunday Law, was first enacted on April 10, 1858, and *People vs. Newman* immediately contested it. Newman, a Sacramento clothing store owner and vice president of Congregation B'nai Israel, challenged the law by keeping his store open on Sunday and was arrested. He pled not guilty on the grounds that Sunday was not the Sabbath but was found guilty and jailed. His lawyer, Daniel Webster Welty, requested a writ of habeas corpus and petitioned the California Supreme Court to overturn the law. In collaboration with Solomon Heydenfeldt, a Jew and former justice of the California Supreme Court (1852–57), Welty succeeding in proving on appeal that the law was unconstitutional in that it favored one religion over others. Chief Justice David Smith Terry and Judge Peter Burnett ruled that the law was based on religious beliefs and thus violated the principle of separation of church and state. Judge Stephen J. Field dissented, however, and three years later a reconstituted court, which included Judge Field, reinstated the law.

Justice Solomon Heydenfeldt, California State Supreme Court judge, 1852–57. Courtesy of the American Jewish Archives.

The Courts.

Supreme Court—Present, Terry, C. J., Burnett, J., and Field, J.

Monday, June 21st. [1858]

People vs. M. Newman.—This case, involving the principle of Sunday Law, came up for hearing on a writ of *habeas corpus*. R. F. Morrison, District Attorney, and Attorney General Williams, appeared for the People; and Welty and Heydenfeldt for the petitioner. [. . .]

Let a writ of *habeas corpus* issue according to the prayer of the petition, returnable before the Supreme Court, at one o'clock, this day of June 21st, 1858.

D. S. Terry, C.J., Supreme Court.

—

STATE OF CALIFORNIA, SS.

CITY AND COUNTY OF SACRAMENTO, June 21st, 1858.

I hereby certify that I have the person of M. Newman in my custody, by virtue of commitment issued by C. H. Hill, Justice of the Peace of the city and county of Sacramento, charged with the crime of keeping open a clothing store on the Christian Sabbath (or Sunday) for business purposes, and having been sentenced on the 19th day of June, to be imprisoned for thirty-five days in the county jail, in default of payment of fifty dollars fine and twenty dollars costs, and to hold the same M. Newman until he be legally discharged.

John Hayes,
Deputy Sheriff.

—

D. W. Welty, in opening the case, remarked that the only question which he should raise was, whether the Act of the Legislature under consideration is in accordance with that provision of the Constitution which gives every person the free exercise and enjoyment of his religious profession and worship without discrimination of preference. Was this act constitutional, so far as a conscientious belief was concerned? Judge Heydenfeldt would follow and argue that the law was unconstitutional *in toto,* but he would consider it only in the view referred to. The petitioner was of the Jewish faith, and held honestly and conscientiously to the belief that the seventh was the day to be observed, and not the first. He was also protected in his rights by the 1st Section of Article 1st of the Constitution:

"All men are by nature free and independent, and have certain inalienable rights, among which are those of enjoying and defending life and liberty; acquiring, possessing and protecting property; and pursuing and obtaining safety and happiness."

SOURCE: "People vs. Newman," *Sacramento Daily Union,* June 22, 1858, 5.

But the main point that he should contend for was that the Act conflicted with the 4th Section of Article 1st of the Constitution, which was as follows:

"The free exercise and enjoyment of religious profession and worship, without discrimination or preference, shall forever be allowed in this State; and no person shall be rendered incompetent to be a witness on account of his opinions on matters of religious belief: but the liberty of conscience, hereby secured, shall not be so construed as to excuse acts of licentiousness, or justify practices inconsistent with the peace or safety of this State." [. . .]

R. F. Morrison followed on the other side. He remarked [. . .] that the case before them was for the sale of goods on Sunday. The law recently passed only requires a cessation of public employment on the first day of the week. It does not violate the Jewish Sabbath. It does not require the Jew to desecrate his Sabbath. He can enjoy, with perfect liberty, his morning prayer and his evening sacrifice. It is said it derogates from the Jewish Sabbath, and makes the Jew observe two days. This was a mistake. It only said to him, "Observe one day." If the law required the Jew to labor six days; there might be some cause for complaint.

Judge Terry—Does not the law violate his constitutional right to acquire property? Cannot it be justly said that there is a Constitution for one man and one for another?

Morrison—There is no Constitution of any State in the Union that does not give its citizens the right to acquire and hold property. There is as much freedom in this respect in South Carolina, Pennsylvania, Ohio, Maine and other States that might be mentioned as in California, and all those States which have had decisions under this law have similar constitutional provisions to our own.

Terry—I would ask whether the Legislature, by this Act, is not interfering with the right of citizens to acquire property? and where is the limit?

Morrison continued: He would not undertake to define the limit. The question had never been raised in the United States before, and it was a strange point to him altogether. In relation to the right to acquire property, the Court here has declared the license law constitutional and the law compelling merchants to pay taxes on goods. Reasoning on the same principle, all these laws abridged the right of acquiring property. If it is a constitutional right the Legislature could not clog it with such laws. [. . .] In conclusion, Mr. Morrison said, he defied those who represented the other side to show any decision that was opposed to this mass of authority, gathered from all portions of the Union. He had not found any adjudication that favored the other side, and the provisions in all the Constitutions of the different States were as full as those of our own. It was strange the obnoxious principle referred to had never been discovered.

S. Heydenfeldt remarked that he should be very brief. There were two questions which he would present: First, Can the Legislature make a civil, municipal rule that imposes a compulsory abstinence from the ordinary occupations of a citizen? And second, Have they intended to do it? He did not wish this point to be confounded with the authority to regulate the relation of master and servant. Could the Legislature compel him to abstain from work one day in the week, when he had every disposition to work from a sense of duty? When Judges in the East had decided this Sunday Law to be constitutional, they had resorted to subterfuges. We had adopted the institution of the Sabbath from the Hebrews, and they had obtained it as far back as the days of Moses. Could anyone say it was adopted for any other than a religious observance? Had not this Act of three sections better be called an Act for the preservation of the human species? It was a religious institution, and it gave preference to one religious sect. Did not these same Judges, in the cases cited, indicate a preference, and did not they make use of subterfuges? If this be the law, he could go to Russia and get the same kind of toleration. Toleration did not exclude preference. They had toleration in England, but they had also preference. The Judges referred to have set up men of straw, only to knock them down. If the law had observed the seventh day they would not have resolved to submit to it so readily. The Act was not to make a civil day of rest, but to provide for a better observance of the Sabbath. Governmentally considered, this was not a Christian country, and the counsel instanced a case in our relations with Tripoli, to show that it could not be so considered. The people of this State had a Constitution to preserve their rights and liberties. How far could the Legislature restrict those rights? There were certain rights which are surrendered, but they were such as were ordinarily given up for the safety of the whole, but not those relating to one's creed or opinion. They must be such as are necessary to sustain society. You cannot go beyond this rule. If the Legislature could enjoin one day of compulsory rest, where would be the limit of the power? They say, in fact, that it is necessary to rest one day for the preservation of the human race, but a man's instinct would teach him this. It was a question of physiology, and one that the Legislature need not dabble in. Nature would teach man to rest. He had heard of men who would not work, but he never had known of men that would work too much. No such event was to be feared, and no remedy was required. This Court was bound to declare whether the Legislature had carried out its power in good faith, or whether they had not exceeded it. The religious question was ignored. If there was no civil evil to be cured, no remedy was desired.

Attorney General Williams followed briefly, in support of the views urged by Mr. Morrison. [. . .]

Judge Terry said:

"It is conceded, that the Act does not conflict with any provision of the Constitution of the United States, or the treaty of Guadalupe Hidalgo. The opinion seems to be predicated on the grounds that the Act is void, because it is in violation of natural justice, and infringes article first of section first of the Constitution of this State. The article is a mere reiteration of a truism which is as old as Constitutional Government. A similar declaration is contained in the Constitution of most of the States of the Union, but, I think has never been construed as a limitation of the power of the Government.

"Such a construction might seriously affect the power of Government to enact laws for the punishment of crime by the incarceration of the criminal, or to enforce the collection of debts by a seizure and sale of property.

"The doctrine that Judges have power to annul a law, because, in their opinion, its provisions are in violation of natural justice, is one of dangerous consequences, tending to destroy that distribution of powers made by the Constitution, by concentrating in the hands of the Judiciary, functions which are, by the Constitution, conferred on different departments, and cannot, I think, be maintained on principle or authority.

"The question, whether a particular law is in violation of natural justice, may be one of difficult solution. Its determination is governed by no fixed rules, and often depends on considerations of policy and public advantage, which are more properly the subjects of Legislative than Judicial exposition."

Judge Terry—This was not the opinion of the Court, Mr. Williams.

Williams—I did not say it was, your Honor. I quoted it as the opinion of a member of this Court, and, in opposition to views which he has just announced.

Mr. Williams continued: The law under consideration only discriminates as it does ever in the regulation of property. The Courts upon principle, and all the authorities, declare this law to be constitutional. If gentlemen are correct in their views, no regulation as to the acquisition or protection of property could be made. People would be thrown back to the first principles of nature. This law was necessary to the well being of society. The Legislature has exercised its discrimination in the matter, and it was not for the Judiciary to interfere with its Acts. The Legislature in its wisdom had a right to go as far as it pleased in its own proper sphere without let or hindrance.

After a little incidental discussion between the respective counsel, the Court announced that it would take the case under advisement, and in the mean time the prisoner might be discharged upon his recognizance in the sum of $100.

89

Kaddish for James King of William

American Israelite, Cincinnati, 1856

The following statement commends Congregation Emanu-El for its generous use of Jewish ritual to express respect for a Christian. In 1855 James King of William (he took his father's name, William, to distinguish himself from others with the name James King), a failed banker, began publishing the *San Francisco Daily Evening Bulletin,* an anti-Catholic newspaper that sided with merchants against what he saw as corrupt local government officials and machine politics. After King made public the fact that county supervisor James P. Casey had served a prison sentence, Casey shot King dead, a crime that led to the founding of San Francisco's Second Vigilance Committee, which promptly hanged Casey. King had been on the executive committee of the first Vigilance Committee in 1851. For the Jews of San Francisco, King's memorial may have symbolized solidarity with King's pro-business position, his Vigilance Committee leadership, and the members of the synagogue.

EMANU-EL, SAN FRANCISCO.

IMPRONEMENTS. A NEW RABBI [written in Hebrew, Kaddish memorial service] FOR THE CHRISTIAN EDITOR OF THE BULLETIN. THE SYNAGOGUE GIVES A NOBLE EXAMPLE OF LIBERALTY.

[. . .]

The death of the late editor of the "Bulletin," a daily paper edited in this city, created as much excitement here in the far West, as on the arrival of Kossuth had produced in the East.[8] On this occasion, the Jewish Rabbi of Emanu El Congregation gave a rare instance of liberty. The first Sabbath of that event, May 24th, the Rabbi in person said the Kadish Yosom for the benefit of the deceased's soul, which he *expressly* declared to have been appropriated for that purpose. Such an act of liberty extended by a Jewish Rabbi to a Christian editor deserves due acknowledgment.

And we congratulate the new Dignitary on the liberality of the administration of his Church, which did not fall short of his own. A Synagogue in mourning! The deep affliction caused to the Synagogue by that sad affair which terminated

---

SOURCE: *American Israelite,* Cincinnati, July 4, 1856, 422.

8. Lajos Kossuth (1802–94) was a leader of Hungary's 1848 revolution against Austria. When he was deposed after serving for a year as president of Hungary, he fled to the United States, where he was enthusiastically received and had many supporters, among them Hungarian Jews.

in the death of Mr. King, threw a cloud of darkness among our people, who, in order to show their sympathy for the unfortunate victim of that combat, independently of the Kadish Yosom said on Sabbath a separate Kadish, appropriated for the occasion, on which the Synagogue was draped in mourning cloth. The shine of the God of Israel in mourning dress on account of the death of a Gentile! And as the Synagogue—as far as is known—was the only fit place for worship amongst about thirty churches of this city, where an extra service was held and was decorated with black, except the Church, where the obsequies were performed, this act showed the liberality of the Jews toward their Christian brethren.

We hope the liberal minded reader will not mistake progress and liberality for levity or profanity. Nay, the very fact of reciting the Kadish Yosom on the one occasion of Sabbath and the Kadish Derabanan after the speech on Sunday when the "extra service" was performed, are a full evidence of the Synagogue's adherence to the Rabbis and the usages instituted by them.

90
A Mosaic Dispensation
Occident and American Jewish Advocate, Philadelphia, 1863

A national Jewish newspaper, the *Occident and American Jewish Advocate,* found this 1862 court case significant enough to reprint it in full. The question addressed in *David Spiegel vs. John Ellis* is whether kitchen utensils and plates taken by the sheriff of San Francisco were exempt from rules of seizure because they were used in a religious ceremony. Little else is known about the plaintiff, David Spiegel.[9]

RELIGIOUS EQUALITY IN CALIFORNIA

THE subjoined has been placed in our hands, and as it illustrates the equality under the law as it is held in California, we place it on record, for future reference. Otherwise the case speaks for itself, and we give it without any comment.

State of California, City and County of San Francisco, *ss.*—In Justice's Court, Fifth Township.—David Spiegel, plaintiff, vs. John S. Ellis, Sheriff, &c., defendant.

OPINION OF THE COURT.

THIS is an action brought by plaintiff against the defendant, the Sheriff of the City and County of San Francisco, for the recovery of certain goods and chattels, alleged to be the personal property of the plaintiff, to wit: his necessary household furniture, seized by the defendant, as such Sheriff, by virtue of an execution issued from the District court of the Fourth Judicial District of this State.

The main question is, whether or not the articles seized are the necessary furniture of the family of the plaintiff, and as such exempt from execution under our statute?

It is in evidence by the testimony of A. Bertheimer, a witness for the plaintiff, that all the property is the necessary household, kitchen, and table furniture, and wearing apparel of the plaintiff and his family, he being the plaintiff in this action, and a judgment debtor in the District Court of the Fourth Judicial District, and that the same does not exceed one hundred and sixty-five dollars and eighty-seven cents. Also, that it does not embrace any article of provision or

---

SOURCE: "David Spiegel vs. John Ellis," *Occident and American Jewish Advocate,* Philadelphia, May 1863, 82–85.

9. This case was reported in Germany; see *Allgemeine Zeitung des Judentums,* July 7, 1863, 434–35.

food, actually laid in for individual or family support, sufficient for one month, nay, not even for one day, all of which is exempt by our statute from sale under execution.

The only articles embraced in the inventory of the seized property in question subject to doubt, are one silver-plated goblet and one silver-plated cake basket, both together of the value of *five dollars*, and by the evidence of the same before mentioned witness, it appears also that these two articles, together with one *extra set* of knives and forks, are a part of the utensils used by the plaintiff's family, and are dedicated as such for their religious exercises, which is the Mosaic dispensation, the family being Israelites; hence the question, or the doubt of these articles being or not *necessary* and *exempt* from sale under execution.[10]

In interpreting the remedial law of our State, we take broad ground for investigating the philosophy of the law, and the motives of this law-giver to enact such relief-law in favor of the judgment debtor, and in so doing we naturally come to the starting point, to wit:

THE OBJECT OF THE RELIEF.

We are a progressive people and are living in the *age of progress*. The American people, as a nation and as the constituted government of the United States of America, is bound to be and will be, under the dispensation of a benign Providence, the model nation on the globe, and by means of its civilization, Christianity, and social element, will attract the admiration and merit the reverence of mankind, and why?

Because we have by our political constitution abolished the feudal system of government, with all its concomitant barbarous practices, and oppressive jurisprudence, and its cruel and vindictive punishments. We have annihilated time and space by electricity, and have substituted steam in lieu of animal power and other insufficient and precarious natural motors. We have economized human strength and vigor from unnecessary and wasteful expenditure by the introduction of the *ten-hour* day labor system, and have established by law a *day of rest,*[11] refreshment, and recreation, for the recuperation of the bodily and mental energies, in every seven days. All this we have done to alleviate the condition of man, and to elevate him above brute creation; and in doing so we have by proper laws added to his comfort; among them prominent is the *Relief Law* under consideration at this time.

---

10. It is unclear whether the utensils were necessary because the family kept kosher dietary laws requiring two sets of utensils, or whether the second set was necessary for Passover observance.

11. A reference to the Sunday Laws that were on the California State Law books until 1883.

Again, by the Constitution of the United States, and by that of this State, we have among other things guaranteed in the most solemn manner to all men *religious liberty,* by declaring that "The exercise and enjoyment of religious profession and worship without discrimination or preference shall forever be allowed in this State," &c. (Art. I. Declaration of Rights, Sec. 4, Constitution of California.) Hence to observe and to maintain this guarantee, we must not only permit the party to exercise and enjoy his religious belief, but we must secure to him the possession and the control of all the paraphernalia, furniture, fixtures, and appurtenances belonging to his family altar or private chapel, when such articles are dedicated and used for that purpose, and especially where they are of inconsiderable value, as the case is now under consideration, and *in primis,* to the Israelite, being of the most ancient and venerable institution among us, and upon which our own religious tenets are predicated, the "Old Testament," the holy vessels, kitchen and table furniture, made use of at New Year, the Atonement Day, and at the Passover especially.[12] To the Greek and the Roman Catholic, the crucifix, the holy water font, the rosary, the Madonna, Sacrafamilia, and other allegorical pictures and paintings of their particular creed. To the Protestants of the various Christian denominations, the Family Bible, with its numerous commentaries, the prayer and hymn books, with such articles of furniture as are dedicated and necessary at their family or social religious exercises, and for the administration of the holy baptism and the eucharist, to wit: the urn, the goblets, the plates, and the font.

We would always in cases as the one now under consideration, exempt the above enumerated articles as coming within the purview and meaning of our statute, as being exempt from execution, and for the reason that if we deprive the owners of these necessary and indispensable articles, we embarrass, prevent, and restrain by force the exercise of a constitutional right.

In the British dominions, under the common law of England, the *heirloom* is exempt from seizure and sale under execution, on the ground of securing to the family reminiscences of its ancestry; whereas at the same time the farmer's husbandry utensils, the mechanic's tools, the professional man's library, instruments, and apparatus, are not, nor is any article of household, kitchen, or table furniture or utensils exempt, not even the family bedstead and bedding, or the child's crib or cradle; and many are the instances on the records of the several European and Hispano-American government courts of justice, where the bed and bedding of the sick and the dying were levied upon and sold under execution, and if not sufficient to satisfy the judgment debt, the

---

12. There was uncertainty about Jewish practice, as the New Year, the Day of Atonement, and Passover are all commonly confused in publications of this period.

debtor's person was attached and incarcerated until ransomed by some friend or relative, or until duly discharged by the course of law.

Such instances have taken place in some of our own sister States, but Heaven be praised, that this barbarous and cruel custom has passed away from our land, and that a more liberal policy has been inaugurated under our humane and philosophic constitution and laws; and that not only the person of the judgment debtor is sacred from incarcerations for debt, but also all his necessary household, kitchen, and table furniture with many other articles enumerated in the statutes, are exempt from forcible sale, to make him and his family comfortable and above want, to enable him to procure an honest livelihood and preserve his social condition, as before his misfortunes, and to insure his happiness and encourage him in the hope of being able to provide for his family by securing him a sweet home, with a happy fireside and all the household goods.

Taking this liberal and enlarged view of the object of our *remedial laws* in favor of the judgment debtor, this Court declares, that the property in question in this action is embraced in the exemption from execution, and that the same is *bona fide* necessary for the support and comfort of the plaintiff's family. Therefore, it is ordered, adjudged, and decreed, that the plaintiff have judgment for the possession of the same, as enumerated in the inventory filed in this case, and for his costs expended in this suit, and that judgment be entered in accordance with this opinion.

GEO. FISHER,
Justice of the Peace, 5th Township.

San Francisco, June 30, 1862

91
"Abraham Lincoln, the Twice Anointed High Priest"
Hebrew, San Francisco, 1865

Word of President Lincoln's assassination reached Rabbi Elkan Cohn of Temple Emanu-El just as he was about to deliver his Saturday sermon. It is evident from the power of the words Cohn used to describe his feelings for the assassinated president and the Union that his congregants on that day felt themselves fully American, though still largely foreign-born.

Just as the Rev. Dr. Elkan Cohn, of the Congregation Emmanuel, on Broadway, was ascending his pulpit, on Saturday, to deliver the usual sermon, a copy of the dispatch announcing the assassination of President Lincoln was handed to him, and on reading the same, he was so overcome that, bursting into tears, he sank almost senseless. Recovering, in broken accents he announced the same to the congregation, and it fell upon their ears like a thunderbolt—the whole being moved to tears. The impression created was beyond description. Dr. Cohn made this very impressive and eloquent address on the character of the National calamity:

"Beloved Brethren! Overpowered with grief and sorrow at the terrible news which just at this moment was communicated to me, I am scarcely able to command my feelings, and to express before you the sad calamity that has befallen our beloved country. Who might believe! our revered President, Abraham Lincoln, the twice anointed High Priest in the sanctuary of our Republic, has fallen a bloody victim to treason and assassination, and is no more. He, who by the indomitable power of his energy, stood amidst us like a mighty giant, holding with his hands the tottering columns of our great commonwealth, and planting them secure upon the solid basis of general freedom and humanity; his great mind full of wisdom, his great heart full of love, his whole being, a true type of the American liberal character. Oh! the beloved of our heart is fallen, and is no more amongst the living. And with his soul departed, the soul and spirit of his council, the great statesman who inspired him with wisdom, and stood on his side with the giant intellect of his mind, William H. Seward.[13] Under the burden of this terrible affliction, we can scarcely realize the truth of our bereavement; our feelings quail under the weight of a most intense grief, and we are more inclined to cry than to speak

---

SOURCE: "Synagogue Emanu-El," *Hebrew,* San Francisco, Apr. 21, 5625 (1865), 4.

13. It was at first believed that William Seward, the U.S. secretary of state, had also been killed.

them out. Two great men have fallen. Arise, my brethren, and bow in humble devotion before God! Arise, and honor the memory of the blessed, whose life was a blessing to us, to our country, to the oppressed and afflicted, and to the human race at large. But though they are dead, their noble persons hushed in ethereal silence, their spirits live—live in thousands and millions of American hearts and souls, a sacred inheritance to them of their great dead—never to die out—never, never! The great principles they so nobly and fully represented are the very nerve and essence of our people, and as long as there is upon our soil a mind to think and a heart to feel, these principles will be defended and upheld with the last drop of blood. Glory in heaven will be the celestial reward of our beloved, whom we mourn as children mourn the loss of a father, and we pray to God to receive their souls in love and mercy, and be gracious to these His most faithful servants. Oh, they served God, in their love to man, the most glorious worship upon earth! And we pray that He, in His infinite love, may graciously avert the dreadful consequences of this calamity, calm the passions of the people, so justly aroused at this atrocious crime, soothe the grief and sorrow so deeply cutting in the very heart of our nation, and speak to the Angel of Destruction: 'Enough! The noblest victims may be the last.' Henceforth, the great work for which they bled stands under my protection. They have fulfilled their mission, they have restored the Union, they have rebuilt the great stronghold of humanity and freedom; I will now seal their work with the great blessing of peace! [']O God! Thou who hast given victory to Thy people, may it please Thee to bless thy people with peace.['] "

92

"Freemasonry Resembles Judaism More
than Any Other Mode of Worship"

Hebrew, San Francisco, 1865

This anonymously written article concludes that Jewish affinity for the Masons may stem from the fact that Masonic rituals share common elements with aspects of Judaism.[14] In San Francisco, in the river towns, and in the mining communities, the Masonic Brotherhood, a fraternal organization with humanitarian goals, counted a disproportionally large number of Jews among their predominantly Protestant membership. In the 1870s, one of San Francisco's four Masonic lodges was largely Jewish, and many leaders of the Jewish community, including officers of both congregations and philanthropic organizations, were Masons. Most Masons were shop owners or businessmen and shared a common social class and economic background. Membership in a fraternal organization such as the Masons gave them respectability and practical advantages. The call for a universal belief became especially attractive to San Francisco's Reform Jews, who were beginning to place as much value on their American identity as they did on their Jewish identity.[15]

FREEMASONRY AND RELIGION

A CONCISE VIEW OF THE ORIGIN, PROGRESS AND ULTIMATE AIM OF

THE MASONIC INSTITUTION.

BY ONE OF THE CRAFT

We now proceed to show that Freemasonry in its progress and its present state bears the marks of being closely connected with the Jewish religion; and in all its rites and ceremonies resembles the Jewish mode of worship more than any other. [. . .] For if the institution took rise among the Jewish nation, it is quite natural that it should rest on the principles of their faith, and be modeled after their rites and customs. But let us test the truth of this assertion by a closer examination and comparison of the two sister institutions. We will not dilate upon any of the characteristics which Jewish and Christian religion have in common—though there is not one of the moral principles taught by the latter which is not included in the former—but we will attend to some of

---

SOURCE: *Hebrew,* San Francisco, Sept. 8, 1865, 4.

14. The author probably chose anonymity, as Masonic rituals were secret.
15. See Tony Fels, "Religious Assimilation in a Fraternal Organization: Jews and Freemasonry in Gilded-Age San Francisco," *American Jewish History* 74:4 (1985): 369–403.

those distinguishing features of the Jewish religion, the reflection of which is so plainly visible in the Freemasonic institution.

The principal and most distinguishing doctrine in Judaism is Monotheism. Israel ever was, and is up to the present day, one nation adoring One Supreme Being. Though on their leaving Egypt the people were more than a million in number, they had but one tabernacle of the congregation, and but One God they worshipped. And this is exactly the same in Masonry. There is nothing in it to inculcate the doctrine of a trinity or polytheism. Dispersed as its members are over the surface of the globe, they form but one society, adoring but one Supreme Architect, the Grand Master of the Universe. The historical parts of its lectures bear an undoubted reference to the Jewish religion. This coincidence is indeed so remarkable, that it would almost convince any unprejudiced mind that Masonry was formed as an exclusive companion for Judaism. The strength of this testimony is increased by the general tendency of its allegorical instruction, and the symbols employed for that end, nearly all of which are borrowed from the Jewish religion and history. It is well known and universally admitted that the Jewish religion abounds in symbols and allegories, as in most of the observances prescribed in the law of Moses symbols are employed; while on the other hand the Christian religion is said by its professors to be perfectly spiritual. The very pass-words and signs by which the secrets of our craft are communicated, are taken from the Hebrew, and connected with some events relating to the Hebrew nation.

Again, the construction and situation of our lodges bear such strong resemblance not only to the temple and tabernacle, but also to the Jewish synagogues of the present time, as to leave no doubt that the former are in close imitation of the latter. Our lodges, like our synagogues, are situated due east and west, because King Solomon's Temple was. In the temple the "sanctum sanitarium" was in the east; in the synagogue the ark containing the holy law, the true light revealed by God to man, is likewise deposited in the east, and in our lodges the W.M. presides in the east to open and adorn his lodge. Israelites worship with covered heads, and so does he. The Jewish festivals and holy convocations are regulated by the lunar months; so are masonic meetings. Among the Jews we have three successive degrees, or three classes of men—ordinary Israelites, the Levites, and the Priests—who as their dignity increases approach nearer to the service of God, and consequently receive more light; corresponding to this we have three degrees of Masonry. It is, in fact, needless to multiply evidence in support of our theory. We might notice many other particulars which point out the intimate connection between Masonry and Judaism, but enough has been said to prove that the institution was planted and reared upon Jewish ground and by Jewish hands.

It now remains for us to show how far Masonry and Judaism correspond in their common object of diffusing the knowledge of God, and promoting the happiness of man.

It is obvious that all increase of knowledge is improvement to the understanding. The more the sphere of our understanding is enlarged, the more must those rational powers, which are the peculiar privilege and glory of man, be in the course of attaining their proper strength and maturity. Ignorance and moral darkness are productive of misery, whilst light, knowledge and understanding, produce happiness. The highest degree of knowledge we can wish to attain to and which is most productive of true felicity, is the knowledge of God: to seek which we are commanded alike by precepts of institution and our religion. It is scarcely necessary to remind the initiated that the acquisition of such knowledge is one of the primary objects of our craft; and it is likewise the religion revealed to Moses and the prophets, which bids us to "know the God of our fathers and to serve him." The teachings of our craft are intended to give us just and proper ideas of the grand Architect of the Universe, defining the relation we bear to Him as creations of his will, teaching that we are in his hands; "as the clay in the hands of Him who fashioneth it," as bricks in the hands of the builder. It is Freemasonry which leads us step by step, and degree by degree, to the more perfect enjoyment of heavenly light and divine truth. And it is the religion taught in the books of the Old Testament, which inculcates those pure and exacted conceptions of the Deity as the only one God, creator and supporter of all things, the Universal Father and Omnipotent Benefactor of all his creatures, and the standard of unspotted perfection. Religion as taught in the Old Testament, has a tendency to improve the social intercourse of men, and to assist them in co-operating for common good. The worship of the true God as revealed in the Mosaic law, introduces the idea of concord, union, and peace. The prophets constantly and repeatedly teach us to look for that happy period when all mankind shall constitute one grand lodge of free and accepted Masons; free in a great measure from the burden of worldly cares and anxieties, free in the possession of a pure heart, and acceptable in the eyes of the world's Grand Master—when "the earth shall be filled with knowledge like the waters cover the sea; when all the peoples of the earth shall know that the Lord he is God, and there is none else; when he shall be universally acknowledged as one, and his name shall be one."

Masonry teaches us to live together in peace, and union and brotherly love, to regard the whole human species as one human family, created by one Almighty Parent. On this principle Masonry unites men of every country, sect and opinion and conciliates friendship among those who might otherwise have remained at a perpetual distance. And so the prophets in the Old Testament teach us that "the day shall come when the mountain of God's house shall be established above all the mountains, and exalted above all the hills, and all the nations shall flow into it; and they shall say, come, let us go up to the mountain of God, to the houses of the God of Jacob: ". . . ." And they shall beat their swords into ploughshares and their spears into pruning hooks: nation shall not lift up sword against nation, neither shall they learn war anymore." Assuredly none

427

will presume to say that we have as yet arrived at that happy period. But it is the design both of Masonry and the Jewish religion to prepare mankind for that happy and glorious time when those rapturous prospects and prophecies shall be realized; when universal knowledge, and peace and brotherhood shall reign among mankind—the children of one Father, the creatures of one God.

We may then look forward to that time when the temples of the Juggernaut of the Lamma and the Japanese idol, the mosque, the church, and the synagogue, and every temple that has an altar raised unto the unknown God, will be in ruins; and one universal temple be erected of which the people will be the living walls, the heart the altar, and the incentive, adoration and gratitude to the true and everlasting God.

93
A Painter's San Francisco Youth
Toby Rosenthal, ca. 1865

Born in Strasbourg, Toby Rosenthal (1848–1917) became the West's first Jewish artist. He grew up in New Haven, Connecticut, and San Francisco, where his father was a tailor. As a child in San Francisco, Rosenthal sold newspapers to help support his family, which included three younger brothers, and played cruel pranks with his friends in the ethnic neighborhoods. At the age of fourteen he began to study drawing and painting with a local artist. In 1865 he continued his studies in Munich, where he settled permanently, returning only twice to the

San Francisco artist Toby Rosenthal, age seventeen, San Francisco, 1865. From William M. Kramer and Norton B. Stern, *San Francisco's Artist: Toby E. Rosenthal.* Courtesy of William M. Kramer.

United States. His portrait paintings, commissioned primarily by West Coast Jews, were displayed in San Francisco galleries. Like other American Jewish artists, Rosenthal often used Biblical motifs and a narrative style in his work.[16] Rosenthal's memoir vividly describes his introduction to art in San Francisco, his boyhood prejudices against the Chinese, and the effects of the Civil War and Lincoln's assassination on his life and on the city of San Francisco. Although written in English, his memoir was first published in German in 1927.

During my free Sunday hours and on other occasions, I constantly practiced drawing. At the beginning my father called it a waste of time, because he regarded painting as did others of his environment as an unprofitable activity. Since everyone was trying to get rich, and because there seemed to be no possible way to give me a chance to study art, his disapproval was understandable.

When I was about fourteen years old, I finally received permission to attend the drawing class of French sculptor, Louis Bacon. Monsieur Bacon had participated too enthusiastically in the Revolution of 1848, and had made active use of his gun behind the barricades. When the uprising failed, he had to flee, finally landing in San Francisco, and here he founded his drawing school.

Indescribably happy, I made my way to the first lesson. My enthusiasm helped me make such progress that soon I was the favorite student. Bacon was a very cultured man, very emotional, but kind. He was married to an Italian, had two children, a son and daughter, whom he treated with tyrannical severity. In excited moments, and these were frequent, he would, always speaking French, use the most vulgar swear-words to the great amusement of his pupils. After a year I had completed a series of large drawings and was urged, on the occasion of a trade and art show, to exhibit some of them. This was very significant, for in the area in which I lived there was almost a total lack of artistic endeavor and production, and my work was bound to attract attention. People were not spoiled, and there was no possibility for comparison. All my father's friends now insisted that my apparent talent should be encouraged. When after a time the financial condition of my family improved, my father finally agreed, and I had the opportunity to continue more intensive study with a painter called Fortunato Arriola.

Fortunato Arriola descended from an old Spanish family. His grandfather had been sent to Mexico on some sort of political mission, and had remained there for the rest of his life. Fortunato's father became wealthy, acquiring

SOURCE: *Rosenthal's Memoir of a Painter,* ed. William M. Kramer and Norton B. Stern and trans. Marlene Rainman (Northridge: Santa Susana Press, 1978), 144–52.

16. Diner, *A Time for Gathering,* 205.

much land and many silver mines, but lost his wealth because of the many political uprisings. Fortunato himself was uninterested in business of any kind. He showed talent for painting early in life and longed to go to Europe in order to study. But his father felt old and lonely after the loss of his fortune, and did not want to be parted from his son. So Fortunato had to stay in Mexico, and since he did not want to forego his cherished desire, he tried to educate his eye and develop his taste through the study of the paintings in churches. He practiced without an instructor and taught himself. When I recall to mind his achievements and the sort of mistakes he made, I can recognize the error in the claim of some writers and critics who say that a course of study at an art academy is not necessary in order to become a capable painter.

The outward appearance of my new teacher was interesting and made a great impression on me as a young boy. Tall in stature, with a pale-yellowish face, large black eyes, and an almost Grecian nose, very red lips, mustache and beard and hair coal black, the total effect resembled a head by Velasquez. He had left his wife and seven children in Mexico and, like all immigrants, had come to San Francisco in order to get rich quickly through his art. Several persons had brought me to his attention, and since from his own experience he had an understanding of my situation, he was prepared to give me a helping hand without remuneration of any kind. Of course I had to agree to render small services from time to time and to prepare the canvases, but I was delighted to accept these conditions.

Arriola painted portraits, landscapes, flags with emblems, and carried out all kinds of painting commissions. I was of help to him in every way possible. Our relationship soon became very friendly and his care for me truly paternal. His studio was the gathering place for all the Mexican adventurers. If an uprising collapsed in Mexico and the leaders (naturally so-called generals) had to flee, they came to San Francisco and put up at Arriola's. I regarded these political highwaymen, with their staffs and mistresses, with burning curiosity. Among them was Captain Gonzaga, leader of the gang who would carry out the execution of the unfortunate Emperor Maximilian.

In this turbulent life there was no avoiding an occasional fight, and where there is much shooting and beating, there are bruises and black eyes, which one does not care to display. One of the injured men once had the idea of hiding the black and blue marks with paint. Lightheartedly he went to my teacher and the obliging Arriola covered the spot with a suitable flesh color, then removed the oily shine of the paint, and the patient went on his way satisfied after having paid two or three dollars. As time went on many a victim of beatings followed this example. It was an incredibly comical sight to see my aristocratic, hidalgo-like teacher carefully wielding his brushes on the face of the patient, while I held the palette.

My first work under Arriola's supervision was a copy of the large self-portrait of my teacher. This, the best work that he ever accomplished, was good and

431

painted in the style of the Spanish masters of the end of the sixteenth century. With love and patience I succeeded in making a convincing copy. This first attempt (I had never before dared to work with colors), to my great satisfaction, evoked a general amazement. This young stripling thus became very cocky. I was beginning to be noticed, and I was entrusted with orders for portraits from photographs, although no one yet dared to order from me a portrait done from life. In addition, no one had the time to sit for a portrait. The customers would bring me daguerreotypes of their deceased fathers and mothers, and with the help of such photographs I did portraits in oil.

For such work I received in most cases a payment of one hundred dollars.

In the midst of my work in my teacher's studio I found much free time and was able to take better care of developing my mind and body. I had to catch up on my learning, and my body had to be strengthened in the gymnasium. An acquaintance of my father's, who owned two riding horses, permitted me occasionally to ride for a few hours. I would ride out over the sand dunes toward the ocean or past the old Mission in the direction of San Jose. Inland, outside the city, stood the old Mission church and the monastery, which Spanish monks had built. The San Jose monastery was surrounded by a high wall, which enclosed about half an acre, that had once served as a vegetable garden for the monks. Since California had once been part of Mexico, until it joined the Union, its language had been Spanish. For a short time the populations of Spanish descent remained in the state, and with it many traditional customs. For instance, the old settlers could not refrain, sometimes secretly, but with the lenient blindness of the police, from staging bullfights in the enclosed garden of the monastery.

One of the most picturesque sights to be seen in those days were the herds of livestock which, destined for slaughter, were driven into the city by buckaroos swinging their lassos. The buckaroos are cowhands, mestizos of Mexican and Indian blood. These brown riders still wore their traditional costume; the flat sombrero with a wide band and multi-colored tassels, the short, richly embroidered jacket, underneath it a colorful, silken waistband, leather trousers to the knee, and with this huge medieval spurs, from which dangled bells. The mustangs were decorated with extravagantly ornamented long saddles with a towering pommel, to which the lasso was fastened; a silver ornamental harness with silver bells and colored tassels completed the highly picturesque impression.

My young fame as a painter, which I exploited fully, found so much respect among my equals that I was considered the ringleader for every stupid prank. Of course I was always enthusiastically ready for such undertakings. One of the main targets for our tricks was Chinatown. There the Chinese lived crowded together, busy, unassuming, tightly knit by the traditional customs of their homeland. In the narrow alleys stood their temples, theaters and gambling dens, their stores and teahouses. We had soon found out how superstitious the Chinese are, and what fear, for example, they have of the broom which, with the sweeping side turned up, signifies all kinds of terrible trouble to them. We marched in solemn procession, our faces serious, I, as leader, carrying the broom through the busiest alleys. We wanted to split with laughter when the Chinese fled from us with an excited "poi, poi." It was too funny a contrast to their otherwise grave behavior. Or on Chinese holidays, when they could be found chatting in the street and were so absorbed in their conversation that nothing could distract them, we, covered by another companion who pretended to be a harmless walker, would sneak up and quickly tie their pigtails together. Then, when the group separated and each wanted to go off in a different direction, we had already make our escape and watched joyously from a distance how they scolded and labored over their pigtails.

Among the deepest impressions of that time are two events which occurred in the years 1859 and 1865. I mean the war between the Southern States and the Union, destined to bring slavery to an end in the United States. The numerous partisans of the Southern States caused serious conflicts. An adventurer who had come from the South[17] attacked the Senator of California, David C. Broderick, a Republican,[18] in the open street. The senator lost his life in an improvised duel. I saw the body lying in a hall as I was passing by. It was the first dead body I had ever seen and the strong impression was intensified by the sensational political significance of the murder.

The second event, which long occupied my imagination and the terror of which recurred in many of my dreams, was the riot which raged in San Francisco when the news of the murder of President Abraham Lincoln was heard. Most of the papers in San Francisco were sympathetic to the Northern States. There were, however, one large and one small paper which defended the interests of the Southern States. There was a tremendous excitement over the death of Lincoln, and the population rushed from all sides into the center of the city. A few fanatical speakers incited the people to occupy the buildings of the hostile papers. In a frenzy of excitement the mob obeyed instantly. It entered a rambling building and blocked off all passages, and within it a horrible uproar started.

Tables, cupboards, papers, all things that came to hand were flung through the windows. The howling mob in the street urged on the vandals with repeated applause. Finally the militia had to be brought in, because the police had been put to flight by scornful derision. The armed troops tried to break through the immense human wall, but only when they closed their formation with fixed bayonets did those closest to the soldiers begin to fall back. I happened to be

---

17. A reference to California Chief Justice David S. Terry; Rosenthal has many of his facts wrong. See Arthur Quinn, *The Rivals: William Gwin, David Broderick, and the Birth of California* (New York: Crown, 1994).

18. Broderick was a Democrat.

433

standing in the place that was attacked by the troops and in the push I landed in the front line. There was no escape. For a half hour the bayonet of a determined-looking soldier flashed at my chest, so that only a casual movement was needed to kill me. I suffered terrible tortures during this half hour and felt the cold steel a hundred times in my chest. For a long time I could not look at armed soldiers without shuddering.

Up to the age of sixteen-and-a-half I painted in Arriola's studio, but my work began to be monotonous and to bore me. Then something happened that changed the direction of my life. The well-to-do friends and acquaintances of my father gradually came to the conclusion that a trip to Europe would be necessary for my artistic training. However, my father's financial circumstances were no secret to anyone, and in order to make my trip possible some of these gentlemen wanted to raise the means for it among themselves. One day they told my father that the sum of $3,000 was at our disposal. This offer aroused my father's opposition. Much as he appreciated it, he felt wounded in the depth of his soul and his pride rebelled against the offer, which carried with it the stigma of charity. He refused the offer with the explanation that it was painful for him to know that I should have others than my parents to thank for my progress. A few weeks later he announced to me his decision to send me to Europe at his own expense, and furthermore that the means he could make available to me for that purpose would be very limited, but that he hoped to be able to keep me from want. This news gave me great delight and made me tremendously excited. I was to start the trip two months later. Meanwhile all preparations were made, all steps were considered, and at the same time we began to feel the sorrow of the imminent farewells.

On the day of departure my father took me into his room. He appeared very excited and worried and unable to keep silent any longer. With his first words he warned me of all the dangers to which I would be exposed out in the world. It seemed to calm him when he could show me the possibilities of avoiding these dangers because gradually he became more composed, and when my mother entered he said a brave farewell to me. This conversation made such a lasting impression on me that I have remembered it clearly all my life. In later years I painted the scene. The painting is called "Departure from Home" and is in the private collection of the iron king, W. D. Wood, in Pittsburgh. When I had said goodbye to my mother and brothers, my father accompanied me to the pier where the great ocean liner was docked.

94

An Interfaith Calendar

Philo Jacoby, 1865

The son of a rabbi, Philo Jacoby (1837–1922) grew up in Pomerania, now part of Poland, where in addition to obtaining a traditional Jewish education he was trained as a printer. In San Francisco he distinguished himself as a journalist, publishing both the *Hebrew* (1863–87), an English and German Jewish weekly, and the *Almanach für Californien*.

For more than fifty years Jacoby was a prominent figure in German-American circles. His *Almanach* familiarized residents, prospective immigrants, and investors with California's natural resources and business opportunities. Each month the *Almanach* included an extensive calendar of Protestant, Catholic, and Jewish holidays, each religion receiving equal space and prominence. The following is a sample page from an 1865 issue.

1865. Mai. 31 Tage.

Tag und Datum.	Protestantischer Kalender.	Catholischer Kalender.	Sonnen- Auf- und Untergang U M	U M	Mondes- Auf- und Untergang U M	U M	Fluth Morgens U M	Abend U M
1 Montag	Philipp. u. Jac.	Philipp. u. Jac.	5 4	6 51	5 44	0 1	3 34	6 8
2 Dienstag	Sigismund	Athanasius	5 3	6 51	6 30	0 40	4 39	6 53
3 Mittwoch	Kreuzes F.	† Erfndg.	5 2	6 52	7 15	1 15	5 48	7 38
4 Donnerst.	Florian	Florian	5 0	6 53	7 58	1 46	6 58	8 22
5 Freitag	Gotthard	Gotthard	4 59	6 54	8 40	2 17	7 59	8 55
6 Samstag	Joh. Pfort.	Joh. v. d. Pf.	4 58	6 55	9 22	2 46	8 58	10 12
7 Sonntag	3. Jubilate	3. Jubilate	4 57	6 56	10 4	3 15	9 28	10 10
8 Montag	Dietrich	Stanislaus	4 56	6 57	10 48	3 46	10 22	10 32
9 Dienstag	Benigna	Gregor v. N.	4 55	6 58	11 34	4 19	11 16	10 50
10 Mittwoch	Victoria	Antonia	4 54	6 59	morg	g. a.	0 5	11 5
11 Donnerst.	Adolph	Florens	4 53	7 0	0 22	8 1	1 13	11 47
12 Freitag	Pankratius	Pankratius	4 52	7 1	1 11	8 56	.....	2 10
13 Samstag	Servatius	Servatius	4 52	7 1	2 3	9 47	0 16	2 53
14 Sonntag	4. Cantate	4. Cantate	4 51	7 2	2 55	10 35	0 53	3 36
15 Montag	Sophie	Sophia	4 50	7 3	3 48	11 18	1 38	4 24
16 Dienstag	Sara	Peregrinus	4 49	7 4	4 40	11 59	2 36	5 22
17 Mittwoch	Jodokus	Bruno B.	4 48	7 5	5 32	morg	3 48	6 21
18 Donnerst.	Venantius	Liborius	4 47	7 5	6 24	0 37	5 7	7 14
19 Freitag	Potentian	Sara	4 46	7 6	7 15	1 14	6 24	7 59
20 Samstag	Theresia	Bassila	4 46	7 7	8 7	1 51	7 35	8 41
21 Sonntag	5. Rogate	5. Rogate Ph. J.	4 45	7 8	9 1	2 28	8 59	9 21
22 Montag	Helena	Helena	4 44	7 9	9 56	3 8	10 11	9 52
23 Dienstag	Desiderius	Desiderius	4 43	7 10	10 53	3 52	11 18	10 19
24 Mittwoch	Johanna	Johanna	4 43	7 11	11 51	g. u.	0 19	10 52
25 Donnerst.	Himmelf. Ch.	Himmelf. Chr.	4 42	7 11	Nchm	8 9	1 18	11 30
26 Freitag	Beda	Beda	4 42	7 12	1 47	9 5	.....	2 24
27 Samstag	Florens	Joh. v. P.	4 41	7 13	2 42	9 53	0 13	3 11
28 Sonntag	6. Eraubi	6. Eraubi	4 40	7 14	3 34	10 35	0 58	3 46
29 Montag	Manilius	Max	4 40	7 14	4 23	10 12	1 52	4 26
30 Dienstag	Wigand	Ferdinand	4 39	7 15	5 9	11 46	3 1	5 15
31 Mittwoch	Petronella	Angela	4 39	7 15	5 54	morg	4 6	5 56

Kalender der Juden.

5,625. Ijar 17—Lag B'omer	13. Mai 1865.
— Sivan 1—	26. — —
„ 6—Erstes Wochenfest	31. — —

Mond-Wechsel.

Erstes Viertel,	2	7 Uhr 54 Minuten	Morgens.
Vollmond,	10	0 Uhr 13 —	Nachmittags.
Letztes Viertel,	17	10 Uhr 30 —	Abends.
Neumond,	24	2 Uhr 40 —	Nachmittags.

95
A Newspaper Man with a Rifle
Philo Jacoby, 1862–1865

Jacoby stood out not only for his publishing accomplishments but for his athletic prowess. Captain John A. Sutter of Sacramento taught him marksmanship, and Jacoby went on to win competitions throughout the United States and Europe. He became a founding member of the Olympic Club as well as a member and organizer of several rifle clubs and shooting festivals. Awarded the title of "Champion Rifle Shot of the World" at the 1876 Centennial Exposition in Philadelphia, he went on to compete in Prussia, Germany, Austria, and Switzerland. With his heavily muscular build, this amateur strongman who sported medals on his chest was a larger-than-life character in both the Jewish community and the world at large.[19] In the following excerpts from his memoir (written in the third person), Jacoby describes the first long-range rifle match in California.

May 15th, 1865, the first long range rifle match in California took place between Alois Schneider, an expert gunsmith and good shot and Philo Jacoby (the writer, that time a young marksman with some skill and more nerve). The match came about through Schneider challenging all marksmen to a contest at 600 yards, globe sight and muzzle rest. [H]e to use a 30 pound rifle of his own make. Jacoby, who owned a good rifle weighing about 12 pounds, made by Schlotterbeck, had the latter make him a high globesight, and by practicing with the aid of an old marksman, A. Beschauman, on a level stretch (now Bryant street between 16th and 22nd) soon found that his rifle, with somewhat larger powder load, shot true, but that the wind deflected his bullets greatly. First he tried to set the sight of his rifle, but soon found it better to hold according to his last shot. The match ($100 a side), was shot near the beach in Alameda. Dr. Pardee being the second of Jacoby and Joseph Hug the second of Schneider, Severin and George Schmidt and John Bach were the judges who measured the shots while Severin Jr., acted as marker. The targets were black, six feet in diameter having a 20-inch white bullseye. There were about 100 interested spectators present when Schneider fired his first shot, scoring

Source: Philo Jacoby, *The Rifle in California* (San Francisco: Self-published, 1910), 9–11.

19. See William M. Kramer and Reva Clar, "Philo Jacoby: California's First International Sportsman," *Western States Jewish History,* part 1, 22:1 (1989): 3–17; part 2, 22:2 (1990): 122–36; part 3, 22:3 (1990): 243–57.

Philo Jacoby, marksman, strongman, and editor of the *Hebrew* ca. 1910.
Courtesy of the California Historical Society, de Young Collection, FN-08607.
Photograph by Taber-Stanford Studio, San Francisco.

a bullseye, Jacoby following with a shot just outside of the bullseye and to the right. Schneider's second shot was also to the right, while Jacoby, who held to the left, scored a good center. The wind then freshened, and Jacoby, who continued to hold towards the wind, in fact he held and pulled his last two shots clear outside to the left of the target, beat Schneider who did not follow the advice of Hug to hold according to the wind, 79 1/2 inches, to the great astonishment of all present. The Sixth (German) Regiment of Militia,[20] commanded by Colonel Fred Tittel, held its annual prize shooting the same day at the Odeon, and as Jacoby had promised to act in the afternoon as their prize Judge he instructed the stakeholder, Mr. O. Wertheimber, the treasurer of Deutsche Schuetzen Club to entertain all present at Fasking's Park, a resort near by. This Wertheimber did to such a good purpose that he spent not only the $200 stakes, but, also a little more in giving the boys a good time. When next day Jacoby asked Wertheimber for an accounting, the latter showed him a receipted bill for $207 from Faskings Park for refreshments comprised of several dozen Rhinewines most expensive liquors, cigars, many roast chicken, ducks, etc., etc. Champagne was lacking only because Fasking did not have any. As the betting had been 5 to 1 in the match in favor of Schneider and Jacoby had taken many bets, he consoled himself.

---

20. Gun Clubs were formed by men of the same national origin; Jews were members of German clubs.

96
"An Independent Little Cuss"
Adolph Sutro, 1840s–1860s

Born in Aix-la-Chapelle (Aachen, Prussia), a city with a small Jewish population on the German-Belgian border, Adolph Heinrich Joseph Sutro (1830–98) became one of the first Jewish mayors of a major American city.[21] Unlike most of his fellow immigrants, Sutro came from a wealthy family and had all the advantages of a secular education and social distinction that went with his background. He arrived in California in 1850, met and married Leah Harris in a Jewish ceremony, and became the father of three children. Sutro became famous for building the Sutro Tunnel under the Comstock Lode through the Nevada mountains to speed production in the silver mines, improve ventilation and drainage for the miners, and create a process for refining silver ore. In 1879, after becoming disgusted with corrupt officials, mining tycoons, and unscrupulous bankers who hindered the project, he sold his mining interests. He returned to San Francisco, where he invested his profits in real estate; in time, he owned one-twelfth of the city's acreage. Sutro gave much of this land to the people of San Francisco, developing the Cliff House, the Sutro Baths, and the Sutro Gardens as places of inexpensive popular entertainment.

A passionate bibliophile, Sutro collected books and manuscripts in many languages, including Hebrew. More than half of his original collection was destroyed in the 1906 earthquake and fire; but in 1943 his collection, thought to be the largest of its kind in the country, was given to the state of California, which established the Sutro Library as a branch of the California State Library. Sutro's many philanthropic efforts endeared him to the people of San Francisco, and in 1894 he ran for mayor as the candidate of the People's Party, defeating the "Octopus" of Huntington and the powerful railroad interests. Unfortunately, his temperament was not suited to public life, and his administration accomplished little.

Although Sutro's early days in California were similar to those of many other Jewish merchants, his drive and education led him down a road far different from that of the mercantile community. This candid self-portrait of Sutro's childhood and early years in California is from an interview with a representative of H. H. Bancroft, for the Bancroft collection.

---

21. For more about Sutro see Robert E. Stewart, Jr. and Mary Frances Stewart, *Adolph Sutro, a Biography* (Berkeley: Howell-North, 1962), and the many unpublished manuscript and papers in the Sutro Collection, Bancroft Library, University of California, Berkeley.

My parents were of the Jewish faith. One of my Uncles was a great Rabbi—honored by the king of Prussia more than any other Rabbi in Westphalia. [. . .] I was brought up in great comfort. My father had a large cloth factory and employed a great many men. We lived in a large house with 30 or 40 rooms in it—kept up a nice establishment, many servants etc.

There were thirteen children. Two died in infancy—all the others lived to grow up. One sister died about 20 years ago and no one has died since. There are ten living now—all in this country, except one brother who has gone back to Europe because he is sick. Seven were brothers—all living now. One of these is in Baltimore, one here; one has a large cigar factory in New York; another one [. . .] has a manufactory in Philadelphia; and one is an invalid now but is interested in a manufactory in New York.

Aix la Chapelle is a very nice place. It is one of the most picturesque places in all Europe. It is visited by tens of thousands every year. The inhabitants are

Adolph Sutro, 1869. Courtesy of the Nevada Historical Society.

SOURCE: Adolph Henrick Joseph Sutro. Autobiography, marked as a dictation. Typescript. H. H. Bancroft Collection, C-D 799:5, Bancroft Library, University of California, Berkeley.

all manufacturing people. The principle manufactures are broad-cloth and fine cloths generally. The population is from 60,000 to 70,000.

I was sort of an independent little "cuss" when I was a boy. Hard to regulate. Had notions of my own as a little child—pretty independent ideas. I had an immense love for mechanics and being surrounded by machinery and steam engines, I spent nearly all of my time with machinery. When I grew up I got the higher branches in school. By that time I knew all about the machinery in the factory-built little steam engines and did everything mechanical that a boy could do.

I had a most extraordinary love for books, as a child. Whenever a public book sale was announced they could not keep me away from it. I started in to buy books when I was 7 or 8 years old. I would go and ask my father's permission to go and buy $2 or $3 worth of books and then I would buy four or five times as much. I got it when I got home but I didn't care for that; I had the books, and that was what I wanted.

I had an extraordinary love for chemistry. When I started to study chemistry I had a little laboratory of my own. When I started to experiment, I came nearly blowing up. If I had known better I would not have done it perhaps.

I had a fancy for astronomy. I had a very beautiful reflecting telescope given me which had a lens of about two inches and a-half in diameter. We had a tower on our house and I used to go up there night after night and study the heavens. I am thoroughly familiar with the constellations now. I never followed it. Had sort of a superficial knowledge of it as a boy.

As a boy I was always in mischief. We had bells hanging on the door and at night we would tie a bone to the bell and the dogs would come and pull on it and when the woman came out she could not see any-one. No boy could have been brought up any better. It was the most harmonious household—intelligent, and simplicity of taste and the highest degree of honor. We lived well and my father kept plenty of servants.

My mother was one of the most extraordinary women I ever saw; intelligent —at 80 she could play a game of chess and beat all the children and everybody who came about; before she died. She was a most extraordinary determined woman. Her whole aim in life was to bring up her large family of children and give them a good education and correct ideas of morality.

In religion she was a very liberal woman—extraordinarily so. She was more so than my father. She was particularly devoted to her family. Of course my father was very much occupied with his affairs and could not devote that time to the children that my mother could.

Aix la Chapelle was a well regulated, well disciplined town—largely Catholic, and influenced a good deal by the Catholic priests. I never was a very strong religionist. My parents were not either; nor any one of my brothers. If you call religion taught as it is generally taught I say no, but when it comes to religious feelings, I think they are strong in the family, if religion consists of charity and kindness, which we considered always the true religion of the world. When it comes to religious rites and superstitions handed down in all directions, you find very little belief in our family—in other words, the whole family were thoroughly liberal in their ideas. I never made any particular distinction between one religion and another; in fact, no one of my brothers was married in the Jewish faith. I did. [. . .]

The school I went to at home (I was 8 years old) is what is called a general school, or citizens' school. The German translation was "bürger-schule." The gymnasium is generally considered to be a preparatory school for the university. The citizens' school is liberal in scientific branches, which brings a young man up to a practical life in all the branches of science, mathematics, and all that sort of thing. That is the school that I would naturally prefer. I went there till I was nearly 17 years of age. I would have liked to have gone longer but my father required me in the factory and I was placed in there.

I was a boy of very strong will. If my mind was made up to do anything, nothing could swerve me from my purpose—no amount of labor would discourage me. If I came across a question that I was not posted on I found out all about it before I quit. If I got hold of any scientific subject, I followed it right up till I mastered it. My investigations were not confined to any one thing, but generally any question of a scientific nature interested me. If I would take up the newspaper and see any new discovery or anything of that sort, I would read that first before I read the news of the day. If I see anything in the papers about Edison and his great invention—the phonograph, I read it at once. [. . .]

I studied specially, the sciences, but I have also a little Hebrew and I studied French and German and I knew some of Spanish, and Italian and could manage to get along wherever I was. I am not a social disposition. I am very much alone. I fall in with the English Poet: "Never less alone than when all alone." I can spend more hours alone than any man you ever saw. I am not a particle lonely. When I am alone, I think about one subject and another that interests me. Any question that comes up, I post up on. My recreation is largely in thinking.

My greatest ambition was for large mechanical works. To accomplish some work that would be generally useful/some benefit to mankind. Something that would last longer than our own poor lives, in the way of improvements that would improve the day and age I was in. That is one of the distinctive features in me—to accomplish something. [. . .] My idea was to get a thorough practical idea, and not go into the abstruse at all, but get a thorough knowledge of what we call natural philosophy—physics. I only employed formal mathematics on account of its bearing on applied mathematics.

At the age of 17 I had the practical control of my father's large factory and soon I began to manage people. In fact, I was pretty successful in managing a large number of people. If you can pick the right man who will help you it is a great benefit. I always believe in giving full responsibility to a man and not interfere with his management, either in hiring men or discharging them. If you interfere with a man it sort of discourages him. I afterwards established a cloth factory in another place on the Baltic and then they would send men from there to our country to this place. I was only 18 then. I had control of about 75 men at that time. My father employed a good many men—several hundred.

In 1848 (my father died in 1847), the whole responsibility of the establishment fell on myself and my older brother. There was only one brother older than I was. There were revolutions in nearly every part of Europe then and the result was that a revolution took place in mercantile affairs and we could not see our way through, so we gave up the establishment and wound it up, making some money—not very much.

My mother with all children (a very wise woman) she concluded to migrate to the United States. It was all our ideas, she consulted with us. The youngest child was 5 or 6. It was general that when anything broke out in Europe they would look to the United States. The whole family landed in New York in October, 1850. I staid one week and then I made for California. [. . .]

I made up my mind to go to California. They thought it was a wild undertaking. I was then 20 years old. I didn't know exactly what I would do. [. . .] We didn't know much about it then, only that it was exceedingly rich in gold. I had an idea I might rely on my mechanical ingenuity. [. . .]

I came by the way of Panama. When in Panama, I didn't have money enough to pay my way first class. I had made the acquaintance of a gentleman, the Swedish consul, and he kindly loaned me enough for cabin passage. I paid him in a few weeks after I got here with difficulty. It took us six days to cross the Isthmus. We were four days in a boat, coming up the Chagres River and we were a day and a half on a mule. At night the mosquitoes, as big as grasshoppers, would nearly eat you up. Alligators all around us.

I made up my mind then that I would not live in that country if they would not make me sole proprietor over all of it.

There were some men on board that were well known. Freemont [Frèmont] was among the passengers. I got acquainted with one gentleman who had been brought up in the Hartz mountains and whom I made my first experiments with. His name was John Randohr. I made my first experiments of treatment of silver ore with him. [. . .]

Of course, coming to a country like this, which was only emerging from savage life, as it were, it struck me very forcibly. But I soon adapted myself to it. After I was here a couple of months, I was just as much a Californian as anybody else. I fall in very easily with people. I have very few close friendships, but a great many friends and acquaintances.

Here it seems to me like home. I look upon it as if I had never been in any other country. I am thoroughly identified with everything in common with the people of the United States and California particularly. If I would go to a new country I would soon see something that ought to be done of the good for the people. It is certainly easier for a man to assert himself in this country than in Europe, because there is more freedom, more liberty. I think some people came to the United States that have become citizens that take more interest than some native born Americans. There are others, old people who hang to their own ways and then again there is another class that are paupers and criminals. [. . .]

When I first came out I went into the commission business. I had some few old goods that I wanted to dispose of, which some friends in San Francisco had furnished me. My great desire was to make a living of my own, independently. I thought I could do a great deal more, if I was independent financially, than if I were clerking. I never clerked in my life, except in father's business, I was too independent to be a clerk. A great many were coming to California. Some were coming to enter into business and some were going into agriculture—anything to make a competency. I was located in Stockton for a while. I went into the mercantile business there. [. . .] I had somebody that went in with me. I stayed there awhile and then I went East again—in 1853. Then I made new arrangements for importing goods. I kept everything—drygoods, groceries, tobacco particularly, I had an immense stock of tobacco. Times were not very good after that for a while and I didn't make any money. That was along '53–4–5.

Afterwards I went into the tobacco business and stayed in that more or less until 1859—having my eye on mining all the time. Finally when the Comstock lode was discovered, I packed up and went to Nevada, and after looking at that, that was my field. I thought I could be successful. I returned to San Francisco and we started in to experimenting working silver ores. We got a little place on Market Street and tried a great many chemical experiments to make this refractory ore amalgamate and we succeeded admirably. I call it refractory, which I ought not to do, because some of the Comstock ore readily yielded to quick-silver, but by chemical processes it yielded very much more.

I then gave up what little affairs I had here and went up to Nevada and built a little mill—an amalgamating mill, at Dayton— I didn't have sufficient money to build a large mill. I only worked with pans at first. I found the refuse ore very rich and I commenced working over the tailings and made a great deal of money. I think I can say that I was the first man that worked the tailings. Sometimes I would get more out of the tailings than they would get out of the ore. I made money enough soon to build a regular stamp mill—10 stamps. I made a contract with the Gould & Curry Co., which was a bonanza for me. I got $75 a ton for working the better class of ores and I could work six tons a day. We made a clear profit of almost $10,000 a month. It was very profitable. We ran the mill by steam. There was lots of cheap wood on the river and with my dealings with the other mines in the Comstock, I was carried to Virginia

City almost daily—generally on horseback. That made me explore the whole country between the Carson River and Virginia City—going over passes and hills and mountains, exploring the county with a view to constructing a tunnel, which had been my idea from the very first, I finally found a place where the valley approaches the Comstock within four miles. I then formed a definite plan for constructing a trench which would supply the working tunnel for the Comstock Lode.

97
Joshua Abraham Norton I,
an Emperor and an English Jew
Benjamin Lloyd, 1876

A bookkeeper for the San Francisco patent agency of Dewey & Co.[22] and a dedicated observer of the city, Benjamin Lloyd chronicled the life of Joshua Abraham Norton (1819–80), a popular Jewish eccentric known as Emperor Norton. Adopted by the citizens of San Francisco and known for the epaulettes on his navy blue uniform, his proclamations, and his two mongrel dogs, Bummer and Lazzaras, Norton frequented lectures, theaters, churches, and synagogues, where the self-proclaimed "Norton I, Emperor of the United States and Protector of Mexico" was welcomed by all. Norton was born in England and raised in South Africa. He came to California for the Gold Rush and entered into real estate and brokerage speculation. After amassing and losing a fortune, as well as some of his mental capacities, he proclaimed himself Emperor in 1859. Well read and informed of current events, Norton printed his own monetary scrip, sought to mediate wars, and even foretold the future when he decreed that a bridge should be built across the bay connecting San Francisco and Oakland.

EMPEROR NORTON

EVERY city has its share of eccentric characters. There are always some persons who, either from a desire to be odd and peculiar, or because of a fancy resulting from a diseased or unbalanced mind, adopt a manner of life entirely different from any other of their fellows.

The forms of this peculiarity are as varied as the persons assuming or bearing it are numerous. With few exceptions, however, they—like many of those who, by the ordinary standard of human intelligence are adjudged to be sane—assume to be persons of much greater worth and importance than they really are, and entitled to greater consideration from their fellowmen than they receive.

Perhaps the most original and best sustained character that is met on the streets of San Francisco is that of "Emperor," adopted by Joshua Norton, an English Jew. To look upon him, knowing his early history in the city, one feels

---

SOURCE: Benjamin Lloyd, *Lights and Shades in San Francisco* (San Francisco: A. L. Bancroft, 1876), 130–34.

22. H. G. Langley, *Guidemap of the City of San Francisco: compiled from the official surveys and engraved expressly for Langley's San Francisco Directory* (San Francisco, H. G. Langley, 1875).

like exclaiming with Ophelia, "how great a mind is here o'erthrown!" His is not merely a character assumed for effect or peculiarity, but results from a disordered mind—a mania or hallucination. Yet there is much of "method in his madness."

His early life is shrouded in mystery. He was born in England, and from there went to the Cape of Good Hope, where he entered the military service as a member of the colonial riflemen. How long or how well he served in that capacity we are not informed.

In 1847 or '48 he came to San Francisco, and is remembered by the early pioneers as having been a shrewd, safe and prosperous man; possessing more than ordinary intelligence, fertile of resource and enterprising. His business pursuits were varied. At one time he was buying partner for three or four mercantile houses in the interior of the State and in this capacity manifested great business ability. Then he engaged in the real estate business, in which he

Joshua Abraham Norton, Emperor of the United States and Protector of Mexico. Courtesy of the California Historical Society, de Young Collection, FN-04268.

continued with apparent prosperity a number of years. While in this business he became a possessor of much valuable real estate, and judging by the frequent occurrence of his name on the city and county records, and the monetary values represented, he was one of the largest land speculators in those early times. [. . .]

It appears that his business career culminated in a grand effort to get a "corner" on rice, which staple was, some ten or twelve years ago, a favorite article for speculation. He purchased all that was in the city and (as rumor has it) all that he could ascertain was in transit, paying large prices with a view of controlling the future market. Of Macondray & Co. he bought a large cargo, to arrive, agreeing to pay fifteen cents per pound (or therabout). Other shipments, however, that he knew not of, were reported in the meantime, and upon the arrival of Macondray & Co.'s cargo the market was so "flat" that he could not meet his contract, and a protracted law suit followed, during which the mania that he was "Emperor" first became manifest. It is said that he proposed to compromise the matter with Messrs. Macondray & Co. by marrying Mr. Macondray's daughter and investing her with the royal title of Empress.

His hallucination is, that he is Emperor of California and Protector of Mexico. In accordance with this belief, his sole purpose in life is to properly administer to his subjects, and like a wise ruler should, do everything possible for the promotion of prosperity and the advancement of his dominions. His diplomatic relations with other countries are not lost sight of, and he profits by closely observing the progress or downfall of other nations, using their experience in his home policy. His power is duly recognized in times of international or civil wars. He alone claims to have reconciled the French and the Prussians, and brought about the peace that was established between them at the close of the late Franco-Prussian war. The war of the Rebellion was terminated through his interference, and the success attending the reconstruction of the Union, is due in great part to his wise counsel.

His own Empire was vigilantly watched. He is not only skilled in the arts of war, but his wisdom extends to the pursuits of peace. The great resources of California are his pride, and to their proper development his greatest exertions are directed. How he gloats over the mineral wealth of his domain, and the agricultural value of his broad acres are a source for delightful contemplation! San Francisco, his favorite city, he calls the "Queen of the Pacific," and the world pays tribute to her. The municipal authorities receive his praise or condemnation as their administration pleases or offends him. By proclamation (sometimes to humor his whim published in the city press) he communicates to his subjects his ideas of progress and justice, and never fails to attach his signature with the imperial seal, "Norton I. Emperor of California and Protector of Mexico *Dei Grata.*" Thus, from day to day, he busies himself with the affairs of his Empire, the belief that he rules most royally being strengthened by the allegiances that all show. On his head his crown rests lightly.

DRESS HABITS

Emperor Norton may be known by his dress, as he pays no attention whatever to the varying fashions. His coat is navy blue, cut in the military style, and lavishly trimmed with brass buttons. On the shoulders are heavy epaulettes usually tarnished from exposure to weather, though sometimes brilliantly polished. His hat, the regular Jehu style, is trimmed with some brash ornament, from which extends two or three waving cock-plumes. His boots are notorious for their size, and are less frequently polished than otherwise.

During the day he passes the time upon the streets, traveling from one part of the city to another, without apparent object, unless it be to see that the policemen are on duty, the sidewalks unobstructed, and the various city ordinances promptly enforced. He occasionally calls at the offices or business houses of acquaintances, stops for a few minutes, talking on general topics, and proceeds on his round—never calling at one place so often as to render his presence offensive, nor remaining so long as to be considered a bore. He is a good conversationalist, and having free access to all the libraries and reading-rooms, keeps well posted on current topics. He will talk readily upon any subject, and his opinions are usually very correct, except when relating to himself. He is more familiar with history than the ordinary citizen, and his scientific knowledge, though sometimes "mixed," is considerable.

Of evenings he may be found at the theater or in the lecture room, a cool observer and attentive listener. His face is a free ticket for him to all places of amusement and public gatherings, and oftentimes he makes quite extended journeys by rail and other public conveyances without expending a dollar. Sacramento is a favorite resort during the sessions of the Legislature, whither he goes to see that legislators do not prostitute their privileges. He is on familiar terms with all officials, high or low, feeling of course that they are only his more favored subjects. He is perfectly harmless, and unless his mind be occupied with some more than ordinarily grave question relating to the Empire, is jocular, and disposed to be humorous.

His living is very inexpensive. He occupies a cheap room, is temperate in his habits, boards at cheap restaurants, which, with many privileges granted him that others have to pay for, reduces his expenditures to a very small sum. When he wants more money he will draw a check on any of the city banks, take it to an acquaintance who humors his delusion, and get it cashed, thinking no doubt, that it is a legitimate business transaction. Some of the merchant Jews contribute to his support, and he is much better cared for than many who labor hard every day for a livelihood. Thus does his affliction secure him a comfortable living happy today, without care for the morrow, and free from all the annoyances that to many renders life a burdensome existence.

98
Should the Lord's Prayer Be Recited in Public Schools?
Joseph R. Brandon, 1875

Joseph Rodriguez Brandon, a Sephardic Jew and fighter for Jewish rights, came to San Francisco in 1855. Born in Barbados on Brandon Island, where his father was a wealthy planter, Brandon was educated in Europe and became a lawyer and businessman. As a member of Congregation Sherith Israel and an Orthodox Jew, he followed kosher dietary laws and strictly observed the Jewish Sabbath and holidays. He became known as a supporter of Jewish causes as president of the Society for the Relief of the Jews in the Holy Land and was instrumental in fund-raising for poor Jews in Jerusalem under the auspices of Sir Moses Montefiore.[23] Upon his death in 1916, he was eulogized as "a fine Hebrew scholar, a writer on ethics and an authority on law."[24]

A strong supporter of the separation of church and state, Brandon opposed Sunday closing laws, prayer in schools, and school texts that were Christian-oriented. In the following statement he responds to the published sermons of John Hemphill, pastor of the Calvary Presbyterian Church of San Francisco.[25] A native of Ireland and a Hebrew and biblical scholar, Hemphill arrived in California in 1870. At a time when Jewish children were entering the public schools in increasing numbers and confronting a largely Protestant-based educational system, the church-state question acquired new importance.[26]

A REPLY

TO THE

REV. MR. HEMPHILL'S

DISCOURSE

ON

"OUR PUBLIC SCHOOLS,"

"SHALL THE LORD'S PRAYER BE RECITED IN THEM?"

---

23. Salo W. Baron and Jeannette M. Baron, "Palestinian Messengers in America, 1849–79," *Jewish Social Studies* 5:2 (1943): 239.

24. William M. Kramer, "Joseph R. Brandon, Activist Lawyer," *Western States Jewish History* 23:1 (1990): 29.

25. See Alonzo Phelps, *Contemporary Biography of California's Representative Men,* vol. 1 (San Francisco: A. L. Bancroft, 1881), 430–32.

26. For a broader discussion of Jewish attitudes toward religion in the public schools, see Jonathan D. Sarna and David G. Dalin, "Religion in the Public Schools," in *Religion and State in the American Jewish Experience,* ed. Jonathan D. Sarna (Notre Dame: University of Notre Dame Press, 1997), 181–226.

There have been two sermons lately published in this city by the Rev. Mr. Hemphill on the above subject, which are so illogical, so intemperate, so full of a spirit calculated to awaken religious dissension, that they seem to call for some reply.

The reverend gentleman's first sermon opens with one of those favorite sophistries of the Christian churchman, a misquoted extract from Scripture garbled to accommodate it to the views of the speaker. He commences with Israel's grand declaration of the Unity of God, and its glorious fundamental principle, speaking of a religion of love, and not of fear. He quotes:—(deut., ch. 6 v. 4–9.)

"Hear, O Israel, the Lord our God the Lord, is One. And thou shalt love the Lord thy God with all thy heart, with all thy soul, and with all thy might. And these words which I command thee this day shall be in thy heart, and thou shalt teach them diligently unto thy children, speaking of them when thou walkest by the way, when though liest down and when thou risest up."

But he does not quote correctly. The words, *"When thou sittest in thy house,"* pregnant with a meaning which would tell against his views, he designedly and artfully omits. And the reason is obvious. They would suggest too plainly what would contradict his proposed interpolation, "When thou teachest in the public schools," and that is that *thy* house—the home of the child—not thy neighbor's, not the co-operative mental training-place of children of diverse faiths, but the *home* was the proper place to receive its religious culture. The whole quotation suggests the great lesson of home and parental religious training—that, like charity blesses both the giver and the receiver. The verb is in the singular throughout, as addressed to each individual; —*thou* shalt speak of them to *thy* children, *thou* shalt talk of them, not *you*, suggesting plainly that the parent should be the agent of the soul's development, as well as the author of its bodily form. It does not speak well for Mr. Hemphill's sincerity, honesty, and fairness as a disputant, that he is detected at the very threshold of the discussion in so designedly garbled a quotation as I have shown this to be; and the utter want of application of this text referring to the teaching in our houses of the unity of God, to the teaching of a contrary doctrine in our public schools, does not bespeak much for the logic we are to meet with in the discourses.

The question Mr. Hemphill proposes for discussion or treatment is, Shall the prayer, known among Christians as the Lord's Prayer, be recited in the public schools?

SOURCE: Joseph R. Brandon, *A Reply to the Rev. Mr. Hemphill's Discourse on "Our Public Schools," "Shall the Lord's Prayer Be Recited in Them?"* (San Francisco: M. Weiss, 1875). Bancroft Library, University of California, Berkeley.

Now, one would think that the only logical treatment of this question would be: First, to show that prayer was a necessary accompaniment to the common school exercises, such as reading, writing, arithmetic, grammar, and geography, etc.; second, to show that this so-called Lord's Prayer was entirely unsectarian, and was not offensive to Jewish and non-Christian children, and repugnant to their religious ideas; and third, its peculiar adaptability as an accompaniment to the aforesaid exercises. Instead of this, the garbled quotation above given is followed by a bitter tirade against Mr. Donovan, one of the School Directors, and his nationality, and against the Catholics generally; dilating on the terrible persecutions which the Jews have endured at the hands of Mr. Donovan's church; seeking to inflame the minds of Israelites against the Catholics, and concluding with the usual language of the Protestant conversionist—"That they, Protestants, must bind up the wounds [. . .]" that Catholics have given the Jews and tell them the "Story of the cross, the true gospel of the peace of God, [. . .] With loving earnestness."

The merest tyro in disputation might well ask, what can this have to do with the question at issue, and well he might. But let me say a few words on these remarks.

Does not a Protestant Christian minister think that his zeal makes him for the moment forget his character, when he seeks to create the bitter feelings of religious hatred, and the spirit of non-forgiveness, by dilating on the sufferings of the Jews at the hands of the Catholics? The Jews, he may be assured, need not the reminder. They remember, too well, all that they suffered at the hands of the Christian Church and its followers—their persecutions, their martyrdoms, their imprisonments, their banishments, with all the accompanying horrors and sufferings, their burning at the stake, their torturing on the rack, — and remembering them as they do, there has seldom been presented to the contemplation of the world a grander, a more sublime picture of religious forgiveness, than do the Jews, practicing and fulfilling the beautiful teachings of their religion "—Thou shalt not revenge nor bear a grudge" (Lev., ch. 19), enunciated nearly fifteen centuries before the Christian era.

The Christian Church and its followers have, indeed, bitterly and terribly wronged the Jew [. . .]

[B]ut he would retaliate upon the doctrines of the Church and not upon its followers, the wrongs he has suffered. [. . .]

[Mr. Hemphill] comes at last to the question at issue, and asks is the prayer sectarian and partisan, and is it contrary to the school law? and here let me follow him. Certainly, as between Christian sects, who acknowledge the divinity of Jesus, who all pray for the coming of his kingdom, there can be nothing sectarian in it; but is it not so to the Jew and to the non-Christian? [. . .] the sectarianism of the prayer—Mr. Hemphill, who certainly ought to be familiar with the explanation and the meaning of so simple a prayer of his church; who certainly should know the meaning of the words "Thy kingdom come," as defined in the Gospel itself; as defined in the commentaries of learned members of the Christian Church; contents himself with a bold *denial* that it is in any way prejudicial to the tenets of the Jewish faith, and the equally bold assertion that there is not one of its petitions that might not be uttered by the strictest Jew; and in these bold denials consists, really, the whole of Mr. Hemphill's argument on the point in issue—the sectarianism of the prayer. Does it not suggest itself to Mr. Hemphill that the very title of the prayer, which although of course not part of it, yet, is always associated with it, and always referred to when it is spoken of, must be offensive to the mind of the Israelite, jealous as he is of his treasure, God's unity; as it should be to the mind of the consistent and true Unitarian, as being from their point of view idolatrous in its ascription of divinity to any one but God? But disregarding the title, what is the meaning of the words "Thy kingdom come?" What was the contemporaneous construction put on these words? In what sense have they been used for eighteen hundred years? In what sense is Jesus himself represented as using them? Surely these considerations have some weight. [. . .]

As to Jewish children not objecting to the prayer, that might well be. Jewish children, I understand, do not pass through a course of theology, including Dr. Lange's and Dr. Charke's Commentaries, before entering the public schools, and might well be unaware of the meaning of the words recited at the command of their teachers; as, indeed, I have found many Christian parents to be, who, however, were truthful and candid enough to admit when the meaning was given that the prayer was certainly sectarian. As to finding whether any Israelites agreed with me or not, I failed to see what that had to do with the question, or what support that would give my quoted authorities. Besides, Mr. Hemphill's biblical reading should tell him that majorities do not constitute right, or the "seven thousand left in Israel," mentioned in Kings, ch. 19, v. 18, "who had not bent the knee to Baal, and whose lips had not kissed him,:" would have been lamentably in error. My former opponent is, I believe, a very worthy gentleman, and therefore I may remark, without any personality, that the argument about his being the son of a Jewish rabbi is not a particularly forcible one, for ministers' sons are not *proverbially* orthodox, nor considered the highest authorities in theological matters. As to my writing under a mask, I have been under the impression that it matters little to the general public, in a discussion of any principle, who may be the advocate on either side. An intelligent public, one would think, would be swayed by the reason and argument in, and not by the signature affixed to the communication, which, doubtless, is the reason why newspaper communications are signed by initials. Sermons in churches, where men, although perhaps opening their hearts, doff their reason, logic, and common sense, with their hats on entering, may be governed by a different rule; and the name and reputation of the preacher may be sufficient endorsement for the doctrines he teaches, however erroneous they may be; which may have been the reason why the reverend gentleman selected this field for his discussion. Faith may be strong in the sheep of Mr. Hemphill's fold, and judging from his logic they need it. [. . .]

Are you convinced, reader, by such arguments, of the dire necessity of the immediate introduction of the prayer into the schools? Or may I not retort on Mr. Hemphill what he says of his dreaded Romanist? No! Mr. Hemphill, it is not prayer, unsectarian prayer, that you want; but it is the opportunity you seek, in the true spirit of the propagandist, and conversionist, to introduce insidiously, the leaven of the doctrines of your church into the impressionable minds of the young. The opportunity, you think, is given to your church which is intensely propagandist, by the attendance of non-Christian and Jewish children at the schools, and you would avail yourselves of it to indoctrinate them with "your gospel of peace, your story of the Cross." Your teachers, animated by the same conversionist spirit, would as has been done, when the prayer was said in the schools, (I state here a fact,) compel Jewish children, against their objection, to kneel and join in your unsectarian prayer for the coming of the "Kingdom of Jesus," and when remonstrated with by the parent of the child, teach it deception by telling it ought not to have told its parent. This, Mr. Hemphill, is what you want, not schools *with religion,* but schools where your Christianity shall be taught, where your gospel of peace, your story of the cross shall be told—perhaps as the Revivalist preachers are now telling it to your children; where your doctrine of faith above reason shall be taught, and the minds of Jewish and non-Christian children emasculated by the destruction of the glorious privilege of reason as to things spiritual, shall be left as powerless in your hands as the followers of your church now are. Judaism fears not the ordeal of reason, and she would preserve the minds of her children in all their vigor and all their strength. With that weapon sharpened and ready for use, they need not fear the insidious approach of the conversionist, nor the doctrines of the materialist.

Mr. Hemphill, in his cry about Godless schools, evidently represents that class of men who must see the name of God stamped upon everything; who are uneasy because it does not appear in the Constitution of the United States, and are continually agitating to get it there, as the first step to sectarianizing the Government. [. . .] And if the name of God does not appear in the Constitution of the United States, surely to him who God in his heart His hand is seen therein, and he may exclaim with the magicians of Egypt, "The finger of God is here."

It is interesting to remember that the very year that saw the perpetration of that atrocious act of religious persecution, the banishment of the Jews from Spain, was that in which America was discovered. Others besides Israel have suffered religious persecution. Others besides Israel have passed through the sea from slavery to freedom—from the slavery of religious persecution to religious freedom and equality. And how history repeats itself continually. [. . .]

Must we, in free, enlightened America, the vaunted home of religious freedom and equality, see re-enacted the scenes that Europe has beheld in the struggles for supremacy of the rival Christian churches? Must we pass through the whirlwind that breaketh in pieces the rocks, desolating earthquake, the ravaging fire, before the STILL SMALL VOICE—in which alone speaks religious truth—can be heard? Heaven forbid it. [. . .]

Education—unsectarian education is the hope and salvation of the Jew, as of all who have passed through religious persecution; for it is from the deep, dark clouds of ignorance, which bespeak its absence among men, that the direst shafts of bigotry and persecution which have fallen upon our people and others have proceeded. Well, indeed, and earnestly may we labor for its diffusion, and seek not to drive children from, but to persuade and invite them to the common schools by removing all obstacles in the way.

Let our education be of the widest kind. Let reason and religion, too long divorced, too long at enmity, be reconciled. Let all of us, with free thought and free, unsectarian education, seek to lift ourselves and our fellows above the clouds of ignorance, sectarianism and prejudice, until these clouds can be dissipated; and although in that clear upper air we may see such men as Spencer, Tyndal[l] and Huxley, the bold, intrepid aeronaughts of science, soaring far above us in search of what is beyond and making our weaker heads swim at the sight, we need not follow them there. [. . .]

No, reader; because sectarian prayer has not been permitted in the schools, the friend of true education and true religion need not wail with Mr. Hemphill—that a battle has been lost—that Rome has conquered. He may rather rejoice that free thought, free education, free religion has gained a victory over the churchmen of all denominations; that the great principle has at last been enunciated, the State, which should be the common parent and protector of all, its children—majority or minority—few or many—will not lend its aid to dispense the particolored light of any particular sect, but only that colorless, illuminating principle which is common to all; and let us fervently hope, and at the same time be vigilant, that sectarianism, whether in the garb of Catholic priest, or Protestant minister, rob us not of the victory.

America's flag—the star-spangled banner—should symbolize the roof of that grand, common, unsectarian, religious temple of all mankind—THE CLOUDLESS SKY!

99
Jews and Chinese: A San Francisco Dilemma
Isaac Mayer Wise, 1877

Isaac Mayer Wise, a leader of American Reform Judaism, traveled west in 1877 to persuade congregations to join the new Union of American Hebrew Congregations and to support his new Hebrew Union College. In that turbulent summer, he visited a San Francisco torn by labor, ethnic, and economic strife. It was also a drought year and food prices were high. Moreover, much of the city's capital had been widely invested in the Comstock Mines. The rabbi's view of the situation captures the mood of the time and place.

EDITORIAL CORRESPONDENCE

NUMBER SIX

SAN FRANCISCO, CAL., July 26, 1877.

I am sitting here high and dry, that is, I sit in the fifth story of the Palace Hotel, and all California is dry, because the latter rain has failed and crops are short. The decline of mining stocks is worse to all commercial interests than all the other causes combined. The business men here look displeased, some gloomy. It is a dull season. There are in this city, they say, ten thousand white men without employment and quite a number of "hoodlums." You do not know who the hoodlums are and I must tell you; they are a class of young loafers who do no work, and are seeking mischief, boys of sixteen to twenty and upward. They are the standing army of disorder and lawlessness. As long as the laboring class is orderly and satisfied the hoodlums are under the control of the police force. Any commotion among any dissatisfied element brings these loafers to the front, and they perpetuate mischief. The chief object of their hatred is the Chinaman, who works for low wages and keeps the white man out of employment. This is true. It is the Chinaman who does the factory work, the house work, the farm work, the railroad work, all sorts and kinds of manual work. But it is equally true that this cheap labor builds up California, and San Francisco especially. Now comes the strike from the East, and this is a city of earthquakes and country of volcanoes, high winds and spring tides, and so are men and feelings, business and all common transactions. The strikers roused the laboring class on this Pacific shore to quite an unpacific state of mind, and the hoodlums appear in front. Down with Chinaman, is the first cry, of course. Several of these poor fellows have been killed, and their laundries ransacked and demolished. The citizens are thoroughly alarmed. A committee of safety

---

SOURCE: Isaac Mayer Wise, *American Israelite,* Cincinnati, Aug. 10, 1877, 4.

457

has been organized, four thousand stands of arms have been procured, a special police organized, the militia armed and augmented, and for the three nights past there was plenty of work on hand. Fires, fights, rows, shooting affrays, etc., meetings of socialists, incendiary speeches, bulletins, crowds at the corners, and excitement are increasing at this moment. A cannon is ready for service in the yard of our hotel, and last night one thousand five hundred militia, horse and foot, passed this house in good order.

It is the general impression here that the railroad strikes in the East are just, although the lawless acts, the destruction of life and property is condemned. It is maintained the railroad managers and officials live in palaces, have become millionaires, one of them here has a salary of $150,000 per annum, are the princes and rulers of the country, have spent millions to corrupt legislatures and Congress for their corporation purposes, have put down the toll on freight and the passenger tariff to the disadvantage of business, and want the laboring man to work for starving wages. Those who have made towering fortunes out of the laboring man, they say here, must be ready now to sacrifice some of it, and not oppress the laboring class. This is the theory here, and it is a fact after all that the Chinaman here is paid better wages than the white laborer in Massachusetts, New York, or Pennsylvania, although victuals are cheaper and fuel hardly necessary, except for cooking purposes. But the working man here has not come and does not come to this coast to make a bare living. Money, wealth, is everything here with everybody, hence also with the laboring class. A million is the unit in estimating a man's wealth, and the rich man is also the great man, the good man, in fact, THE man. Others are of very little account. Hence everybody feels the necessity of getting rich, very rich, because he wants to be somebody. Therefore this universal stock in gambling in which everybody and his nurse or hostler, all men of all professions and avocations, and all women of all positions are engaged. Therefore this gambling, as an amusement, to lose or win from $100 to $30,000 an evening. Therefore the laboring class here is as dissatisfied as it is elsewhere. Wealth being everything, it must be gained by everybody, and those who fail are in a constant state of despair. The sympathy with the railroad strikers by millionaires in this city is an evidence that there is a feeling of justice among the rich in this city. They are also inclined to ameliorate the condition of the laboring class here; but here is the Chinaman who works for low wages, and so he is chiefly in the way of the laboring class.

It appears, however, that the fifty to sixty thousand Chinese in their quarter, which is in the heart of the city, are as little afraid there as the Germans, across the canal in Cincinnati were in 1855 of the enraged Know nothings. I was in that quarter yesterday and saw divers things. I think if the hoodlums venture in there they will meet fists, clubs, pistols and rifles in rather uncomfortable positions. The quarter is small, not too large for ten thousand Caucasians, the streets are narrow, connected by narrow passages, and the inhabitants are as numerous as the sands on the sea shore, nine-tenths of them are laboring people. The hoodlums cannot manage them.

This trouble, I am afraid, will interfere with my mission here. The depression in commercial and financial circles is a stumbling block and the present excitement bewilders the mind, and all ideal interests are here below zero anyhow. I preached on Saturday last in the Temple Emanu-El (Rev. Dr. [Elkan] Cohn's) to a very large congregation—the largest, I am told, that has filled that gorgeous building since the last *Kippur day*. My friends were there, and their number is considerable. The president, Mr. Selig,[27] is an enthusiastic, religious and genuine Israelite, who is very strongly in favor of the Union [Union of American Hebrew Congregations]. In fact, the leading men of the four congregations, the rabbis included, are in favor of the Union.

I spoke Monday evening in the hall of the Columbia Lodge, I.O.B.B., and listened there to some very enthusiastic speeches in favor of "Union and College," and have been invited to the Ophir Lodge for last evening, although on account of the disturbance the meeting was postponed. [. . .] The press, and especially the Jewish press, is in my favor, so are numerous men and friends. I have good reason to believe that all the congregations here will join hands with the Union of American Hebrew Congregations, to which the Council at Philadelphia and its brilliant results, the telegram of Mr. Peixotto and the letter of Alfred T. Jones, Esq., all of which the *Progress* published, will contribute largely.[28] Still I can not tell whether I will meet with any signal success here. [. . .]

While writing, the most alarming reports from Chicago reach here, and it is feared rioting will be the order of the night. Rev. Dr. [Elkan] Cohn, who has just left my room, also tells me that a turbulent night is expected; seven to eight thousand safety men and militia have been armed and provided with ammunition, and the Mayor has issued a second proclamation, cautioning rioters and idlers that firearms will be freely used, if necessary, for the maintenance of order, and requesting all peaceable citizens to remain within doors after nine o'clock this evening.

Some of our most prominent and wealthiest Israelites are very badly frightened by the threatened rows, and most all young men are among the defenders of the city just sworn in. The cause of this special fright is, because many of them are extensive property holders, and the city, according to the laws of this State, is held responsible for all property destroyed by mobs in any shape or form. Besides this, one or more Chinese are engaged in almost every house

---

27. Moses Selig, a kosher butcher, was president of congregation Emanu-El from 1871 to 1880.

28. Benjamin Franklin Peixotto and Alfred T. Jones were leaders of B'nai B'rith. See chapter 11 for more about Peixotto.

and in many business places, so that every family almost is threatened by the hoodlums. But the main cause of the fright is this: some of our Jews here are largely engaged in manufacturing woolen goods, shoes, and boots, clothing, etc. I will give a description of factories in another letter. Factories here in order to compete with Eastern establishments must have cheap labor, hence it is necessary to engage Chinamen. In some factories three hundred and even five hundred are at work. These are supposed to be the objective points of the rioters. Another objective point is the Pacific mail wharves, where the steamers land with Chinamen, 1,700 of whom were said to have arrived to-day. To burn down these wharves, it is supposed, is one of the objects of the rioters, and several Jews are interested in that property. Therefore the commotion and disturbance of ease and peace among all to-day. Let me close here to continue to-morrow with more favorable news.

I. M. W.

11
A Part of the Jewish World

A LITTLE-KNOWN ASPECT OF CALIFORNIA'S EARLY HISTORY IS THE prominent role assumed by members of its Jewish community in the moral and financial support of less fortunate Jews around the world. The Gold Rush made this so, as news of phenomenal riches circled the globe from San Francisco to London and Jerusalem, inspiring not only newspaper articles promoting continuous immigration but also solicitations for aid.

The first document in this chapter records the proceedings of an extraordinary meeting held to protest a notorious incident of religious intolerance, the abduction by papal guards in Bologna, Italy, on June 24, 1858, of Edgardo Mortara, a six-year-old Jewish boy. The story of this child, who was allegedly baptized by a young servant, united Jews around the world. As the pope was losing land and influence due to the birth of modern Italy, emancipated Jews around the world rallied to the family's side in an effort to recover young Edgardo. At the mass meeting in San Francisco, Jewish and Protestant speakers declared their abhorrence of the child's abduction and tried to marshal public opinion against the pope, to no avail.[1]

Beyond protesting, a special connection was formed between the Jews of northern California and the Jews of Palestine in the 1860s and 1870s, as California was singled out as a destination for messengers' travels. In California, the busy young merchants had little time to pray, while in Jerusalem the poverty-stricken older men had time for prayer but could not work; and so

---

1. See David I. Kertzer, *The Kidnapping of Edgardo Mortara* (New York: Knopf, 1997).

a symbiotic relationship developed in which one community raised funds and the other studied and prayed.[2]

Palestine in the mid-nineteenth century was a province of the Turks, and its residents were subject to the whims of their tax collectors. Eight thousand Jews, divided into eight congregations, lived in the old city of Jerusalem. They lived off charity from the Diaspora, which was stimulated by emissaries who traveled the world offering the promise of fervent prayers from the Holy City in return for financial aid.[3]

It seems only natural that northern California and Jerusalem would develop this kind of reciprocal relationship. Both of these unique communities experienced significant growth between 1850 and 1880, and both owed their growth to some of the same technological forces. The steamship facilitated migration to both the United States and Palestine. It shortened the trip from Odessa to Palestine to a mere week rather than many weeks of sailing the pirate-ridden Mediterranean.[4] The steamship also allowed news to travel and to be printed in Jewish newspapers, which spread the word of the Gold Rush as well as of the poverty of Jerusalem's Jews.

European visitors to Jerusalem wrote accounts that were reprinted verbatim in the Jewish press of San Francisco, ensuring that even Jews in the remote foothills became aware of the hardships endured by their coreligionists in the Middle East.

As rabbis in Jerusalem learned of the prosperous new communities of California, they looked to the west for financial support. So great was their interest that in 1860, when four elders of the Ashkenazi community sent Abraham Nissan (Weinstein) to the United States, they addressed their appeals to all Jews "residing in peace in all the States of gracious America and the magnificent State of California." Nissan advocated the formation of societies for the support of the Jews of Jerusalem, requested that synagogues begin annual subscriptions, and asked that collection boxes be placed in both synagogues and homes. In return, he promised that donors who entered their names in the messenger's record book would have prayers said for them by the congregations in Jerusalem.[5]

On November 22, 1861, Nissan lectured at congregation Sherith Israel. Three days later the rabbis and lay leaders of Sherith Israel and Emanu-El and the publisher of the *Weekly Gleaner,* Rabbi Julius Eckman, met to discuss the

---

2. Jonathan D. Sarna, "A Projection of America as It Ought to Be: Zion in the Mind's Eye of American Jews," in *Envisioning Israel: The Changing Ideals and Images of North American Jews,* ed. Allon Gal (Jerusalem: Magnes Press, Hebrew University, 1996), 42.

3. Yehoshua Ben-Arieh, *Jerusalem in the Nineteenth Century* (Tel Aviv: MOD Publications, 1989), 32.

4. Ben-Arieh, *Jerusalem in the Nineteenth Century,* 36.

5. Baron, "Palestinian Messengers in America," 145.

founding of a charitable society at the kosher St. Nicholas Hotel. Although these men harbored opposing opinions on reforming worship services and family seating in synagogues, they were of one mind about the need to contribute funds for the relief of the indigent in Palestine. It took only one meeting, and Ohabai Zion was born in San Francisco.

In the following years, messengers visited not only San Francisco but also the small supply and mining communities. Nathan Neta Notkin visited Marysville, Grass Valley, and Nevada City in search of support. In Sacramento he received seventy-five dollars from Congregation B'nai Israel for their coreligionists in Jerusalem. The B'nai B'rith Grand Lodge in San Francisco and the individual lodges of northern California also sent $460 to Palestine.[6] From 1876–79, Notkin made a second "mission to the U.S. of America and California."[7] This time he spoke not only for the Jerusalem Ashkenazi community but for the entire Yishuv, including the Sephardic and Ashkenazic leadership of Jerusalem, Hebron, Safed, and Tiberias.[8] Notkin again journeyed to Marysville, where on "March 6, the Hebrew Benevolent and Congregational Society of Marysville donated $25.00."[9]

This close relationship between the golden land and the promised land did not last. It was changed dramatically by two events in 1885—the death of Sir Moses Montefiore, the Jewish community's conduit to Jerusalem, and the issuing of the Pittsburgh platform by the Reform movement, which de-emphasized Israel's importance in Jewish practice. At this time, the Jews of California, especially of San Francisco, were adopting reforms, and the messenger system fell out of favor. The relationship between the promised land and the golden land had changed.

However, for a period of more than twenty years it did not matter whether Jewish life in Jerusalem was the antithesis of life in San Francisco or not. They were tied together by the love of a land that the Californians only hoped to see when the Messiah came. In addition to supporting their brethren in Jerusalem during these years, northern Californian Jews also worked to help Jews in parts of Europe and Africa, especially Morocco.

Benjamin Franklin Peixotto, who saw himself as the quintessential Jew and American, and therefore as the ideal American consul to Romania, labored to

---

6. "To an appeal from the Most Worthy Grand Saar, Brother B. F. Peixotto in behalf of our suffering brethren in Palestine all our Subordinate Lodges answered generously." "Quarterly Report of the General Committee, for the Quarter Ending January 19th," 1866 B'nai B'rith Grand Lodge Number 4. *Proceeding of the District*, 34, Western Jewish History Center.

7. Baron, "Palestinian Messengers in America," 251.

8. Baron, "Palestinian Messengers in America," 248.

9. Baron, "Palestinian Messengers in America," 258.

aid oppressed Jews. But his work was inadequately sustained and his mission lasted only five years. The San Francisco Jewish community also showed concern for the Jews of Bulgaria, as is evident in the letter of Isaac Adolphe Crémieux, president of the Alliance Israélite Universelle, to Rabbi Elkan Cohn. Here, in a small corner of the world, in a very short time, California's Jews, firm in their historic Jewish and new American traditions, joined to help others in the world. California's Jews were not unique in this, but because of the dramatic nature of the Gold Rush and the attention it generated, California Jewish communities became more visible, and their voices were heard more loudly, than their counterparts elsewhere.

100

A Thousand More than New York

Mortara Affair Mass Meeting, 1859

In June of 1858, papal guards abducted six-year-old Edgardo Mortara from his home in Bologna. Pope Pius IX held that the child, secretly baptized years earlier by a teenage Catholic servant, was now a Christian and could not be raised in a Jewish home. Demonstrations were held throughout the United States in reaction to the kidnapping. The largest rally of all was held in January of 1859 in San Francisco, attracting three thousand participants, a thousand more than attended a similar protest in New York City. The largest assemblage to date to respond to a Jewish issue, the rally was presided over by Solomon Heydenfeldt, the former justice of the California Supreme Court, and brought the local press out in full force. Copies of the resolutions approved at the meeting were sent to Sir Moses Montefiore in London, coordinator of the worldwide protest, and to members of the United States Senate and House of Representatives.[10]

If few Catholics joined Jews and Protestants in protesting the Mortara affair, Rabbi Julius Eckman insisted that the public "must not identify Catholics with Catholicism."[11] Although Jewish leaders in Europe and the United States joined the Mortara family in protest, the child, raised and inculcated by the church, became a priest and was active in Catholic missions throughout the world, though he occasionally met with members of his family. In 1940 at age eighty-eight, he died in Liège, one month before the Nazi invasion.[12]

PROCEEDINGS AT THE MASS MEETING.

The meeting was called by Messrs. Seligman, Solomon, Ashim, Helbing, Davies and King—the first two Presidents of Hebrew Congregations in this city,

---

10. Sir Moses Montefiore (1784–1885), longtime president of the Board of Deputies of British Jews and virtually the Jewish emissary for the British government, sent a circular letter to Jewish congregations in the United States asking them to urge their government to intercede with the pope. The U.S. response to the Mortara case was inevitably influenced by party politics. President Buchanan and Secretary of State Lewis Cass had to take into account Catholic support for the Democratic Party; Buchanan declared a policy of nonintervention. The anti-Catholic Know-Nothing Party and the new Republican Party, formed with strong Protestant support, used the Mortara issue to seek Jewish votes.

11. For more about Rabbi Julius Eckman, see chapters 3 and 9.

12. See Jacob Rader Marcus, *United States Jewry 1776–1985*, vol. 2, *The Germanic Period* (Detroit: Wayne State University Press, 1991), 297–305, and Korn, *Eventful Years and Experiences*, 75.

and the three last named Presidents of Hebrew Benevolent Societies. The call, as published in the daily papers, was as follows:

THE MORTARA ABDUCTION.—We, the undersigned, feeling deeply incensed at the injury recently perpetrated upon Mr. Mortara, of Bologna, (Italy,) in the abduction of his son, and recognizing the peril which attaches to the social and religious condition of all those antagonistic to the Catholic faith involved in such a precedent, make this call upon the Israelites of San Francisco, and others of our fellow citizens whose sentiments and sympathies are kindred to our own, to unite with us in Mass Meeting, at Musical Hall, on Saturday evening, the 15th instant, at 7 o'clock, for the purpose of publicly expressing their feelings upon this grievous wrong.

Henry Seligman, President Congregation Emanu-El; Israel Solomon, President Congregation Sherith Israel; August Helbing,[13] President Eureka Benevolent Society; J. P. Davies, President First Hebrew Benevolent Society; L. King, President C.B.C.U.;[14] M. B. Ashim, President I. O. Benai Berith.

At half past seven o'clock, Henry Seligman, Esq., called the meeting to order.

Isaac S. Josephi, Esq., nominated the Hon. Solomon Heydenfeldt as President of the meeting.

Mr. Heydenfeldt was unanimously elected, and, on taking the chair, spoke as follows:

FELLOW CITIZENS:—The object of your meeting to-night has been made known in the call which has brought you together. I am not fully acquainted with the transaction upon which you are here to express your opinions. The details of it will, doubtless, be given to you by the other gentlemen who are present. The general aspect seems to be that, on a recent occasion, in the town of Bologna, Italy, a child of Hebrew parentage—an infant child—was snatched from the protection of his home by the ecclesiastical authorities, upon the pretense of his having been admitted, by rites of baptism, to the faith of the Church of Rome. The question does not appeal alone to the sect to which the child belongs. It is a direct attack upon the principles of humanity and civilization (Applause,) and persecution of one, to-day, which may be the fate of another tomorrow. (Applause) It was an act of tyranny which, in the very nature of things, must be adverse to the common sentiments of both Catholics and Protestants. It is strange, indeed, that, in the middle of the nineteenth century, we should be

---

SOURCE: *Proceedings in Relation to the Mortara Abduction Mass Meeting at Musical Hall* (San Francisco: Towne and Bacon, 1859). Western Jewish History Center of the Judah L. Magnes Museum, Berkeley, California.

13. For more on Helbing and the Eureka Benevolent Society, see chapter 4.

14. Founded in 1857, Chebra Bikur Chdim Ukedisha was a society that cared for the sick and needy and buried the dead.

called upon to denounce such an outrage as this—strange that, in the midst of this age of advancement, any man should be molested in his own theory of the future or the past—strange that we should still have an example of the existence of a power to enforce religious faith. But, it may be asked, what good can come of this meeting here, and the passage of resolutions! The answer is, we are uniting our voices to those of the rest of the civilized world, in forming a grand public opinion against this invasion of the rights of humanity, of liberty, and the social relations of mankind. (Applause.) Our Government may not have, according to the law of nations, the material power to stretch forth its hands with sufficient potency—rescue the child and restore him to the arms of his parents—but we have another power, which is irresistible—the power of public opinion, which, if excited properly in this instance, the Mortara case will be the *last* of the kind that the world will ever see. (Applause.)

The following named gentlemen, on motion of Mr. M. M. Noah,[15] were elected Vice Presidents:

H. Seligman, I. Solomon, L. King, Aug. Helbing, J. Davies, M. B. Ashim, B. Schloss,[16] A. C. Labatt,[17] B. Reinhart, J. Michael, Jacob Rich, A. Hollub, A. Wolf, Louis Cohn,[18] A. Tandler, D. Rgeensburger [Roggenburger], A. Wasserman, A. Godchaux, M. Mayblum, Eli Lazard.

On motion of Mr Louis Cohn, the following named gentlemen were elected Secretaries:—G. S. Goodman, Isaac S. Josephi, B. Hagan, Seixas Solomons, S. L. Simon, S. Uhlfelder.

The Rev. Dr. Henry, (Congregation "Sherith Israel,") in moving that a committee of ten be appointed by the Chair to draft resolutions expressive of the sense of this meeting, offered some very appropriate remarks upon the subject which had called them together. The resolution being carried, the following named gentlemen were appointed:

Rev. Dr. Henry, M. M. Noah, G. S. Goodman, Isaac S. Josephi, Seixas Solomons, Rev. Dr. Scott,[19] Rev. Dr. Anderson, Rev. Dr. Peck, Dr. Wozencraft, L. B. Mizner.

The committee retired, to discharge the duties assigned them.

---

15. Manuel Mordecai Noah, the son of Mordecai Manuel Noah, was a San Francisco journalist and an editor with the *Daily Evening Argus,* the *San Francisco Call,* and the *Daily Alta California.*

16. Born in Reckendorf, Bavaria, Schloss was a member of Congregation Emanu-El and a president of the Eureka Benevolent Society.

17. Abraham Labatt was the first president of Congregation Emanu-El.

18. Louis Cohn was a charter member of Congregation Emanu-El and its first religious schoolteacher.

19. William Anderson Scott was pastor at the Calvary Presbyterian Church.

Mr. S. Solomons then read the following letter from the Rev. Dr. Cutler,[20] which was received with marks of evident gratification:

To the Committee of Israelites, Mortara Case:
SATURDAY, JANUARY 15, 1859.

MR G. S. GOODMAN, *Secretary:*—Owing to a temporary affection [*sic*] of the eyes, I cannot, I regret to say, be present this evening, to respond, in person, to your call. But let me say, I shall none the less be present in spirit, feeling and interest, and in a hearty and indignant remonstrance against the cruel wrong, and the act of high-handed tyranny which calls you together. I have read, with thousands of others, doubtless, the account of the Mortara outrage, with deep mortification for the men who perpetrated the act, and for those of the Christian Church who now sanction and approve it.

It is a deed of shame, which casts a shadow over the Christian name, and which every Christian believer should be anxious to disown. It is an act of religious intolerance, which is incapable of any vindication and admits of no apology. It militates alike against the spirit of the age, against the whole spirit and precept of the Christian religion, and against the fundamental principles of the Protestant faith. And all Christendom must, if true to the great founder of its religion, for ever repudiate this, as well as every attempt to make disciples, from either Jews or Gentiles, by force and acts of violence.

As Christian believers we ought to feel shame, at this unchristian act—falsely done in the name of Christ—and sympathy, too, for the suffering parents and child, who were driven asunder by Christian dictation, and who are kept apart by Christian power.

As a man, I would lift, with my fellow citizens, and with the whole Hebrew race, in every latitude and land, (14,000,000 in number),[21] the voice of indignant remonstrance against this mean act of tyranny; nay, this most disgraceful crime.

As it is an act in conflict with the whole spirit and religion of Jesus, it deserves the rebuke of all Christian people. And as it is an act at war with humanity, the Christian body who commits it should be held to strict account, at the bar of public opinion, and the deed be branded with reprobation by the whole civilized world.

Yours, most respectfully, R. P. CUTLER.

[. . . Rabbi Julius Eckman spoke while the resolutions were being drafted.] Dr. Eckman, [sought] to remove the onus of the case from any existing sect, [which] endeavored to throw the fault wholly on the superannuated Roman Canon Law. [. . . He believed that] the deed of the Roman Executive [must

---

20. Rev. R. P. Cutler led the Unitarian Church in San Francisco.
21. The accepted number is around 4 million.

not] be instrumental in raising any ill-feeling against Roman Catholics. We must not identify *Catholics* with *Catholicism*. For, if the Mortara case has, as yet, not produced any other benefit, it has opened the eyes of Christianity—of the world, and of Rome, and showed the great chasm which exists between the *living* and the *dead*—between Catholics and the Catholic Canon Law. [. . .]

Mr. Seixas Solomons then read the [. . .] Resolutions:

Resolved, That the Israelites and other citizens of San Francisco, in mass meeting assembled, denounce this act of the papal authorities at Bologna, as being sacrificial of the dearest rights of humanity—social, political, and religious.

Resolved, That we regard with apprehension and regret this revival of a power whose intolerance and oppression history and experience teach as prejudicial to mankind, and to a just enjoyment of their natural rights.

Resolved, That we appeal to the recognized intelligence, virtue, and humanity of the head of the Roman Catholic Church, to discourage the enforcement of a canon which is opposed to the enlightenment of the present century, and which must lead to consequences fraught with discord, evil, and danger.

Resolved, That we deeply sympathize with Mr. Mortara in his severe affliction, and are ready to contribute every means at our command necessary to effect the restoration of his child, and to secure the household of others from a similar visitation.

Resolved, That we fully appreciate the spirit of liberality and tolerance manifested by a large and enlightened portion of the Christian world in the expression of their disapproval of this act of tyranny.

Resolved, That a copy of the proceedings of this meeting be transmitted to our Senators in Congress, with the request that they urge upon that body the moral power of our Federal Government, to co-operate with the several European powers in their endeavors to suppress religious intolerance and persecution, such as exhibits itself in the Mortara case.

Resolved, That a copy of these proceedings be transmitted to Sir Moses Montefiore, President of the London Committee of Deputies, as a response to the address made to the Israelites of America, dated October 25th, 1858.

Resolved, That the cordial thanks of this meeting be, and are hereby, tendered to the press for its liberal and kind co-operation in the cause of civil and religious liberty.

[the meeting was then addressed by Rev. Dr. Scott.]

101
Sir Moses Montefiore Salutes Sacramento
Sir Moses Montefiore, 1859

Contributions to the poor Jews of Palestine were often sent through Sir Moses Montefiore (1784–1885), the accepted leader of British and world Jewry. Beginning in 1827, Montefiore made seven trips to Palestine and became associated with the movement to support the community, encouraging its members to move outside Jerusalem's city walls. A letter from Montefiore acknowledging receipt of a contribution from Sacramento's congregation B'nai Israel is one of the first documented connections between the Jews of California and the Jews of Jerusalem.[22]

London
Grosvenor Gate, Park Lane
4 Oct. 5620 [or 21][1859]

Sir

In compliance with your request, I have forwarded your remittance of £6 to the Representatives of the different Congregations in Jerusalem for the benefit of the poor residing in the Holy City—I entreated them to acknowledge the receipt of the same to you at their earliest convenience, which I have no doubt, they will cheerfully do With fervent prayers that the God of Israel may grant you, and all our Brethren in your Congregation every prosperity

I have the honor to be
Sir
Your obedient servant
Moses Montefiore

Moses Hyman Esq
Sacramento, Cal.

SOURCE: Sir Moses Montefiore to Moses Hyman, Esq., Oct. 4, 1859. Western Jewish History Center of the Judah L. Magnes Museum, Berkeley, California.

22. This letter reached San Francisco on November 17, 1859, and was then forwarded to Sacramento. Reinhart, *Diamond Jubilee,* 8. Moses Hyman hosted the first Jewish religious services in Sacramento and served the community as a *mohel* (see chapter 7).

102
For the Love of Zion
Weekly Gleaner, San Francisco, 1861

Created by a diverse group of leaders of the San Francisco Jewish community, Ohabai Zion was founded at a meeting called by Henry Seligman, president of Temple Emanu-El, at the St. Nicholas Hotel in November of 1861.[23] The catalyst for the organization may have been the visit of Abraham Nissan, an emissary from Jerusalem, who was soliciting funds on the West Coast. The first officers of the organization included Rabbi Elkan Cohn of Emanu-El, president, Rabbi Henry A. Henry of Sherith Israel, and Rabbi Julius Eckman, editor of the *Gleaner* and director of the Hepzibah school, vice presidents. Its goals were to take the "initiative in procuring relief for the wants of their suffering brethren in the distant East."[24] On December 20, 1861, the *Jewish Messenger* of New York reported the founding of Ohabai Zion. "Our California brethren," it concluded, "have a favorable opportunity of manifesting that active benevolence for which they have so fairly earned a reputation."[25] The organization faltered in the late 1860s and was reformed by new officers in 1868, after which it became known alternately as the Society for the Relief of the Jews of Palestine or the Friends of Zion or, in Hebrew, the original Ohabai Zion.[26]

The Palestine Charity Fund

While the recent inundations in the interior[27] have made a sad havoc with a number of our people, in destroying their property and business prospects for some time to come—while charity appeals to our men for those in their immediate neighborhood—while our people are now daily called upon to contribute for the suffering poor of this State—we are not unmindful of the indigent poverty-stricken of our race in Palestine, who look to the West for succor. In the midst of this clamor for aid for those who have recently been driven from their homes

---

SOURCE: "The Palestine Charity Fund," *Weekly Gleaner*, San Francisco, Dec. 20, 1861.

23. The St. Nicholas was a kosher hotel.
24. Julius Eckman, *Weekly Gleaner,* Nov. 29, 1861.
25. Baron, "Palestinian Messengers," 158. Funds had been sent to Jerusalem by individual members of the San Francisco Jewish community in 1858 (*Weekly Gleaner,* Apr. 2, 1858). Many of the other officers were members and/or officers of Sherith Israel and Emanu-El.
26. In 1870 the by-laws of Ohabai Zion were placed in the cornerstone of the new Sherith Israel synagogue building.
27. This was probably a reference to the 1861 flood of the Sacramento River.

and comforts, and while thousands of dollars have been given by our Israelites alone to those of their brethren in [t]he interior who are in need of immediate assistance (one Hebrew firm, besides contributing largely to the wants of his people, has forwarded two large cases of clothing to the Howard Benevolent Association of Sacramento)[28] we still have not been loath to meet on Saturday last, at the St. Nicholas Hotel for the purpose of aiding our poor brethren in the far off land—a work auspiciously begun and, to all appearances,—judging from the readiness of individual members—destined to become of material benefit to our brethren in Palestine. It is, therefore, highly gratifying to note that the society, "FRIENDS OF ZION" numbers already more than three hundred members, and promises a respectable increase from the interior. To this hope we are justified on consideration of the members elected as managers for the ensuing year, viz:

Rev. Dr. Elkan Cohn, President.
Dr. Julius Eckman and Rev. H. A. Henry, Vice-Presidents.
Mr. M. Mayblum, Treasurer.
" J. [I.] N. Choynski, Secretary.
" L. King,   Trustees.
" J. S. Rothchild,
" Henry Seligman,
" S. Morgenstern,
" Louis Sharp,
" S. Marx,
" C. Meyer,

It must also be highly gratifying to Rev. A. Nissan, the worthy Messenger from Jerusalem, to be able to bring these tidings of our endeavor to aid those who are so needy and so near us by the ties of religion and nationality, to the Promised Land. May Mr. Nissan prove a [mevaser tov, messenger of good blessings] wherever his steps may lead him. And may Israel on this coast and everywhere else feel for the woes of their fellow men until Jerusalem again shall be the home of all Israel and the abode of the chosen ones of the Lord.

---

28. The Howard Benevolent Association was a Sacramento-based association founded in 1857 to serve the sick and needy and, in times of fire and flood, everyone. The association was supported by donations from its members, other voluntary contributions, and, in its early years, by funds appropriated by the state legislature (*Thompson and West's History of Sacramento County, California* [1880; reprint, Berkeley: Howell-North, 1960], 176).

103
From Golden Land to Promised Land
Rabbi Henry A. Henry, 1861

Rabbi Henry Abraham Henry hosted Nissan during his San Francisco visit. As the following letter from the emissary's notebook demonstrates, not only did Rabbi Henry develop a personal relationship with Nissan but he also won the commitment of his congregation, Sherith Israel, to make an annual donation to the Jewish community of Jerusalem.[29]

San Francisco, Cal
Decr 1861 [Tebet 5622, written in Hebrew]
I have had the pleasure of perusing the documents in the possession of Rabbi Abraham Nissan which show that he is the accredited Emissary from the Holy Land, and deputed to solicit subscriptions towards the support of our suffering Brethren in the City of Jerusalem viz. the [Ashkenazim Perushim,[30] written in Hebrew] I also acknowledge the receipt of Letters of introduction from the Revd. Dr. Raphall and Revd. Mr. Isaacs of New York[31] strongly recommending the Rabbi to my especial notice to aid him in his praiseworthy mission. I therefore considered it my duty as an Israelite in the first instance, to extend to him that hospitality becoming his exalted position, and I am pleased to record that during his stay at my House, his uniform Conduct as a pious and learned Israelite has confirmed him in my opinion, as fully verifying all that he himself states, and what has been said by others in his behalf. It shall ever be my study D.V. [*Deo volente*] to use my humble influence for the benefit of my Coreligionists in the land of Promise. It is gratifying to me to be enabled to record the ready response which was given to the application of the Rabbi to my Congregation [Sherith Israel, written in Hebrew] of this city, who resolved unanimously to award *One*

SOURCE: Rabbi Henry A. Henry, letter. Emissaries Notebooks 4 (quarto) no. 90:38. Jewish National University Library, Jerusalem, Israel.

29. The emissaries' notebooks contain letters of authorization from the elders in Jerusalem, testimonials by American and British supporters, and letters and notations from contributors.

30. The Perushim, followers of the Vilna Gaon, were among the first Ashkenazi Jews to settle in Jerusalem after arriving from Europe in the late eighteenth century. From the 1830s on they maintained a relationship with European Jews, especially with Moses Montefiore.

31. Rabbi Morris Raphall was the rabbi of B'nai Jeshurun, where Mr. Isaacs was the *hazzan*. These two men also wrote letters of recommendation for I. J. Benjamin when he traveled to California.

hundred Dollars p. Annum from its funds for the poor of Jerusalem, with the promise to do all in their power to collect as heretofore and transmit the result of their labors as often as possible.

In addition to the above a Society has been formed in this City called [Ohabai Zion, written in Hebrew] "Friends of Zion" for the relief of our Brethren and is now at this time fairly organized, particulars of which will shortly be published and issued to the world, which will show the feeling of the Israelites of California towards their foreign Brethren in distress. It is confidently hoped that a very handsome sum will be annually raised for the Amelioration of the Condition of ahenu bene Yisrael baarets hakadoshah, [written in Hebrew, Our Fellow Israelite brethren in the Holy Land] and it will be the Constant study of the Board of Trustees to see that the funds so collected shall be applied to its legitimate purpose.

H. A. Henry

104
"The Accredited Messenger of
My Brethren in Jerusalem"
Abraham Nissan, 1861

On December 20, 1861, the *Weekly Gleaner* published Abraham Nissan's letter of thanks to his California friends.[32] From New York Nissan also wrote that "Every footstep I have trod from New York to San Francisco, has reminded me that Israel has not changed, for in every way have I been received with true Jewish kindness."[33] Upon his return to Jerusalem, the elders of the Perushim wrote letters of appreciation as well. According to the *Jewish Messenger,* "the societies which have been organized in California in behalf of the poor of the East, appear to afford the greatest satisfaction."[34]

(From the Hebrew.)

Thanks.

To my brethren in San Francisco.

By the Grace of God who has endowed his peculiar people, the children of Israel, with humanity and brotherly love; as, called by the wise men of old, "Merciful and the children of the Merciful," I greet you as the accredited Messenger of my Brethren in Jerusalem, and appeal to the benevolence of our people in California. I gratefully acknowledge the hearty welcome received at the hands of my co-religionists of San Francisco. Their sympathies have been awakened to the distresses of their brethren of Jerusalem, who are engaged in the study of the Law. For the more effective matter of affording the due support, they have organised a Society—and in a kind spirit one brother has said to another, "Take courage and strengthen yourself for the sake of our brethren who dwell in the Promised Land."

Abraham said, "Blessed be you to the most High," and God will bless you with riches and with honor, with children and with grandchildren, and in your days and in our days shall Judah be saved and the Redeemer come unto Zion speedily in our days, Amen!

And our brethren who dwell in Jerusalem shall pray continually for you on the spot where our forefather Jacob ejaculated, "How tremendous (holy, awful,

---

SOURCE: Abraham Nissan, "The Accredited Messenger of My Brethren in Jerusalem," *Weekly Gleaner*, Dec. 20, 1861, 4.

32. The letter was translated from the Hebrew by Rabbi Julius Eckman.
33. Baron, "Palestinian Messengers," 159.
34. Baron, "Palestinian Messengers," 159.

reverential)" this place by the Western Wall and all other holy places, that your days may be prolonged and the days of your children; and that they may be laden with riches and honor and that your eyes may behold the rebuilding of Jerusalem.

I trust in you, from the many acts of kindness received, to strengthen yourselves and to arm yourselves to enlarge this Society and to publish it throughout the State of California. The leaders of the Society will assume the labors thereon depending upon your support to enable us to live in the "land of our delight"—And may your righteous actions bring you peace and prosperity. Amen!

And me, your servant and friend, may you remember in kindness.

Your obedient servant

ABRAHAM NISSAN

Messenger from the "*Ashkenazim*" and "*Perushim*" of Jerusalem.

105

Jerusalem Discovers Marysville

Hebrew, San Francisco, 1868

After arriving in San Francisco in February of 1868, Nathan Neta Notkin journeyed to Marysville, where the hundred-member Hebrew Benevolent and Congregational Society donated $75.[35] Notkin's letter of recommendation from U.S. Consul H. Victor Beauboucher stated, "The situation of Jews in Jerusalem being such as to require the assistance of their brethren and others in the West on account of their extreme poverty, the bearer of this present is strongly recommended to the Charitable feeling of all Americans."[36]

MARYSVILLE—Rabbi Nathan Watkin [Notkin], from Jerusalem, visited this city on Tuesday and Wednesday, as accredited Messenger to the Continent of America to gather contributions from the Israelites for the relief of their suffering brethren in the Holy Land. He is accredited from six different Congregations at Jerusalem; also the American Consul-General at that city, and the great English philanthropist, Sir Moses Montefiore. The Marysville Hebrew Benevolent Society, as well as individual members, contributed liberally to the distinguished Rabbi's benevolent object. He paid a visit to his people in Oroville, February 7th, intending to return and go to Grass Valley and Nevada [City], where he will undoubtedly be liberally received.

SOURCE: *Hebrew*, San Francisco, Feb. 21, 1868, 4.

35. Baron, "Palestinian Messengers," 275; Benjamin, *Three Years in America*, vol. 2, 25.

36. Baron, "Palestinian Messengers," 228. According to Baron, who inspected his notebooks, Notkin kept poor records of his journey.

106
To Help the Jews of Morocco
Jewish Chronicle and *Hebrew Observer,* London, 1860

In the 1860s the Board of Delegates of American Israelites (BDAI) sent money to help Moroccan Jews who had become refugees, fleeing to the Straits of Gibraltar in the wake of the Moroccan-Spanish wars (1859–60).[37] Formed after the Mortara incident to protect Jews worldwide and work for civil and religious rights, the BDAI sent circulars to American congregations to request support for the Moroccan community. The San Francisco Jewish community responded and its generosity was noted in London.

California.—The Collection.—We have before us a file of the "Gleaner," the organ of our Californian co-religionists, and we are exceedingly gratified to learn from it the alacrity with which the Californian Jewish community responded to the appeal made to it in behalf of the Jews of Morocco by our Board of Deputies, through the instrumentality of the American Board of Delegates. Immediately on receipt of the appeal at San Francisco, a meeting was convened, and a committee for the collection of funds appointed. The committee displayed extraordinary zeal in the discharge of its duties, and of the 54 circulars issued by it (we suppose to as many congregations), only two, we are assured by our contemporary, remained without response. It is particularly pleasing to read the copies of letters which accompanied the remittances, in the first instance, by the donors to the San Francisco committee, being expressive of the warmest sympathy and of a truly fraternal spirit.

SOURCE: *Jewish Chronicle* and *Hebrew Observer*, London, Apr. 20, 1860, 8.

37. One of the reasons for the war was the 1844 execution of Victor Darmon, a Moroccan Jew and consular agent representing the Spanish government in Morocco.

107
An American and an Israelite
Benjamin Franklin Peixotto, 1870

The relationship between the messengers from Jerusalem and the Jewish community of San Francisco produced unexpected results in 1870. Traveling in the West in search of support for his Jerusalem Hasidic community, Rabbi Hayyim Zvi Sneersohn, the great-grandson of the founder of the Lubavich dynasty, had more than Jerusalem on his agenda. In the aftermath of the Crimean War, the Jews of Romania had become victims of riots and persecution, and the Board of Delegates of American Israelites (BDAI) persuaded President Grant to appoint an American consul to Bucharest. In the following letters, Benjamin Franklin Peixotto urges the president of the BDAI, Myer Isaacs, to help him get the appointment.

Born in Philadelphia in 1834 to an old Sephardic family, Peixotto, a lawyer, lived in New York before moving to San Francisco. With Sneersohn's encouragement and the financial support of the San Francisco Jewish community, especially the Seligman banking family and BDAI, he was awarded the unsalaried consulship. Sustained by support from the Seligmans and from B'nai B'rith, which he had served as president in the 1860s, Peixotto labored at his post for five years, but without significant effect.[38]

1

Law Office
Benjamin F. Peixotto
302 Montgomery St.

S.F. N.E. CORNER PINE

San Francisco June 7th 1870

My dear Friend:

I am about to greatly surprise you in the communication this letter will convey. To speak at once of that which is nearest my heart will be to fulfill what hath been written:

SOURCE: (1–2) Benjamin Franklin Peixotto to Myer Isaacs, June 7, 1870, and June 28, 1870, box 3, folder "Correspondence, N–R," Board of Delegates of American Israelites Records, American Jewish Historical Society, Waltham, Mass., and New York.

38. For insight into Peixotto see Lloyd P. Garter, "Roumania, America, and World Jewry: Consul Peixotto in Bucharest, 1870–1876," *American Jewish Historical Quarterly* 58:1 (1968): 25–117.

—"Out of the abundance of the heart the mouth Speaketh"—The dreadful news from Roumania telegraphed from Constantinople and rec[eived] here Thursday last filled me with profoundest grief and though it has since been contradicted—and later dispatches have thrown grave doubt upon the reliability of those first rec[eived]—the fact remains that our poor unhappy people have been and are being mercilessly persecuted—their property and lives treated as so much paper.

In this emergency—aware of what has taken place the past four years—the political schemes of Russia and The Viceroy of Egypt—The fears of Turkey and much Else which the limits of time now at my command will not Explain, deeply affected and feeling moreover that as an *American* and an *Israelite* I can be of great— incalculable service—*I am ready and willing to go to Bucharest.* This is the startling communication. You will say "but you have not calculated the situation and do not know what it is you would do!" Yes I do know. I know there are nothing but fees and those but trifling connected with the office—but I know more that the Israelites of America are rich and that among these are men who will sustain a representative there. This suggestion comes to me from Abraham Seligman of this city brother of Jesse & Joseph [Seligman]—it has been his thought he tells me for sometime and you my Friend may if you so wish put it into life and serve a great cause by prompt action.

In a word: get me the appointment first, if possible have Congress Salary the office & makit [*sic*] Consul-General. The Seligmans can get this through, the more important office the more efficient & potent the mission & the *power. But get the appointment the rest will take care of itself—*. I have written Wolf and Adolphus Solomons. I fear the former overestimates his influence—the latter is a *true man.* It would not be too much in such a cause for you to go to Washington to go armed with letters from the Seligmans & those whose power is potent with the Pres[ident] and the Senate. I tell you my Friend that mighty interests lie involved in this mission. That a man read in the institutions of America, an American by birth *an Israelite to the core,* possessing the confidence and wide acquaintance of so many eminent Christian Americans and of his own people can be, must be, will be a *power* there.

But why do I argue the question, *it is sufficient that I tell you I will go and that I am Earnest.* If you do not know the question at issue, or know sufficiently of my capacity for the work—*it is useless to speak.* This I must say I am told by Rabbi Sneersohn who has been with me for the past month (my constant companion and counsellor) that Adolph Buchner is in no way fitted & must not be confirmed if the appointment has been (as stated by Telegram) given him.

Action—prompt and decided is called for. The Board of Delegates may or may not secure a Consul General at Bucharest. Telegraph or write—I will be ready.

B. F. Peixotto

2

San Francisco June 28, 1870

My Dear Friend

Your brief letter of the 17th, is rec[eived] I have to thank you and dear Adolph for the interest you take in the suffering of our brethren of Roumania, it is *them* not *me* you serve by any and all you do to promote the success of the appointment made by the President.

No "Empty" Acceptance would do those wretchedly persecuted people any good. Authority in name and not in fact would be a gross outrage, a mockery. Not only would the fair fame of our country be tarnished but that which is still dearer, *Israel's* would be blurred and disgraced. The Consul to Roumania to do good must have the means with the official Varnish. He must be American Consul for outward form and what prestige such position may possibly confer— but *American Israelite* and Jew to the core to do practical good. His work lies in winning the love of those poor people of his of whom there are countless hundreds, of doing them charity in many ways, by money, by words of counsel, of going down to them not being above their reach. His main instrumentality for good would be in his successful inauguration of schools, among them *a la Alliance Israelite.* Disseminating modern thought, liberalizing the mind, reaching into their hearts by showing them how they may still be Jews without the frightful social *costumes* and customs which they persist in retaining. I believe when my thoughts for these people are placed before the *Alliance* of Paris[.] Cohn and Cremieux will warily sustain me. But is it not possible for the B[oard] of D[eligates] of Am[erican] Israelites to inaugurate something for them. Cannot a Roumanian School Fund be Established? Must we go abroad to the B[oard] of Deputies of London or the Alliance of Paris? Or cannot all three of these be united in the work—contributing thereto? Will not the Board of Delegates of American Israelites second the Government of the United States. The Govt. gives the shadow—the official trappings,—will not the Board make that shadow substance—afford the means to make effectual the good the office may be made to do?

A meeting of some 12 or 15 of the prominent Israelites of this city has been called for to-morrow evening at the instance of Rev Dr Elkan Cohn, Abraham Seligman, Alexander Weill and A. Hollub[39] who have issued a private note which reads as follows: "The present unfortunate condition of our brethren in Roumania exciting deep sympathy, and the President of the United States, having exhibited commendable interest in their behalf, we have thought it our duty to call together a few prominent co-religionists with a view of sustaining the Government. To this end you are invited to attend a meeting Wednesday

---

39. Most were members of Emanu-El.

evening 8 O'ck"—this is signed by the gentlemen I have before named. You will please make no use of this communication other than to a similar private end. The object of the meeting is to determine if concert of action cannot be had through which the leading public spirited Israelites of the principal cities can be united in the object of sustaining the mission to Roumania. Of course my reaction to the mission will preclude my presence, but I will let you know the result as soon as I hear it.

If New York Phila Cincinnati Chicago St Louis & perhaps one or two other cities can be reached through enough of their public-spirited men who are possesessed [sic] of ample fortune— it is not designed to approach any others— then this mission may prove a success—provided, the nomination is confirmed. Did I not believe it possible that some practical good—decided and positive— could be accomplished I would not urge this undertaking. Nor would I urge it did I in this view stand *alone*. But when eminently practical men like Abraham Seligman and Alexander Weill believe in it and urge it with all their hearts, I am confirmed in my belief. At the same time I am anxious to know how *you* view the matter and how it is viewed by others. In this you must separate the *personal man* from the man whom the mission calls, if there be a better man than the one whose name is now before the Senate let him stand forth or be brought forward, and gladly willingly will I withdraw. I am not afraid of the consequences of this mission upon myself. When it shall please Heaven that I return from it, if I go—my power for good will be so greatly and potently advanced that I shall be richly repaid for the sacrifice. Nor will those who I love best on Earth my wife and children suffer from it—a few years in Europe—the benefit of a European Education for my darlings will be an *advantage* not a disadvantage.

I have tried to look at this question in all its aspects and the result is— my determination to go if it be possible I can have the mission so placed as to make it potent for good. I have very grave doubt however of their being sufficient disinterestedness and unselfishness existing to secure the end desired and while I shall lament for the unhappy ones of Roumania that they could not have secured a *friend,* I shall probably rejoice in the sacrifice *Saved me.*

One word more. I am told by an Enlightened Hungarian who lived six years in Bucharest that Adolph Buchner is the son of an unprincipled man, that he himself was a dissipated young man Educated & having the Entree to many Boyar[40] families—a Secy to Mr Czapky formerly our Consul there who came also from this city—who lives now in Europe. I cannot believe it would be well in any event to have such a person represent this country

---

40. Of the Romanian privileged class.

or Am Israelites. One, who has never trod our soil or knows nothing of our institutions[.]

My dear wife thanks you for your ever kind remembrances. So do I. To yours remember *us*. And to Adolph—Kind friend—good heart. And to you brother Isaac—and to your venerable Father.

Ever Most faithfully Your friend B. F. Peixotto

108
The Alliance Israélite Universelle

Isaac Adolphe Crémieux, 1877

The following letter, sent to Rabbi Elkan Cohn, president of the San Francisco chapter of the Alliance Israélite Universelle, by Isaac Adolphe Crémieux (1796–1880), illuminates one of the many ties between the Jewish community of San Francisco and European Jewry. A lawyer, statesman, and leader of French Jewry, Crémieux served as the president of the Alliance for fifteen years and worked to aid Jews in Morocco, Russia, Turkey, Romania, and Palestine, as well as in Bulgaria.[41]

ALLIANCE ISRAÉLITE UNIVERSELLE

COMITE CENTRAL
RUE DE TRÉVISE, 37

Paris, le 25 October 1877

No 2727
5267
Rev. Dr. Elkan Cohn
Rabbi of Congregation
Emanu-El, San Francisco
Dear Rabbi,
We have the honor to acknowledge receipt of your letter of October 2, and of a sum of two thousand four hundred eighteen francs comprising the balance of the subscriptions obtained through your good offices for the Israelites of Bulgaria. The Central Committee thanks you deeply for this new remittance, which brings the total of the San Francisco donations up to twelve thousand four hundred eighteen francs, and asks you to reiterate to the honorable donors the expression of its heartfelt gratitude. [The fact of providing] such a large share in the relief work we are engaged in is eloquent testimony to the feelings of Jewish fraternity that inspires the Community of San Francisco and does great honor to it.

The hope you give us that the Alliance may soon be restored in your city causes us heartfelt pleasure, and we need not add that we will be extremely grateful to anyone who chooses to contribute to this end.

SOURCE: Isaac Adolphe Crémieux to Rabbi Elkan Cohn, Oct. 25, 1877, trans. Orin Gensler. Copy in possession of editor.

41. For more about the Alliance Israélite Universelle, see Hyman, *The Jews of Modern France.*

We hasten to send you, in accordance with your wish, a certain number of bulletins, of the two half-years of 1876 and of the first half-year of the present year, to which we are adding, along with copies of our monthly bulletins of September and October, the society's statutes, membership forms, and printed instruction for the formation of Committees, administration etc. Finally, we have the honor to convey to you also a few lines which our President wishes to address to you himself.

Please accept, my dear Rabbi, the assurance of our highest esteem,

For the Central Committee

The President

Ad. Crémieux

VI
Looking Backward and Forward

12
Maturity

APPROPRIATELY, TWO OF AMERICA'S MOST RENOWNED RABBIS VISITED California as it approached maturity, and they wrote with great enthusiasm of the rapid growth of its cities, of its expanding economy, and of the diversity of its Jewish communal institutions. Max Lilienthal saw himself as a witness for the Midwest and East, reporting on the social and business atmosphere of the West and noting the prominence of his fellow Bavarian Jews. Isaac Mayer Wise also went west to observe but primarily to enlist support for his growing movement of reform congregations. Together these reports provide an outsider's picture of the early decades of Jewish life in northern California.

109
Pioneers of the Pacific Coast
Rabbi Max Lilienthal, 1876

After his visit to San Francisco, Rabbi Max Lilienthal wrote a glowing description of the California economy and, probably more important to his Cincinnati readers, gave this account of the role played by German Jews.[1]

OUR BRETHREN IN THE WEST AND SAN FRANCISCO

BY DR. LILIENTHAL

IV.

Concluding my report of my trip to California, I have yet to speak of the social position of our brethren on the Pacific Coast. Here, too we must exclaim: California is a land of wonders indeed! We, in the Eastern and Middle States, have hardly an idea of the rapid growth of this young State. We do not know what to admire the most: nature, with her bounty and inexhaustible resources, or the energy, daring enterprise and astonishing success of her men. We all have met Californians in our Eastern and Western homes, and when we had listened to their reports, we thought them to be mere exaggeration, and shook our heads incredulously. But when one comes to San Francisco, and gets convinced of the truth of their statements, they stand bewildered before sterling matters of fact, before a wealth that reminds us either of the wonderful tales of the Arabian Nights, or the modern story of a Monte Christo.

Arriving at Sacramento City, my son, Philip, the Cashier of the Anglo-California Bank, at once introduced me to a crowd of millionaires, who in the depot had awaited the arrival of our train. They had either come down from their mines, or had been looking after their banks in the country-towns, and they were a motley crowd of both Jews and Gentiles.

The Christians are the richest on the Pacific Coast. The Jew can no longer be reproached with that he has got all the money of the world. There are four Irishmen who stand at the head of the millionaire list, namely: Flood and O'Brien, Mackee and Fair. They are the owners of the consolidated Virginia gold and silver mines. Twelve years ago Flood and O'Brien kept a barroom. The other two were common miners; now they are considered worth over sixty million dollars, and these millions are daily increasing beyond all mercantile proportion and calculation.

SOURCE: Rabbi Max Lilienthal, *American Israelite*, Cincinnati, June 23, 1876, 6.

1. For more about Rabbi Lilienthal, see chapter 2.

VIEW OF MONTGOMERY STREET, SAN FRANCISCO, 1878

Montgomery Street, San Francisco, 1878. Courtesy of Wells Fargo Bank.

Mr. Fair lately stated to a reporter: "A residence of 27 years on the Pacific slope has given me an opportunity of watching developments in that quarter. The Comstock Lode, which underlies Virginia City, is about four miles long and from 400 to 800 feet wide. We have been raising about 800 tons of ore daily, valued at from $80,000 to $100,000. We did rather better in March, the value reaching $3,600,000, and expect to increase it during the summer to $5,000,000 per month."

This statement is not fabulous, but it is literally true! I spent one evening in the Exposition building, where Gilmore's Band, of New York, gave a concert. During the recess my attention was called to a gentleman who promenaded with his lady, both plainly dressed. "Look at him," said my son, "there is one of our millionaires; it is Mr. Donohue. He began at the foot of the ladder, as a blacksmith, then started an iron foundry, which he has sold. And now he owns the splendid steamer which plies between this city and Vallejo, and then a railroad of ninety-six miles, down to Cloverdale, on which there is neither a loan nor a mortgage." "How is that for high, sir?" smiled one of the young men who accompanied us.

491

I could go on with such marvels, but who can repeat and remember them all? I shall add but one more, which seems almost incredible, but is a stern fact. There are in San Francisco two Christian butchers, Chas. Lux and Henry Miller, one hailing from northern Germany, and the other from Wurtemberg. They own in Santa Clara County, south-east from San Francisco, so much land that the fence of pinewood, around their land costs over half-a-million dollars. Who would believe such a fact in our homes on the Old Continent?

I had once in an evening a company of well-informed business men assembled in my room at the Palace Hotel. I begged them to write down the names of the men in San Francisco, who are worth one million or more, excluding all those who count their fortunes only by the hundred thousands. In less than ten minutes they wrote down fifty-seven names, and among them seventeen Jewish ones. On the next morning they remarked to me that they had omitted at least twenty more names.

I have the list before me; I could give the names of our Jewish brethren, but I fear I would omit some one, and therefore only state a well-authenticated fact. Men, who count their fortunes by the hundred thousands, can be found here in any number among our co-religionists, and what they and I with them, value more than their fortunes is the sterling integrity and unimpeachable honesty which characterizes them. They, therefore, occupy a high position in the mercantile community, and his Honor, Mayor Bryant, told me, "We have ample reason to be proud of our Hebrew fellow-citizens.["]

Our brethren flourish not only in the usual business lines, in which we see them everywhere engaged, but I was most agreeably surprised to see that in the young State of California they have established large and important factories, and are also engaged in agricultural pursuits. I will give your readers only some of the names I could pick up from my informant, having been unable, on account of my short stay, to obtain all desirable details.

The "Alaska Fur Company." Three of its principal partners are Mr. Louis Sloss, from Under-Eisenheim; Mr. Louis [Lewis] Gerstle, from Ichenhausen, and Mr. Simon Greenewald, from Neuhemsbach, in Bavaria. This company has taken the place of the former renowned Hudson Bay Company, and is in a most flourishing condition. They have been given the privilege both by the American and Russian governments to carry on the seal fishing in Alaska and in Russian waters; and in this time of star-chamber investigation, the committee in Congress reported that the company not only strictly conforms with all the conditions of the contract, but has done a great deal more for the inhabitants than could be required according to the letter of the law. They have built houses for the Alutes; have established schools and churches, and all with their money and for their own account. The company, of which many influential Christians are members, is an honor to the Jews. It has now two splendid steamers and fine large schooners, its own property, engaged in the seal-fisheries.

In their shoe factories, Messrs, Hecht & Bros., employ 300 to 400 men; Einstein Bros., 250 men; Rosenbock, Oppenheimer & Co., have a large shoe and hat factory. Levy, Straus & Co., a large factory of gentlemen's furnishing goods; Neustadter Bros., a very large shirt factory; Lewis & Co., one of the largest cigar factories in which nearly 500 Chinese are employed; Rosenbaum & Brandenstein, a large furniture factory, and besides them there is quite a host of others, who give employment to thousands of hands.

Our brethren are large property-holders, not only in San Francisco, but also in the State of California. I again can only give you a few names, which my reporter had on hand.

Messrs. Scholle, Sachs, Straus, Lippman and Lengersheim, have in Los Angelos County, Sixty thousands of acres of land, which they have bought of Gov. Pito, of Mexico, for $125,000. They have, since they have bought it, greatly improved it. They have six thousand acres in grain, and have introduced all the modern improved agricultural implements. It will be, in course of time, one of the model farms of California. On their pastures they have 45,000 sheep, and expect to sell this year a quarter of million pounds of wool to the Eastern States.

Blachman & Cerf, have got in San Lonis Opispo, [San Luis Obispo] in Lower California, over 12,000 acres of land. They have on their pastures over 10,000 sheep and over 5,000 heads of cattle.

Schwabacher & Bros., of Zirndorf, near Fuerth, in Bavaria, have got over 3,000 acres of land in Washington Territory. They have built thereon a flour mill, and in their cooperage factory they finish daily over two hundred barrels. They have, moreover, 2,000 acres of wood-land in Idaho, and shall open in the neighborhood coal mines, splendid coal having been discovered on their property.

Oppenheimer Bros., one of the prominent tobacco firms of San Francisco, a few years ago bought some thirty thousand acres of land, and will greatly improve it, too. Thus, we see, that our brethren in all branches of agricultural, industrial and commercial pursuits, take a most lively interest and occupy a prominent position. They can share with others the glory of having been the pioneers of early civilization on the Pacific Coast. I am sorry that the space allotted to me in the AMERICAN ISRAELITE will not permit me to give all the names of our prospering brethren; may it suffice to say, they all are an honor to their State and to their race.

That Israelites, and especially German Israelites, will not forget and neglect the pleasures of social life, is a matter of course. I have visited two of their clubs, the "Verein," which consists of Jewish and Christian members, and the "Concordia," which consists only of Jewish members. Both are most elegantly furnished and excellently managed, and fully rival even the "Harmony," of New York.

That "All is not gold that glitters," holds as good of the Golden State of California as of any other corner of the world, but I have been told that any one who is willing to work, can there earn a good and honest living. Drones, idlers and professional beggars must suffer everywhere.

In conclusion; I shall never forget this trip to California. I shall always cherish it as one of my most agreeable recollections. I have learned a great deal. As soon as the traveler has crossed the Missouri, and has entered the cars of the Union Pacific Railroad in Omaha, he is ushered into new scenes, and meets with a new life. I rejoice in having seen our great country, stretching from the Atlantic to the Pacific, and having witnessed the truth of Bishop Berkeley's saying: "Westward the course of empire takes its way." I have seen the blessings and results of our free institutions, where the free citizen, not hampered by official red-tape, displays his indomitable energy and forces the seed of progress and civilization through untrodden areas of wilderness. The American heart glories in these American victories won without strife and bloodshed.

And as an Israelite I gloried in the prosperity of our brethren, in the prominent position they have won and hold among their fellow-citizens. May they continue to prosper in the noble work they have begun, not only in their domestic life, but as the pioneers of our religion on the Pacific. Thanks, thousand thanks, and Heaven's best blessing for their liberal exertions on behalf of Judaism.

May the Congregations prosper, and act in peace and harmony for the honor of our religion. May the Sabbath-schools continue in the instruction of our youth to prepare a rich harvest for the future generations. May the numerous charitable institutions, as heretofore, verify the truth of that charity is considered among Israelites the cornerstone of all religion. There is a future of bright success before them all, and Californians know the word: Perseverance, energy and union will achieve a glorious victory over difficulties heretofore thought to be unconquerable. May they live long and prosper.

110
"A New Edition of an Old Country"
Isaac Mayer Wise, 1877

In the following article and report to the executive committee of the Union of American Hebrew Congregations, Isaac Mayer Wise, leader of the American Reform movement, reflects on his 1877 trip to San Francisco. Wise explains Jewish institutional achievements in detail and expresses his concern about the negative influence of wealth and materialism on religious thought and observance.[2]

1
JEWISH INSTITUTIONS OF SAN FRANCISCO

During my travels I saw and heard so much which I wished to describe that I could not reach many an interesting subject and must now bring it up as a sequel. I have not spoken of the Jewish institutions of San Francisco and propose to do it now.

California is a new edition of an old country. The old institutions were planted in a new country with a rich and remunerative soil, improved upon in many instances. The Israelites of San Francisco support five regular congregations and a number of temporary *minyanim*. Four of these congregations have synagogues of their own and the fifth made preparations to build a new house of worship; they occupy now a rented church. The smallest of these congregations is the oldest, called *Share Tzedek*, with sixty members; Mr. Samuel Polack is its president, and Rev. Aaron Brown, minister. Its synagogue on Stockton Street was finished in 1872. The next oldest congregations are the Temple Emanuel Congregation and the *Sherith Israel*, both established in 1851. The Emanuel Congregation has a magnificent temple on Sutter Street with choir, organ and family pews; its president is Mr. M Selig; its rabbi, Rev. Dr. [Elkan] Cohn, who has occupied that position for eighteen years past, and its Hazan, Rev. Mr. [Max] Wolf, is as eminent and accomplished in his part of the service as Rev. Dr. Cohn is in the pulpit. The congregation counts upward of 260 members, each paying $100 per annum. The temple was dedicated in 1866, and ranks among the most prominent buildings in the city.

SOURCE: (1) "Jewish Institutions in San Francisco," *American Israelite*, Cincinnati, Sept. 14, 1877, 5; (2) *American Israelite*, Cincinnati, Sept. 7, 1877, 6.

2. For more about Isaac Mayer Wise, see chapter 9. Not all of Wise's information is correct.

"A Temple for all the World to See," Emanu-El, 1867. Courtesy of the San Francisco Public Library.

The Sherith Israel Congregation, H. W. Hyman, president, and Rev. Dr. [Henry] Vidaver, rabbi, has upward of 200 members. Its synagogue (*Minhag Polen*) is a very elegant building at a prominent corner in the heart of the city, with a seating capacity of 1,500 to 1,600, the galleries included.

The next is the second German congregation, with choir, organ and family pews, the Ahabath Shalom [Ohabai Shalome], with 125 members. Col. Ab.[raham] Newman, president, and Rev. Dr. [Albert (Aaron) S.] Bettelheim, rabbi. Its synagogue, but lately finished, is a handsome building, pleasantly located, and the congregation is fairly under way to adopt Minhag America.

The next is the second Polish congregation, [Beth Israel], S Zemansky, president, and Rev. Dr. [A. J.] Messing rabbi. This congregation is young and a year ago had but eighty members, but since Rev. Dr. Messing preaches there the membership has increased to nearly 200. This is perhaps the only orthodox congregation in the city, with a considerable German element among the Polish.

In all these places of worship sermons are preached once a week, or once every other week. Rev. Dr. Cohn, as a rule, preaches German, on every other Sabbath, and on exceptional occasions, English. Rev. Dr. Vidaver always speaks English, Rev. Dr. Messing always German, and Rev. Dr. Bettelheim alternately

English and German. These four eloquent preachers are each in his way perfectly qualified to do justice to the sacred cause of Israel, and the Israelites of San Francisco are well provided with competent expounders of the Law as any city we have visited in this or any other country. Public service is conducted in an excellent manner, which must be satisfactory for every party. I heard the best choir in Dr. Bettelheim's synagogue, and the best Hazan in the Emanuel Temple.

The Sabbath-schools attached to these congregations are of special excellency, well provided with good teachers and a large attendance. I have been exceedingly pleased in the schools which I visited by the zeal of their officers, the competency of the teachers, the intelligent looks and good discipline of the pupils. These institutions do special credit to the San Francisco congregations and are the best conservators of Judaism. There is taught in those schools religion, mostly from Wise's book, Jewish history, and the Hebrew language. The latter, however, is taught more thoroughly than is usual in Sabbath schools. In some of the schools the pupils of each class have two extra hours weekly for Hebrew exclusively. The rabbis, of course, are the superintendents of these schools and the teachers of the confirmation classes. I found under Dr. Vidaver's superintendency one of the best disciplined schools in this country.

San Francisco supports three weekly Jewish papers, *The Hebrew Observer,* edited and published by Mr. [William] Saalburg; *The Hebrew,* by the two brothers Jacobi [Jacoby], and *The Progress,* by Mr. Bachrach. Besides, the AMERICAN ISRAELITE has quite a number of patrons in that city. Jewish literature is provided for that community by I. N. Choynski, who moved his valuables into a new and elegant store, where he sells good books and writes bitter reports of things generally. He flatters none and displeases many.

The charitable institutions of San Francisco are, besides the B.B. [B'nai B'rith] and K.S.B. [Kesher Shel Barzel] Lodges, with their respective District Grand Lodges, the Orphan Asylum, the Eureka Society, and a number of similar benevolent societies of ladies and gentlemen, including one sewing society of young ladies, who also do the sewing for the Orphan Asylum. The Orphan Asylum, Mr. W. Levy, president, and the zealous and generous Mr. [Alfred P.] Elfelt, secretary, supports and educates forty-two children by the annual contribution of members and donations of generous friends and life members (for $125). The building lately erected between the city and the Golden Gate Park is a handsome frame, large enough for the purpose and well furnished, on a lot which is already very valuable and will be only more so in a few years. This institution is the pride of San Francisco, to which everybody points with particular satisfaction. It is a point not only of laudable charity, but also of unity and good will.

The Eureka Benevolent Society has 500 to 600 members, each paying $15 per annum, including 100 to 150 life members, each having paid $125. They pay $3 from each member's annual dues to a widow's and orphan's fund. Needy widows receive $30 or more per month, and $7.50 for each child. The balance of the society's income is distributed among the poor and needy. Mr. Martin Heller is its president; B Hagan, vice-president; Leo Eloesser, secretary, and Aaron Kahn, treasurer.

The First Hebrew Benevolent Society, with 300 members, C. Meyer, president, was established in 1849, and is the most important after the Eureka. There are another number of similar societies in existence which could do much more good if they were united in one with a regular bureau, as in St. Louis, New York and elsewhere.

There are, perhaps, in San Francisco as many Israelites outside of the congregations as are within them. Many of them rent seats in synagogues for *Rosh Hashonah* and *Yom Kippur,* and after those days they are to be found in their respective places of business. There are in this city quite a respectable number of zealous and working Israelites who deserve credit for their work and laudation for their success, but as a general thing the ladies must maintain Judaism. They are three-fourths of the congregations in the temples every Sabbath and send their children to the Sabbath-schools. With a very few exceptions, the men kept no Sabbath, keep nothing besides Rosh Hashanah and Kippur, and although charitable in general, they are not used to pay[ing] as much to congregations or charities as some of our people do in small towns, whose wealth does not begin to compare with any of them. Two hundred dollars per annum pays a millionaire's bills to the congregation, charities, lodges, and orphan asylum, all told. Every congregation is in debt, except the [Emanu-El] temple, whose debt has been assumed by its members advancing the money. If it was not for a few good and zealous working men, the whole of Jewish affairs would rapidly go down in that city, because materialism is so prominent and absorbing that hardly any room is left for ideal interests. This is the case among Jews and gentiles alike. So, for instance, there is but one public library in this city and that is not very large. The schools as a general thing are good, but the higher institutions are in their infancy. The same is the case with the churches. They are all in debt and poorly attended. "I take no interest in Jewish affairs," is a remark which you hear ten times a day made by men of prominence. One told me he was so indifferent to Judaism and Christianity that he would embrace either to suit his interests or do without both of them and the man is considered good and respectable. There is not one Jewish wholesale merchant in San Francisco who could not observe his Sabbath without any loss or inconvenience, for in the most instances the Jewish merchants govern the market in their particular branch; but they do not from sheer frivolity and indifference. I have told them all that in their synagogues.

Commercially and financially, however, they are very prominent and prosperous. The two great and celebrated woolen factories are in the hands of Israelites, so are the shoe and boot factories, so is the Alaska Fur Company, a large portion of the grain, grocery, tobacco, dry goods and clothing trade.

Every other house almost in the wholesale quarter of the city is occupied by a Jewish firm in all departments of business. They are very prominent in industry, finance and commerce, some living in princely mansions and occupying high positions in society. As a class the San Francisco Israelites are more prominent than the Hebrews as a class are in any other city I have visited.

Last, though perhaps not least, among the institutions is the Concordia—a Jewish club-house where gay people seek amusement. It is an elegant place, of the same character as Allemania, Phoenix, etc., in other cities.

To my numerous friends in San Francisco I send my love and best wishes.

I. M. W.

2

Cincinnati, Ohio, September 2, 1877.

To the Executive Committee of the Union of American Hebrew Congregations.

Mr. President and Gentlemen:—In compliance with your resolution of June last, your obedient servant went to California in order to work for the Union of American Hebrew Congregations, and now begs permission to report to you the result of his labors.

I left Cincinnati July 1st and returned August 30th. During this time I have visited the Israelites of Omaha and Lincoln, Neb.; Denver, Col.; Salt Lake City, Utah; Eureka, Virginia City and Carson City, Nevada; San Francisco, Sacramento City, San Jose and Santa Cruz, Cal. I had been invited to Portland, Oregon, by Rev. Mr. [Moses] May, but could not undertake the journey and be home at my post in proper time (September 1st). I proposed to go to Los Angeles, Cal., but the president of that congregation would not have me come there, and the president of the congregation in Oakland Cal., also did not want me to address the congregation. I have not seen the congregations at Stockton and Marysville, Cal., on account of want of time.

During this time I have delivered fourteen public speeches, and have besides addressed every individual of whom I supposed he had any influence with the congregations in behalf of the Union of American Hebrew Congregations.

Your messenger was received and treated everywhere with distinction, respect and kindness, and his appeals were listened to with much attention and consideration. The rabbis and ministers everywhere, especially of San Francisco, as also the presidents and honorary officers of the congregations have assisted and encouraged me in a manner truly generous and fraternal.

In San Francisco the four large congregations (there are a number of smaller ones), the presidents of the four large congregations, have positively promised me that at the next general meetings of their respective congregations they will propose and advocate the proposition to join the Union of American Hebrew Congregations, and those presidents are gentlemen of high position and influence. Likewise the rabbis of those congregations and many influential members have promised me to give their support to this proposition, so that I have little doubt of its success. The same promises have been made me by the respective presidents and ministers of San Jose and Sacramento City, Cal., of Denver, Col, and Omaha, Neb. The congregation of Eureka, Nev., belongs to the Union. There is no other congregation in Nevada. However influential members of the B'nai B'rith Lodge, of Virginia City, Nev., have promised a $500 donation from that lodge to the sinking fund of the Hebrew Union College, for which I have brought two students from San Francisco, *viz.*: Masters Henry and Messing.[3]

I am entitled to the hope that within a month or two the congregations of the states of California, Nevada, Colorado and Nebraska, will be united with the other sister congregations in our Union of American Hebrew Congregations, which then will reach from the Atlantic to the Pacific, as it does now from the Gulf to the Lakes. Our Hebrew brethren from the Pacific Coast and the states named will certainly be an honor to the Union and true to the faithful champions of the sacred cause which engages our attention and devotion. It will be a glorious day when the congregations of the Pacific Coast will join hands and hearts with those of the Atlantic Coast and the Mississippi Valley. It will be a day of fraternization to Israel and of glory to the Most High.

I did not consider it advisable to solicit subscriptions now to the sinking fund of the Hebrew Union College and did not commence. Besides Mr. [Abraham] Anspacher, formerly of Evansville, Ind., who subscribed $100, and a young gentleman of San Francisco, who subscribed $25, none came to me to offer any subscriptions, and I did not start the matter, because: 1. The subject was foreign to most and entirely unknown to many, who looked upon it as a matter far away from home concerning them but little. 2. In consequence of two years' short crops and the decline in mining stocks there is now, as eminent friends told me, a very inopportune time to open a subscription list in any of those cities. 3. In consequence of the Strike and its re-echo in San Francisco there was depression in all business circles, so that subscriptions to any purpose could hardly be expected. 4. None of the wealthiest men of San Francisco was ready to start the list with a considerable sum, or to take the matter in hand just then, and without their aid success appeared to me impossible.

This, however is not to be understood to the effect that our brethren in San Francisco or the states named will not in time contribute their mite to the great enterprise of the Hebrew College. On the contrary, I found that very many are generally very liberal and generous, that they contribute freely to

---

3. Marcus M. Henry was the twenty-one-year-old son of Rabbi Henry A. Henry; Herman Messing was the fifteen-year-old son of Rabbi Aron J. Messing.

charities and other public enterprises. Many, very many, indeed are public-spirited and munificent, and some very prominent gentlemen told me that they well understand that in the proper time something must and will be done for the Hebrew Union College; but that was not the time to start it, and I acted on their advice.

So far God has helped, and that I was able to do no more. Mr. President and gentlemen, I am glad that I have seen the brethren of the Far West, and I must confess that I feel attached to them and fully convinced that they will be with us, for God and Israel, for His Torah and eternal truth; for they are men and brethren, our flesh and our blood, our God is theirs and their people ours.

In the name of God and His Torah,

Your most obedient servant,
Isaac M. Wise.

Glossary

Ashkenazi (pl. Ashkenazim, adj. Askenazic)
Jews of western, central, and eastern European ancestry

Bar Mitzvah (pl. Bnei Mitzvah)
A boy of thirteen who takes on the obligations of following the commandments of Judaism; also the ceremony recognizing a boy as a bar mitzvah

Chevra Kadisha (chevra kadusha)
"Holy society," the society that provides all religious functions relating to funerals and burials according to Jewish law

Chuppa
Marriage canopy

Hazzan (chazan, hazan)
Cantor or prayer leader at a Jewish religious service

Kehillah
Autonomous Jewish community organization or congregation

Kesher Shel Barzel
"Band of Iron," a fraternal organization

Ketubah (kethubah, pl. ketuboth)
A Jewish marriage contract

Landsmanschäften
Organization of people who come from the same region

Matzoh (pl. matzoth)
A crackerlike bread made without yeast that is eaten during Passover

Metaher
The house where dead bodies are "purified" (washed) before burial

Mezuzah or mezuza (pl. mezuzot)
A scroll of Jewish prayers in a container placed by Jews on the doorposts and gates of their homes

Mikvah
Ritual bath

Minhag
A Jewish ritual or social custom, usually referring to a style of prayer

Minhag Ashkenaz
The style of prayer used by German Jews

Minhag Polen (minhag polin)
The style of prayer used by Polish Jews

Minyan
A quorum of ten adult Jews required for public prayer. In Orthodox practice, all must be men

Mishnah
A part of the Talmud containing Rabbinic law. First codification of Jewish oral law.

Mitzvah (mitzvot)
A commandment or a good deed

503

Mohel
A person who performs ritual circumcision on Jewish boys when they are eight days old

Ophir
A country that was known in biblical times for its gold (see 1 Kings 9:20, 10:11; 2 Chronicles 8:18, 9:10)

Parnas
The leader of a Jewish community or congregation

Pesah
Passover

Rosh Hashanah
The Jewish New Year, a time of prayer

Schule (shule, shul)
Synagogue (Yiddish)

Seder
A traditional ritual dinner and religious service held the first two nights of Passover

Shema Yisrael (Semah Yisroel)
"Hear, Israel," the creed that is central to Judaism and affirms one's faith in one God

Sephardim
Jews of Spanish and Mediterranean ancestry

Sephar ha Torah
The books of the Torah

Shaar Hashamayim
Gates of Heaven

Shaar Zedek (shaari zedeck, sharay zedek)
Gates of charity

Shabbat
The Jewish Sabbath, lasting from sundown on Friday to sundown on Saturday

Shamash (shammash, schamis)
A sexton, one who looks after the synagogue

Shochet (schochet, schohet, shokhet)
A Jewish ritual slaughterer of meat

Shomer Shabbat
"Guards of the Sabbath"; refers to Jews who observe the Sabbath laws

Shomrai Shabbes
"Guard the Sabbath"

Shofar (shophar)
The ram's horn that is sounded on religious holidays, including Rosh Hashanah and Yom Kippur

Simchat Torah
The holiday that joyously celebrates the end of the annual reading of the Torah and the beginning of the next year's reading

Torah
The Pentateuch or scroll of the Pentateuch

Trafe (trafa)
Unkosher, or forbidden according to Jewish law

Tsitsis (tzitzit)
The fringes on a four-cornered garment worn by religious Jews

Tzedakah
Charity

Verein
Association or club (German)

Yad

"Hand," the pointer used when reading the Torah

Yigdal

"May He be magnified": the first word of the liturgical hymn used in daily prayer based on the Thirteen Articles of Faith of Maimonides

Yishuv

The Jewish settlement in Palestine before the state of Israel was established in 1948

Yom Kippur

The Day of Atonement, the most solemn and introspective day of prayer for the Jewish people, marked by a twenty-five-hour fast

Bibliographical Essay

HUNDREDS OF PRIMARY AND SECONDARY SOURCES WERE CONSULTED in preparing this book. What follows is a discussion of the most important research tools and secondary works; for additional primary and secondary sources see the annotations to individual documents.

Long before Frederick Jackson Turner's frontier thesis, and even longer before Hollywood's cowboys-and-Indians West came to be fixed in the public mind, California elicited an extraordinarily individualistic mystique that continues to conjure up images of anarchy, freedom, and wilderness. While some historians have persisted in promoting this romanticized version of the West, others, most notably Patricia Nelson Limerick, have labored to de-romanticize western history. Yet Limerick, who portrays the region as an "intersection of ethnic diversity with property allocation," neglects its religious and communal dimensions and in doing so marginalizes the role of Europe's immigrants, including its Jews, and their descendants in the shaping of western society (Limerick, *The Legacy of Conquest* [New York: Norton, 1987]: 27). Other historians of the West, including Paula Mitchell Marks in *The American Gold Rush Era, 1848–1900* (New York: William Morrow, 1994) and Malcolm J. Rohrbough, *Days of Gold* (Berkeley: University of California Press, 1997) have assimilated Jews into an amorphous group simply labeled "white" or at times "immigrant," but have not viewed them as a distinct ethnic group. This approach is widespread, as Matthew Frye Jacobson notes in *Whiteness of a Different Color: European Immigrants and the Alchemy of Race* (Cambridge: Harvard University Press, 1998), when he demonstrates how Jews came to be described as Caucasians in the late twentieth century.

To contemporaries, certainly, California's European diversity was immediately apparent. Indeed, a visitor to San Francisco in 1859 exclaimed that he "had not been on shore two hours before [he] had conversed with members of every European nation" (Henry Arthur Tilley, *Japan, the Amoor, and the Pacific* [London: Smith, Elder, 1861]: 252). A century later, Moses Rischin called for a concerted study of the long experience of cultural diversity in California and the West, arguing that "no region of the United States has seen from its beginnings, so great and so varied a mingling of peoples, and nowhere has the need for a sense of history and identity been more nakedly and more decisively felt" ("Beyond the Great Divide: Immigration and the Last Frontier," *Journal of American History* 55:1 [1968]: 42).

Yet even today the primary materials available for the studying of Jews in the West await examination. There are three key bibliographical aids for researching Gold Rush Jewry. First and foremost is Ruth Kelson Rafael's *Western Jewish History Center: Guide to Archival and Oral History Collections* (Berkeley: Western Jewish History Center, Judah L. Magnes Memorial Museum, 1987), a vital starting point for locating primary sources in the rich collections of the Western Jewish History Center, where many of the original documents in this book are housed. Rafael's guide is complemented by two meticulously annotated bibliographies prepared by Sara G. Cogan, *Pioneer Jews of the California Mother Lode, 1849–1880: An Annotated Bibliography* (Berkeley: Western Jewish History Center, Judah L. Magnes Memorial Museum, 1968) and *The Jews of San Francisco and the Greater Bay Area 1849–1919: An Annotated Bibliography* (Berkeley: Western Jewish History Center, Judah L. Magnes Memorial Museum, 1973). These books primarily describe the collections in the Western Jewish History Center, the Bancroft Library at the University of California, Berkeley, and the California Historical Society, though they also include some collections at the American Jewish Archives, Hebrew Union College, and local northern California libraries. The guides include bibliographical aids, contemporary records, family histories and biographies, city and county directories, and select secondary sources. Without these three exemplary research tools, the compiling of this book would have been a far more arduous task. A bibliography of collateral value for northern California, prepared by Norton B. Stern, is *California Jewish History: A Descriptive Bibliography— Over Five Hundred Fifty Works for the Period—Gold Rush to post–World War I* (Glendale, Calif.: Arthur H. Clarke: 1967). Another helpful work is Louis J. Rasmussen's *San Francisco Ship Passengers List,* vol. 4 (Colma, Calif.: San Francisco Historical Records and Genealogy Bulletin, 1970), which documents arrivals by ship. Various archives and libraries have also published guides to their own collections. Soon most libraries, archives, and virtual archives (such as the Jewish Women's Archive), will have finding aids on the web. At present, the most useful websites for western Jewish history are those of the American Jewish Archives; the American Jewish Historical Society; the Bancroft Library; Jews in the Wild West; Rochlin-Roots-West; the Jewish Women's Archive; and the Jewish Women's Web Site at the University of Wisconsin, which inventories many archival and library resources.

Next to the archival collections, newspapers are perhaps the single most vital source of information about Gold Rush Jews, as they put the period in cultural and social context. San Francisco's venerable *Daily Alta California,* which is available on microfilm, aids the researcher in understanding state and local politics as well as economic and social conditions, while the Jewish weeklies, the *American Israelite* of Cincinnati and the *Occident and American Jewish Advocate* of Philadelphia, provide a national perspective on Jewish community development. Moreover, both the *American Israelite* and the *Occident and American Jewish Advocate,* always eager to report on the far West, employed regular western columnists in addition to asking their readers to contribute descriptions of communal life. Although there were as many as four Jewish newspapers in San Francisco in this period, their existing files are fragmentary. The best known, the *Weekly Gleaner,* published in English by Rabbi Julius Eckman, presents the editor's religious and educational agenda, while the *Hebrew,* more culturally than religiously oriented, published by Philo Jacoby, chronicled community events (especially those of interest to German Jews) and enthusiastically supported integration into American society. In addition to its English columns the *Hebrew* published articles in German, the preferred language of the educated elite and of immigrant women who were often homebound and had no opportunity to learn English. Both papers are essential resources for California Jewish history. The other San Francisco Jewish weeklies should not be overlooked, however—the *Hebrew Observer, Jewish Times, Jewish Times and Observer* (a merger of the two previous newspapers), *Kol Yisra'el* (Voice of Israel), the *Progress,* and its successor, the *Voice of Israel.* The best collections of San Francisco Jewish newspapers on microfilm can be found at the Western Jewish History Center and at the American Jewish Archives. A small collection is also available at the Bancroft Library.

Aside from archival collections and newspapers, there are two travel books by nineteenth-century Jewish authors that merit serious attention. The most notable of all American Jewish travel accounts is I. J. Benjamin's *Three Years in America, 1859–1862* (Philadelphia: Jewish Publication Society of America, 1956). First published in German in 1862, it was translated into English some ninety years later by the poet Charles Reznikoff. Highly opinionated and at times inaccurate, this memoir does convey feeling for the era and especially for California. Benjamin visited Jewish communities throughout the United States, although he gave his main energies to California, where he spent a year and a half, and wrote in great detail about what he saw, whom he talked to, and what he learned of its history. David A. D'Ancona's more modest travelogue, *A California-Nevada Travel Diary of 1876: The Delightful Account of a Ben B'rith,* edited by William M. Kramer (Santa Monica, Calif.: Norton B. Stern, 1975) records D'Ancona's impressions of his visits with the B'nai B'rith lodges in the state. Not to be neglected is a useful little book by Alexander Iser, *The California Hebrew and English Almanac for the Year 5612 [1851–1852]* (San Francisco: Albion Job Press, 1851); it was the first to list California's congregations, kosher boarding houses, and Jewish communal institutions.

The early histories of San Francisco Jewry were produced by Congregation Emanu-El's rabbis. However filio-pietistic, sectarian, and incomplete, Jacob Voorsanger's *The Chronicles of Emanu-El* (San Francisco: Temple Emanu-El, 1900) and Martin Meyer's *Western Jewry: An Account of the Achievements of the Jews and Judaism in California* (San Francisco: Temple Emanu-El, 1916) are valuable for their reproduction of original sources, which were often destroyed by the 1906 earthquake and fire. Meyer's work, recently reissued, is in large part a wonderful "mug book" of San Francisco Jewry, with biographies and personal sketches of many of the city's pioneers.

Two recent secondary works, Robert Levinson's *The Jews in the California Gold Rush* (Berkeley: Commission for the Preservation of Pioneer Jewish Cemeteries and Landmarks of the Judah L. Magnes Museum, 1994) and Rudolf Glanz's *The Jews of California: From the Discovery of Gold until 1880* (New York: Southern California Jewish Historical Society, 1960), provide good starting points for the study of the role of Jews during the Gold Rush era. Of the two, Levinson's volume is the more useful resource. Although not analytical or fully contextualized, it provides a clear narrative history and quotes original sources at length, often giving clues for further research. Glanz's book, although a bit more analytical, comprehensive, and wide-ranging, is loosely organized.

Fred Rosenbaum's *Visions of Reform: Congregation Emanu-El and the Jews of San Francisco, 1849–1999* (Berkeley: Judah L. Magnes Museum, 2000) is a revised and expanded version of his *Architects of Reform: Congregational and Community Leadership Emanu-El of San Francisco, 1849–1980* (Berkeley: Western Jewish History Center, Judah L. Magnes Memorial Museum, 1980). Together with *Free to Choose: The Making of a Jewish Community in the American West* (Berkeley: Judah L. Magnes Memorial Museum, 1976), these books are thus far the definitive works on the histories of Congregation Emanu-El in San Francisco and the Oakland Jewish community, respectively. *Visions of Reform* ably chronicles Emanu-El's history rabbi by rabbi, paying particular attention to the changes in religious practices.

An excellent introduction to Jewish history in California and in the American West more generally is *Jews of the American West* (Detroit: Wayne State University Press, 1991), edited by Moses Rischin and John Livingston. This collection of essays by nine leading historians addresses questions of regional and national as well as local history. Especially important for California history are the essays by Moses Rischin, Fred Rosenbaum, and Earl Pomeroy. In the book's opening piece, "The Jewish Experience in America: A View from the West," Rischin establishes the singular role of San Francisco Jewry and raises questions for future study.

Two carefully researched, popular, large-format works are especially useful. Irena Narell's *Our City: The Jews of San Francisco* (San Diego: Howell-North Books, 1981) is devoted to telling the story of the founding elite families for well over the course of a century and is richly embellished with photographs and genealogical charts. Far more extensive in scope, *Pioneer Jews: A New Life in the Far West,* by Harriet and Fred Rochlin (Boston: Houghton Mifflin, 2000), a thematically organized and abundantly illustrated book, demonstrates the role of Jewish men and women in the creation of dozens of western cities and towns.

For special aspects of northern California history, see Ruth Kelson Rafael, *Continuum—A Selective History of San Francisco Eastern European Jewish Life, 1880–1949* (Berkeley: Judah L. Magnes Memorial Museum, 1977);

Bibliographical Essay

Harold F. Reinhart, *Diamond Jubilee: The Seventy-fifth Anniversary of the Consecration of the First Synagogue Building in the West 1852–1927, Temple B'nai Israel* (Sacramento: Temple B'nai Israel, 1927); Rabbi Joshua Stampfer, *Pioneer Rabbi of the West: The Life and Times of Rabbi Julius Eckman* (Portland: Self-published, 1988); Harold I. Sharfman, *Nothing Left to Commemorate—Story of the Pioneer Jews of Jackson Amador County, California* (Glendale, Calif.: Arthur H. Clarke, 1969); and Bernice Scharlach, *House of Harmony: Concordia Argonaut's First 130 Years* (Berkeley: Western Jewish History Center, Judah L. Magnes Memorial Museum, 1983).

Also worthwhile is the informative and well-researched *A Traveler's Guide to Pioneer Jewish Cemeteries of the California Gold Rush* (Berkeley: Commission for the Preservation of Pioneer Jewish Cemeteries and Landmarks of the Judah L. Magnes Museum, 1996) by Susan Morris, which narrates the stories of the seven Gold Rush Jewish cemeteries maintained by the Commission for the Preservation of Pioneer Jewish Cemeteries and Landmarks of the Judah L. Magnes Museum. More than a guide, the book supplies detailed information and photographs of the cemeteries and of the individual graves and suggests historical tours of Gold Rush communities. For a visual understanding of the period, the video "Birth of a Community: Jews and the Gold Rush," directed by Bill Chayes of the Judah L. Magnes Museum (Berkeley: Judah L. Magnes Museum, 1994), pictorially and with scholarly illumination depicts the first years of community life. Its accompanying teacher's manual, *Birth of a Community: Jews and the Gold Rush—A Teacher's Resource Guide for Grades 4–6, 10–Adult* (Berkeley: Western Jewish History Center, Judah L. Magnes Museum, 1995) written by Leslie Brenner and edited by Ava F. Kahn, provides related activities for students.

An indispensable journal for the study of California Jewish history is the *Western States Jewish Historical Quarterly*, renamed *Western States Jewish History* in 1983. Intended for a popular audience and indexed from 1968 to 1999, this journal publishes both original articles and carefully edited primary sources. The annotated scholarly apparatus throughout the journal constitutes a treasure trove that no researcher can afford to bypass. Its prolific editors, William M. Kramer and the late Norton B. Stern, have also written and edited numerous books and articles documenting individual and community life in the West.

For this era of American Jewish history there are several solid secondary works that incorporate the most recent historical scholarship and provide a national context for the California story. Especially important is Hasia R. Diner's *A Time for Gathering: The Second Migration 1820–1880* (Baltimore: Johns Hopkins University Press, 1992). Despite the weakness of her treatment of California Jewry, the book is an excellent general introduction to American Jewish history during this period. Important works on American Jewish women also deserve special note, especially *The Jewish Woman in America* (New

York: New American Library, 1975) by Charlotte Baum, Paula Hyman and Sonya Michel, pioneers in the field of Jewish women's history. See also Jacob Rader Marcus, *The American Jewish Woman: A Documentary History* (Cincinnati: American Jewish Archives, 1981) and *The American Jewish Woman, 1654–1980* (Cincinnati: American Jewish Archives, 1981), and especially the monumental *Jewish Women in America*, 2 vol. (New York: Routledge, 1997), edited by Paula E. Hyman and Deborah Dash Moore, which includes profiles of representative western women Mary Ann Cohen Magnin, Hannah Solomons, and Mary Goldsmith Prag.

For a close reading of specific documents see Daniel J. Elazar, Jonathan D. Sarna, and Rela G. Monson, eds., *A Double Bond: The Constitutional Documents of American Jewry* (Lanham, Md.: University of America Press, 1992). A rich context for many of the documents in this collection is provided by Lance Sussman's *Isaac Leeser and the Making of American Judaism* (Detroit: Wayne State University Press, 1995). Alan Silverman's *The Alternatives to Assimilation: The Response of Reform Judaism to American Culture 1840–1930* (Hanover, N.H.: University Press of New England for Brandeis University Press, 1994) gives a comparative analysis for San Francisco's Congregation Emanu-El, while Frank E. Manuel's *The Realities of American-Palestine Relations* (Washington, D.C.: Public Affairs Press, 1949) portrays the philanthropic activities of the American Jewish community in Palestine, a favorite of California's Jewish community. Lastly, "Jewish 'Forty-Eighters' in America," in Bertram Wallace Korn's *Eventful Years and Experiences: Studies in Nineteenth-Century American Jewish History* (Cincinnati: American Jewish Archives, 1954), insightfully discusses the impact of the 1848 European revolutions on immigration to the United States in general and to California specifically.

Other works, most notably in California and western history, ethnic and community studies, and women's history, shed light on this period. Kevin Starr's *Americans and the California Dream 1850–1915* (New York: Oxford University Press, 1973) depicts the birth and early maturation of the California ideal. William Issel and Robert W. Cherny's *San Francisco, 1865–1932: Politics, Power, and Urban Development* (Berkeley: University of California Press, 1986) chronicles the unique interplay between the city and its people. Glenna Matthews's "Forging a Cosmopolitan Civic Culture: The Regional Consciousness of San Francisco and Northern California," in *Many Wests: Essays in Regional Consciousness*, ed. Michael Steiner and David Wrobel (Lawrence: University Press of Kansas, 1998), illustrates San Francisco's singular cosmopolitan character. *Religion and Society in Frontier California* (New Haven: Yale University Press, 1994) by Laurie F. Maffly-Kipp delineates the failure of religious leaders to replicate eastern Protestant patterns in the far West. Erwin G. Gudde's *California Gold Camps: A Geographical and Historical Dictionary of Camps, Towns, and Localities Where Gold Was Found and Mined, Wayside Stations and Trading Centers*, ed. Elisabeth K. Gudde (Berkeley: University of

California Press, 1975) provides a virtual directory of the gold country, while Gladys Hansen's *San Francisco Almanac: Everything You Want to Know about Everyone's Favorite City* (San Francisco: Presidio, 1995) does the same for the city.

With the current interest in ethnicity, historians have begun to incorporate the European immigrant dimension into the California and western story. See Peter R. Decker's *Fortunes and Failures: White Collar Mobility in Nineteenth-Century San Francisco* (Cambridge: Harvard University Press, 1978); R. A. Burchell, *The San Francisco Irish 1848–1880* (Berkeley: University of California Press, 1980); Dino Cinel, *From Italy to San Francisco: The Immigrant Experience* (Stanford: Stanford University Press, 1982); Ralph Mann, *After the Gold Rush: Society in Grass Valley and Nevada City, California 1849–1870* (Stanford: Stanford University Press, 1982); Earl Pomeroy, "On Becoming a Westerner: Immigrants and Other Migrants," in *Jews of the American West,* ed. Moses Rischin and John Livingston (Detroit: Wayne State University Press, 1991); and Frederick Luebke, ed., *European Immigrants in the American West* (Albuquerque: University of New Mexico Press, 1998). Other scholars have produced thoughtful monographs on the importance of Chinese and blacks to the region. See Judy Yung, *Unbound Feet* (Berkeley: University of California Press, 1995); and *Unbound Voices* (Berkeley: University of California Press, 1999); Rudolph Lapp, *Blacks in Gold Rush California* (New Haven: Yale University Press, 1977); Douglas Henry Daniels, *Pioneer Urbanites: A Social and Cultural History of Black San Francisco* (Philadelphia: Temple University Press, 1980); and Albert Broussard, *Black San Francisco: The Struggle for Racial Equality in the West, 1900–1954* (Lawrence: University Press of Kansas, 1993).

The integral role of women in the history of the West calls for special emphasis. Historians Joan M. Jensen and Darlis A. Miller, in "The Gentle Tamers Revisited: New Approaches to the History of Women in the American West," *Pacific Historical Review* 49:2 (1980): 173–213, were among the first to assert that there is an abundant source of materials available for the study of the West's multicultural women's history. Good works on western women include Ruth B. Moynihan et al., *So Much to Be Done* (Lincoln: University of Nebraska Press, 1990), and Lillian Schlissel, *Women's Diaries of the Westward Journey* (New York: Schocken, 1992). For a classic contemporary account, see Louise A. K. S. Clappe's *The Shirley Letters* (Salt Lake City: Gibbs-Smith, n.d.).

Index

Index

Books in the American Jewish Civilization Series